SOUL
FLIGHT

About the Author

Donald Tyson (born 1954) is a Canadian who lives just outside Halifax, Nova Scotia. His books cover the full spectrum of the Western esoteric tradition, including topics such as the Tarot, runes, the Kabbalah, Enochian magic, the Golden Dawn, and the Necronomicon. He seeks in his writing to make ritual magic both comprehensible and relevant to modern readers, and believes that magic could not have survived for so many thousands of years unless it offered something essential to the human experience. He is the author of nearly two dozen nonfiction books on practical occultism and several novels related to the supernatural.

To Write to the Author

If you wish to contact the author or would like more information about this book, please write to the author in care of Llewellyn Worldwide and we will forward your request. Both the author and publisher appreciate hearing from you and learning of your enjoyment of this book and how it has helped you. Llewellyn Worldwide cannot guarantee that every letter written to the author can be answered, but all will be forwarded. Please write to:

Donald Tyson
℅ Llewellyn Worldwide
2143 Wooddale Drive, Dept. H0-7387-1087-3
Woodbury, Minnesota 55125-2989, U.S.A.

Please enclose a self-addressed stamped envelope for reply,
or $1.00 to cover costs. If outside U.S.A., enclose
international postal reply coupon.

Many of Llewellyn's authors have websites with additional information and resources. For more information, please visit our website at http://www.llewellyn.com.

DONALD TYSON

SOUL FLIGHT

ASTRAL PROJECTION
& THE MAGICAL UNIVERSE

Llewellyn Publications
Woodbury, Minnesota

First Edition
First Printing, 2007

Book design by Steffani Chambers
Editing by Brett Fechheimer
Cover design by Kevin R. Brown
Interior diagrams courtesy of the author
Llewellyn is a registered trademark of Llewellyn Worldwide, Ltd.

Library of Congress Cataloging-in-Publication Data
Tyson, Donald, 1954–
    Soul flight: astral projection & the magical universe / Donald Tyson. — 1st ed.
        p. cm.
    Includes bibliographical references (p.   ) and index.
    ISBN-13: 978-0-7387-1087-7
    ISBN-10: 0-7387-1087-3
        1. Astral projection. 2. Parapsychology. 3. Occultism. I. Title.

    BF1389.A7T97 2007
    133.9'5—dc22

Llewellyn Publications
A Division of Llewellyn Worldwide, Ltd.
2143 Wooddale Drive, Dept. H0-7387-1087-3
Woodbury, Minnesota 55125-2989, U.S.A.
www.llewellyn.com

Printed in the United States of America

Other Books by Donald Tyson

1-2-3 Tarot
Alhazred
Enochian Magic for Beginners
Familiar Spirits
Necronomicon
Portable Magic
The Power of the Word
Ritual Magic
Scrying for Beginners
Three Books of Occult Philosophy

CONTENTS

INTRODUCTION

The Astral World

Astral projection is usually understood to be the act of separating the subtle or astral body from the physical body, so that the astral body can travel away from the physical body, carrying with it the consciousness of the traveler. It is held that the astral body can be projected any desired distance by the force of the will, even to the farthest corner of the universe, unrestricted by the physical laws that govern the movement of matter, such as the limitation of the speed of light. Vast distances are crossed instantly. The physical body remains behind, as though asleep or in a trance state. The astral body stays connected to the physical body by an astral umbilical cord known as the silver cord that can stretch to an unlimited degree, and when stretched to its thinnest has the appearance of a strand of spider web. The link of the silver cord allows the astral body to return at once to the physical body at any moment that the traveler conceives of the desire to return.

That is the popular modern concept of astral projection, which was formalized by the Theosophists and spiritualists during the latter half of the nineteenth century. The word *astral* can be a bit misleading. It means "from or like the stars," and signifies a subtle substance that possesses form without matter, or at least without the gross matter with which we are familiar. It is sometimes described as a subtle fluid, and may be conceived to be somewhat similar to moonlight: silvery and faintly glowing. The general idea is that this astral body lies within the physical body, taking the shape of the physical body, but at times, either by accident or by deliberate choice, it may be dislocated from the physical body to roam freely through the world.

No Traveling in Astral Travel

It is necessary to understand this nineteenth-century Theosophical concept of astral projection because it persists as the common view to the present day. Unfortunately, it is completely wrong. There is no projecting involved in astral projection, and no traveling in astral travel, not in a physical sense. The astral body is not a separate physical envelope for the consciousness, but is a part of the mind, and it never leaves the mind. Astral projection involves the transition of consciousness from one state to another—from the normal everyday waking state we are all familiar with, to an altered state that may be called the astral world.

The astral world is not a place in space; rather, it is a dimension of the mind that resembles very closely the dream state. Indeed, the astral world and the dream world are one and the same. Consciousness is a part of the mind, and never leaves the mind. When you think about it, the very idea that it could somehow separate itself from the rest of the mind and go wandering around the material world is absurd. We might as well suppose that our liver, an essential part of the body, could tear itself out and go bouncing away on a journey of self-discovery, leaving the rest of the body behind it.

To accept that our awareness can never leave our minds is not to impose a limitation, but to strip all limitations away. Each individual human mind is a part of the universal mind that shapes and sustains all things. There are no limits within the mind because mind underlies everything, extending not merely to every corner of space, but into the past and future as well, and into other realms of reality that are not a part of the realm we understand as the physical world, which we believe ourselves to inhabit.

Astral projection is a real phenomenon. It has existed since the early beginnings of the human species, and descriptions of it are found in the myths and tales of every culture and historical period. Please do not feel that I have somehow diminished it when I tell you that there is no physical travel involved in astral travel. Astral travel is what it is, and what it has always been. How we describe it does not change its nature. Our understanding of it may be more useful or less useful, depending on how well we model the underlying reality of astral travel. At the end of the nineteenth century, it was possible to think of it as the physical projection of some material envelope or shell of the body that carried consciousness with it, but our understanding of reality has advanced in the past hundred years, and this simplistic, mechanistic view of astral travel is no longer to be accepted.

The Mind Creates Reality

We now understand that the mind itself creates the reality we perceive to surround us, not in a passive way but actively, constructing its parts and interrelating them from moment to moment as we experience our reality. The mind builds up the physical world just as surely as it builds the mental world of dreams. This process was not clearly understood in the nineteenth century by the average person, who would have viewed the notion that the mind affects physical reality as absurd. To that citizen of the nineteenth century, there was clearly an outside objective world and an inside subjective world, which were divided from each other and which did not interact.

As comforting as this absolute division between the world of material things and the world of mental states may have seemed, it was a false division then just as it is now. The material world is as much within the mind as the dream world, or the astral world. Granted, the material world obeys slightly different laws, which we ignore only at our peril. It is not as malleable as the astral world, nor is it amenable to wishful thinking. If we decide we can fly in our material body and step off a cliff flapping our arms, we will have a very brief time to contemplate our error. Yet the cliff is as much a construction of our mind as our personality. It is merely a construction of a different type.

The modern understanding that mind pervades everything, that there exists no "inside the mind" or "outside the mind," is essential to a clear view of astral projection. What we have are various levels of the mind that can be occupied by consciousness. When we occupy a level, we become aware of it just as if we had entered a dark room and turned on the light. Astral projection is the process of projecting consciousness from the physical level of reality to the astral level of reality.

Astral World Similar to the Dream World

It has already been pointed out that the astral world is similar to the dream world. Perhaps the only difference is that when we inhabit the astral world, we do so with full self-awareness. In dreams there is a tendency to forget ourselves, and to accept the circumstances of the dream without analysis. Within the dream world, we are usually an actor in a play, or perhaps a more accurate metaphor would be a puppet on a string. Our actions, words, emotions, even our thoughts, are not under our control. We are swept along wherever the dream takes us. By contrast, in the astral world we remain ourselves, and are able to respond independently of the circumstances in which we find ourselves. We walk through the scenes, interacting with the players, but we are not required to play a part in the drama, although we may choose to do so.

There is a condition known as lucid dreaming, in which a dreamer is able to become fully conscious while asleep and dreaming, so that he realizes that he is dreaming, and can by an act of will change the direction of the dream. Lucid dreaming does exist and has been recognized by psychologists. What is not generally realized is that lucid dreaming is a type of astral projection. The dream world becomes the astral world when we enter it with full conscious awareness, because the two are at root the same.

Those who have read descriptions of astral travel, or who have experienced it themselves, may object with indignation that it is nothing like dreaming, that the astral world is completely different from the dream world. They may assert that an astral traveler is able to move about the physical plane of existence like an invisible ghost, interacting with other human beings who inhabit their bodies of flesh and blood, and that the astral world is in every respect like the physical world.

True Nature of the Astral World

Yes, so the astral world is like the physical world, sometimes. At other times, it is completely different from the ordinary world we inhabit while we perceive ourselves to remain within our material bodies. The astral world is not fixed in the same way the physical world is fixed. It is subject to rapid and radical mutation in response to our emotional states and our unconscious fears and desires. It can be altered consciously by acts of will. It does resemble very closely the physical world much of the time—because astral travelers have the expectation that it will resemble the physical world. When an astral traveler projects his astral body with the purpose of sending it to some remote location in the physical world, it is little wonder that the astral world through which he projects is much like the physical world, since it is constrained to resemble the physical world by the expectation in the mind of the traveler.

Although the astral world usually appears similar to the physical world because it shapes itself in response to the presumptions of the traveler, anomalous intrusions occur of a surrealistic nature, things that could not exist in the physical world. The astral traveler, while seeming to walk down the street in front of his house in his astral body, might encounter a dog with two heads, for example. The dog might grin at him and ask for the time. To the traveler, the street has the appearance of the same street in the physical world, but because of the plasticity of the astral world, the figure of the dog is able to intrude itself into the landscape, just as it might during a dream.

The astral world is often described as parallel to the physical world, overlying or interpenetrating it, so that a traveler on the astral plane, as it is sometimes called, has access to all parts of the physical plane. This is a useful way to think of astral travel, as long as it is clearly understood that both the astral plane and physical plane are constructions of the mind, and exist within the mind. The important point is that the astral world is not isolated from the physical world, but is able to interact with it, because both are mental levels. Astral travelers can gather useful information about the physical world during their travels. However, they do not experience the physical world directly during astral projection, but rather they interact with an astral reflection of the physical world, which may not correspond with the physical world in every detail.

This astral reflection of the physical world that is perceived during astral travel accounts for the factual errors that occur in descriptions of the physical world by travelers. It is not a direct passive reflection, such as the reflection in a mirror, but a simulacrum of physical reality actively constructed by the mind. Part of the construction is based on the memories of the traveler. Other parts may be drawn from the minds of other human beings on the unconscious level, and from sources the nature of which is as yet completely unknown. As a result of this patchwork construction of the reflection of everyday reality perceived by the astral traveler, some of the information gathered about the physical world during astral travel is accurate, and some of it is inaccurate. Even when the information is not strictly true, it can be of value, because it contains symbolic meaning of importance to the traveler.

This point is important, so I wish to make it crystal clear. When you travel on the astral level to visit the house of your Aunt Sara who lives in Milwaukee, you should not assume that everything you see there is factually accurate, even though to you it seems you are actually standing in Aunt Sara's living room. Sara may appear completely her usual cheerful self as she goes about her daily tasks, unaware that you are watching her in your astral body, but there may be curious anomalies in the scene, departures from the physical reality. For example, you might see a black-and-white cat sleeping on her sofa, only to find out later when you talk to her long distance on the telephone that Sara doesn't own a cat. Yet it may be that Sara has been thinking about how nice it would be to have a cat around the house to keep her company.

Astral Spirits

The astral world has been called the realm of spirits. That view is a bit simplistic. It would be better to think of the astral world as the common meeting place for spirits and human beings. Spirits in their essential natures no more inhabit the astral world than we do, but they are adept at using its underlying mind substance to shape bodies for themselves that we can perceive and with which we are able to interact. When a spirit appears to a human being who is fully conscious, the astral body of the spirit intrudes itself into the physical world of the person perceiving it. This is possible because, as has been explained, both the astral world and physical world are levels of the mind, and interconnected. It is the same reason that when we are very tired, we sometimes dream while we are awake, and see dream images with our eyes open.

A significant though often overlooked component of astral travel is interaction with spiritual beings. Those who mistakenly believe that astral projection involves nothing more than the astral body moving through the ordinary, everyday physical landscape are often terrified the first time they encounter a spirit on their travels. Some have tried to explain such meetings by saying that while in the astral body, we are more sensitive to the impressions of spirits, which we would pass unnoticed in our waking condition. But it is not the case that the astral body has more sensitive eyes than the physical body; it is rather that the entire astral world through which we travel is innately congenial to the manifestation of spirits, who are able to shape their substance to express themselves to human beings. When traveling through the astral world, we travel through a landscape that lends itself more readily to spiritual beings than it does to human beings.

Spirits are much more likely to appear to astral travelers who expect to encounter them, and even more so to those travelers who actively seek to communicate with them. A materialistically minded traveler who has the firm expectation that he will see nothing more than streets and trees and houses and cars on his astral excursion unconsciously tends to exclude spirits from the astral landscape shaped within his mind. He may still see a spirit from time to time, but his expectation that he will see only the ordinary physical world tends to exclude spirits from his awareness. When a spirit does spontaneously show itself, the traveler is apt to be utterly terrified, even though the dangers in such an encounter are small. It may afford the spirit some moments of amusement to watch the astral traveler flee.

Only a select few human beings are aware that the human race coexists with an infinite multitude of spiritual beings. Those who happen to perceive a spirit on rare occasions in their waking conscious state often do their utmost to avoid having the experience repeated. They may mislabel the harmless and bemused spirit as a ghost, or even as a demon, even though it exhibited no malice of any kind. It would not be strange if spirits as a group considered the human race quite mad. Spirits have no trouble being aware of human beings, even though few humans can easily see or hear spirits. Many of them seek active communication and interaction with humans, as a way of experiencing the physical world through human perceptions.

Nowhere is interaction between spirits and humans easier than in the astral world, and historically this has been the prime use for astral projection. Shamans engaged in soul flight to travel to what they believed to be the dwelling places of the spiritual beings who instructed them. Each hierarchy of spirits has its own astral realm. The interest of the shamans was focused on the inhabitants of the astral world, and the landscapes through which they traveled were merely obstructions that had to be crossed in order to reach those dwellers in the astral world with which they interacted.

During the twentieth century, attempts were made by various government agencies both in Western and Communist countries to use astral projection as a tool of military intelligence. A rigorous scientific outlook tended to exclude meetings with spirits on these experimental astral excursions across enemy lines. Science does not recognize the existence of spiritual beings. The results were mixed, due to the plasticity of the astral world and its responsiveness to human emotions and unconscious urges. The scientists in charge of the experiments thought that their travelers were viewing the actual physical environments to which they were sent, when they were actually seeing distorted astral reflections of those environments constructed in the mind. Little wonder the results of the experiments tended to be uneven.

Reasons For Writing This Book

There is no underlying difference between the soul flights of prehistoric shamans and the remote viewing used in the secret government intelligence-gathering projects of the Cold War. Astral travel has always been with us from our earliest beginnings as an intelligent species. It expresses itself in such diverse forms as lucid dreaming, near-death experiences, alien abductions, the bilocation of saints, doppelgängers, remote viewing, and the occult practices of ascending the planes and scrying in the spirit vision. Because of this wide diversity of forms, I have employed the general term *soul flight* to embrace both conventional concepts of astral projection and its many divergent expressions.

One of the main reasons that I decided to write this book was to demonstrate that even though astral travel has expressed itself in numerous seemingly distinct ways over the centuries, it always relies on a similar underlying process. The ancient shaman and the modern Cold War spy each used the same basic techniques to shift their consciousness from the physical world to the astral world. The experiences of medieval witches at their mountaintop sabbat gatherings and modern alien abductees in the bellies of spacecraft from the stars are not unlike each other even though they are called by different names.

Another reason I felt a need to write this book was to dispel some popular misconceptions about the nature of astral projection, many of them fossilized relics of Theosophy and the spiritualism movement of the nineteenth century. There are numerous other texts available on astral travel, but they tend to repeat the same concepts that were formulated more than a century ago. The Theosophical theory of astral travel is both antiquated and simplistic in its slavish adherence to a materialistic view of reality. As any architect will attest, when you attempt to build from badly drawn blueprints, the result is bound to be a disappointment. This book presents a new blueprint of soul flight that the astral traveler can build on with confidence.

A third important reason for writing it is the tendency of most modern books on the subject to discount or ignore the use of a ritual structure during astral travel. Even though rituals were employed in ancient times to achieve the separation of the astral body, modern writers on the subject largely exclude this useful aid. When dealing with malicious astral spirits and safeguarding the security of the traveler, ritual is not merely useful but can be essential for success. The general ritual of projection that I present near the beginning of the second part of this work is what might be called the modern magician's method of astral projection. It is not the only ritual pattern that may be used, but it provides a good working framework for a ritual of projection that not only facilitates astral travel but also ensures that it is done safely on all levels.

The astral world is not some alien or distant land; it is present in each of us every moment of every day of our lives. To enter it, we need only alter our level of consciousness. Then we discover to our delight that we have no need to travel out of ourselves because we were there within the astral landscape all along, but did not know it. Astral projection is a process of opening the eyes inward. It is attainable by everyone, because everyone possesses the astral world within themselves. What was accomplished by the soul flights of shamans thousands of years ago can be experienced today. Whether or not an individual claims that birthright depends on expectation, belief, and persistent practice. No one can prevent you from entering the astral world if you are determined to do so.

How To Use This Book

The first part of this book relates the history of astral travel through the ages, beginning with the ritual practices of the tribal shamans who were the forerunners of the priests, physicians, and magicians of later times, and proceeding up to the modern experiences of remote viewing and alien abduction, both of which are forms of soul flight. The second part is devoted to practical techniques with which to experience soul flight reliably and safely on a personal level.

Those impatient to get started with the practice of projecting the astral body need not read all the chapters in the first section, but may move directly to the second part of the book and begin ritual training. Later, if you wish, you can always go back and finish those chapters about history that you skipped. They are well worth reading, since they give an overview of soul flight through the ages that is not to be found elsewhere. In my opinion, the first part of the book is even more valuable than the second part since without a clear understanding of the true nature of soul flight, it is difficult to achieve its greatest utility or to fully understand what is happening during the projection of the astral body.

PART
ONE
HISTORY

CHAPTER
ONE

Shamanic
Soul Flight

It has been written that shamanism is ten thousand years old, but that is only a vague guess—a nice round number meant to signify, in the biblical sense, a very long time. When the first tribes started to gather in caves and chant songs of the hunt, there were shamans to lead them in their chants. When hunters were brought back to the cave dead or dying, shamans presided over their burials or called upon spirits to heal them. Shamanism is older than religion, perhaps as ancient as magic itself. There has never been a time since the human race discovered fire that shamans have not practiced their arts somewhere on this planet.

Each developing culture has had its own form of shamanism, unique in its details, but certain practices are common to all shamans around the world. Among these is the power to control spirits, to communicate with the dead, to heal the sick, to foresee the future, and to communicate with and control beasts. Most important of these shared practices is soul flight, the ability to leave the physical body during ecstatic trance and travel to the realms of spiritual beings for the purpose of acquiring wisdom or occult essences. Feathers frequently form an important part of the shaman's costume because the feather is the universal symbol for flight. It has been asserted by anthropologists that soul flight is one of the defining qualities of shamanism. All shamans possess the power of astral projection.

> What concerns us in this instance is the fact that sorcerers and shamans are able, *here on earth* and *as often as they wish*, to accomplish "coming out of the body," that is, the death that alone has power to transform the rest of mankind into "birds"; shamans and sorcerers can enjoy the condition of "souls," of "disincarnate beings," which is accessible to the profane only when they die. [1]

Shamans leave their bodies during trance for two main purposes: to communicate with spirits and to gather information across great distances. The shaman of a tribe enjoys a special relationship with spirits who are linked to his family line, or the line of his clan. One or several of these spirits single him out at an early age for the shamanic profession, and then visit with him to communicate his future path in life. The shaman sees these spirits in dreams or visions. After he has accepted his fate, the spirits become his teachers and instruct him in the ways of shamanism. Frequently the shaman marries one of the spirits. He has other lesser familiar spirits who act as his assistants.

Although I use the male gender for convenience, there have been many female shamans in different cultures. It is not exclusively a male profession. Female shamans also engage in soul flight, and sometimes wed the spirits who guide their progress and instruct them in their arts. A shamaness named Thorbjorg is described in detail in the Norse saga of *Eric the Red*. She was probably typical for her time and culture, although the appearance of the shamaness varied widely around the world. Many of her garments and ornaments were not merely decorative but had a magical function.

> When she came in the evening, with the man who had been sent to meet her, she was clad in a dark-blue cloak, fastened with a strap, and set with stones quite down to the hem. She wore glass beads around her neck, and upon her head a black lambskin hood, lined with white cat-skin. In her hands she carried a staff, upon which there was a knob, which was ornamented with brass, and set with stones up about the

---

1. Eliade, *Shamanism*, 479.

knob. Circling her waist she wore a girdle of touch-wood, and attached to it a great skin pouch, in which she kept the charms which she used when she was practicing her sorcery. She wore upon her feet shaggy calfskin shoes, with long, tough latchets, upon the ends of which there were large brass buttons. She had catskin gloves upon her hands, which were white inside and lined with fur.[2]

Beast and Spirit Relations

In soul flight, the shaman is able to assume at will the shape of a beast such as a wolf, a bear, or an eagle, in order to more swiftly progress to his destination. The animal forms selected are those of beasts who have a magical relationship with the shaman or his tribe, and are believed by the shaman to be linked to him by ties of blood; a shaman might take on the form of a wolf if he believed his family line descended from wolves because the wolf form would confer upon him heightened abilities.

In primitive cultures, there is difficulty in distinguishing between physical reality and spiritual reality. Members of the shaman's tribe believe that the shaman can actually change his body into the body of a reptile, animal, or bird. Sometimes even the shaman believes this to be so because he is in trance when it occurs and, in any case, it is in his interest to inflate his own reputation by maintaining this fiction of physical shape-changing, the better to awe and control the tribe. The transformation from human to animal form really takes place on the astral level. The entire astral world is easily molded by the mind, and this applies also to the astral body of the traveler himself.

Shamans during soul flight do not meet spirits in the ordinary world, but rather they do so in the higher realms in which the spirits dwell. The shaman possesses an extraordinary fiat to travel unhindered between the intermediate human realm and both the higher realm of the spirits and the lower realm of the dead. He does so for the purpose of carrying out the duties of his profession, which is of vital interest not only to the members of his tribe but also to those classes of spirits who are related by ties of ancient blood to the tribe. In primitive cultures, it was often believed that humans and spirits could interbreed. The idea that a person might have a family connection with a particular spirit was not seen as absurd. The value in such beliefs is that it joined humans and spirits in bonds of mutual support.

---

2. Anderson and Buel, *Norse Discovery of America*, 36–7.

Contrary to what might be assumed, this belief in the interbreeding of spirits with humans has not died out in modern Western culture, but has merely taken on a new form that is acceptable to the prejudices of the modern world. This belief has existed continuously throughout history. We will encounter it again when we examine witchcraft, the fairy faith, and alien abductions. It is also a part of the religious rapture of the saints, and relations between spirits and mediums in spiritualism, although in these cases it is less overt. It has never ceased to be believed from ancient to modern times because there is an underlying basis of truth to support it.

Shamans were the only members of the tribe who could go to the homes of the spirits of the forest, the spirits of the waters, and the spirits of the air, and enlist their aid either with gifts, reasoned argument, or threats. The use of threats was uncommon because shamans considered spirits to be their kin, and treated them with respect and even affection. When a shaman married a spirit, he became a part of the clan of that spirit, just as the spirit became a part of his clan. If the crops were dying of blight, the game animals had vanished from the usual hunting grounds, or the fish no longer filled the nets, it was the shaman's duty to discover the reason, and to use his knowledge and his connections with both the animals and the spirits to solve the problem.

Axis of the World

Access is often made to the higher spiritual via a tree or post that is climbed by means of a spiral series of notches. The notches, called *tapti* or *tapty* by the tribes of Siberia, are usually seven, nine, or twelve in number, although they may be more numerous. Each notch represents a successive heavenly level or plane. Seven is the most common division. When we examine Theosophy, we will again encounter this concept of the spirit realms divided into a series of seven successive planes. The tapti do not correspond, as might be supposed, with ruling deities, but rather with successive levels of spiritual reality.

The Altaic shaman climbs a tree or a post notched with seven or nine *tapty*, representing the seven or nine celestial levels. The "obstacles" (*pudak*) that he must overcome are really, as Anokhin remarked, the heavens that he must enter. When the Yakut make blood sacrifices, their shamans set up a tree with nine notches outdoors and climb it to carry the offering to the celestial god Ai Toyon. The initiation of shamans among the Sibo (related to the Tungus) includes, as we have seen, the presence of a tree with steps; another, smaller tree notched with nine *tapty* is kept in his yurt by the shaman. It is one more indication of his ability to journey ecstatically through the celestial regions.[3]

The tree represents the living axis of the world that has its roots in the underworld and its branches in the heavens. It is found in Norse legends in the form of Yggdrasill, the World Ash, the roots of which run so deep not even the wise god of the shamans, Odin, knows their endings. One of the many names of Odin is Yggr—he was named after the shamanic tree. In the religion of Voudoun, transplanted from Africa to the New World by black slaves, it appears in the form of the central pillar (*poteau-mitan*) of the ritual space that holds up the roof, representing the starry heavens.[4] During his ecstasy, this tree or post becomes for the shaman the central channel of the universe that he is able to ascend or descend at will, with the aid of his familiar spirits.

The ritual of ascent, performed before the watching members of his tribe, can be extended and elaborate. At each notch in the trunk of the tree, the shaman chants his attainment. In the Altaic ritual of ascent described in detail by Mircea Eliade, when the shaman reaches the sixth notch in the tree, he salutes the moon. When he ascends to the seventh, he salutes the sun. Having attained the "head" of the tree, he collapses to the floor of the ritual enclosure in a trance, and his soul leaves his body to soar through the heavenly regions he accessed in a symbolic way during his climb.

Descent to the Underworld

Descent into the underworld of the dead was achieved by passing through an opening in the ground, reached by means of a soul flight across the astral plane. Shamans descended to the underworld either to escort there the soul of a member of the tribe who had died, or sometimes to retrieve a soul in order to bring the newly dead back to life. Such descents were considered dangerous by shamans, and few records of the rituals they used still exist. In one such rare description, an Altaic shaman descended vertically down through seven subterranean levels called *pudak*, a word that means "obstacles." In this task, he was accompanied both by spirits of his ancestors and by familiars. At the seventh level, he reached the place where the nine subterranean rivers have their mouths and met the lord

---

3. Eliade, 275.
4. Deren, *Divine Horsemen*, 36.

of the dead, Erlik Khan, to whom he uttered a prayer. If the prayer was accepted, he was permitted to return to the surface.[5]

Sometimes a shaman who went down to rescue the soul of one who had died was not so fortunate. There is a tale in the *Chronicon Norvegiae* of a shaman who attempted to bring back the soul of a woman who had suffered a sudden death. In the middle of this work, a severe wound appeared on the shaman's abdomen and he fell lifeless to the ground. A second shaman revived the woman. She related how she had seen the astral spirit of the first shaman crossing a lake in the form of a walrus, and that someone had struck the animal with a weapon, causing the wound that was visible on the corpse.[6]

This story may not be a complete fiction. The appearance of marks or wounds on the physical body of someone engaged in astral travel is a common feature both of legends of the werewolf and other were-animals, and of the lore of spiritualism and Theosophy. It is known as repercussion. Werewolves are astral projections. The astral body can take any form desired, since its shape is not fixed but reflects the expectations and emotions of the traveler. Regarding repercussion, Charles W. Leadbeater wrote:

> The principle of sympathetic vibration mentioned above also provides the explanation of that strange and little-known phenomenon called repercussion, by means of which any injury done to, or any mark made upon, the materialized body in the course of its wanderings will be reproduced in the physical body. We find traces of this in some of the evidence given at trials for witchcraft in the middle ages, in which it is not infrequently stated that some wound given to the witch when in the form of a dog or a wolf was found to have appeared in the corresponding part of her human body.[7]

Repercussion appears when the projected body is of so dense an astral composition that it acquires an almost physical reality, and is seen by others as though it were a solid material body. This happens most often when it is projected in animal forms, since the emotions involved are of the most primal and powerful sort, and enable this seeming density of the astral vehicle. Repercussion is uncommon in ordinary projection of the astral double, and is not a consequence to be greatly feared by those experimenting with astral travel.

---

5. Eliade, 200–1.

6. Ibid., 383.

7. Leadbeater, *Astral Plane*, 123.

Shamanic Mind-Altering Techniques

In order to engage in soul flight, shamans needed to induce an altered state of consciousness. Because their role in their societies was so vital, shamans used whatever techniques were found to be effective, even those that might result in permanent injury or death. A shaman was expected to get results and often sacrificed the health of his mind and body in order to live up to his reputation. Mind-altering techniques used by shamans generally fall into three groups: (1) pain, (2) music, and (3) drugs.

Pain

Exalting the mind through pain or fatigue inflicted on the body takes the form of trials of endurance. The discomfort is sustained for prolonged periods, allowing normal consciousness to slip gradually into the entranced state necessary for the separation of the astral body. Frequently, the shaman denies himself water and food, denies himself sleep, exposes his body to the elements, and may even inflict injuries of various kinds upon himself, or have his disciples inflict these injuries. For example, the shaman might have his body bound in an uncomfortable position, or slash his arms and chest to deliberately make himself weak with blood loss and the pain of the cuts. Other forms of endurance include sitting for extended periods near a hot fire to induce dehydration and to overheat the body. The famous sweat lodge of the Plains Indians of America fulfilled the same function. Suspension of the body was also used by shamans.

Ordeals are usually most severe during initiation. Among the Manchu, nine holes were made in the ice and a person seeking to become a shaman was forced to dive into the first hole, come out of the second, and continue in this way to the end. If the spirits were with him, they would protect him. Another Manchu initiation involved fire walking. If the candidate was able to achieve contact with his tutelary spirits, it was believed they would shield his feet from the glowing embers.[8] A member of the Jivaro tribe of South America is forced to go for days without food, and drinks large amounts of tobacco juice. When a spirit finally appears to him, the master who is controlling the initiation proceeds to beat the initiate into unconsciousness.[9]

In ceremonies of initiation, there are two factors at work. One is the use of pain, hunger, and fatigue to induce an altered state of consciousness that is conducive to the

---

8. Eliade, 112.

9. Ibid., 84.

perception of spiritual beings. The other factor is the ordeal as a barrier that must be overcome in order to demonstrate worthiness to gain admission into the society of shamans. Even in the second case, the spirits play a part, for if the spirits have embraced the initiate and support him through his ordeals, he is able to pass the ordeals with ease. The candidate's successful fulfillment of the ordeal shows the older shaman overseeing the trials that the spirits have accepted him.

Such an extreme approach to soul flight as a trial of endurance is not recommended for the modern astral traveler, who will seldom be faced with the same degree of necessity that confronted the primitive shaman trying to solve a problem vital to the survival of his tribe. However, this method of altering consciousness is not unpracticed in modern Western cultures, although it is almost never linked with astral travel by those who practice it. It occurs during extended scenes of bondage in sadomasochistic sexual play—what is generally known as the BDSM scene. Those who have been bound and whipped for hours as a way of heightening their sexual response report a sense of leaving their own bodies, accompanied by an intense euphoria. For some recipients of the physical abuse, this is the ultimate objective, more important than any sexual release.

From the early centuries of the present era until the Renaissance, it was common for monks and nuns to chastise their bodies, or to have others inflict chastisement upon them, and also to engage in prolonged trials of endurance and deprivation. The most famous example is that of the Christian fanatics known as Stylitës, or Pillar Saints, who lived on the tops of stone pillars, exposed to the elements both day and night. Simeon the Stylite of Syria (died AD 460) spent thirty-seven years of his life on various pillars, the final one sixty-six feet in height. It has been speculated that those monks and nuns receiving punishment derived sexual pleasure from it, and this is no doubt true, given how closely chastisements of the flesh used by the religious parallel the sexual play of submissives and masochists. However, sexual pleasure was not the primary goal, but rather freedom from the yoke of the body by inducing spontaneous astral projection, which resulted in visions that were interpreted as divine revelations.

Music

The second general technique employed by shamans to transform their consciousness involves rhythm and sound. It is the least dangerous of the three, but perhaps the most effective since it can be replicated with exactitude and does not reduce to a serious degree the vital energies of the body. A shaman undergoing an extreme trial of the flesh may be brought so near death when he finally achieves separation of the astral body that he is unable to fulfill his tasks in the astral world. The musical technique avoids this unfortunate outcome.

As might be expected, rhythm is the most important component. The European shaman is renowned for his drum: a broad, flat instrument resembling a large tambourine that is beaten with a curved stick. It was believed to have been cut from the trunk of the World Tree that is the axis of the universe.[10] The shamans of the North American Indians used a similar drum. Rhythmic beating of this drum is able to change the heart rate and other more subtle bio-rhythms of the body. The drumming is often accompanied by singing or chanting, using either words or repetitions of sound patterns. Another component that often appears in this induction technique is rhythmic dancing to the beat of a drum or drums, or the clapping of hands. Dancing has the added effect of inducing fatigue in the body, so it is in part a pain technique. There is no rule that the three categories I have defined can never overlap. Shamans used whatever they found to be effective, without regard to formal classifications.

Chanting was a popular form of rhythmic induction. The same phrase or phrases would be repeated in a low voice, sometimes for hours, accompanied by rocking motions of the body. We see the same technique employed in modern society by religious groups during prayer. Catholics chant on their rosaries. Jews chant in their synagogues and at the Wailing Wall in Jerusalem. Muslims chant the verses of the Koran. The result is not always the separation of the astral body, but often this type of prolonged chanting induces an elevated mental condition or even an ecstatic state.

A less well-recognized induction technique employed by shamans is the use of extended pure tones in the form of whistling. When formed by the lips, the notes are sounded as long as there is air in the lungs, then at once renewed when a new breath is drawn. In this way, the notes can be repeated indefinitely. Sometimes flutes or whistles are employed. This method can be highly effective. The mind is able to glide along on the extended musical note, which extends away from the shaman who forms it almost like a flowing river of sound. It is possible to ride this sound away from the physical body, to use it as a vehicle of separation.

The tones used were originally arrived at in an intuitive way. The shaman used what he had found to give the best result in altering his consciousness. Repeated usage establishes a

---

10. Eliade, 270.

ritual and a tradition within the culture in which certain notes are perceived to be magical or possessed of a heightened occult potency. This process is always how rituals are established. Individuals perform actions that they intuit to be effective, and these become institutionalized and passed down through generations. Those who disparage the religious rituals of modern Western society as empty forms should bear in mind that rituals only come to exist in a society because those who institute them perceive them to have practical value. They do not arise from nothing, or without purpose.

Drugs

The third technique used by shamans to separate the astral body is the use of intoxicating substances derived from herbs, mushrooms, roots, bark, berries, and other natural sources. By far the most popular and common is alcohol, in the form of wine or beer. In ancient times, the Greeks considered wine a gift from the gods, to be employed only for sacred purposes such as communicating with the gods and receiving their inspiration. The Greeks held the same views regarding theater, dance, and music, since all were found to alter and exalt consciousness. This attitude is shamanic to the core. Needless to say, wine was soon debased for common purposes of pleasure, as was music and theater, but in their most ancient forms, they were sacred.

Most individuals who get drunk in a bar on a Friday night probably don't consider that, at one time, intoxication was held to be an important pathway to the spirit world. Used with careful moderation, in company with drumming and chanting, alcohol can be highly effective. Excessive indulgence overwhelms the mind completely and no useful result is possible. Carried to its extreme, alcohol is a deadly poison. The wine brewed in primitive cultures was fairly weak, and was limited by the concentration of alcohol that the yeast excreting the alcohol could endure. Wine has its own natural limit on alcohol percentage, and above a certain point the yeast that makes the alcohol becomes poisoned by it. Only when wine is fortified—having additional alcohol added to it—can that limit be exceeded. To make fortified wine requires distilling, something unknown to simple shamanic cultures. Therefore, we know that the wine or beer used to induce an exalted mental state for the purpose of soul flight was quite mild by the standards of modern excess.

Another popular drug employed by the shamans of the New World—and, after the voyages of discovery of the early Europeans, in the Old World as well—was tobacco. Our modern culture has so abused and debased this plant that it is sometimes difficult to realize that it was sacred for the American Indians. They regarded it as sacred for its mind-altering properties. Tobacco was found to sharpen and focus thoughts, while at the same time relaxing the body; it enhances mental clarity in part by widening tiny blood vessels in the brain, a process known as cerebrovasodilation, so that more blood can flow through them, feeding the brain with increased levels of oxygen. Yet, paradoxically, by acting on the nervous system, tobacco constricts blood vessels in the body and raises a person's blood pressure, which further enhances this mental sharpness by pumping blood through the brain under increased pressure. In addition to these remarkable qualities, tobacco is an analgesic that reduces pain in the body, an anti-psychotic, and an effective anxiolytic that reduces anxiety levels.

The shamans of the northern and central regions of the Americas relied on tobacco, rolling the dried leaves of the plant or putting them into pipes to smoke, chewing them, or drinking the extracted juice. But the shamans of the southern region of the Americas preferred the leaves of the cocoa plant, from which the modern illegal narcotic cocaine is derived. As is true of fortified wine and the hard spirits of alcohol, the ancient shamans never experienced the effects of cocaine because they did not possess the technology to manufacture it. They chewed the fresh cocoa leaves, mingling the juice gradually with their saliva, which they swallowed. The leaves of the cocoa plant induce euphoria, coupled with a temporary freedom from pain or weakness. The cocoa leaves were often used, or abused, by the common members of the tribe in order to carry heavy loads for long distances, or to cross large tracks of countryside with unnatural swiftness.

A mind-altering substance occurring naturally in the central part of the New World is peyote. Extracted from several species of mescal cactuses growing in what is now Mexico and the southwestern United States, it was used to induce visions and, thanks in large part to the books of Carlos Castaneda, is perhaps the most famous of the naturally occurring drugs employed by shamans. Castaneda wrote:

> My basic assumption in both books [*The Teachings of Don Juan* and *A Separate Reality*] has been that the articulation points in learning to be a sorcerer were the states of nonordinary reality produced by the ingestion of psychotropic plants.
>
> In this respect don Juan was an expert in the use of three such plants: *Datura inoxia*, commonly known as jimson weed; *Lophophora williamsii*, known as peyote; and a hallucinogenic mushroom of the genus *Psilocybe*.[11]

---

11.   Castaneda, *Journey to Ixtlan*, 7.

If history teaches us anything, it is that the excessive use and abuse of a substance or technique for exalting consciousness will not produce a useful result. We have learned this in the uses of music, theater, dance, poetry, alcohol, tobacco, cocaine, and it certainly applies to peyote and other mind-altering substances such as LSD. Castaneda goes on to write in *Journey to Ixtlan* that he was wrong in his assumption, and that it is possible to learn to induce states of "nonordinary reality" by means other than drugs. I will go still further and assert that outside of a rigorously controlled traditional ritual context, it is almost impossible to use drugs in a useful spiritual way, such as for the exaltation of consciousness and the separation of the astral body.

Even within such a context, the use of drugs to force the astral shell from the body can have dire consequences. Both the minds and bodies of traditional shamans have been severely degraded by the habitual use of powerful drugs, and even by the use of milder drugs in massive quantities. For example, tobacco was not only smoked and chewed, but ingested by shamans in the form of concentrated juice from the leaves. Even today the shamans of the Campa people of the eastern Peruvian rain forest drink large amounts of tobacco syrup as an intoxicant. In large enough amounts, tobacco juice is a deadly poison, as those who have worked on tobacco farms, handing the cured leaves, will testify. Given a long period of exposure, enough nicotine can be absorbed through the skin of the hands to kill those who are not habituated to it.

Music and Dance Recommended

Of the three classes of technique used by shamans to induce soul flight that I have described, I must strongly recommend against the first and third classes. Both have been proven effective over centuries yet both carry serious risks that the modern soul flyer does not need to take. In the first class, abuse applied to the body can easily result in permanent injuries that will disfigure or hinder those who experiment with pain techniques for the rest of their lives. The danger of the third class, drugs of various kinds, is so amply illustrated by the fate of addicts that little more need be written. Even the very mild natural drugs used in traditional shamanic cultures can be abused, and this is doubly true of the enhanced and concentrated drugs produced by modern chemistry. For example, the tobacco plant that is transformed into cigarettes has a much higher concentration of nicotine than any tobacco plant used by the shamans of pre-Columbian America.

Some modern drugs are so absurdly powerful that those who experiment with them might as well put a loaded gun to their heads and blow their brains out. LSD is so potent that the smallest speck will cause a psychotic state that endures for many hours. Those who have used LSD and believe themselves to have survived the experience intact may laugh at this caution, but in addition to the well-known genetic damage that LSD causes, those who have interacted with habitual users are aware of the more subtle mental damage the abuse of this drug can inflict. LSD burnout is a real phenomenon and the consequences are tragic.

In contrast to physical self-abuse and drugs, the use of dancing, chanting, percussive rhythms, and musical tones is relatively safe. When coupled with ritual, as they invariably were when employed by shamans, they can also be effective at generating an out-of-body experience. Ecstasy through dance and song is an uplifting experience that has no negative repercussions, apart from perhaps a gentle fatigue of the body that is without lasting effect.

CHAPTER TWO

Witches' Flying Ointment

Traditional European witchcraft descends from shamanism, which is evident when we compare the abilities attributed to witches during the medieval witch trials with the powers of shamans. Witches healed the sick. They performed divination and augury. They conversed with spirits and kept familiar spirits as their servants, usually in the forms of small animals such as cats. Witches were able to bewitch beasts, cause storms, and affect the growth of crops. Spirits instructed them in the technical details of their profession. Most significantly, it was believed that they had the power of flight. All these abilities are shamanic.

Sixteenth-century English author Reginald Scot gave an extended catalog of the supposed powers of witches in his *Discoverie of Witchcraft*, including the following talents:

Some write that with wishing they can send needles into the livers of their enimies. Some that they can transferre corne in the blade from one place to another. Some, that they can cure diseases supernaturallie, flie in the aire, and danse with divels. Some write, that they can plaie the part of *Succubus*, and contract themselves to *Incubus*; and so yoong prophets are upon them begotten, etc. Som saie they can transubstantiate themselves and others, and take the forms and shapes of asses, woolves, ferrets, cowes, apes, horsses, dogs, etc. Some say they can keepe divels and spirits in the likenesse of todes and cats.[12]

Why Most Witches Were Women

The term *witch* is gender neutral, as is the term *shaman*. Even so, today most people think of witches as exclusively women. There is a reason for this error. Throughout history witches have been presented in literature and in art as female. Medieval Christian theologians held that women were by their nature more susceptible to evil influences than men. They derived this belief in part from the biblical fable of Adam and Eve because it was Eve who was seduced by the Serpent. Due to this imagined vulnerability of women, theologians believed that more women than men became witches. However, many men were also accused of witchcraft and executed for it. An examination of the long lists of witch names in Appendix III of Margaret A. Murray's *Witch-Cult in Western Europe* shows a ratio or roughly one man for every ten women.

Since the practice of shamanism in pagan times was divided between men and women, it may be wondered why witchcraft, its descendent, came to be associated predominantly with women. A possible answer lies in tracing what became of the role in society that had been filled by male shamans. It is apparent that their functions of intermediaries with the spirit world and healers of the sick were assumed, respectively, by priests and physicians—and neither profession was open to women in medieval Europe. To be a healer, a woman had to become a witch. To converse with the spirit realms and work magic, a woman had to become a witch. Or, at least, women who healed and made charms were understood to be witches by the general population, and may have considered themselves to be witches also.

---

12. Scot, *Discoverie of Witchcraft*, bk. I, chap. 4, p. 6.

How Many Witches Were There?

It is impossible to know how extensive the practice of witchcraft was in Europe prior to and during the Renaissance, when the persecution of witches by the Catholic and Protestant churches reached its height. The records of the witch interrogations and the literary works of witch finders, demonologists, and priests of the Inquisition certainly exaggerated their number outrageously, but when this exaggeration is discarded, it must be concluded that traditional shamanic skills passed down from generation to generation as a cultural heritage of rural European communities formed the basis for the genuine practice of witchcraft.

It is currently estimated that around forty thousand men, women, and children accused of witchcraft were executed in Europe over a span of three centuries—roughly between the years 1450 to 1750, the approximate duration of the witch mania that gripped the Christian churches. Rossell Hope Robbins gives a much higher estimate of executions, around two hundred thousand,[13] but even this is very conservative when compared with the ridiculous numbers that have circulated, some of them in the millions! These higher estimates are quite absurd. It is unlikely the number of executions exceeded one hundred thousand, and it was probably less than half this amount. C. L'Estrange Ewen, author of *Witchcraft and Demonianism*, guessed that only about one thousand accused witches were hanged in England. The numbers executed on the Continent were much higher, but they have been wildly overestimated by many authorities.

Executions for witchcraft, even were the numbers known with assurance, would be a perilous way of computing the actual number of practicing witches. The majority of those executed had nothing to do with witchcraft and no knowledge of it, other than what they may have picked up in general gossip, or during the interrogations of their torturers. They were accused of witchcraft by spiteful neighbors or hysterical children. Practicing witches were vulnerable to discovery because it was the nature of their art that they had dealings with common people, so undoubtedly many of the accused were true witches. But we can only guess just how many genuine witches were burned or hanged for witchcraft. It was a small percentage of the total number executed.

What can be stated with some assurance is that there were indeed witches—men and women living alone or in family groups in villages and towns, offering such services as the healing of disease, fortunetelling, protection from evil spirits, communications with

---

13.   Robbins, *Encyclopedia of Witchcraft*, 180.

the dead, and the sale of charms for various purposes such as compelling love or finding treasure. They used a mixture of folk magic and folk medicine. Whether such a person was known locally as a wise woman or a witch probably depended on how highly they were regarded in the community. Until recent times, *witch* was a wholly pejorative term. The Bible mandated a sentence of death for witches (Exodus 22:18), so to accuse some-one of being a witch was to condemn them to execution, particularly toward the close of the Renaissance when the furor against witchcraft reached an hysterical frenzy.

Witch's Familiar

The witch's familiar was held by the demonologists who wrote against them during the witch craze to be either an animal possessed by an evil spirit, or an evil spirit in the shape of an animal. In the second case, the familiar spirit was believed to have actually assumed a material body, composing it from the moisture of the air and from the dust and smoke in the air. Matthew Hopkins, the Witchfinder General of England, wrote in his *Discovery of Witches* (1647) that Elizabeth Clark possessed a familiar named Vinegar Tom that had the power to change its shape. He saw it first in the form of a greyhound with a head like an ox and large eyes, and before his sight it transformed into a child of about four years with no head that went running madly around the house, then vanished at the door.[14]

The usual assumption is that Hopkins was lying in order to ensure the conviction of Elizabeth Clark for witchcraft. However, it is possible that he was in such a heightened state of anxiety and hysteria while he interrogated the woman that he saw the familiar in the form of an astral vision. Contrary to what Hopkins believed, the spirit he identified as Vinegar Tom had no material body, and it may not even have been connected in any way with Elizabeth Clark. It is possible that it was a spirit linked to Hopkins himself, that chose to represent itself as a familiar of the accused witch in order to fulfill the expecta-tions of Hopkins. If any man was haunted by evil spirits, it was surely Hopkins, who was responsible for the deaths of hundreds of innocent women.

Goddess of the Witches

As is the case with legends and stories about shamans, there is often confusion between the physical and spiritual in the medieval accounts of witchcraft. Many records of the witch trials declare witches to have the power to physically fly through the air, as well as

---

14. Robbins, 192.

the ability to vanish from sight or transform themselves into cats or other creatures. The theologians, unwilling to grant any power to the witches themselves, ascribed the power of flight to the Devil. Francesco Maria Guazzo wrote: "Further I hold it to be very true that sometimes witches are really transported from place to place by the devil who, in the shape of a goat or some other fantastic animal, both carries them bodily to the sabbat and himself is present at its obscenities. This is the general opinion of the Theologians and Jurisconsults of Italy, Spain, and Catholic Germany; while a great many others are of a like opinion."[15]

Guazzo substituted the ubiquitous Devil in place of the lunar goddess Diana, as referred to in the much older ninth-century decree of the Council of Ancyra, recorded in the *Canon Episcopi*, which mentions that "certeine wicked women following sathans provocations, being seduced by the illusion of divels, beleeve and professe that in the night times they ride abroad with *Diana*, the goddesse of the *Pagans*, or else with *Herodias*, with an innumerable multitude, upon certeine beasts, and passe over manie countries and nations, in the silence of the night, and doo whatsoever those fairies or ladies command."[16]

Herodias is the daughter of Diana, the moon, by her brother Lucifer, the sun, according to the Italian witches' gospel published in 1897 under the title *Aradia* by the folklorist Charles G. Leland. Herodias is the ruling tutelary spirit of all witches, who is commanded by Diana to descend to the earth to communicate the secrets of witchcraft to human beings. The shamanic overtones are overt and undeniable:

'Tis true indeed that thou a spirit art,
But thou wert born but to become again
A mortal; thou must go to earth below
To be a teacher unto women and men
Who fain would study witchcraft in thy school.[17]

By "go to earth below," manifestation to human perceptions is intended, so that witches will be able to see and hear Herodias, or Aradia, allowing her to instruct them in Diana's forbidden arts. Until spirits manifest on the astral level, they have no existence to human

---

15. Guazzo, *Compendium Maleficarum*, 34.

16. Scot, bk. III, chap. 16, p. 37.

17. Leland, *Aradia*, 4.

consciousness. There is also an echo here of the Gnostic myth of Sophia, goddess of wisdom, who incarnated as a mortal woman in order to aid human souls mired in ignorance to regain their divine birthright to dwell among the stars.

Witch's Power of Flight

Witchcraft is ancient in Italy, and even in its pagan beginnings involved soul flight. The second-century Roman writer Lucius Apuleius, in his novel *The Golden Ass*, described the flight of the witch Pamphilë, who smeared her body with a magic ointment and transformed herself into the form of an owl:

> And when midnight came, she led me softly into a high chamber and bid me look thorow the chink of a doore: where first I saw how shee put of all her garments, and took out of a certain coffer sundry kindes of Boxes, of the which she opened one, and tempered the ointment therein with her fingers, and then rubbed her body therewith from the sole of the foot to the crowne of the head, and when she had spoken privily with her selfe, having the candle in her hand, she shaked the parts of her body, and behold, I perceived a plume of feathers did burgen out, her nose waxed crooked and hard, her nailes turned into clawes, and so she became an Owle. Then she cried and screeched like a Bird of that kinde, and willing to proove her force, mooved her selfe from the ground by little and little, til at last she flew quite away.[18]

Notice that the metamorphosis from woman to owl was not effected solely by means of the ointment, but was triggered with the muttering of an incantation. This suggests that it took place in a ritual context, although Apuleius does not bother to describe any other aspects of the ritual. Elizabeth Style, accused of witchcraft in Somerset, England, in 1664, gave her version of the flying incantation to her inquisitors. After anointing her forehead and the insides of her wrists with a greenish, raw-smelling oil that was brought to her by a spirit, she spoke the words "Thout, tout a tout, tout, throughout and about" and was carried away. To return to her house, she spoke the words "Rentum, Tormentum."[19]

In the novel of Apuleius, the transformation is physical. Pamphilë actually becomes an owl, the better to fly through the air. This is nonsense, as it should be needless to point out. The flight of witches as owls certainly did occur, but it was an astral—not a physi-

---

18. Apuleius, chap. XVI, 67.
19. Murray, *Witch-Cult in Western Europe*, 101.

cal—flight. We can be quite certain about this from a few eyewitness accounts of witches when they actually were engaging in soul flight. These accounts, small in number, are remarkably uniform. The witch is observed lying unconscious for an extended period of time. Sometimes she is seen to apply an ointment to her naked body before lying down or falling down and going to sleep. Attempts to rouse her from her trance are usually futile. When at last she recovers her senses, she declares that she was on a journey, and may believe that the journey was taken in her physical body, although it is evident to the witness that this was not the case.

The demonologist Johann Weyer, who was the pupil of Cornelius Agrippa, quotes Giovanni Battista Porta (1535–1615) on this matter. Porta recorded in the second book of his work *Magia naturalis* (*Natural Magic*) how an elderly witch offered to give him an account of the things she experienced during her magical flight, which was effected by means of an ointment that she applied to her body.

> Removing her clothing, she vigorously rubbed herself all over with some ointment, while we observed through cracks in the door. She collapsed under the force of the soporific juices and fell into a profound sleep. We opened the doors, and struck her repeatedly, but her sleep was so deep that she felt nothing. We returned to our position outside, and now the strength of her remedy began to weaken and grow feeble. Awaking from sleep, she began a long raving story of crossing seas and mountains, and she brought forth false responses. We denied her story, but she insisted upon it. We showed her the black-and-blue marks, but she became all the more stubborn.[20]

The same sort of account occurs in the 1525 *Tractatus de strigibus sive maleficus* of the Dominican monk Bartholomaeus of Spina (1465–1546), who relates the story told to him by his friend, Augustus de Turre of Bergamo. While still a young man, Augustus returned late one night to his rented house in the university town of Pavia, where he was studying to become a physician. For a long time he pounded on the door, but nobody answered. In frustration, he climbed the side of the house to a balcony and entered through an open window, and then went looking for the maid who was supposed to have been ready and waiting to unbolt the door when he knocked. He found her in her room, lying unconscious on the floor, and left her to her sleep. The next day, when he asked her what she had been doing on the floor, she replied that she had been "on a journey."

---

20. Weyer, *On Witchcraft*, 114.

Writing about the astral flight of witches in his 1597 work *Daemonologie*, King James VI of Scotland, who would later be crowned King James I of England, observed:

> And some sayeth, that their bodies lying stil as in an extasy, their spirits will be rauished out of their bodies, & carried to such places. And for verefying thereof, wil giue euident tokens, aswel by witnesses that haue seene their body lying senseles in the meane time, as by naming persones, whomwith they mette, and giuing tokens quhat purpose was amongst them, whome otherwaies they could not haue knowen: for this forme of journeing, they affirme to vse most, when they are transported from one Countrie to another.[21]

The Sabbat Gatherings

It was the general belief of the demonologists that witches flew through the air, either in body or in spirit, to attend the great gatherings of witches known as sabbats, which were supposed to be held at certain times of year, most notably All Hallow's Eve (October 31) and Walpurgis Night (April 30), usually on high places such as the tops of mountains. The Brocken or Blocksburg in the Hartz Mountains of Germany was the most famous location for this gathering.

More fascinating from the point of view of astral travel and the astral world is the gathering place supposed to have been used by the witches of Mora, in Sweden, who attracted the ire of the clergy and of the Swedish monarch Charles XI in the year 1669. The accused witches called the place the Blocula, according to their inquisitors, who described it as "a delicate large meadow, whereof you can see no end. The place or house they met at had before it a gate painted with divers colors; through this gate they went into a little meadow distinct from the other, where the beasts went that they used to ride on."[22] A schoolteacher who claimed that the Devil had carried him there described it as an island.

In 1730, long after the accused witches of Mora had been executed, a thirteen-year-old Norwegian girl named Siri Jørgensdatter claimed that when she was seven, her grandmother had taken her to visit the Blocula. "Siri told them that when she was seven years old, her grandmother took her to a pigsty, where she smeared a sow with some ointment she took from a horn, whereupon they both mounted and after a short ride through the

---

21. James I, bk. II, chap. 4, pp. 39–40.

22. Robbins, 349–50.

air arrived at a place that her grandmother called Blaakullen."[23] The sow was left outside the building. They entered and sat down at one of seven tables next to the Devil, who was referred to as "grandfather" by Siri's grandmother.

This child's accusation of witchcraft came to nothing, and it was dismissed by the bishop who reviewed it. It contains a number of interesting details. The flying ointment was kept in a horn, which because of its crescent shape is symbolic of the moon. The sow is a lunar beast. It was the sow that was smeared with the ointment, but the girl and her grandmother straddled it, bringing their sexual parts into contact with the ointment. The mention of a pigsty recalls an incident related by Bartholomaeus de Spina, who in his *Tractatus de strigibus sive malificis* told of a notary from Lugano who missed his wife when he arose one morning and went searching for her around his estate. He located her naked and dirty, lying unconscious in the pigsty. When he interrogated her, she tearfully admitted that during the night she had gone "on a journey."[24]

The Blocula, insofar as it can be said to have had any existence, is clearly an astral place. The beasts supposed to have carried the witches there were astral beasts, carrying their astral forms. It is doubtful, however, that Swedish witches ever traveled to the Blocula, either physically or astrally, to attend large sabbat gatherings. The whole concept of the great witch sabbat was an invention of the inquisitors of the church. Rossell Hope Robbins wrote: "The conception of the sabbat seems to have been fabricated during the fourteenth and fifteen centuries, largely by the investigators and judges connected with the Inquisition."[25] Witches were solitary practitioners of their shamanic traditions, or at most family practitioners, and never met in large groups. However, it is possible that the story of the Blocula as an astral place was derived by the inquisitors from some traditional belief among Swedish witches, perhaps a belief that descended from a pagan myth of paradise.

Methods of Flight

An interesting aspect of the soul flight of traditional European witches is the methods supposed to have been used to carry them through the air. Citing Nicolas Rémy's *Demonolatry* as his source, Guazzo mentions numerous forms of transportation:

---

23. Robbins, 288.

24. Hansen, *Witch's Garden*, 87.

25. Robbins, 414–5.

But it must be known that before they go to the Sabbat they anoint themselves upon some part of their bodies with an unguent made from various foul and filthy ingredients, but chiefly from murdered children; and so anointed they are carried away on a cowl-staff, or a broom, or a reed, a cleft stick or a distaff, or even a shovel, which things they ride. At times they are mounted upon an ox or a goat or a dog, and so are carried to their feast. And yet again they go on foot when the place is not far distant.[26]

In earliest times, it was by transformation into birds, as the quotation from the novel of Apuleius demonstrates. By the tenth century, the prevailing belief was that witches flew on the backs of beasts sacred to the lunar goddess Diana. In the fanatical eyes of the medieval church, pagan Diana was only one step away from Satan, so it was maintained that witches flew on beasts controlled by the Devil, or sometimes were carried through the air by the Devil or by his demons. A later evolution gives the witch a stick to ride upon. This stick takes several forms. It can be a simple forked twig—forked to indicate duality and thus duplicity, after the manner of the forked tongue of the serpent. Or it can be a homely farm implement such as a pitchfork, which had two prongs in early times, or a corn broom.

Witches are shown in old woodcuts straddling the broom or sitting astride it side-saddle. Usually the bush of the broom points forward, but there is no rule about this, and sometimes the handle of the broom is depicted foremost. This is the archetypal image of the flying witch that has come down through the centuries to our modern celebrations of Halloween. More than any other single visual image, it embodies the popular conception of the witch of folklore. That the witch is flying in the image is significant. Flight is an absolutely essential part of the archetype.

Sometimes witches were said to fly to the sabbat on wands or simple rods, which they held between their legs for the purpose. This may refer to autoerotic stimulation by the witch to help achieve the altered consciousness necessary to separate the astral body from the physical body. It is possible that witches masturbated with some form of dildo to aid in soul flight. Such powerful archetypes as the witch on her broom have astonishing persistence and show up in the culture in curious ways. Recently a company was forced to stop making vibrating *Harry Potter* flying brooms for children. It was discovered that older girls were taking the toys from their younger siblings and playing with

---

26. Guazzo, 34–5.

them alone for prolonged periods of time. Whether astral travel was achieved by these girls is doubtful.

There seems little difference between the soul flight of the shamans of primitive cultures—frequently induced by intoxicating drugs such as alcohol, nicotine, and peyote—and the astral flight of medieval European witches, which was often provoked by what has come to be known as flying ointment. This ointment was sometimes applied to the wands or rods that witches held between their legs during flight. If these wands were used as dildos, absorption of the active components of the ointment through the mucous membranes of the sexual parts would have been rapid. The witch's ointment was also used to cause the illusion of shape-shifting, an activity closely related to soul flight since witches as well as shamans sometimes believed themselves to fly through the air in the forms of birds, or run swiftly over the ground in the forms of wolves or other beasts.

Nature of Flying Ointment

Exactly how the flying ointment worked was beyond the understanding of the times. The uncommonly enlightened Francis Bacon (1561–1626) in his *Sylva Sylvarum*, a treatise written in his last year of life, expressed his conviction that flying ointment induced a hallucination by means of "soporiferous medicines" such as the juices of smallage, wolfbane, and cinquefoil. He was undoubtedly correct, as we may surmise from our modern vantage. By contrast, Henry More wrote in his 1653 work *Antidote Against Atheism* that the ointment sealed up the pores of the skin, and in this way preserved the heat of the body while the soul was absent, allowing it to survive until the soul's return.[27] He believed the ointment incidental to the projection of the soul, but necessary to preserve the life of the body. Eyewitness accounts of witches lying in trance, who later claimed to have been flying, indicated to enlightened men such as Bacon and More that no physical flight was involved, but the more credulous continued to believe that witches actually flew.

A surprising number of recipes of witches' flying ointment have survived down to the present in written form. Hansen mentions that sixteen of them are "comparatively reliable."[28] The active ingredients were the juices from narcotic or psychotropic plants. The inactive ingredients were occult in nature, and probably played no part in the effectiveness of the ointment. These include such things as soot and bat's blood. The base

---

27.   Robbins, 365.

28.   Hansen, 90.

of the ointment was rendered fat, into which the active and inactive ingredients were blended.

The priests of the Inquisition and the demonologists such as Guazzo maintained that the fat was obtained from murdered babies. This should probably be regarded as little more than a slander against witches, who likely used the same type of lard they employed for cooking. However, it is possible that when this slander became common knowledge, some men and women who fancied themselves witches, as the Inquisition understood witches—that is, as agents of Satan —may have actually used the fat of infants. An alternative base to fat was oil, which would have been less effective since the ointment would more quickly run off the body, or be wiped off by the movements of the limbs. Some scholars suppose the "oil" specified in the formulae to be a euphemism for baby fat.

The other major inactive ingredient, soot, would have the effect of coloring the ointment black. When smeared over the entire naked body it would make an effective concealment for travel at night, when the ointment was applied for the purpose of shape-shifting. As mentioned, shape-shifting is an astral event, but those who believed themselves transformed into wolves, bears, stags, or other beasts, and intoxicated by the effects of the ointment, may have run through the fields and villages in their physical bodies beneath the light of the moon, under the delusion that they had changed into the bodies of beasts. In the tale related by Bartholomaeus de Spina concerning the wife of the notary from Lugano, who found his wife unconscious in the pigsty, it may be significant that the wife is described as dirty. The dirt could have come from the sty, or perhaps if she used a flying ointment, it was from soot in the ointment.

The method of applying the ointment, according to Lucius Apuleius, was to rub it vigorously into the skin all over the body from the soles of the feet to the hairline. For this purpose, the witch was more or less forced to make herself naked. The common image of a nude witch applying the ointment to her body promoted the myth of the lustfulness of witches. Reginald Scot wrote that the ointment was rubbed into the skin until the skin was reddened by the friction, bringing the blood to just beneath the surface and warming it so that the pores were opened.[29] It is likely that it was also rubbed into the genitals.

---

29.   Murray, 100.

Three Recipes for Flying Ointment

Margaret A. Murray provided three simple recipes for flying ointment in the final appendix of her *Witch-Cult in Western Europe* that are translated into English from an unnamed French source, or sources.

1. Parsley, water of aconite, poplar leaves, and soot.

2. Water parsnip, sweet flag, cinquefoil, bat's blood, deadly nightshade, and oil.

3. Baby's fat, juice of water parsnip, aconite, cinquefoil, deadly nightshade, and soot.[30]

The active ingredient of the first formula is aconite, which is derived from a root and was a poison well-known to the Romans. It is an alkaloid that causes irregularity and stopping of the heart. A. J. Clark, who wrote the appendix to Murray's book, points out that the parsley (*du persil* in the French text) may actually have been hemlock, which he says closely resembles parsley. Hemlock, a poison used in classical times, produces paralysis of the body that is sometimes accompanied by delirium.

The second formula contains the active ingredient deadly nightshade, or belladonna. In moderate doses, it generates excitement or delirium, but eating as few as fourteen berries is known to have caused death. Clark suggests that water parsnip, which is harmless, may actually refer to the poisonous water hemlock or cowbane.

The active ingredients of the third formula are aconite and deadly nightshade. Together they would cause irregularity in the heartbeat and emotional excitement.

Notice that two of the recipes contain soot, which has no active function but would blacken the ointments. The first may have been thickened by a paste made from ground and pulverized poplar leaves, or more probably fresh green poplar buds, which yield a thick juice when crushed that was employed for the making of ointment. The second was liquid and used an oil as its base. The third relied on human fat taken from an infant. In the medieval European world, infant deaths were commonplace. Woman had many children, and the majority of them died in infancy. It is impossible to know if baby fat was ever used in a flying ointment, but it was not an unobtainable substance, and would not necessarily have required murder. Human fat is perhaps more readily absorbed through the skin than animal fat, since it is so similar to the fat beneath the skin of the person applying it.

---

30. Murray, 279.

Active Ingredients

Harold A. Hansen lists twenty-seven ingredients that occur either once, or multiple times, in traditional flying ointment recipes. Most would seem to have no active properties, but it is possible that their inclusion created a catalytic effect, enhancing, limiting, or otherwise modifying the power of the active substances. Soot appears in seven of the sixteen recipes that Hansen regards as reliable. The only ingredient that is found more often is cinquefoil (*Potentilla reptans*) which occurs in eight.

The main active ingredients appear to be water hemlock (*Cicuta vivosa*), hemlock (*Conium maculatum*), monkshood (*Aconitum napellus*), opium poppy (*Papaver somniferum*), deadly nightshade (*Atropa belladonna*), henbane (*Hyoscyamus niger*), black nightshade (*Solanum nigrum*), mandrake (*Mandragora officinarum*), thornapple (*Datura stramonium*), darnel (*Lolium temulentum*), poison lettuce (*Lactuca virosa*) and black poplar (*Populus niger*).

Hemlock and water hemlock have similar poisonous effects. It was a concoction of hemlock that was used to execute the Greek philosopher Socrates. Hansen asserts that the juices of the two hemlocks, when rubbed into the skin, cause the sensation of gliding through the air.[31]

Monkshood is poisonous when applied to the surface of the skin. The naturalist Pliny the Elder wrote in his *Natural History* that the Roman Calpurnius Bestia murdered a succession of wives by rubbing aconitine on their sexual parts as they slept. "It is established that of all poisons the quickest to act is aconite, and that death occurs on the same day if the genitals of a female creature are but touched by it."[32]

The juice of the opium poppy causes languor and hallucinations. In modern times, we are familiar with the power of the opium poppy's concentrated extract, heroin, but the raw gum that seeps from cuts in the seed pods can be smoked, or the plant can be eaten, to produce a less potent effect. Opium was known about and used by physicians in Europe during the Middle Ages. It is possible that witches mistakenly assumed that they could get the same effect from the common corn poppy (*Papaver rhoeas*), but both types of poppies are listed in one recipe for flying ointment. Of the corn poppy, Nicholas

---

31. Hansen, 74.

32. Pliny, (bk. XXVII, chap. 2), vol. 7, p. 391

Culpeper wrote: "The herb is Lunar; and of the flowers and seeds is made a syrup, which is frequently, and to good effect, used to procure rest and sleep in the sick and weak."[33]

Mild poisoning by deadly nightshade brings on high spirits, a sense of timelessness, and deep sleep that is often accompanied by erotic dreams. Its common Italian name, *belladonna* (beautiful lady), refers to the historical practice of women applying drops of its juice diluted in water to the surface of their eyes to dilate their pupils, in order to lend themselves a more fascinating and seductive appearance.

Henbane contains throughout its parts the alkaloid hyoscyamine, and its seeds also contain scopolamine. Hansen asserts that henbane by virtue of these alkaloids "can produce in its victims the illusion of having been turned into an animal."[34] The herbalist John Gerard wrote that "to wash the feet in the decoction of Henbane causeth sleepe; or giuen in a clister it doth the same; and also the often smelling to the floures. The leaues, seed and iuyce taken inwardly causeth an vnquiet sleepe like vnto the sleep of drunkennesse, which continueth long, and is deadly to the party."[35]

Mandrake was known to be both a soporific and an aphrodisiac. No plant has a greater occult reputation. It was fabled to render the possessor of its dried root invulnerable in battle, to cure him of all sickness, to aid in the discovery of hidden treasure, and to induce any woman he desired to make love to him. By comparison, the actual physical effects of the root are mild. Wine in which the root was boiled was used to cause sleep. The same effect was achieved by smelling the fruit of the mandrake and by drinking its juice.

The very scent of the flowers of thornapple in the air can induce stupefaction, and when the root is taken internally thornapple causes hallucinations and temporary insanity. A larger dose can produce permanent insanity and a still larger dose, death. Pliny called it *manicon*, the maddening herb.[36]

The seeds of darnel induce dizziness when eaten, and may perhaps have some similar effect when their active component is leeched from them into the ointment and absorbed through the skin. "When Darnel has been given medicinally in a harmful quantity, it is

---

33. Culpeper, *Culpeper's Complete Herbal*, 125.

34. Hansen, 45.

35. Gerard, *The Herbal*, 355.

36. Pliny (bk. XXI, chap. 105), vol. VI, p. 287.

recorded to have produced all the symptoms of drunkenness: a general trembling, followed by inability to walk, hindered speech and vomiting."[37]

Poison lettuce is said to bring on sweet dreams. The Latin name *Lactuca virosa* signifies "poisonous milky juice." At one time, the juice was collected by cutting the tops of the plants and scraping the milky juice that welled forth into a cup several times a day. The juice in the cup became congealed, and was knocked out in the form of a patty. It was used to cut or adulterate opium because its properties are similar to those of opium. "The drug resembles a feeble opium without its tendency to upset the digestive system. It is used to a small extent as a sedative and narcotic."[38] Water distilled from lettuce (*eau de laitue*) was used in France as a mild sedative, but larger doses given to animals in the form of injections have caused death.

Francis Bacon listed the leaves of the black poplar as a soporific. Gerard, writing in 1597, reported that the buds of the new leaves were made into "that profitable ointment called *unguentum populeon*."[39] It is worth noting in passing that the juice of the mandrake was also put into this ointment,[40] and that the ointment was sometimes combined with crushed henbane leaves.[41] Gerard further wrote that "the leaues and yong buds of blacke Poplar doe asswage the paine of the gout in the hands or feet, being made into an ointment with May butter."[42]

Given the potent qualities of many of the active herbal ingredients in flying ointment, it would be foolish in the extreme to experiment with their manufacture and use. One of the first men to do so in modern times, Dr. Karl Kiesewetter, died of poisoning as the result of one of his experimental soul flights.[43] Will-Erich Peuckert, who in 1927 experimented in spite of the dangers with one of the flying ointments described by Giovanni Battista Porta in his *Magia naturalis*, reported that it first induced a sensation

---

37. Grieve, *Modern Herbal*, 372.

38. Ibid., 476.

39. Gerard, 1486.

40. Ibid., 352.

41. Ibid., 355.

42. Ibid., 1488.

43. Hansen, 95.

of rapid and wild flight, followed by the impression of being jostled amid a great throng of revelers, and finally of participating in a chaotic sexual orgy.[44]

There can be little doubt that some of the flying ointments worked in the intended way, at least some of the time. In the absence of a rigorous control over the amounts and potencies of the ingredients that made them up, their effects probably varied wildly from batch to batch. There is no way to know if their use was harmless, or caused cumulative damage to the organs and nervous system. The latter case appears more likely in view of the malicious effects of some of the herbs that the ointments contained. Fortunately for those who desire to project their astral bodies, drugs are not necessary to achieve useful results.

---

44. Hansen, 99.

CHAPTER
THREE

The Land
of Fairy

The description of the vast meadow of the Blocula, with its central meeting house
and smaller enclosed grassy space for the keeping of horses and other mounts, that
we met with in the previous chapter in connection with the testimony of the accused
witches of Mora, Sweden, is relevant in illustrating the strong connection that exists
between traditional European witchcraft and the fairies. The Blocula is certainly an astral place, and is very similar to numerous descriptions of the land of fairy. The accused
witches characterized it as "a delicate large meadow, whereof you can see no end," and the
enclosed grounds of the meeting house possessed a gate painted with many colors.

King James VI of Scotland, who would later become James I of England, when writing about the connection between witchcraft and fairies, observed:

That fourth kinde of spirites, which by the Gentiles was called Diana, and her wandering court, and amongst vs was called the *Phairie* (as I tould you) or our good neighboures, was one of the sortes of illusiones that was rifest in the time of *Papistrie*: for although it was holden odious to Prophesie by the deuill, yet whome these kinde of Spirites carryed awaie, and informed, they were thought to be sonsiest and of best life. To speake of the many vaine trattles founded vpon that illusion: How ther was a King and Queene of *Phairie*, of such a iolly court & train as they had, how they had a teynd, & dutie, as it were, of all goods; how they naturallie rode and went, eate and drank, and did all other actiones like naturall men and women: I think it liker Virgils *Campi Elysij*, nor anie thing that ought to be beleeued by Christians, except in generall, that as I spake sundrie times before, the deuil illuded the senses of sundry simple creatures, in making them beleeue that they saw and harde such thinges as were nothing so indeed.[45]

In his epic poem *The Aeneid,* the Roman poet Virgil described Elysium, the land of the dead visited by the hero Aeneas, as a pleasant place of smiling lawns and happy groves. "Here a bright sky robes the fields with fuller radiance and with dazzling light: and they know their own sun, their own stars. Some exercise their limbs on grassy wrestling-grounds; in sport they contend, and struggle on the yellow sand: some mark the measure with their feet, and sing songs."[46]

Fairyland is the astral realm where human beings who have projected their consciousness out of the physical world perceive and interact with the race of spirits known in Europe, and particularly in Celtic countries, as fairies. It is commonly thought to be the place where fairies live, but since human beings only are aware of fairies in this place when they themselves are present, this is not something that can be stated with assurance. It is certainly one of the astral meeting places between fairies and humans. But who can say what forms fairies may have when they are not interacting with human consciousness, or if they have any form at all? If they are formless in their essential nature, they would scarcely require a three-dimensional dwelling place.

---

45.   James I, bk. III, chap. 5, pp. 73–4.

46.   Virgil, *Works of Virgil,* 172.

Under the Hill

There seem to be two predominant descriptions of the land of fairy. One, as suggested by King James I with his reference to Virgil's Elysium, is a bright and sunny meadow, often the slope of a large and gently rounded hill, where fairies are observed to dance and play. The other is sometimes called the Underworld, and is described as brightly illuminated and lavishly appointed caverns beneath the surface of the earth, in which are set fine houses and dining halls. The two come together in the descriptions of the portals to fairyland, which often open into the sides of low and grass-covered hills. Such hills are common in southern England, rising from the flat plains. They are not natural, but were build for religious purposes by the ancient race that erected Stonehenge and other great cosmic circles and spirals such as Avebury.

The center of fairy activity in Ireland is a similarly shaped, grass-covered hill. It is named Tara, and was the residence of the ancient kings of Ireland. Tara Hill in the County of Meath stands about 510 feet in elevation, and is crowned with a series of six circular earthen works, known as raths. The largest is called the king's rath (*rath-na-riogh*), and within its boundary is the meeting place (*forradh*), a flat-topped mound on which important gatherings of the people were held. It contains the sacred stone of destiny (*lia fail*), a phallic standing stone on which the ancient kings of Ireland were crowned. The stone is not in its original location, but was moved and re-erected. It was fabled to roar when a rightful king stood upon it. Also upon the hill of Tara was a great banqueting hall some 759 feet long by 46 feet wide. For centuries, kings ruled and made their laws here. When Christianity came to Ireland, the priests condemned Tara as a seat of druidism and idolatry, and around the year AD 560 it was cursed by Saint Ruadan, and was abandoned by the Irish in fear of the curse, leaving it as the habitation of the fairies.

Fairies were closely linked by the Celts to the souls of the dead, so both Virgil's sunny meadow of Elysium where the dead sing and sport, and the large and splendid caverns in which they reside in other myths, can be applied to the fairies. Many of the recognized fairy knolls or hills are barrow mounds where lie the bodies of dead heroes, although many others are natural hills. In ancient times, it was not unheard of for whole Celtic clans to live in large caves and even to keep their cattle in the caverns with them, so it would have seemed natural to place the race of fairies in caverns, as a way of explaining how fairies could appear and disappear in moments as though from the thin air. The sides of fairy hills are said to open up like great doors to allow the passage of the fairy host going to and from the wild hunt of Diana or Herodias, and at other times the fairies ride on their miniature horses directly into the slope itself and disappear.

The Good Neighbors

Fairies are not the harmless, tiny pixies in gauzy gowns with dragonfly or butterfly wings that usually illustrate children's books. They are spiritual creatures who can at times be both dangerous and terrifying, which no sane person would ever wish to anger through imprudent action or careless words. They were known by various euphemistic titles, among them the Good Neighbors, the Good People, the People of Peace, the Fair Family, and the Gentry. This might lead someone coming across these titles to conclude that fairies are a jolly and pleasant band of spirits with whom to have dealings. However, if that person thought for a moment, and reflected that in Greek mythology the Furies, or *Erinyes*, were commonly known as the *Eumenides* (the Gracious Ones), and if he considered why this should be so, he might begin to see fairies in a less rosy light.

Robert Kirk, who wrote about fairies and fairyland in 1691, made this important point in the opening paragraph of his treatise, in which he describes the nature of fairies.

> THESE Siths, or FAIRIES, they call Sleagh Maith, or the Good People, it would seem, to prevent the Dint of their ill Attempts, (for the Irish use to bless all they fear Harme of;) and are said to be of a midle Nature betuixt Man and Angel, as were Dæmons thought to be of old; of intelligent fluidious Spirits, and light changable Bodies, (lyke those called Astral,) somewhat of the Nature of a condensed Cloud, and best seen in Twilight. Thes Bodies be so plyable thorough the Subtilty of the Spirits that agitate them, that they can make them appear or disappear att Pleasure.[47]

Kirk, who was the minister of the Scottish parish of Aberfoyle, rightly observed that the bodies of fairies are astral, not material, in nature. He came to know only too well the dangerous nature of fairies on a firsthand basis. Kirk was a seventh son, and possessed the second sight that allows perception of fairies and fairyland. The year after writing his important work on fairies, he was found lying dead on the slope of the local fairy hill (*dun-shi*) in Aberfoyle, called the Fairy Knowe. Aberfoyle was the place of Kirk's birth, where he had returned to preach following the death of his father, the minister of the

---

47. Kirk and Lang, *Secret Commonwealth*, 5.

parish, so it may be presumed that he had enjoyed some familiarity in his boyhood with the local spirits under the hill.

The legend surrounding his death asserts that he did not really die, but that he was spirited away and a lifeless duplicate of his body put in his place. His successor, the Rev. Dr. Graham, wrote in his book of local history, *Sketches of Picturesque Scenery*, that Kirk's ghost appeared to one of his relatives shortly after his abduction and declared that he would come again at the baptism ceremony of his child—his wife having been pregnant at the time of his supposed death—and that his cousin must cast his dirk over Kirk's head, and then Kirk would be released from his captivity in fairyland. True to his word, Kirk made his reappearance at the baptism, but his cousin was so startled and frightened by the apparition that he forgot to throw the knife, and so Kirk remains a prisoner of the fairies to this day.[48]

Fairies were known as the Fair Family and the Good Neighbors because the country folk who interacted with them were terrified of them. The flattering names were a way of placating their wrath. They were believed to possess considerable power in the material world, such as the ability to blight or otherwise hinder crops; to sour milk; to lame horses; to take away sight, hearing, the strength of the legs, and the power of speech; to bewitch and cause fantastic visions; to lift men and women into the air and deposit them in treetops or on roofs; to transform the shapes and appearances of humans into those of beasts; and, most sinister of all, to cause sickness or death.

In spite of these and other dangers, many men and women sought to interact with fairies, not only because of their wondrous spectacles of music, dancing, and feasting, but also because of the benefits fairies could confer on humans if they took the capricious inclination to do so. Fairies controlled both good and evil fortune. A person favored by the fairies would enjoy marvelous luck, whereas one who earned their disfavor by some ill-considered act, such as the cutting down of a thorn tree beloved by the fairies, would remain unlucky to his dying day.

Appearance of Fairies

There is more than one kind of fairy, and their natures differ from country to country. In Ireland, they are known as the *Sidhe* (pronounced "Shee"). Some assert that even within Ireland they are divided into several species, the Tuatha de Danann, the Fir Bolgs, and

---

48. Kirk and Lang, xii–xiii.

the Milesians.[49] The Welsh know them as *Tylwyth Teg*, the Fair Folk. In Scotland, they are known as the *Sith*. Although they can cause their size and appearance to change, they generally appear in human forms, sometimes of normal human stature, but more commonly smaller than the average adult person. The height of fairies generally ranges between two feet and four feet.

Shamans have described many of the spirits with whom they communicate as being of smaller than normal human stature,[50] and the familiar spirits of witches are often diminutive. Why fairies and other similar spirits should be of less than normal height when they come in human forms is not apparent. Fairies are known as the "little people" on this account, and elves and dwarfs, who appear along with fairies in old tales, are also usually described as of less than normal height. The more noble and exalted a fairy, the more likely it is to be of human, or nearly human, dimensions. Fairies of royal or noble blood possess an inhuman beauty, but common fairies resemble common farmers and other country folk.

Those scholars incapable of accepting any other than a material explanation for a mystery have asserted that fairies are a mythic remembrance of an ancient race of people who inhabited the British Isles before the coming of the Celts. This primitive people, called Picts, were smaller than the Celts who displaced them, and were driven underground to live in caves, venturing forth only at night or in remote places where they would not be observed. It is a seductive explanation for the materially minded, but there is little or nothing in hard evidence to substantiate it. Fairies are said to exist in many lands where there were no Picts.

Another peculiar aspect of the appearance of fairies is that they are frequently described as wearing antique or very out-of-date clothing. If there is no underlying basis for these spirits, it is difficult to see why they would be so often seen in antique dress. My own suspicion is that both their smallness of stature and the antique clothing have a basis in the mechanism of the mind through which fairies are perceived. Perhaps there is a distortion of space, a dislocation in time, during the astral perception of this kind of spiritual being. The smaller stature and antique garments are not invariable in the appearance of fairies, but they are habitual.

---

49. Evans-Wentz, *Fairy-Faith in Celtic Countries*, 32.

50. Eliade, 72.

The Fairy Queen

Fairy society is a monarchy. They are ruled by a king and queen, but the king is much less prominent than the queen, and perhaps less powerful. This is not true in all the accounts of fairies, but it is so in the majority of tales. Shakespeare's play *A Midsummer Night's Dream* (c. 1595), in which King Oberon and Queen Titania rule fairyland together as equal partners, does not reflect the countless encounters with the fairy queen that occur in more simple folktales. Sometimes the queen is met on the road mounted upon a fine white horse, accompanied only by her hunting dogs, as she appeared to Thomas Learmont of Ercildoune, who went with her to fairyland and there acquired the occult knowledge that caused him to be remembered by Sir Walter Scott as the "Merlin of Scotland." At other times she passes by travelers in a splendid procession, composed of hundreds of guards and courtiers and ladies in waiting.

The prominent, active role of the fairy queen, in contrast to the more authoritative yet passive role of the king, expresses the feminine nature of all energy or force, which is recognized in the Tantra texts of the Hindus as the goddess Shakti. The god Shiva, the initiating spark, is essential and yet to some extent impotent, in the sense that he acts only in a secondary way through his agents, whereas Shakti acts directly of her own accord. We see exactly the same dynamic in the game of chess. The king is the most important piece on the board—when the king is lost the game is forfeited—yet he has little power of his own. The greatest active power in chess is held by the queen.

Queen Elizabeth I of England was often compared with the queen of fairies, an association she played up to the hilt as a way of impressing her less educated subjects. Her mother, Anne Boleyn, had been rumored to be a witch, so it was not such a leap to believe that Elizabeth herself had commerce with the fairies, or even commanded their realm, just as she commanded the realm of England. The poet Edmund Spenser (c. 1552–1599) wrote the epic poem *The Faerie Queene* in 1590 in order to do homage to Elizabeth.

Contrary to popular belief, Queen Mab was not the fairy queen of England. "When Mab is called 'queen' it does not mean sovereign, for Titania was Oberon's wife, but simply female; both midwives and monthly nurses were anciently called queens or queans. *Quen* or *cwen* in Saxon means neither more nor less than woman; so 'elf-queen' and the Danish 'elle-quinde' mean *female elf*, and not 'queen of the elves.'"[51] Shakespeare described Queen Mab as "the fairies' midwife," a diminutive creature that rides her tiny

---

51. Brewer, *Dictionary of Phrase and Fable*, 535.

wagon across the faces of sleepers to bring them dreams. This is in sharp contrast to the grand lady Queen Titania.

Fairy Abductions

It is a persistent theme in fairy legends that human beings are abducted or otherwise deceived by fairies into entering under the hill through the magic gateway into the fairy world. Those taken by fairies may be absent from their homes and family for years, and then suddenly return having no memory of where they have been or how much time has elapsed. It was fabled that they profited greatly from their time in the land of fairy, because the fairies taught them many secret arts, and continued to watch over them and assist them after their return to the human world.

When fairy abductees are asked what transpired in the land of fairy, they discover that they cannot remember, or remember but refuse to speak about it, or try to speak and find themselves unable. Commonly, the elapse of time is greater in the human realm than in the fairy realm; a man who believes himself gone but a day may find that a year has passed. This is the case in the Scottish folk tale *Cnoc An T-Sithein* (*The Fairy Knoll*). A man on the Isle of Barra was out walking when he heard beautiful music coming from under the ground. He lifted a broad, flat stone and descended the hidden stair beneath to discover the piper, who kindly invited him to stay for a meal. After eating, the man returned to his home, only to discover that four generations had passed. Less frequently, the time distortion is reversed, and those who believe themselves to have spent years living in fairyland discover that only a few hours have elapsed in the human world.

Scholars commenting on this time distortion have observed that the mind-altering drugs taken by shamans and witches to induce soul flight—such as mescaline, opium, and peyote—sometimes distort time. Opium addicts have written that in certain opium dreams, years seem to pass—or even entire lifetimes. If the brains of those believed to have been abducted by fairies were affected by their astral journeys in a manner similar to the way that these psychotropic drugs affect the brain, it might explain the time-distortion effect. Even if the fairy abductees did not consume or apply mind-altering substances prior to their experiences, if their brains responded in a way similar to the responses provoked by shamanic drugs such as the flying ointment, they may have experienced similar effects, among them time distortion.

It is said that fairies have no use for old men and old women. The reason may be that the vital energies of the elderly are limited. Fairies abduct or lure men and women to their world, and are particularly eager to obtain infants, which they then raise as their own, taking care to substitute a duplicate in the place of the real child so that the theft will go unnoticed for as long as possible. These duplicates are called changelings. It is not certain why fairies should want to abduct babies. One explanation put forward is that fairies have difficulty conceiving children of their own. Or, as seems more likely to me, fairies draw upon the pure, intense vital essences of the child for their nourishment.

The fable of the changeling should be understood in a spiritual rather than in a physical sense. The fairies abduct the personality and true identity of the child, substituting in its place a false identity that pretends to be the child. The deception is discovered when the child becomes increasingly strange and uncouth as it grows older. Changelings are wise beyond their years, are sly of manner, and their bodies develop an unnatural strength and vitality. They sometimes become malicious and even dangerous. Modern medicine would dismiss the changeling as a folk explanation for mental illness, yet to dismiss it in this cavalier fashion is not to explain it. The changeling is an integral part of the fairy mythology.

A related type of abduction was that of nursemaids, who were taken to fairyland for the purpose of nourishing fairy children at their breasts. When their duties were fulfilled, they were either permitted to return to the human world, or were allowed to stay on in the fairy world. This myth suggests that fairies are nourished in some way on the vitality of human beings, which in the tales of the abduction of nursemaids is represented by human milk. We see in this an echo of the witch's familiar imp, asserted by the demonologists to nourish itself by sucking the blood of the witch at a small protrusion similar to a mole that was known as the witch's teat. In both instances, it is vital energy, not the physical materials of milk or blood, that provides the nourishment for the spirit—although the vital force may be said to be present within the blood, and to a lesser degree within the milk.

When attempting to abduct a man who is resting on a fairy knoll, the sidhe may come with a pair of large shears and, while they believe themselves to be wrapped in a cloak of invisibility, attempt to roll up and cut off his shadow. At least, that is how the process has been interpreted by those who have witnessed it. The shadow represents, in a symbolic way, the soul. By rolling it up and cutting it off at the feet, the fairies are able to steal away the essence of personality. Perhaps the result would be coma or death. Or perhaps the man or woman whose shadow was stolen and carried off to the underworld would slowly waste away, a fate that sometimes befalls those who displease the fairies.

Quarters of the Year

Abductions are more common on the solstices and equinoxes that fall on the quarters of the year. These are the days when the fairies leave their land and move abroad on the roads used by mankind. It is very unlucky to travel at these times.

> THEY remove to other Lodgings at the Beginning of each Quarter of the Year, so traversing till Doomsday, being imputent and [impotent of?] staying in one Place, and finding some Ease by so purning [Journeying] and changing Habitations. Their chamælion-lyke Bodies swim in the Air near the Earth with Bag and Bagadge; and at such revolution of Time, SEERS, or Men of the SECOND SIGHT, (Fæmales being seldome so qualified) have very terrifying Encounters with them, even on High Ways; who therefoir uswally shune to travell abroad at these four Seasons of the Year, and thereby have made it a Custome to this Day among the Scottish-Irish to keep Church duely evry first Sunday of the Quarter to sene or hallow themselves, their Corns and Cattell, from the Shots and Stealth of these wandring Tribes;[52]

The quarters of the year are the transitions from season to season, when the length of the day is noticed to change. On the Winter Solstice (December 21), the shortest day occurs in the Northern Hemisphere and on the Summer Solstice (June 21), the longest day. On the Spring Equinox (March 21), the day goes from being shorter than the night to being longer; on the Fall Equinox (September 21), the opposite occurs, and the day goes from being longer than the night to being shorter. The dates given for these quarter days are nominal; they vary slightly from year to year.

These changes or transitions open occult doorways that allow the fairies to wander the surface of the earth. The astral world of fairies and the material world of mankind overlap in some way on the quarters of the year. They are magic days laden with possibilities. For example, there is a myth that on the equinoxes you may stand an egg up on end on any flat surface, and it will not fall over. While not true physically, it conveys a mythic truth that the equinoxes are days on which magic happens.

In the quotation above, Robert Kirk expressed the opinion of his century that women are less adapted to seership than men. This was a prejudice of the same sort that once held men to be better weavers than women, and that continues to assert that they make better cooks. Experience has demonstrated the falsehood of all these beliefs. If anything,

---

52. Kirk and Lang, 7–8.

the spiritualist movement has proven women better seers than men—at least, there seem to be more female mediums in modern times than male mediums, and they have attracted a larger share of attention.

The same walking abroad of the fairies occurs, on a smaller scale, at twilight, the transition between day and night, when fairies are most often to be glimpsed or their music and laughter heard in the fields and woods. The Scots call this transition period of the day the gloaming. Fairies are also to be seen in the early mornings, when the mist lies close to the ground. However, just as the wheel of the year has four gateways, so does the wheel of the day, and the other two are at noon and midnight. Sir Walter Scott wrote in a magazine article of the Boddach of the Highlanders, "who walk the heath at midnight and at noon."

John Walsh of Netherberry, Dorset, when interrogated for witchcraft in 1566, was asked how he knew when a man was bewitched. "He sayth that he knew it partlye by the Feries, and saith that ther be .iii. kindes of Feries, white, greene and black. Which when he is disposed to vse, hee speaketh with them vpon hyls, where as there is great heapes of earth, as namely in Dorsetshire. And betwene the houres of .xii. and one at noone, or at midnight, he vseth them. Whereof (he sayth) the blacke feries be the woorst."[53] These three types of fairies perhaps correspond to another triple classification: those that do only good (the white), those that do only evil (the black), and those that do both good and evil (the green).

Stone Circles

A more material kind of doorway into fairyland was the stone circles that are to be found scattered throughout Britain and continental Europe. Fairies were supposed to dance about these circles to open the gateway to the astral world. It was located between two of the stones in the circle, but which two was not evident when the gateway remained inactive. How the fairies opened the gate is a mystery, unless it is revealed in the practice of one accused witch, who testified that he opened the door into a fairy hill by walking around it three times widdershins—against the course of the sun. In magic, clockwise circumambulation winds up and focuses energy, whereas counterclockwise circumambulation unwinds and releases it. Passage between two pillars of stone is symbolically

---

53. Murray, 240.

akin to being born between the legs of a woman, and passing from a place of darkness into a place of light.

At one time, the stone circles were thought to have been erected by the priestly and scholarly order of Druids that was great in power in Britain and northern France just prior to the time of Christ. Archeology has revealed that they are much older than the Druids, older even than the Celts themselves. They were built by the prehistoric Neolithic people who inhabited Britain before the coming of the Celts from the mainland. Work on the earliest version of Stonehenge began around 2180 BC. It did not achieve its final form until 1550 BC, still long before the coming of the Celts to Britain, which occurred no earlier than around 600 BC.

The truth of the matter is that even after all the research that has been done on stone circles, no one knows with certainty why they were built. It seems reasonable to assume that such enormous investments of time and labor must have had a purpose that was of vital importance to the people who built them. One theory is that they were great cosmic clocks, but it seems improbable that such immense, permanent structures would be needed merely to keep track of the phases of the moon and the change of the seasons. Such timekeeping might just as well have been accomplished with smaller wooden constructions similar to sundials, or with wooden staves driven into the earth, which could easily be renewed when necessary.

On the other hand, if the people who built the stone circles and the great earthen mounds considered them gateways to an underworld that was inhabited by spirits and the souls of the dead, it might well have been necessary to place them on specific power points on the surface of the earth, and to make them large enough to accommodate their sacred functions. They may have acted as junctions between our material world and the astral world, where spirits and humans could meet and hold commerce of various kinds. It is possible that the Celts did not originate the mythology of the fairies that is so closely bound up with Celtic culture, but instead inherited it along with the stone circles of the much more ancient inhabitants of the lands they occupied.

CHAPTER
FOUR

Religious Bilocation

Descriptions of soul flight and communications with spirits are often encountered in the writings of saints, martyrs, priests, monks, and nuns. The church accepted the reality of the projection of the astral double, and sometimes relied on testimony of the event as proof of saintliness. It was known as bilocation, the seeming appearance of an individual in two places at once. One is the physical body and the other is the astral double, which at times can be observed and is mistaken for the physical body. It is not a projection through space, as was wrongly assumed by the church, but a projection through mind, for all human minds are connected, and the astral traveler does not travel anywhere, in a physical sense.

Allan Kardec related the case of Saint Anthony of Padua, who was preaching in Spain on the same day his father in Padua, having been falsely convicted of murder, was being led to his execution. Just before the execution, Anthony appeared and pointed out the real murderer. It was ascertained that Anthony had never left Spain.[54] Brewer described the same event somewhat differently, writing that Anthony was in Padua when his father was in danger of being put to death for manslaughter in Lisbon. According to Brewer's source, Kinesman's *Lives of the Saints* (1623), an angel carried Anthony to Lisbon while the trial was in progress. Anthony ordered the corpse of the victim brought into the court, and asked the corpse if his father was guilty. The corpse denied it, and Anthony's father was released, whereupon the angel carried Anthony back to Padua that same night.[55]

Saint Anthony pulled much the same trick while preaching at the Church of Saint Pierre de Queyroix at Limoges on Holy Thursday, 1226. He suddenly remembered that he was due that same hour to perform a service at a monastery on the other side of town. He drew his hood over his head and knelt while the congregation watched and waited with puzzlement. At that moment, he appeared in the monastery chapel, read the passage of the service that he had been assigned to read, and immediately disappeared. This is clearly a case of deliberate astral projection. Similar events are recorded in the lives of Saint Severus of Ravenna, Saint Ambrose, Saint Clement of Rome, and Saint Alphonsus Liguori, who while in prison at Arezzo, took no food and went into a kind of trance state for five days. When he awoke, he stated that he had been at the bedside of the dying Pope Clement XIV. His statement was later confirmed.[56]

Joan of Arc

Historically, Christianity has had an ambivalent attitude toward projections of the astral body into other realms and communication with spiritual beings. When it is done by someone outside the authority of the church, it is almost invariably condemned as occult and devilish. However, when it is experienced by a member of the church hierarchy, or by someone regarded by the church as favored by God, public knowledge of the event is either suppressed, or if that is impossible due to the prominence of the person who had the experience, it is embraced and upheld as a prophetic miracle.

Nowhere is this double standard more evident than in the tragic life of Joan of Arc (1412–1431). As a young girl, Joan heard voices telling her to be a good girl and to pray

54. Kardec, *Mediums' Book*, 130–1.

55. Brewer, *Dictionary of Miracles*, 75.

56. Fodor, *Encyclopædia of Psychic Science*, 100.

regularly. When the wars against the invading armies of England began to go badly against the French, and the city of Orléans was laid under siege by the Earl of Suffolk, the voices changed their message and told Joan that she must go to King Charles VII, who was as yet uncrowned, and have him place her at the head of an army, which she was to use to liberate Orléans. At first, she was ignored, but when she accurately predicted a defeat of French forces, she was granted an audience with Charles. She won his favor by relating the content of a private prayer he had recently made to God.

Charles had her examined for orthodoxy before a panel of theologians at Poitiers. After a two-week interrogation in the spring of 1429, they found no fault with her. Their conclusion reads, in part: "The King ... must not prevent her from going to Orléans with his soldiers, but must have her conducted honorably, trusting in God. For to regard her with suspicion or abandon her, when there is no appearance of evil, would be to repel the Holy Spirit and render himself unworthy of the aid of God."[57] The king gave his consent, and Joan rallied the army that liberated Orléans, turning the tide of the war against the English.

Captured outside the city gates of Compiègne by the French forces of the Duke of Burgundy, who was in alliance with the English against Charles VII, she was sold to the English by the Burgundians, interrogated by the Inquisition, and put on trial for heresy. The voices in her head that had previously been accepted by the theologians as the voices of saints were now declared to be the voices of demons. She was accused of having consorted with fairies as a young girl, a common charge against witches. This contact with fairies supposedly took place at the site of a fairy tree, known as the Charmed Fairy Tree of Bourlemont, near Joan's home village of Domrémy. It was a giant beech, also called the Ladies' Tree, located on the property of Seigneur Pierre de Bourlemont, and accepted as the gathering place of "fairy-ladies."[58]

Joan was accused of having danced around the tree, and of having made garlands for it, along with the other girls of her village. Joan admitted to having heard the rumor that she had received her divine mission to liberate Orléans from the fairy-ladies of the Ladies' Tree, but she did not confirm or deny the rumor. She stated that she had never seen fairies (but did not state that she had never heard them). She admitted that her grandmother had seen the fairy-ladies, but said that her grandmother was held to be a good woman, not a

---

57.   Paine, *Joan of Arc*, vol. 1, p. 112.

58.   Murray, 238.

witch. She admitted that Saint Katharine and Saint Margaret spoke to her at the spring beside the Ladies' Tree, "but would not say if they came to the tree itself."[59] Perhaps most significantly, she refused to acknowledge that she believed fairies to be evil spirits.

It was not the weak charges of witchcraft that condemned Joan, but rather her custom of wearing men's clothing, which she had adopted after taking up the role of a warrior. For a woman to wear the clothing of a man was against the laws of the church, except in circumstances of dire necessity. The English deliberately took away Joan's dress and left only male apparel in its place, forcing her to either fend off her jailers in the nude, or put on the clothing of a man. She was condemned as a heretic and burned alive at the stake in 1431. The executioner, Geoffroy Therage, confided to others shortly after the execution that he was in great fear of being damned, for "he had burned a saint." In 1920, Joan was canonized by the church and transformed into Saint Joan.

The case of Joan of Arc is particularly interesting for the way it shows how the same behavior might be looked upon by the Catholic Church as either divine or devilish, depending on the circumstances of the moment. The theologians who examined her at Poitiers came close to proclaiming Joan a messenger of God. The Burgundians and the English, good Catholics all, conspired to have her burned as a witch by the Inquisition. Centuries later, she was elevated to sainthood. The voices in Joan's head that helped the Dauphin Charles finally be anointed as king of France at Reims were naturally viewed as holy by Charles VII and his followers, since they worked to the advantage of Charles, but the English and French opponents of Charles took the opposite view.

Soul Flight in the Bible

There are many examples of soul flight in the Bible, but they are always presented as divine miracles that fulfill the purposes of God. The experience of the prophets is the same as that of shamans and witches, with the difference that the soul flights of prophets were usually spontaneous, whereas those of shamans and witches were often induced. An exception is the ascent of Moses to the top of Mount Sinai, where he remained forty days and forty nights (Exodus 24:18). He engaged in this trial of physical endurance for the purpose of altering his state of consciousness, in a way little different from that of countless shamans around the world, who go alone into the wilderness and endure hunger and thirst to achieve what is called a "vision quest." Success came in the form of the

---

59.   Murray, 239.

astral vision of the laws inscribed by Moses himself on the stone tables that he carried down from the mountain.

All the great prophets of the Old Testament exhibit many of the characteristics of shamans. They lived alone, outside the customs of their society, and they went into the wilderness where they received detailed visions while traveling out of their bodies on the astral plane. They acted as intermediaries or mediums, carrying the messages of spiritual beings to humanity. The true nature of the spirits that inspired their prophecies is as much a matter of conjecture as the question of whether the spirits who spoke to Joan of Arc were saints or fairies.

The astral journey of Isaiah involves his great vision of the throne of God. In the final year of the reign of King Uzziah, the prophet entered the presence of God, whom he perceived sitting on an elevated throne within a temple. Above it stood the angels known as Seraphim, each with six wings, chanting "Holy, holy, holy is the Lord of hosts: the whole earth is full of his glory" (Isaiah 6:3). We know this vision involved astral projection because Isaiah was actually present before the throne in his astral body. He protested that his lips were too unclean to repeat the words of God, so one of the Seraphim flew down and took a live coal off the altar fire, where the offerings to God were consumed in flame, and touched it to Isaiah's lips to cleanse them.

The bewilderingly complex vision of Ezekiel also involves the throne of God, but it is more concerned with flying mechanisms that are constructed of wheels within wheels. Like the vision of Isaiah, it appears to have occurred spontaneously. These biblical prophets did not choose to have visions but were chosen by the spirits to receive them. However, once they were acknowledged as prophets, and had accepted this role as their calling in life, it is possible they learned how to encourage the occurrence of these soul flights using chanted prayers and physical austerity.

The astral landscape seen by Ezekiel was inhabited by four strange angels who were characterized by the prophet as "living creatures" (Ezekiel 1:5). They had six wings, as did the Seraphim seen by Isaiah, but in addition they had four faces: that of a man, a lion, an ox, and an eagle. Again, we can be certain it was a soul flight because God gave the prophet a book in the form of a written scroll and told him to eat it. Ezekiel wrote, "So I opened my mouth, and he caused me to eat that roll" (Ezekiel 3:2).

The prophet Elijah is significant for another reason. He is one of only a handful of men said in the Bible to have ascended into heaven while still inhabiting his body of flesh. Out walking with his son, Elisha, who was also a prophet, beside the River Jordan, he saw a chariot of fire drawn by fiery horses descend from the sky, and was lifted up into the heavens by a whirlwind (Second Kings 2:11). This physical ascent may be compared with the disappearance of men, women, and children presumed by their neighbors to have been abducted by fairies. Such disappearances in the body might be permanent, or they might endure anywhere from a few hours to tens of years.

It is intriguing to consider whether, on vary rare occasions, the separation between the astral world and the physical world may be crossed—not only with the mind, but with the physical body as well. It would be easy to dismiss all such transitions as either willful falsehoods or errors in perception, but there are enough of them recorded throughout the history of mankind to cause a thinking person to wonder if such a passage of the body from physical to astral has ever happened. Reports of identical abductions in the flesh are still being generated in modern times, but the context has shifted from divine whirlwinds and fairy gateways to alien UFOs. People continue to vanish into thin air, without warning and without explanation. The investigator into the strange, Charles Fort, who was a newspaper reporter by profession, collected a number of these more recent unexplained and inexplicable vanishings in his books.

In addition to the patriarch Enoch, who was believed to have been taken up to heaven by God while still alive and in the body so that he vanished utterly from the earth (Genesis 5:24), there is the most famous of all such translations to a higher sphere, that of Jesus after his crucifixion (Mark 16:19). Jesus is unique among them in that he died and came back to life in his body before that body was lifted alive into heaven. He is supposed to have predicted his ascent to heaven. The event had no eyewitnesses. This is generally true of fairy abductions and UFO abductions—a person mysteriously vanishes, sometimes to reappear at a later date, but the actual disappearance is seldom witnessed.

Descent into Hell

It is the dogma of the church that Jesus came back to life after his crucifixion and ascended in the living body to heaven. The apocryphal Gospel of Nicodemus relates the legend that after his ascent to heaven, he subsequently descended into hell to free all the souls who had been imprisoned there since the fall from grace of Adam. After shattering the gate of brass and bars of iron that closed the entrance to hell, Jesus caused the chains to fall off those languishing in hell and led them up to heaven, where they encountered two others who had ascended in the flesh.

Thus he went into Paradise holding our forefather Adam by the hand, and he hand-
ed him over and all the righteous to Michael the archangel. And as they were entering the gate of Paradise, two old men met them. The holy fathers asked them: "Who
are you, who have not seen death nor gone down into Hades, but dwell in Paradise
with your bodies and souls?" One of them answered: "I am Enoch, who pleased God
and was removed here by him. And this is Elijah the Tishbite. We shall live until the
end of the world."[60]

There is no way to know if the author of the Gospel of Nicodemus related an astral vision
of Christ in hell, or merely invented a charming fable. That is also true of all written accounts of descents into hell, ascents to heaven, and indeed descriptions of astral journeys
of any kind, including those attributed to the biblical prophets such as Enoch, who is
supposed to have been conducted through both heaven and hell by the angels. The author of the Book of Enoch, writing in the voice of Enoch, bore this witness of hell: "And
beyond that abyss I saw a place that had no firmament of the heaven above, and no firmly
founded earth beneath it: there was no water upon it, and no birds, but it was a waste
and horrible place."[61] The hell of Enoch appears to have been largely a zone of negation,
where the good things of the world are not.

Much of what has been written concerning heaven with its choirs of angels, and hell
with its legions of demons, has been obtained through soul flight. Visions of both heaven
and hell were common among the saints, who saw them firsthand, being present within
the landscapes in the astral body. Saint Frances of Rome (1384–1440), while in her cell
at the convent, one day at around four in the afternoon fell into an ecstatic trance in
which the archangel Raphael came to her and carried her away on a guided tour of hell.
Above the gates of hell she read the inscription: "Hell, without hope, without cessation
of torment, without repose."[62] Beyond the gates, she entered a deep abyss from which
emanated cries and a terrible stench. Hell was divided into three levels, the highest being
the least unpleasant and the lowest the most horrifying.

The lowest level was filled with damned souls of the worst kind who suffered intricate and imaginative forms of torture. Usurers were stretched over tables of red-hot brass
while demons poured molten metal down their throats. Blasphemers had their tongues

60. Barnstone, *The Other Bible*, 377.

61. Charles, *Apocrypha and Pseudepigraphia*, vol. II, p. 200.

62. Brewer, *Dictionary of Miracles*, 412.

stretched out of their mouths on hooks. Apostates were sawn in half. Murders wandered forever from a bath of boiling blood to a bath of thick-ribbed ice, and back again. Traitors had their hearts torn out of their chests and then replaced, only to be torn out again over and over.

It is difficult not to suspect that the hell of Saint Frances was influenced in no small part by the hell described in the *Inferno* of the Italian poet Dante Alighieri (1265–1321). So plausible was Dante's description of the nine levels of hell that many simple religious readers were convinced that he had actually been there. This belief is not unique to medieval times. A university professor once confided to me that a student of hers, a young nun, told her quite seriously that Dante had really visited hell, and that the scenes he described were those he had seen with his own eyes. Whereas Frances was conducted by the archangel Raphael, the poet Dante was led through hell by the Roman writer Virgil, who in this office of astral guide acted the part of the tutelary spirit of the shamans and the familiar of the witch. Dante described ingenious torments for the damned souls similar to those described by Saint Frances. His poem reads very much like an astral journey.

Both heaven and hell as related in the prophetic books are astral realms, and for this reason it is quite possible for ordinary men and women to visit them while traveling in the astral body. Safe passage through hell is often secured by means of spirit guides, who have the power to shield the astral traveler from harm. Jesus, having all wisdom and all power unto himself, was without need of either a guide or a protector. Despite superstitions to the contrary, there is no direct physical danger to the body while projecting astrally, but it is possible that the intense shock of scenes in hell might cause a nervous reaction, resulting in emotional or even physical damage in a secondary way by repercussion. The spirit guide acts as a kind of shield, reducing the intensity of the astral experience when necessary, or in extreme cases causing it to be lost from the memory.

Levitation

For the religiously devout, astral projection often takes the form of levitation. Ezekiel told how he was lifted up by the hand of God from a lock of his hair. "And he put forth the form of an hand, and took me by a lock of mine head; and the spirit lifted me up between the earth and the heaven, and brought me in the visions of God to Jerusalem . . ." (Ezekiel 8:3). From the wording of the verse, "in the visions of God," it appears that Ezekiel realized he had not levitated through the air physically, but only in an astral sense.

The assertion has been made by numerous witnesses that, on various occasions, prophets and saints of the church have risen up physically into the air. In the case of saints, this levitation occurs most often during prayer. For example, Saint Agnes of Montepulciano (1268–1317), while only fifteen years old, was many times lifted up five feet or more into the air, an event witnessed by the entire Convent del Sacco. Similarly, Saint Angela of Brescia (1474–1540), who founded the order of Ursuline nuns, was in 1529 seen to levitate during holy services by the entire congregation of the church, and remained suspended for "a long time."[63]

A primary accusation of those giving eyewitness testimony against women thought to be witches is that they flew through the air. As pointed out earlier, the power of flight is essential to the archetype of the witch. Astral flight was mistaken for physical flight when those who observed witches to fly involuntarily shared their astral vision. The ability to see the astral world overlapping the physical world can be contagious, and can be passed through a group of onlookers. It almost seems that the strong belief of the shaman or witch in the reality of the event is able to transform the perception of others who are present, causing them to believe in the experience. It is a kind of group hypnosis, for want of a better term, that takes place under unusual and infrequent conditions. One person seeing a UFO can sometimes pass that conviction on to others present, so that others think they see it also, even when it does not physically exist. Similarly, one person witnessing a miracle can convey to others by the strength of faith the ability to see the same miracle.

Perhaps as a deliberate echo of the Old Testament account of the hand of God reaching down to lift Ezekiel up by the hair, the author of the New Testament book of Matthew told of Jesus walking across the sea. The apostle Peter wanted to imitate him and, encouraged by Jesus, stepped from his boat onto the surface of the water, but became afraid and began to sink. Jesus reached down his hand and drew him up, while still standing on top of the water (Matthew 14:31). It is an Eastern belief common in India that the holy men called fakirs can so reduce the weight of their bodies through prayers and devotions that they are blown about like dry leaves on the breeze, or are able to stand upon the surface of water without sinking. Since this would seem to be physically impossible—for how can the mass of an object be lessened without otherwise changing the object?—it is more

---

63. Brewer, *Dictionary of Miracles*, 215.

likely a shared astral experience akin to the famous Indian rope trick, during which onlookers partake in a group hallucination at the direction of the fakir.

Projections by Saints

A definite case of astral projection is related in the *Little Flowers of St. Francis of Assisi*, an Italian work (*Fioretti*) based on a medieval Latin manuscript. It concerns the nun Saint Clare, who was so ill one year that she was unable to go to church on the feast of the Nativity, which was a source of great vexation to her.

> But Jesu Christ, her spouse, desiring not to leave her thus disconsolate, caused her to be miraculously carried to the church of S. Francis and to be present at the whole of the office of Matins and the midnight Mass, and beyond all this to receive the Holy Communion and then be carried back to her bed. When the nuns came back to S. Clare, after the office in S. Damian's was over, they said to her: "O our mother, sister Clare, what sweet consolation have we had on this holy feast of the Nativity! oh, would that it had pleased God that you had been with us there!" And S. Clare replied: "Praise and glory do I give unto our Lord Jesu Christ, the blessed One, my sisters and daughters most dear; for that with much consolation to my soul I have had part in all the solemn rites of this most holy night, and even more than ye: sith through the loving care of my father S. Francis, and the grace of our Lord Jesu Christ, I have been present in the church of my venerable father, S. Francis, and with the ears of my body and my mind have heard all the office and the sound of the organs that was made there, and in the same place have taken the most holy Communion."[64]

A clearer and more perfect case of astral projection could scarcely be found. Saint Clare achieved an altered state of consciousness due to her fever, and her strong desire to be present in the church of Saint Francis carried here there in her astral body, or at least bore her astral body to the astral reflection of the church, where she was able to perceive all that transpired, and according to her testimony, even believed herself to participate in the taking of communion. Yet it is evident that she was not present in her physical body, or else she would have been observed by the other nuns.

It sometimes happens that those who project their astral body to locations in the physical world are observed by other human beings, but that is not the usual case. Usu-

---

64. Arnold, 103.

ally the astral form is able to pass unseen among human beings on its travels. However, at times those close to the person projecting the astral body, such as friends or family members, observe the astral form and mistake it for the physical form of the person engaged in the projection. There have even been cases when individuals have carried on entire conversations with astral projections, never realizing until being informed later that the other was not physically present.

As a young girl, Blessed Columba of Rieti (1467–1501) was in the habit of scourging herself three times every night: the first time for her own transgressions, the second for the conversion of sinners, and the third time to help souls in purgatory. When not whipping her own body, she passed the entire night in fervent prayer. Not surprisingly, she was subject to astral visions. Once, she traveled on the astral level through space and back in time to the scene of the chastisement of Jesus by the Roman soldiers. She was so overcome with anguish at the sight of his blood flowing from the strokes of the lash that she began to scourge herself in an identical manner. Her mother, hearing her screams, ran into her chamber and begged her to stop before she killed herself, but Columba was in a state of ecstasy and did not even hear her.

In this case, it was not sickness but self-chastisement and prayer that triggered the change of consciousness allowing astral travel to occur. Next to prayer, pain was the trigger for soul flight most often employed by the religious. It may be suspected that Columba's enthusiasm for the lash had a sexual component, but such things were not well understood at the time of the Renaissance, and Columba's self-abuse was regarded as a sign of an admirable piety.

> Sometimes, in her ecstasies, her soul quitted her body. One day her mother entered her chamber, and saw her daughter sitting on her altar, like one asleep. She lifted her down, in order to lay her on her bed, when all her limbs and head fell as if the body was lifeless. The mother thought she was dead, and screamed. Some of her neighbors came, and they also thought she was dead. All blamed the confessor, and accused him of murdering his victim by enforced abstinence and austerities. No doubt, in their irritation, they would have committed some breach of the peace; but all of a sudden the damsel revived.[65]

---

65. Brewer, *Dictionary of Miracles*, 310.

The deathlike state of the body during soul flight, and the near impossibility of awakening those entranced, is mentioned in connection with the astral projections of both witches and shamans. On another occasion, while Columba was seeing the star of Bethlehem on one of her astral excursions, her confessor noticed a globe of fire above her house and hurried over to learn the cause. The girl told him she had just seen the star of the Magi, which had filled her chamber with light and left behind it a sweet scent.[66] The intensity of her astral vision communicated itself to the priest who, being close to her on an emotional level, was able to see a reflexive manifestation of the same vision.

This sort of sharing of an astral vision between the person actually having the vision and others who may be present, or who are emotionally linked with the astral traveler, is common enough that it leads to the suspicion that human minds are linked together on some unknown level beneath that of the physical brain. The strong vision in an individual appears to be capable of creating echoes or harmonics in the minds of other people. Just as one harp string when plucked will cause another tuned harmonically to it to begin to vibrate and emit sound, so one mind powerfully moved by an astral experience can cause other minds in a receptive state to perceive a shadow of the vision. It is not always possible to explain this sharing of an astral vision solely by suggestibility of mind and the physical transmission of hints and cues from one individual to another. In the incident above, the priest had no prior knowledge of what Columba would see, and was not even present in the same house at the time it occurred.

Emanuel Swedenborg

With the dawn of the Protestant Reformation, the rigid and complete control over the relationship between the common individual and the deity passed out of the hands of the clergy. This event gave rise to ordinary men and women having astral journeys of the kind that previously had only been experienced by priests, nuns, saints, and others involved in the church. The best known is Emanuel Swedenborg (1688–1772), a Swedish mystic who wrote entire books describing his astral travels to heaven and hell, and his interactions with angels. He was a prominent scientist who in the year 1743 believed that he had received a mission from God to reveal a new doctrine of Christianity to the world. He was instructed by angels during astral journeys, and wrote more than forty books on

---

66. Brewer, *Dictionary of Miracles*, 310.

the subject. These books formed the basis for the Church of New Jerusalem, also called the New Church, which was established in London in 1778.

Swedenborg distinguished several types of astral perception. The state he experienced most of the time was what he called being "in the spirit." In this condition, his spirit was taken to the realms of the angels, and to the spheres of the planets as well.

> Since by the spirit of man his mind is meant, therefore by being "*in the spirit*," which is sometimes spoken of in the Word, is meant a state of the mind separate from the body; and because in this state the prophets saw such things as exist in the spiritual world, it is called "the vision of God." Their state was then like that of the spirits and angels themselves in that world. In this state the spirit of man,—like his mind as respects the sight,—can be transported from place to place, the body remaining in its position. This is the state in which I have been now for twenty-six years; with the difference that I have been in the spirit and at the same time in the body, and only sometimes out of the body.[67]

What Swedenborg meant is that when he traveled astrally to spiritual realms in this condition of mind, he remained aware of being also present at the same time in his own body. He did not fall into a trance state and lose complete awareness of his body, as shamans and witches usually did.

Swedenborg experienced the other two forms of soul flight he described only at infrequent intervals. The first, which he called being "taken out of the body," is the soul flight of the shaman and the witch. The second is a form of abstraction or daydream in which he lost awareness of his own physical location and actions while being focused on astral visions. He may have been possessed by a spirit on these occasions, although he does not indicate this to be the case, perhaps because he remained completely unaware of it.

> There are two kinds of visions out of the common course, into which I was introduced only that I might know the nature of them, and what is meant by that which we read of in the Word, that some were "*taken out of the body*," and some were "*carried by the Spirit into another place*."
>
> As regards the first, namely, being taken out of the body, the case is this: The man is brought into a certain state which is intermediate between sleep and wakefulness.

---

67. Swedenborg, *Compendium*, 625.

While he is in this state he cannot know but that he is quite awake; all the senses are as much awake as in the completest state of bodily vigilance, the sight as well as the hearing, and what is remarkable, the touch, which is then more exquisite than it can ever be in bodily wakefulness. In this state spirits and angels have been seen exactly to the life, and also heard, and what is amazing, touched; and almost nothing of the body then intervenes. This is the state described as being "taken out of the body," and of which it is said of those who are in it that, "whether in the body or out of the body, they cannot tell." Into this state I have been introduced only three or four times; merely that I might know the nature of it, and that spirits and angels enjoy every sense,—even the touch, more powerful and more exquisite than the touch of the body.

With respect to the other, the being carried by the Spirit into another place, what this is and how it is was also shown me by living experience; but only twice or three times. I may merely relate an experience:—Walking through the streets of a city and through the country, and in conversation at the same time with spirits, I was not aware but that I was equally awake and in the enjoyment of my sight as at other times, walking thus without error; and all the while I was in a vision, seeing groves, rivers, palaces, houses, men, and many other objects. But after I had been walking thus for some hours, suddenly I was in bodily vision, and observed that I was in a different place. Greatly amazed at this, I apperceived that I had been in such a state as they were in of whom it is said that they were "carried by the spirit to another place." For while the state lasts there is no reflection respecting the way, and this although it were many miles; nor upon the time, though it were many hours or days; neither is there any sense of fatigue. Then, the man is led also through ways of which he himself is ignorant, until he comes to the place intended.[68]

All three types of experiences may be classed as soul flight. The first is astral projection with a divided awareness, part of which is conscious of the normal physical world, while the other part visits spiritual worlds on the astral level. It can be called partial projection. The second is what might be called classic astral projection, in which there is a complete forgetfulness of the body, which sits or lies as though entranced, insensible to pain and almost impossible to arouse from the trance. The third is astral projection with forgetfulness of the body, which however does not remain sitting or lying in one place but

---

68. Swedenborg, 625–6.

continues to function in the normal way, even though there is no conscious awareness of it at the time. This may involve spirit possession.

From Swedenborg's descriptions, it seems that when he projected in the first way, he sent his consciousness to astral worlds, but was not aware of possessing an astral body while he experienced them. He did not merely see these worlds as images but was present within them and was able to converse with their inhabitants, while lacking any sense that he was embodied. In the second case, he was acutely aware of his astral body, and was amazed to find that all its senses, particularly the sense of touch, were heightened to a degree above that of his physical senses. In the third case, he believed himself present in the astral landscape in his physical body, as though he had been transported in the flesh into the astral scene. So real was his impression of the astral environment that he could not distinguish it from the everyday physical environment.

William Blake and the Angels

The English artist and poet William Blake (1757–1827) was also subject to astral visions and journeys to astral landscapes of a religious or spiritual nature. His perception appears to have been very similar to what Swedenborg described as habitual for himself— the dual vision of the astral world overlaid on the physical world, so that he could move through both simultaneously. Once, when accidentally locked into Westminster Abbey, Blake witnessed an entire procession of monks in ancient habits, moving across the floor of the church. His wife remarked to a friend, "I have very little of Mr. Blake's company; he is always in Paradise."[69]

Blake had angels visit him in his home, and sometimes caused them to sit while he drew their portraits. He told Thomas Phillips, a fellow artist who was doing Blake's portrait at the time, about a visit from the archangel Gabriel, who came to his room and offered to sit for Blake. Suspecting that it might be a spirit merely pretending to be the archangel, Blake demanded proof of his identity, and gave Phillips the response of the spirit:

> "You shall have good assurance," said the voice, "can an evil spirit do this?" I looked whence the voice came, and was then aware of a shining shape, with bright wings, who diffused much light. As I looked, the shape dilated more and more: he waved his hands; the roof of my study opened; he ascended into heaven; he stood in the

---

69. Bentley, *Blake Records*, 221.

sun, and beckoning to me, moved the universe. An angel of evil could not have done that—it was the arch-angel Gabriel.[70]

His visionary illustrated books such as the *Marriage of Heaven and Hell*, *The Book of Los*, and *The Book of Urizen* are extraordinary in their poetic genius and subtlety of meaning. Like Swedenborg, he believed that he had been chosen by God for the purpose of conveying a higher spiritual wisdom to mankind. On a number of occasions, Blake stated quite simply that his poetry was not composed, but was received without effort as dictation from angels. He and his wife became members of the Swedenborgian New Church in 1789. Although his artistic works bring prices of hundreds of thousands of dollars today, in his own time they were not understood. He died in poverty, dismissed as an eccentric.

---

70. Cunningham, *Cabinet Gallery of Pictures*, 11.

CHAPTER
FIVE

Spiritualism

It is generally agreed that the modern spiritualism movement started in the spring of 1848, at Hydesville, a small community in New York state located twenty miles or so from the city of Rochester. As with most things generally agreed upon, this information is only partially correct. Communications with spirits have occurred continuously since the beginning of human history, and the incident that marked the nominal start of the spiritualist movement was in many ways typical of its kind, though given more publicity than had previously been the case. Uncanny rappings were heard by the family of John D. Fox, who had just moved into a house in Hydesville that had been vacated by the previous tenant due to strange noises in the middle of the night. Efforts made to find a natural cause of the sounds were met with failure.

The youngest daughter, Kate Fox, who was seven years old at the time, discovered that the raps would respond to her in kind when she snapped her fingers or clapped her hands. Her mother began to ask for responses to questions, such as the ages of her children, as a way of testing the unseen maker of the sounds, and then asked if the source of the noises was a spirit. The answer was yes. By causing the spirit to respond with two raps for yes, and silence for no, she determined that the spirit was of a man of thirty-one years who had been murdered in the house and was buried in the cellar. The spirit indicated that his family consisted of a wife and five children—two sons and three daughters—and that his wife had died since his own death. If nothing else, Mrs. Fox deserves a certain admiration for extracting extemporaneously such specific facts from a simple yes-no oracle.

Soon Mrs. Fox and the spirit were putting on shows for their neighbors, and their neighbors' friends. The house became a kind of theater of the absurd. The cellar was dug up. Eventually, human hair and bits of human bones were discovered. It was not until 1904, when a cellar wall collapsed in the house, that an entire skeleton was found, supporting the information provided by the spirit.[71] The conjecture was that the murderer had buried the body in the middle of the floor, then had decided to move it under a wall, and had left a few fragments of the remains at the first site.

The two young Fox girls, Kate (1841–1892) and Margaret (1838–1893), were taken out of the house to live with relatives, but the rappings followed them. Along with a third sister, Leah, who had not lived in the haunted house when the raps started, they began to give séances that featured tapping sounds and table tipping. The first séance took place on November 14, 1849, at which the spirits conveyed the message: "Dear Friends, you must proclaim the truth to the world. This is the dawning of a new era; you must not try to conceal it any longer. When you do your duty God will protect you and good spirits will watch over you."[72] The news spread like wildfire, and the girls had to turn away curious hordes. Horace Greeley, editor of the *New York Tribune*, was one of their first clients, and he advised the Fox sisters to charge five dollars per person, as a way of limiting the crush of those seeking admission to the events. Free séances open to the general public were arranged by the benefactor, H. H. Day, who paid young Kate Fox twelve hundred dollars a year to conduct them.

---

71. Fodor, 146.

72. Ibid.

Shades of the Dead

Spiritualism soon developed into a kind of alternative religion that gave evidence of survival beyond the grave, and allowed the living to communicate with the beloved dead. It is significant that almost all of the spirits who spoke through spiritualist séances identified themselves as souls of the dead. This is a departure from the spirit communications of preceding centuries. In earlier times, the spirits who communicated had identified themselves more frequently as angels, or spirits of the natural world, or even as demons, but seldom as the dead. However, the religion of spiritualism, and its French version known as spiritism, are based on the premise that the entities that communicate during the séances were once living human beings. Those attending séances did not wish to communicate with the archangel Gabriel; they wanted to talk to Aunt Flora and Uncle Jim, and the mediums, who conducted the séances as increasingly formalized and elaborate performances, accommodated them.

Allan Kardec (1804–1869) identified several kinds of spirits that interact with humanity. He understood all of them to be the spirits of once-living human beings:

> The spirit-protector, good genius, or guardian-angel, is the one whose mission it is to follow each man through the course of his life, and to aid him to progress. His degree of advancement is always superior to that of his ward.
>
> Familiar Spirits attach themselves to certain persons, for a longer or shorter period, in order to be useful to them. Within the limits (often somewhat narrow) of their possibilities they are generally well-intentioned, but sometimes rather backward, and even frivolous. They busy themselves with the everyday details of human life and only act by order, or with the permission, of the spirit-guardians.
>
> Sympathetic spirits are those who are drawn to us by personal affectation, and by a similarity of tastes in good or in evil. The duration of their relationship with us is almost always dependent on circumstances.
>
> An evil genius is an imperfect or wicked spirit who attaches himself to a man for the purpose of perverting him but he acts of his own motion, and not in virtue of a mission. His tenacity is proportionate to the more or less easy access accorded to him. A man is always free to listen to the suggestions of an evil genius, or to repel them.[73]

---

73. Kardec, *Spirits' Book*, 240 (para. 512).

Spirit Mediums

Mediums became essential to spiritualism. It was discovered that not just anyone could elicit useful responses from the spirits, in spite of their eagerness to communicate, but only those with a gift of second sight. As the name implies, the medium acted as an intermediary between the spirits and the people attending the ritual of the séance, just as the shaman acted as an intermediary between the totemic spirits of the tribe and its members. Like the shaman, the medium usually entered a kind of trance during which the spirits of the dead communicated through her using her voice to speak, or her hands to write. The overwhelming number of mediums were women, just as in centuries past a much greater number of witches had been women. However, some of the male mediums, such as William Stainton Moses (1839–1892) and Daniel Dunglas Home (1833–1886), achieved notable success, particularly in the production of physical events, such as the levitations or sudden apports (materializations) of physical objects.

Like the witch, the spiritualistic medium relied on a guiding spirit, called a control. It fulfilled duties similar to the familiar of the witch and the tutelary spirit of the shaman. However, in keeping with the religious beliefs of the spiritualists, the control was the spirit of a dead person, who aided the medium in finding and communicating with the spirits of other dead. The control also protected the medium from the malice of evil spirits—the dead who found pleasure in deceiving and giving emotional distress to the living. Sometimes, an evil spirit would attempt to take over the medium through possession, and the control of the medium defended her against the attack, drawing on her vital reserves to increase its own power so that it was stronger than the malicious attacker. It was a general belief that a spirit allied with a medium was able to overcome any spirit without such a connection, due to the animal energy the control could siphon off from the physical body of the medium.

There are many more parallels between shamanism and spiritualism. The medium does not choose her profession, but is chosen for it by her innate gift, and by visitations of the spirits, who urge her to use that gift. This differs from the priest of a conventional religion, who has no special talent of his own, but receives his power from his office. Threats are sometimes employed by the spirits to ensure that the medium does not shirk from her calling. Similar threats were used by spirits to compel reluctant men and women to adopt shamanism. Both medium and shaman form a close bond of trust and affection with one or several spirits. In both cases, this bond may become sexual.

The familiar spirit of both shaman and medium acts as guide, teacher, and protector. Séances are conducted in a ritual context, as is the work of the shaman. Both shaman and medium usually enter an altered state of consciousness. Both are supposed to have power to heal and to foretell the future, derived from the spirits. In both shamanism and spiritualism, the spirits announce their presence by physical events such as loud noises, sounding musical instruments, sudden breezes, chilling cold, lights, and so on.

Spiritualism might be called shamanism reborn, or perhaps a better way to put it would be shamanism reinterpreted for Christians of the Industrial Age. It was shamanism materialized in a way that was palatable to the nineteenth century, when every event was expected to have an immediate physical cause, generally one activated by steam power. Hence, the phenomena of the séance were physical phenomena—ectoplasmic projections, voices, lights, movement of objects. It was expected that the spirits could be photographed and their words recorded on wax cylinders. The astral body was characterized as an envelope or shell composed of a subtle physical substance.

Nature of the Astral Double

Nandor Fodor described the experiments of Dr. Hector Durville (1848–1923), who succeeded through the use of animal magnetism to draw out the astral body from a suitable "exteriorizing" subject. He also used a "seeing" subject in order to learn the subtle details of its appearance, although he apparently possessed enough mediumistic ability to see it himself. Durville wrote that the double resembled the medium out of whom it was drawn, varied in luminosity, and was united to the body of the medium by a little cord. He asserted that it could see through distant opaque bodies, and most surprisingly, that it caused a calcium sulfide screen to glow when it approached the screen. "The sensory organs of the medium were seated in the phantom. At close approach it produced a sensation of cold, was humid to the touch and made the fingers luminous in the dark."[74] This material appears in Durville's book *Les fantômes des vivants*, and was referred to with great interest by Hereward Carrington.[75]

Durville concluded that astral projection proved, beyond a doubt, not only the existence of the human soul, but also the survival of the soul after death. He summed it up in two statements:

---

74.   Fodor, 100.

75.   Muldoon and Carrington, *Projection of the Astral Body*, 31–2.

1. Projection of the astral body is a certain fact, capable of being demonstrated by means of direct experiment. This also demonstrates to us that the living force is independent of matter, and that our Individuality is composed of a physical body and an intelligent Soul—and a vital link, the astral body.

2. Since this phantom can exist and function apart from the physical body, it may also exist after death. That is, Immortality is a fact which is thus proved scientifically.[76]

Reality of the astral body was equated by spiritualists with tangibility. It does not seem to have occurred to the experimenters that a thing might appear tangible to the senses, yet not be physically present in space. They were obsessed with capturing the material characteristics of the astral body. Two researchers named Malta and Van Zelse actually claimed to have weighed it! According to their findings, the astral body weighs just under seventy grams (just under two and a half ounces)—although it might be assumed that a fat person would project a heavier double than a thin person, if it were to be assumed that the astral body had any weight at all. They reported that the double is affected by gravity and is of the same density as air, that its molecules are held together by an unknown force, and that the atoms composing it are small and heavy but widely separated.[77]

To the modern reader, raised on the theory of general relativity and familiar with the weirdness of quantum mechanics, chaotic systems, and multidimensional space, the idea that an astral projection can be weighed appears quaint. We are not quite so chained to a materialistic outlook as the generation that believed that Isaac Newton had written all there was to know about the physics of the universe. If it were possible to weigh the astral double, its existence would long since have become an accepted fact of science. It is not, since the astral double has no material existence. It appears to be material. It can be seen, felt, even conversed with, but it is not material. It is always projected into the astral world, never the physical world. It merely appears at times to be present in the physical world.

It is difficult to know how to view the physical manifestations that are almost the invariable accompaniment of the spiritualist séance. They are a part of the materialism of the spiritualists—their need to reduce everything to the physical level while at the same time preening themselves on their enlightened emancipation from a materialistic

---

76. Muldoon and Carrington, *Projection of the Astral Body*, 32.

77. Fodor, 100.

outlook. Most of the phenomena can be dismissed as deliberate and conscious frauds on the part of the mediums. The stage magician Harry Houdini spent a large part of his free time exposing the tricks mediums used to make their séances more material, and thus more plausible, to their audiences. Nonetheless, after having dispensed with the obvious frauds, there still exists a body of events that do not appear to have been consciously contrived. Perhaps a few are genuine paranormal events, but most may be explained with Occam's razor as either unconscious deceptions or shared illusions.

In the same way that individuals witnessing a miracle can, in some unknown manner, cause others to see the same vision, even though it has no physical reality, the trance medium, perhaps with the aid of her control and other spiritual beings, can at times induce a shared vision in the minds of most, if not all, of those attending the séance. It also happens on rare occasions that the medium is temporarily possessed by a spirit without her awareness or permission, and the spirit then uses the body of the medium to produce an effect through hidden physical means as a way of deceiving the audience. The medium later protests with complete honesty that she did not contrive the effect, since she retains no memory of having done it.

The Silver Cord

The silver cord was an extremely popular concept in spiritualism. It is the one thing the average person is apt to know about astral projection. The fable is that the projected astral body is always attached to the physical body by a kind of vital conduit that maintains the life of the body while the spirit or soul is absent. Should the cord be cut, and the astral body separated from the physical body, the physical body will die. It is supposed to be infinitely elastic, becoming thinner the more it is stretched, so that on distant travels of the astral vehicle it is drawn as thin as a strand of spider web. It is supposed to glow with silver radiance, an obvious reference to moonlight—the projection of the astral body is a lunar activity, connected as it is with dreams, visions, and the astral world.

Allan Kardec asserted that it is possible for the physical body to survive when the astral body, carrying the spirit, is projected. "How can the body live while the spirit is absent? We reply that it is possible for the body to live with only the organic life, which is independent of the spirit's presence."[78] You may recall that one of the later demonologists, Henry More, theorized in 1653 that the flying ointment of witches preserved the

---

78. Kardec, *Mediums' Book*, 130.

life of the body while the spirit was out of it by filling the pores in the skin and thus seal-ing in its heat. This was a vexing puzzle for those convinced that the spirit and the flesh physically separated during astral projection, since they believed that without the spirit, the body must die. The solution of the writer More was the preservation of the heat of the body, which was its life, by trapping it inside the body. Kardec's solution was that the body had its own life independent of the life of the spirit.

However, hedging his bets, Kardec wrote, "But we must add that, during earth-life, the spirit is never completely detached from the body. Spirits, as well as certain seeing mediums, perceive that the spirit of one in the flesh, when away from the body, is united to it by a luminous trail, which reaches to the body; a phenomenon that never occurs when the body is dead, for then the separation is complete."[79] We can gather from this that the silver cord is not always visible when the astral double is visible. It can be per-ceived by spiritual beings as well as mediums possessed of the second sight, but is not seen by everyone who sees the astral body.

The Method of Saint Alphonsus Liguori

Kardec was puzzled as to how the astral double, projected out of the physical body, could appear not only visibly but also tangibly to others in their normal waking state. He decid-ed to ask an expert, Saint Alphonsus Liguori (1696–1787), who was made a saint largely on the strength of his powers of bilocation. The evoked spirit of Alphonsus gave a useful and instructive method of astral projection. He told Kardec that a man who had achieved a "certain degree of dematerialization" as a result of his advanced moral condition could project his double just prior to falling asleep, by praying to God that his spirit be given the ability to transport itself to the desired location.

> If his request is granted, his spirit abandons his fleshly body, as soon as the latter falls asleep, and accompanied by a part of his perispirit, leaves the gross material body in a state closely bordering on death. I say bordering on death, because there still remains in the body a link which cannot be defined, but which keeps up its union with the perispirit and the soul. The perispirit then appears in the place where the spirit desires to show himself.[80]

---

79. Kardec, *Mediums' Book*, 130.

80. Ibid., 131.

The method of astral projection described by the spirit that assumed the identity of Saint Alphonsus was the method most often used by spiritualist mediums during the nineteenth century, without the component of prayer or the advantage of moral improvement. Fodor wrote, "The usual method of such experiments is to determine before going to sleep to visit someone during the night. The experiment may succeed when the least expected, and the agent may be totally unaware of the success."[81] The male medium Stainton Moses decided to visit a friend one night. Without informing the friend of his intention, he went to bed and fixed his thoughts intently on that individual, than drifted into sleep. He had no awareness of success, but several days later when he asked the friend if anything unusual had happened on that night, the other replied that he had seen the medium sitting in his rooms in a chair by the fire. The friend stared intently at the astral double of the medium, and after a time it slowly faded away.

The spirit assumed by Kardec to be that of Saint Alphonsus went on to explain to him that the astral double can make itself tangible "by a special action on matter," but it neglected to describe that action. It also asserted that the double can be projected while awake, but that during projection the body is never in a completely normal state; it is always more or less entranced.

Notice that the spirit characterized the link between the projected astral body and the physical body as one that "cannot be defined," suggesting that the silver cord, so popular with the spiritualists of the last two centuries, is no more than a visual metaphor for the actual connection. Trying to investigate another myth of astral projection popularized by spiritualism, Kardec asked the supposed shade of Saint Alphonsus what would happen if a person whose astral double was away from the body were to be suddenly awakened. The popular belief was that the person would die. The spirit denied the possibility of awakening the body without the presence of the spirit, assuring Kardec that the spirit would know of the attempt and would instantly enter the physical body before consciousness returned.

Consciousness Cannot Be Divided

Kardec summed up his understanding of astral projection thusly:

> The individual who appears simultaneously in two different places has, then, two
> bodies; but, of these, one alone is real, the other is only an appearance: we may say

---

81. Fodor, 101.

that the first lives with the organic life, and the second, with that of the soul; on awaking, the two bodies reunite, and the life of the soul re-enters the material body. We have no reason to suppose that, in this state of partial separation, the two bodies can possess active and intelligent vitality, simultaneously, and in the same degree. It follows, moreover, from what we have just said, that the real body could not die, and the apparent body still remain visible; the approach of death always recalling the spirit to the body, if only for an instant. It also follows that the apparent body could not be killed, because it is not organic, and is not formed of flesh and bone; it would instantly disappear, if anyone tried to kill it.[82]

Although the double state enjoyed by Swedenborg and Blake, which Blake called his "two-fold vision" and characterized as always active within him—that sense of being both in the body and in the spirit simultaneously, of viewing the physical world and the astral world at the same time —appears to be a division of the mind between the astral body and physical body, reflection shows that this cannot be the case. Consciousness occupies only one point in space and time at any given instant. Although it is possible for the point of view to jump back and forth between two places or two states with great freedom and rapidity, it cannot occupy both at the exact same instant. Kardec is correct that both the astral body and the physical body cannot possess "active and intelligent vitality, simultaneously, and in the same degree." The consciousnesses of Blake and Swedenborg danced between the astral and the physical with great facility, but cannot have resided in both at once.

Neither visionary was conscious of an astral body in the usual course of affairs, but both believed themselves to reside in their physical bodies, and that their awareness focused alternately on the material world and on the astral world. However, the physical body cannot occupy the astral world. When they became aware of the astral world, their consciousnesses resided in their astral bodies even if they did not at the time perceive a separation between astral and physical bodies. It is possible to project the astral body in the same location as the physical body, so that the two overlap—that is, it is possible to make them distinct without separating them.

Sylvan Muldoon

The man most responsible for the two popular myths about astral travel examined above—that of the silver cord, and the belief that to awaken the body when the astral double is

---

82. Kardec, *Mediums' Book*, 133.

absent causes death—was the darling of the spiritualists, Sylvan Muldoon (1903–1971), perhaps the greatest astral traveler, at least by his own accounts, who has ever lived. The well-respected psychic researcher Hereward Carrington (1880–1958) devoted a good portion of his career to studying Muldoon's ideas concerning soul flight.

As a boy and young man, Muldoon suffered from weak health. His first experience of soul flight occurred when he was twelve years old. He woke up in the night and found himself unable to move his body. Later he would characterize this condition, which we now call sleep paralysis, as "astral catalepsy" and would experience it frequently, but the first time it terrified him. He became aware of a floating sensation, followed by rapid vibrations of his body and a pain at the back of his head. Suddenly he found himself lying on the air five feet or so over his bed. An unseen force pushed him into a standing position, and when he looked back at his bed he realized that his body was still lying on it. A glowing white cord stretched between the center of the forehead between the eyebrows of his physical body and the back of the head of his astral body. He tried to wake other members of his family but found that his hands passed through their bodies. After fifteen minutes or so, the silver cord contracted and pulled him back into his body in a reversal of the stages by which he had left it.

In this account, we find all of the main features of Muldoon's later experiences of astral travel—the catalepsy, the exit of the astral body in a horizontal position above the physical body, the silver cord, the automatic assumption of an upright posture, the pull on the cord signaling a return to the body. How many of these details actually occurred to him during that first projection at age twelve, there is no way to know. It is possible that his abilities were mature and fully formed the first time he experienced projection of the astral double. Or he may have modified his memory of the first experience to correspond more exactly with his later technique.

Muldoon found during subsequent projections that when he stood near to his physical form, the silver cord tended to try to draw him back into his body. He called this distance the cord activity range. The pulling sensation went away as soon as he moved more than a dozen feet or so from his body—the distance varied from eight to fifteen feet, depending on his state of vitality at the time. When his physical body was less strong, it was easier to project the astral body. This corresponds to what the spirit that claimed to be Saint Alphonsus told Allan Kardec. The spirit said that a man who had achieved a "certain degree of dematerialization" could project his double—that is, a refining or weakening of the gross animal spirits of the physical body, which the saints of the church achieved through austerity and denial of the urges of the flesh such as sexual desire, hunger, and fatigue.

It is certainly the case that spontaneous astral projection happens most often to those who are either ill, and thereby weakened in the body, or who experience a sudden intense shock to their physical systems, such as a fall or a car accident. In the first class of spontaneous separation, the spiritualists assumed that the lowering of vital energy allows the astral body to slide out of the physical body. Muldoon theorized that it was because the lowered vitality made the silver cord weaker. In the second class of spontaneous separation, the astral body seems to be violently knocked out by a great nervous shock. Of course, the astral body is not really outside the physical body any more than it was ever inside the body—both astral body and physical body are part of the mind, and always remain part of the mind. It is the conscious awareness that shifts from one mental state to another, from physical to astral.

Muldoon and Carrington were obsessed by the silver cord. They believed it was the same as the silver cord described in the Bible. Muldoon probably derived the expression, and perhaps the concept, from the biblical verse, "Or ever the silver cord be loosed, or the golden bowl be broken, or the pitcher be broken at the fountain, or the wheel broken at the cistern:" (Ecclesiastes 12:6). Carrington wrote:

> The astral and the physical bodies are invariably connected by means of a sort of cord, or cable, along which vital currents pass. Should this cord be severed, death instantly results. The only difference between astral projection and death is that the cord is intact in the former case, and severed in the latter. This cord—the "Silver Cord" spoken of in *Ecclesiastes*—is elastic, and capable of great extension. It constitutes the essential link between the two bodies.[83]

This would seem to imply that the cord can be cut during astral projection, resulting in the death of the body. This is not the case. The cord is a metaphorical link between the physical body and the astral body, a symbolic representation of their inescapable connection. There is probably no danger the astral body can encounter during soul flight, and no action it can take, that can directly cause physical death. Prior to the rise of spiritualism in the nineteenth century, most of those who wrote accounts of astral projection did

---

83. Muldoon and Carrington, *Projection of the Astral Body*, 16.

not mention the silver cord. If it were as prominent a part of the experience as Muldoon claimed, it is difficult to understand why it would be omitted from these accounts.

The cord is seen by those who, consciously or unconsciously, expect to see it. It is equivalent to the mythic thread of Ariadne that guided Theseus out of the Labyrinth. Since it is natural to imagine some tangible link between the physical body and the apparently detached and separate astral body, perception of a cord, beam, cable, rope, thread, ribbon, channel, pathway, trail, or conduit of some sort may arise in a natural way, as the consciousness struggles to make sense of the experience, but its perception is not an essential feature of soul flight. Spiritualists would explain away the absence of the silver cord from many records of soul flight by saying that it requires a heightened and unusual degree of psychic perception to see it. However, after the ideas of spiritualism concerning astral travel permeated the culture and became predominant over older concepts, such as those involving witchcraft and fairies, accounts of the silver cord began to appear in a great number of the recorded descriptions of astral projection.

Muldoon describes three speeds at which the externalized astral body may travel, depending on its needs. The first is the normal speed of movement enjoyed by the physical body, a walking or at most a running speed. The second level is an accelerated motion in which objects appear to approach and flash past with great rapidity. This second intermediate speed would have been difficult for his Victorian readers to visualize, but we are all familiar with it from modern cinema. When the film of a movie is speeded up, we get exactly the impression described by Muldoon, apart from the streaks of light that trail after the astral body moving at this velocity, which Muldoon wrote were similar to the scintillations that trail after a meteor. The third supernormal speed involves an instantaneous, or apparently instantaneous, transition from one place to another.

Muldoon's Methods

The primary method used by Muldoon to induce soul flight was autosuggestion. Just prior to falling asleep in his bed he imagined that he was rising or climbing up to a higher level, and tried to induce a dream with this same content that would play out after he fell asleep. The action in the dream was imitative—the rising up of the body within the dream simulated the rising of the astral body out of the physical body. One visualization he had good success with involved imagining himself lying on the floor of an elevator as it ascended in a tall building. Another successful visualization involved climbing up a ladder.

Muldoon also observed that unrelieved stress or tension, when carried into sleep, sometimes had the effect of causing the astral body to separate from the physical body in an attempt to perform the action that would relieve the stress. He gave the example of going to sleep very thirsty one night, and finding himself in his astral body, standing at the kitchen tap trying to turn it on so that he could fill a glass with water.[84] As an example of stress induced by the urge of habit or routine, he wrote that a keen amateur golfer obsessed with his sport might find himself practicing his golf swing in his astral body.

He suggested using stress actively by heightening it before retiring to bed, and then visualizing the action that would relieve it. Using thirst as his trigger, he would take an eighth of a teaspoon of salt immediately before retiring for the night, and then visualize himself going to some place where there was water so that he could get a drink. In this way he was able to induce several recurrences of the projection in which he found himself standing in his astral body at the kitchen sink, trying to turn on the faucet.[85] Certain factors encouraged success in these experiments—total darkness, silence, cool but comfortable temperatures, light bed coverings.

The spiritualists such as Muldoon did more to investigate astral travel in a practical way than any other group, but their work resulted in a set of false conclusions because they were based on the false premises that the astral body is composed of a subtle material substance that occupies space and may be photographed and otherwise recorded mechanically, and that the astral body actually separates from the physical body in distance during astral projection. They were largely unaware that the phenomena of astral projection were just as much subjective experiences as the astral landscapes themselves. The other great error was to regard all of the spirits encountered during astral travel as the souls of dead human beings. This second error rendered spiritualism not only a failed science, but a failed religion as well.

---

84. Muldoon and Carrington, *Projection of the Astral Body*, 177.

85. Ibid., 193.

CHAPTER SIX

Theosophy

At the same time that the spiritualists were conducting their experiments into the projection of the double and forming their materialistic theories concerning the weight of the astral body and the elasticity of the silver cord, the new religion of Theosophy was doing its own more theoretical work in the same field, supported by the wisdom teachings of India and Tibet. Spiritualists held a low opinion of Theosophists. Hereward Carrington wrote that although the literature of Theosophy was filled with references to astral projection, he was unable to find in it any practical instructions on how to actually project the astral body.[86] There is a mingled tone of impatience and contempt when Carrington writes of Theosophy.

---

86. Muldoon and Carrington, *Projection of the Astral Body*, 25.

Theosophists, for their part, gave forth a remarkable account concerning the origins of spiritualism that indicates by its content the condescending attitude with which they regarded the spiritualist movement. It is related by Charles Webster Leadbeater (1854–1934) in his book *The Astral Plane: Its Scenery, Inhabitants and Phenomena*. According to Leadbeater, the modern spiritualism movement began as an experiment conducted by the enlightened spiritual chiefs of a secret occult lodge known as the Divine Rulers of the Golden Gate, which Leadbeater claimed was associated with Atlantis. Appalled by the creeping materialism of the nineteenth century, these powerful spirits decided to make it possible for the average person to converse with the dead, and thereby gain direct proof of the survival of the soul after death:

> The method adopted was to take some ordinary person after death, arouse him thoroughly upon the astral plane, instruct him to a certain extent in the powers and possibilities belonging to it, and then put him in charge of a Spiritualistic circle. He in his turn "developed" other departed personalities along the same line, they all acted upon those who sat at their séances, and "developed" them as mediums; and so spiritualism grew and flourished. No doubt living members of the original lodge occasionally manifested themselves in astral form at some of the circles—perhaps they may do so even now; but in most cases they simply gave such direction and guidance as they considered necessary to the persons they had put in charge. There is little doubt that the movement increased so much more rapidly than they had expected that it soon got quite beyond their control, so that, as has been said, for many of the later developments they can only be held indirectly responsible.[87]

The antagonism that grew up between spiritualism and Theosophy was a natural result of the competition of these two popular movements to redefine the afterlife for those who had rejected the conventional Christian framework. Spiritualists viewed Theosophy as theoretical, unscientific, over-elaborated, and foreign. Theosophists regarded spiritualism as simplistic, crude, and potentially dangerous—an unfortunate attitude considering that Theosophy was a direct outgrowth of spiritualism.

---

87. Leadbeater, *Astral Plane*, 101.

Helena Petrovna Blavatsky

Theosophy was founded by the Russian spirit medium Madame Helena Petrovna Blavatsky (1831–1891) as a way of bringing Eastern wisdom to the West. It began in New York in 1875, but established a second branch in Bombay in 1879, and soon shifted its headquarters from the United States to India. Blavatsky was an accomplished spiritualist who produced many of the physical phenomena that were regarded as a necessary part of any séance at the time. She was particularly adept at apports—the sudden appearance of objects out of thin air. Later it was proven that her apports were frauds. The letters supposedly written by enlightened spiritual masters known as Mahatmas that regularly popped into existence over her head were found to have been slipped through a crack in the floorboards of the room above by an accomplice.

In spite of the obvious fraud of her physical effects, there is little reason to doubt that she was in communication with spiritual beings, or that she received her most significant writings from them while in a trance state. Even as a sickly young child, Blavatsky was strongly gifted with mediumistic abilities. She was a sleepwalker, and was given to fits of uncontrollable fury that caused her nurses to accuse her being possessed by devils. In order to drive them out, she would later say, she was "drenched with enough holy water to float a ship."[88] Her favorite playmate was a spirit that came in the form of a small hunch-backed boy. When others told her that they could not see him, she became irritated by their lack of perception. As she grew into her teens, her mediumistic gifts flowered, and she performed such tricks as locating lost objects and predicting the date of death of visitors to the house.

At seventeen, her governess told her that she was so headstrong, she would never find a man who would consent to marry her. In defiance, the teenager talked an elderly general named Blavatsky into proposing, and she accepted. Almost immediately she changed her mind, but she was compelled to go through with the ceremony. After three months of constant bickering, she fled her bewildered husband on horseback and never returned. Her biographer, the Theosophist A. P. Sinnett, wrote: "Thus Madame Blavatsky abandoned her country at seventeen and passed ten long years in strange and out-of-the-way places—in Central Asia, India, South America, Africa, and Eastern Europe."[89]

---

88. Kuhn, *Modern Revival of Ancient Wisdom*, 45.

89. Sinnett, *Incidents in the Life of Madame Blavatsky*, 39–40.

There is undoubtedly much more myth in the unobserved portions of the life of Blavatsky than fact. She had no intention of telling the truth about herself when a more exciting lie would add to the aura of mystery and romance that she deliberately cultivated. This hidden period in her life, the ten years after her first marriage in which she is supposed to have wandered among the mystic masters of Tibet and India, was probably a good deal more squalid than she preferred to acknowledge. She traveled on the fringes of the law, taking advantage of the foolish, and it was during this period that she acquired the tricks of the séance that served her so well as the leader of the Theosophical movement. The hardship of her vagabond life was undoubtedly mitigated by the regular sums of money sent to her from her father whenever she wrote and requested funds.

Even after she reconciled with her family, she continued to wander the world on various wild excursions, seeking to learn occult mysteries. There is little point in giving a full account of her adventures, the details of which as related by Blavatsky are to be regarded with the most intense skepticism. But one incident has a bearing on astral travel, and is worth relating. In 1856, while passing through Tibet in the company of a shaman, Blavatsky had the shaman leave his body as he lay in trance in their tent, and carry by soul flight a message to a woman friend living in the principality of Wallachia, in what is presently Romania. "Madame Blavatsky later verified the long distance phenomenon by receiving in writing, in response to an inquiry by mail, a letter from the Rumanian friend stating that at the identical time of the Shaman's concentration she had swooned, but dreamed she saw Madame Blavatsky in a tent in a wild country among menacing tribes, and that she had communicated with her. Madame Blavatsky states that the friend's astral form was visible in the tent."[90]

In 1870, while living in Cairo, Blavatsky decided to found the *Société Spirite*, for the investigation of spiritualism along the lines set forth in the books of Allan Kardec. This first effort to form an organized society ended poorly when two of Blavatsky's mediums ran off with all her money. "To wind up the comedy with a drama, I got nearly shot by a madman—a Greek, who had been present at the only two public séances we held, and got possessed I suppose, by some vile spook."[91] This effort, abortive though it was, shows the debt the early stirrings of Theosophy owe to Kardec and spiritism.

---

90. Kuhn, 52.

91. Sinnett, 125.

While living in Paris in 1873, Blavatsky was directed by spiritual overseers to go to New York and meet with a man named Henry Steel Olcott (1832–1907). She followed their directive, and was soon living with Olcott in a seven-room apartment in New York that they referred to as the Lamasery. Their union appears to have been intellectual rather than sexual. An intense period of mediumship and writing culminated in the formation of the Theosophical Society. Olcott was elected as chairman and became the organizational genius responsible for the rapid spread of the Society.

Blavatsky's two greatest works, *Isis Unveiled* (1877) and *The Secret Doctrine* (1888), are bewildering in their scope and complexity. Somehow, from their confusion, and from subsequent spirit messages received by Blavatsky during séances, she and her closest followers were able to extract the essential ideas of Theosophy.

Seven Astral Levels

Madame Blavatsky claimed to receive her wisdom from a hierarchy of highly evolved human souls that were referred to collectively first as the Brothers, and then later as the Masters. When Theosophy shifted its center from America to India, this title was changed to Mahatmas, a word meaning "great souls."[92] Although Blavatsky undoubtedly faked the physical letters supposedly received from these spirits by apports, the actual teachings of the Mahatmas written on the letters may have been psychically received. Theosophy involves numerous sevenfold divisions of humanity, the universe, and its spiritual creatures, most of which do not concern us. We are interested in those that pertain to the astral world and its inhabitants.

The astral world, which Theosophists preferred to call the astral light, is divided by them into seven levels or degrees. They are not to be thought of as one above the other, or even as concentric shells like the layers of an onion, but rather as different rates of vibration that interpenetrate and exist simultaneously in the same place. According to Theosophical doctrine, they are all physical but possess graduated degrees of density—from the most gross, which is not much removed from common matter, to the most refined, which is akin to spirit.

> So when we speak of a man as rising from one plane or subplane to another, we do not speak of him as necessarily moving in space at all, but rather as transferring his consciousness from one level to another—gradually becoming unresponsive to the

---

92. Judge, *Ocean of Theosophy*, 7.

vibrations of one order of matter, and beginning instead to answer to those of a higher and more refined order; so that one world with its scenery and inhabitants would seem to fade slowly away from his view, while another world of a more elevated character would dawn upon him in its stead.[93]

The densest seventh level is described as a shadowy reflection of the lowest aspects of life, where nothing wholesome or pleasant is able to subsist. It may be conceived as a kind of astral underworld, or hell, in which the evil impulses and inclinations of humanity take on murky shapes. "Most students find the investigation of this section an extremely unpleasant task, for there appears to be a sense of density and gross materiality about it which is indescribably loathsome to the liberated astral body, causing it the sense of pushing its way through some black, viscous fluid, while the inhabitants and influences encountered there are also usually exceedingly undesirable."[94]

Level six is identical in appearance to the physical world. Those who project their astral bodies into this level may not know that they are on an astral plane, but may believe themselves to be traveling through the ordinary material environment of everyday life. Levels five and four are similar to level six but are more refined—so that, as the astral traveler ascends through these levels, the landscapes begin to diverge in their details from the corresponding locations in the material world. The remaining levels—three, two and one—are also similar in nature and form a second triplet. The astral beings who live on these levels have little contact with the material plane, so the landscapes of these three higher levels have almost no correspondence with the physical world, but are created by the astral beings that dwell there.

The three highest astral planes of Theosophy appear to correspond with the land of fairy, which has been described in various folklore accounts to have its own roads, towns, rivers, mountains, trees, and other features distinct from the material world. The spiritualists referred to this astral place as Summerland. Leadbeater wrote that it contains "forests and mountains, lovely lakes and pleasant flower-gardens, which are at any rate much superior to anything in the physical world."[95] These higher astral levels in the Theosophical system have a kind of magical, living beauty about them that entrances

93. Leadbeater, *Astral Plane*, 17–8.
94. Ibid., 26.
95. Ibid., 27.

the visitor and makes him reluctant to leave. This has often been said of fairyland, where everything is more perfect and more beautiful than in life.

Spiritualist mediums did not see this level of astral complexity when traveling out of their physical bodies. Naturally, Theosophists had an answer for this discrepancy, one which managed to both dismiss and, at the same time, disparage the spiritualists.

> It may be objected by some readers that no such complexities as these are described by most of the psychics who occasionally get glimpses of the astral world, nor are they reported at *seances* by the entities that manifest there: but this is readily accounted for. Few untrained persons on that plane, whether living or "dead" see things as they really are until after very long experience; even those who do see fully are often too dazed and confused to understand or remember; and among the very small minority who both see and remember there are hardly any who can translate the recollection into language on our lower plane. Many untrained psychics never examine their visions scientifically at all; they simply obtain an impression which may be quite correct, but may also be half false, or even wholly misleading.[96]

Human Souls in the Astral Planes

Theosophy differs from spiritualism in its understanding of the astral world—not only in its complexity, but also in the acknowledgement that not all of its inhabitants are human. Spirits other than human are scarcely to be met within the accounts of astral journeys given by spiritualist mediums. In contrast, Theosophists recognize wholly inhuman astral beings, and astral beings created—either deliberately or unconsciously—by human thought.

Theosophists believe that immediately following death, the souls of human beings go to whichever astral level best suits their degree of spiritual evolution, after first passing briefly and unconsciously through the lowest seventh level. Only the most debased souls become trapped in the seventh level of darkness. The souls of average people remain on the astral planes for periods ranging from hours to centuries, and may rise or fall on the planes as they become more or less advanced during their residence. "The average man has by no means freed himself from all lower desires before death, and it takes a long period of more or less fully conscious life on the various subdivisions of the astral plane to allow the forces which he has generated to work themselves out, and thus release the higher ego."[97]

---

96. Leadbeater, *Astral Plane*, 24–5.

97. Ibid., 39

Departed souls who were very attached to worldly matters are apt to remain for an extended term on the sixth level, which closely resembles the material world and allows them to most easily interact with the still-living human beings that they knew during life. Those advanced enough to turn their backs on material existence—but who have not evolved enough to escape the astral levels—live on the third plane, where they build their own cities and establish their own societies. These cities of the third plane are said to persist in the same way that the cities of our world continue from generation to generation of their inhabitants and builders. This is the Summerland, so similar in many respects to the descriptions of the land of fairy, and fairies have indeed always been mythically linked with the human dead. The second astral plane is inhabited by dogmatic religious believers, and the first plane by intellectuals.

There are two particular forms of astral inhabitants that are cast off from the souls of the dead as they finally free themselves from the astral world entirely and rise above it. The first is called a shade, and the second a shell. Their difference is a matter of degree. Neither one has any trace of human soul remaining with it. The shade is composed of the collection of habits, thoughts, impulses, and so on that bound a soul to the lower astral levels. As the soul at last rises, these are cast off, or torn away, and retain the lower aspects of human personality. For a period of time they persist, and often appear to mediums at séances, where they are mistaken for the actual souls of the dead. Blavatsky referred to this as the Spook body: "Our Theosophists know well enough that after death the *higher* Manas unites with the *Monad* and passes into Davachan, while the dregs of the *lower* Manas or animal mind go to form this Spook."[98] The shells are less animated than the shades, and are merely the final remnants of those who have passed through the astral planes on their ascent to heaven after death. Shells retain no consciousness, and nothing resembling the genuine personality. They are like astral zombies that can, briefly, be animated into an illusion of awareness by the power of the medium during a séance.

On rare occasions, enlightened beings who were once human, but who have long since cast off their astral bodies, find it necessary to descend to the astral planes, and for this purpose they take on astral substance and build temporary astral bodies for themselves. Among these beings are the Nirmanakaya, "the 'spirits' (in the sense of an individual, or *conscious* spirit) of great sages from spheres on a higher plane than our own, who voluntarily incarnate in mortal bodies in order to help the human race in its upward

---

98. Blavatsky, *Studies in Occultism*, 187.

progress."[99] The same descent into the astral is sometimes undertaken by the adepts, who have risen beyond the astral but who are not quite so exalted as the Nirmanakaya.

Astral Projections of the Living

Among these human inhabitants of the astral planes are the astral projections of the living, which fall into several classes. The most numerous are those who send their astral doubles forth during sleep or illness without intending to do so, or who find themselves suddenly knocked out of their physical bodies by some traumatic shock. The second type of living traveler on the astral planes is made up of those possessing psychic abilities who deliberately experiment with the projection of the astral double, such as the Theosophist Oliver Fox and the spiritualist Sylvan Muldoon. Another type is the student of the esoteric mysteries who is taught to travel the planes by a spiritual master. His dark reflection is the student of a black magician, also taught to negotiate the planes by his master.

Some souls of a debased nature are so transformed in the astral levels that they are scarcely recognizable as having once been human. Among these are souls of an extremely lustful and base disposition, who after death inhabit the seventh level and become incubi and succubi. There is an even worse fate than this, according to Theosophists. Souls in whom all traces of decency and humanity have been deliberately suppressed and erased, so that during life they cannot be said to be human at all, are too material and corrupt in their natures to be able to remain in even the lowest level of the astral planes. "The lost entity would very soon after death find himself unable to stay in the astral world, and would be irresistibly drawn in full consciousness into 'his own place,' the mysterious eighth sphere, there slowly to disintegrate after experiences best left undescribed."[100]

As a desperate attempt to avoid the fate of the eighth sphere, a few of these damned souls preserve the life of their bodies in a cataleptic trance, by feeding their bodies blood drawn while in semi-materialized astral form out of the veins of the living. These are the true, corporeal vampires, the existence of which Theosophy acknowledges. They can most easily be destroyed by burning their bodies.

Another astral inhabitant scarcely to be recognized as human is the werewolf. When a human being of a particularly brutal and cruel nature, who has some knowledge of the occult, manages to project his astral body, it may be seized upon by "other astral entities"

---

99.   Blavatsky, *Secret Doctrine*, vol. 2, p. 636.

100.   Leadbeater, *Astral Plane*, 59.

the nature of which Leadbeater does not describe. These transform the astral body of the traveler into that of a beast such as a wolf, and materialize it to such a degree that it is able to roam the countryside, hunting and killing livestock and human beings for the purpose of satisfying not only its own craving for fresh blood, but also the craving of the entities that materialized it. A wound inflicted upon the materialized astral body in animal form will be reflected on to the living physical body of the projector. This is known as repercussion—when something done to the astral body instantly occurs to the physical body.

Inhuman Inhabitants of the Astral Planes

The completely inhuman inhabitants of the astral planes are the elementals, the nature spirits, and the thought-forms. The elementals of Theosophy are not the same as those understood in Western occultism. They are spirits formed and differentiated out of a single elemental essence, which can express all of the qualities we generally recognize as elemental—Fire, Water, Air, and Earth. They arise from random thoughts, and have a brief and mindless existence. At their lowest level, these are the hypnogogic images of faces, seen on the borders of sleep. They can no more be called independent beings than the waves on the surface of a lake, stirred into motion by a passing breeze, can be said to exist independently of the lake.

Only when an elemental is deliberately shaped by sustained concentration and willpower, as is sometimes done by magicians, does it develop any sort of permanence or individuality. Then it attains the capacity to express through its nature either good or evil, and is no longer properly speaking an elemental, in the sense that Leadbeater uses the term. "When we read of a good or evil elemental, it must always be either an artificial entity or one of the many varieties of nature-spirits that is meant, for the elemental kingdoms proper do not admit of any such conceptions as good and evil."[101]

The nature spirits of Leadbeater include what most of us would conceive as elementals—spirits composed of only one of the four elements. His mingling of elementals with nature spirits would not be accepted by most modern Western occultists.

> Many writers have included these spirits among the elementals, and indeed they are the elementals (or perhaps, to speak more accurately, the animals) of a higher evolution. Though much more highly developed than our elemental essense, they have yet certain characteristics in common with it; for example, they also are divided

---

101.   Leadbeater, *Astral Plane*, 72.

into seven great classes, inhabiting respectively the same seven states of matter already mentioned as permeated by the corresponding varieties of the essence. Thus, to take those which are most readily comprehensible to us, there are spirits of the earth, water, air and fire (or ether)—definite intelligent astral entities residing and functioning in each of those media . . .

In mediaeval literature, these earth-spirits are often called gnomes, while the water-spirits are spoken of as undines, the air-spirits as sylphs, and the ether-spirits as salamanders. In popular language they are known by many names—fairies, pixies, elves, brownies, peris, djinns, trolls, satyrs, fawns, kobolds, imps, goblins, good people—some of these titles being applied only to one variety, and others indiscriminately to all.[102]

According to Theosophy, they are completely inhuman and have no connection with our line of spiritual evolution. Leadbeater described them as "frequently human in shape and somewhat diminutive in size." They can take on any forms they like, being able to mold their astral substance at will, but prefer forms that suit their essential inherent natures. They usually pass invisible to human sight, but can if they wish materialize their forms to such a degree that they become visible. Most types want nothing to do with humanity and avoid the habitations of man.

Leadbeater observed that fairies are masters of illusion and are capable of deceiving not only an individual but whole groups at one time. He rightly compared this talent to the similar sensory deception practiced by Hindu fakirs, who during their public performances are able to fool their audiences into seeing whatever they will them to see. The power of these spirits to manipulate human senses is seldom accorded the importance it deserves in accounts of their natures and abilities.

Another inhuman class of beings sometimes found on the astral planes is the devas—what we in the West would call angels. Theosophists use the term in a more restrictive sense than it is used in the East, where a deva might be any of various types of nonhuman entity. Theosophists believe that human beings, when they evolve sufficiently, can if they wish become devas, but that they can also at their discretion bypass the deva state.

The last type of astral entity in the Theosophical catalog that will be touched on here is the artificially formed entity, which may be created unconsciously or deliberately. The unconsciously formed are usually what in Theosophy are called elementals. They come into being in response to strong thoughts. The thought creates an astral shape from

---

102. Leadbeater, *Astral Plane*, 77–8.

the elemental essence that corresponds with it. The artificial being formed possesses its own shadow of existence for as long as the thought that sustains it persists. A repeated thought, mulled over and brooded upon with intensity, can give rise to an astral form that can endure for days.

The unpleasant situation may arise in which a person who has the same thoughts of a hurtful, malicious type that return over and over for months, or even years, may create an entity that attaches itself to him, feeding on his emotions like a kind of astral vampire. Since the hurtful thoughts sustain this creature, it does all in its power to encourage them. A metaphor for this astral leech would be the black cloud that is sometimes said to follow individuals around wherever they go. Such creatures can leave their creators, when they become too weak to be of use, and attach themselves to others, provoking similar obsessive thoughts in their new hosts for nourishment, and in this manner can sustain their existence.

The opposite kind of artificial astral entity is created when a person sustains loving and protective thoughts toward another human being, such as those that might be held in the mind of a mother for her child. They shape themselves into a kind of benevolent spirit that travels to the person who is the object of the love, and protects that person. This is even true when those who have died, and who inhabit the astral planes, think strong thoughts of love about those they have left behind. It is the belief in Theosophy that the love of departed parents, siblings, and lovers can help and sustain the living.

Magicians are able to deliberately shape such artificial astral entities with the power of their thoughts and their will, creating beings with highly specialized personalities and abilities for specific forms of work, and even for individual tasks. Adepts of magic sometimes create astral guardians for their disciples, which remain with them as a kind of familiar spirit. Deliberately formed astral beings may escape the control of their creators, and move from person to person seeking the vital energy that sustains them. The deliberate creation of thought-forms—known in Tibet as *tulpas*—that take on a life and purpose of their own is described by Alexandra David-Neel in her *Magic and Mystery in Tibet*, and it is undoubtedly to this type of creation that Leadbeater referred. David-Neel observed on this subject that once the *tulpa* has been infused with enough vitality to simulate an independent being, it tends to seek freedom from its maker's authority.[103]

---

103. David-Neel, 313.

There are other astral inhabitants and visitors recognized in Theosophy, but these are the most important classes. It is useful to have an overview of them in order to see how the Theosophical concept of the astral world differed from that of the spiritualists who came before them, and from that of the ritual magicians of the Golden Dawn who followed.

The Astral Body

Theosophy divided the human body into seven degrees or levels. We need only concern ourselves with the lowest three. The lowest body is the material or physical body of flesh and blood. Next above it is what is called the etheric body, which resembles the material body closely but is formed of a more subtle substance. Slightly more refined than the etheric body is the astral body, with which human beings are enabled to travel the astral planes. Just as, after death, the human body decays and eventually falls to nothingness, so Theosophists believe that the etheric and astral bodies also break down and fall to nothing with the passage of sufficient time. The body of flesh is the first to disappear, followed by the body of the etheric, and then by the body of the astral, and so on up to the higher bodies.

Theosophists believe that the etheric body is able to separate from the physical body during life no more than a couple of feet. It is connected with the physical body by its own cord that has very little elasticity. It cannot travel far from the physical body.[104] During the séance, it is the etheric body that becomes visible near the trance medium. It is always seen hovering near her. It can take various forms, and is dense enough to be readily felt by those who touch it. The cord that links the astral body to the physical body is elastic to an almost infinite degree. This allows the astral traveler to venture far away from the physical vessel, yet always be assured of finding his way back.

A useful description of the Theosophical understanding of the astral body was given by William Q. Judge:

> The astral body is made of matter of very fine texture as compared with the visible body, and has a great tensile strength, so that it changes but little during a lifetime, while the physical alters every moment. And not only has it this immense strength, but at the same time possesses as elasticity permitting its extension to a considerable distance. It is flexible, plastic, extensible, and strong. The matter of which it is composed is electrical and magnetic in its essence, and is just what the whole world was

---

104. Fox, *Astral Projection*, 28.

composed of in the dim past when the processes of evolution had not yet arrived at the point of producing the material body for man.[105]

Theosophy understands the astral body to be the template upon which the physical body is formed. It exists before the existence of the physical body, and when the physical body dies, it continues to survive for some time on the astral planes. The etheric body remains closely linked to the corpse, and is said to be responsible for ghosts seen in graveyards and near the bodies of the dead. It decays more quickly than the astral body.

Surrounding the human body is the aura, which Theosophy divides into seven layers that distinguish themselves by different colors and varying densities. Those projecting on the astral planes carry their aura with them. It is said to be plainly visible to spirits and to those possessed with psychic ability. The state of health, and also the level of spiritual advancement, is revealed by an intelligent interpretation of the aura.

The Akashic Records

Theosophists also believe in the existence of what is known as the akashic records—a perfect and complete impression of every event that has occurred in the universe. Leadbeater likened it to the memory of God.[106] The akashic records are not, strictly speaking, an astral phenomenon at all, but are merely reflected in the astral light from the higher spiritual level where they have their true existence. Because they are only a reflection, when seen on the astral levels they are imperfect, and those who attempt to read the akashic records during astral projection invariably make mistakes.

Oliver Fox

In view of the almost perfect understanding Theosophists claimed to have of the astral planes, the astral body, and astral travel, it is surprising that so few of them experimented with it in a practical way. As Hereward Carrington observed, useful books on astral projection written by Theosophists are scarcely to be encountered. The exception is the work of the Theosophist Oliver Fox (1886–1949), whose real name was Hugh Callaway. Like his contemporary, the spiritualist Sylvan Muldoon, Fox had been a sickly child with mediumistic abilities who received his first memorable experiences of projection at a young

---

105. Judge, 44.

106. Leadbeater, *Astral Plane*, 27.

age. These usually took the forms of dreams, but they were dreams in which he was at least partially conscious.

When he was seven or eight years old, Fox began to have a recurring dream that came to him several times a year throughout his childhood. In the dream, he sat talking with his mother, when she suddenly fell silent and stared at him strangely. The firelight and lamp-light dimmed, and the air suffused with a kind of golden radiance. The door of the parlor opened and the double of his mother, exact in every detail, walked in and stared at him silently. This terrified Fox into a screaming fit, not because it was frightening in itself, but because he could not tell which version of his mother was real and which was the double.

Sometimes before falling asleep, he saw a strange background of small, misty-blue or mauve circles that vibrated. To his young mind, they resembled a gelatinous cluster of frogs' eggs, and were on the limit of visibility. The blue circles would fill with tiny grinning faces having piercing steel-blue eyes, and Fox would hear a chorus of mocking voices chant in rhythm to the vibration of the circles, "'That is it, you see! That is it, you see!'"[107] The background of blue circles persisted into adulthood, minus the faces, and occurred during many experiences of astral projection.

Fox also had, during his early childhood, numerous dreams in which objects seemed to be stretched or expanded. This sense that "things went wrong" sometimes intruded into his waking life. He gave the example of having one hand on the table and the other on the back of a chair, and suddenly being unable to move them, while having the sense that the table and chair were slowly moving apart and stretching him between them.

Fox found that he could put himself into a light trance by staring at the flame of the lamp in his bedroom, although he had no awareness that he was in a trance state. He only knew that the room around him would suddenly "go wrong." First, the gas flame dimmed, and the room filled with a pale-golden brightness. Miniature bursts of blue lightning crackled and snapped from the corners of the room. This was followed by an apparition of a grotesque or frightening appearance. On one occasion, he saw a man with a horrifyingly distorted face. At other times, it was a wolf with burning eyes, a lion, a giant serpent, or a bear that reared up on its hind legs. These visions caused the boy to scream at the top of his lungs, but the moment his mother entered his bedroom, the apparition vanished and things "came right" again.[108]

107.   Fox, 19.

108.   Ibid., 20–1.

The most interesting of these apparitions involved a fairy, which to the eyes of the young Fox looked like a garden gnome. He described it as "a funny little fellow dressed in brown" that climbed up on his bed with a reassuring smile and pointed to a nearby screen, in which a bright circle of light appeared. Within this circle, the mist cleared to reveal the scene of a farm, in bright colors, with all the animals moving as in life. A woman in a blue dress waved her hand from the doorway of the house. After a while, the scene faded and the fairy gave a nod and a smile before vanishing.

All these early experiences of Fox are connected. They were attempts by spiritual beings to awaken and develop his natural psychic abilities. The dreams of his mother's double directed his mind toward astral projection. The dreams and impressions of being stretched resulted from partial separation of his astral double. The golden light that suffused the air is an event I have experienced during soul flight, and it indicates an astral rather than a physical perception of the scene. The faces in the blue circles, although terrifying to the young boy, were intended to call his attention to the circles and to inform him, "That is it, you see!"—that when he became aware of the background of nebulous blue circles, he was in a suitable mental state to see into the astral. The fairy that visited his bed adopted a non-threatening shape for the purpose of teaching him how to use his ability to see into the astral world.

It appears that some higher intelligence was deliberating pushing the young Fox to explore and develop his innate, latent talent for astral projection. If we were to credit the existence of the adepts of Theosophy, we might suspect that Fox was being guided by a Master from a higher spiritual plane to explore his talent, so that later in life he could write about it and share it with the world.

Lucid Dreams and the Pineal Doorway

The main technique developed by Fox was that of the lucid dream. Fox found that if he became aware during a dream that he was dreaming, then he could move around in it consciously, and step outside it while remaining asleep to travel to other places on the astral level, such as to the rooms of people he knew, or to familiar streets. He passed other people unseen and unheard during these travels, but found that if he touched them, they could feel his touch. The difficult part was becoming aware within a dream. He accomplished this by trying to notice any incongruous detail that would alert him to the fact that he was dreaming. Once he noticed a detail that would not exist in reality, he instantly became conscious, and was able to leave the dream on his astral journey.

He used three kinds of locomotion during his astral excursions. The first was a gliding step that covered large distances, so that he seemed to float across the ground. The second was a swimming motion with his arms that allowed him to rise into the air to a height of from fifty to a hundred feet. The third motion Fox called "Skrying," although it has nothing whatsoever to do with crystal gazing. It was a vertical ascent into the air at a high rate of speed, accomplished by an act of will, which Fox found to be difficult, and believed to be dangerous, although exactly why he felt it posed a danger, he did not write. It terrified him and he did not experiment with it further. As we will later see when we examine the Hermetic Order of the Golden Dawn, Fox had independently discovered the astral technique known as Rising on the Planes.

The single time that Fox saw his silver cord was when he detached his astral body while under the influence of ether. This was also an experience of the type of travel he called Skrying. "After a few sniffs, it seemed to me that I shot up to the stars, and that a shining silver thread connected my celestial self with my physical body."[109] On a few occasions, he felt a pull that seemed to draw his astral body back into his physical body, but he never saw the cord before or after this drug experience. This caused Carrington and Muldoon to doubt very much that Fox had ever achieved the full and complete experience of astral projection. However, merely because Fox's experiences were different from those of Muldoon does not in any way suggest that they were inferior.

Another peculiarity of Fox's astral excursions was his complete inability to see his physical body while in the astral body, even when standing over his bed on the astral level, and looking down at the place where he knew his physical body was still lying. The bed appeared empty to his astral sight. After his marriage, he was able to see his wife's sleeping form in the bed, but never his own. This appears to me to have been some sort of mental block, probably caused by an unconscious fear on the part of Fox that to view his own body while outside of it would result in his death. It is a common superstition that when a person sees their own double, they are soon to die. By unconsciously blinding himself to his physical body while in the astral body, Fox avoided this fictitious danger.

He discovered by accident one afternoon in July 1908 that he was able to project while lying in a light trance state without entering a lucid dream. He propelled his astral body out of his physical body by an act of will so that it shot forth through the walls of his house and into the sky. The first method, through the intermediation of a lucid

---

109. Fox, 68.

dream, he called the dream of knowledge method, but the second trance state method he referred to as the instantaneous method.

Later in the course of his experiments, Fox developed a technique of separation that he described as the pineal doorway technique because he associated it with the pineal gland of his brain. While in a trance state, he focused his consciousness inward on the center of his forehead between his brows. This is the place known in Eastern lore as the third eye, the location of the *ajna* chakra. When the technique was successful, he seemed to feel a click in that place in his head, as though a door had closed behind him, and at once he was released into the astral world with a much greater degree of clarity of mind and freedom of action than he had enjoyed when traveling through his lucid dreams.

Presentiments of Danger

During these experiments, Fox often heard his wife calling to him, pleading for him to come back, telling him that he was in danger. This was an illusion—his wife never really called out to him. He also sometimes felt intense apprehension. It appears that he was being actively discouraged from employing this technique, perhaps by some higher spiritual intelligence. His last successful projection through the pineal doorway took place on April 10, 1916. During this excursion, he tried to visit a temple in India in a past century, but for some reason he was unable to achieve his purpose. The projection ended abruptly. Always thereafter, when he tried to use the pineal doorway technique, Fox saw the vision of a mysterious black Egyptian ankh hanging in the air, as though to bar his way. With his eyes shut, the ankh appeared to be painted on the inner surface of his eyelids, and with his eyes open, it seemed to float in front of him. It would not let him pass.[110]

It is clear that Fox's experiments along this line were stopped for him by some intelligence other than his own. Who can say whether it was his unconscious mind that forced him to cease the pineal doorway method for his own safety, or if it was the protective action of some higher spiritual teacher, equivalent to one of the Masters of Theosophy, who stepped in for his own best interests? Perhaps a spirit of power and authority simply decided that his experiments had gone as far as they could be permitted to progress, and placed a block on his mind to prevent them in the future. Although he was still able to use the instantaneous method of projection, he could no longer use the pineal doorway method.

---

110. Fox, 100.

CHAPTER SEVEN

The Golden Dawn

The Hermetic Order of the Golden Dawn was founded in an official way in 1888 with the establishment of the Isis-Urania Temple in London, although members of the Order such as the poet William Butler Yeats (1865–1939) had begun to receive initiation the previous year.[111] The Theosophical Society of Blavatsky and Olcott was only thirteen years old. At that time, Madame Blavatsky was living in London. Just as spiritualism had its influence on Theosophy, so Theosophy in its turn contributed to the mental climate that allowed the Golden Dawn to flourish. Ellic Howe observed that a kind of underground explosion of interest in the occult took place in Great Britain and France during the latter part of the 1880s. "The explosion itself was hardly noticed by the Establishment,

---

111. Howe, *Magicians of the Golden Dawn*, 69.

but it was felt by many who were no longer satisfied with conventional religious beliefs. The influence of Helena Petrovna Blavatsky's Theosophical Society was notable in this context."[112]

The Order of the Golden Dawn was a Rosicrucian society that admitted both men and women. Its purpose was the revival of the occult wisdom of the past—not merely the teaching of the esoteric philosophies of Greece, Rome, Persia, Egypt, and Judea, but also the revival of the practice of ritual magic both for the perfection of the individual and the advancement of the human species. Even though it made use of numerous pagan gods and goddesses in its rituals, it was fundamentally Christian, as all Rosicrucian societies must be. The primary symbol of the Golden Dawn was the rosy-cross—a cross with a red rose at its intersection.

Many of the early members of the Golden Dawn were also Theosophists. At first this troubled Blavatsky, who prohibited Theosophists from joining the Golden Dawn or other occult societies, out of apprehension that they practiced black magic. But when members of her own Society appealed to her to rescind her decision, she relented and permitted Theosophists to also belong to the Golden Dawn. As a gesture of fraternity, a group of twenty-one Golden Dawn members joined the Theosophical Society.[113]

History of the Golden Dawn

The Golden Dawn was founded by three master Freemasons: Dr. William Robert Woodman (1828–1891), Dr. William Wynn Westcott (1848–1925), and Samuel Liddell Mathers (1854-1918). Woodman suffered from ill health and lived some distance from the center of London, and so played little active part in the running of the Golden Dawn in the Outer, as the more or less publicly accessible lower grades of the Order were known. He died before the Second Order, the *Roseae Rubae et Aureae Crucis* (Ruby Rose and Cross of Gold), where the higher mysteries of practical magic were taught to carefully selected initiates, came into being in 1892.[114] The work of running the Golden Dawn fell to Westcott and Mathers.

According to the history of the Order presented by its three Chiefs, the Golden Dawn was originally founded as an extension of a German secret society of the same name, *Die*

---

112.   Howe, xxiii.

113.   Ibid., 55.

114.   Colquhoun, *Sword of Wisdom*, 172.

Goldene Dämmerung, run by an adept named Fräulein Anna Sprengel. Westcott claimed to have received a written charter from Sprengel permitting him to establish a branch of the German Rosicrucian society in England, and maintained that he was in constant correspondence with the Chiefs of the German Order from 1887 to 1890. This is what those joining the Golden Dawn were taught, and what they believed in the early years. It was not until friction arose between the leaders of the Order that it was revealed that this history was a fiction concocted by Westcott, perhaps with the collusion of Woodman.

Mathers was not a part of the original deception, which was admitted to him by Westcott only after he gave Westcott his solemn word that he would not divulge the truth to any other member. In 1900, he wrote a letter hinting about Westcott's deception to the actress Florence Farr (1860–1917), who was a leading member of the Golden Dawn. "He has never been *at any time* either in personal or in written communication with the Secret Chiefs of the Order, he having *either himself forged or procured to be forged* the professed correspondence between him and them, and my tongue having been tied all these years by a previous Oath of Secrecy to him, demanded by him, from me, before showing me what he had either done or caused to be done or both."[115]

The Secret Chiefs

Mathers was concerned that Florence Farr not be misled into thinking that Westcott was responsible for the esoteric teachings of the Golden Dawn because he himself, aided by his wife, was at that time receiving psychic communications from the Secret Chiefs, a hierarchy of enlightened beings, and it was Mathers who transcribed their dictations into the rituals and teachings that would later constitute the Second Order. Exactly who or what these Secret Chiefs were, Mathers always remained uncertain. He was not really sure if they were living adepts who had discovered the alchemical elixir of eternal life, or spiritual beings dwelling on higher planes who descended to the material world for the purpose of teaching him, although he tended to believe they were living men.

In an extraordinary manifesto written in 1896, Mathers referred to himself as "Chief Adept and Ambassador of those Secret and Unknown Magi who are the concealed Rulers of the Wisdom of the True Rosicrucian Magic of Light," and he wrote about the nature of the Secret Chiefs:

---

115. Howe, 210.

Concerning the Secret Chiefs of the Order, to whom I make reference and from whom I have received the Wisdom of the Second Order which I have communicated to you, I can tell you *nothing.*

I do not even know their earthly names.

I know them only by certain secret mottoes.

I have *but very rarely* seen them in the physical body; and on such rare occasions *the rendezvous was made astrally by them* at the time and place which had been astrally appointed beforehand.

For my part I believe them to be human and living upon this earth; but possessing terrible superhuman powers.

When such rendezvous has been in a much frequented place, there has been nothing in their personal appearance and dress to mark them out as differing in any way from ordinary people except the appearance and sensation of transcendent health and physical vigour (whether they seemed persons in youth or age) which was their invariable accompaniment; in other words, the physical appearance which the possession of the Elixir of Life has traditionally supposed to confer.

On the other hand, when the rendezvous has been in a place free from easy access by the Outer World they have usually been in symbolic robes and insignia.[116]

Both Mathers and his wife, the former Mina Bergson, sister of the famous French philosopher Henri Bergson, were strongly mediumistic. They communicated with the Secret Chiefs through a variety of methods familiar to spiritualists—Mathers specifically mentions astral projection as a key method in his manifesto, but he and his wife also used other techniques.

Almost the whole of the Second Order Knowledge has been obtained by me from them in various ways; by clairvoyance, by Astral projection on their part and on mine—by the table, by the ring and disc, at times by a direct Voice audible to my external ear, and that of Vestigia, at times copied from books brought before me, I know not how, and which disappeared from my vision when the transcription was finished, at times by appointment *Astrally* at a certain place, till then unknown to me; and ap-

116. Howe, 129–30.

pointments made in the same manner and kept in the same manner as in the case of those rare occasions when I have met them by appointment in the physical body.[117]

Vestigia is part of the Latin motto by which his wife, whom Mathers otherwise preferred to call by the Celtic-sounding name Moïna, was known within the Golden Dawn. The full Latin motto of Moïna Mathers was *Vestigia Nulla Retrosum* (No Traces Behind), the choice of which perhaps suggests why she was willing to allow her husband to remake her identity by giving her not only his surname in marriage, but a new Christian name as well. The "table" refers to the familiar table-turning antics of the spiritualist séance, during which the spirits cause a table under the hands of those attending the séance to move and emit raps. The "ring and disc" was a method of divination popular within the Golden Dawn, by which a ring was suspended from the hand on a short length of silk thread over a piece of paper inscribed with a circle.

Francis King, commenting on Mathers' manifesto in *The Rebirth of Magic* (1982), believed the "ring and disc" to be a complex device consisting of a painted cardboard ring suspended on a silk ribbon above a disk inscribed with Hebrew letters and occult symbols.[118] However, in a footnote in the earlier work *Ritual Magic In England* (1970), King described the device more simply as a gold ring on a silk thread, held suspended above a disk on which were written the letters of the alphabet.[119]

It is possible that Mathers and his wife used a complex wheel of Hebrew letters patterned after the mystic alphabet rose that was the central part of the rosy-cross symbol of the Golden Dawn, wherein the Hebrew alphabet is inscribed on twenty-two petals arranged in three concentric circles. I believe it is just as likely that a simpler yes-no oracle made up of a cross surrounded by a circle was employed. If so, the movements of the ring swinging on the thread, either forward and back along the vertical arm of the cross, or side to side along its horizontal arm, would be interpreted as a *yes* or a *no* response.

The astral meetings between Mathers and the Secret Chiefs exacted a terrible toll upon his physical health. It is this detail that convinces me, more than anything else, that his communications with the Secret Chiefs were genuine and not in any way fabricated by him. I have myself often communicated with spiritual beings, and I have felt the seeming transformation in the quality of the air and the intense and very odd strain that is

---

117. Howe, 130–1.

118. King and Sutherland, 95.

119. King, 45.

brought to bear on the body during those contacts. The strain on Mathers was much greater because the beings he communicated with were of a high order, and his communications were prolonged and conveyed detailed, specific information of a technical nature. Indeed, the strain was so great that I suspect, based on my personal experience, that it very nearly killed him.

Mathers described the strain of what he believed were physical encounters with the Secret Chiefs as much greater than the mere physical exhaustion that follows the depletion of nervous energy that is so familiar to trance mediums. He wrote in his manifesto: "The sensation was that of being in contact with so terrible a force that I can only compare it to the *continued* effect of that usually experienced momentarily by a person *close* to whom a flash of lightning passes during a violent storm; coupled with a difficulty in respiration similar to the half-strangled effect produced by ether; and if such was the result produced in one, as tested as I have been in practical Occult Work, I cannot conceive a much less advanced Initiate being able to support such a strain even for five minutes, without Death ensuing."[120]

Leaving aside the question of whether Mathers had ever experienced the effect of a close lightning strike, his description effectively conveys the strain on his body of direct face-to-face communications with the Secret Chiefs. His reference to "difficulty in respiration" is accurate; I have often experienced it when communicating with spirits. The very air around the body seems to thicken or become viscous, resulting in great difficulty inhaling. Elsewhere in the manifesto to the members of the Golden Dawn, Mathers wrote: "The strain of such labour has been, as you can conceive, enormous; in especial the obtaining of the Z ritual, which I thought would have killed me, or Vestigia, or both, the nerve prostration after each reception being terrible from the strain of testing the correctness of every passage thus communicated; the nerve prostration alluded to being at times accompanied by profuse cold perspirations, and by severe loss of blood from the nose, mouth, and occasionally the ears."[121]

The poet William Butler Yeats, who was a leading member of the Golden Dawn, wrote of Mathers in his *Autobiographies*, "Every Sunday he gave to the evocation of spirits, and I noted that upon that day he would spit blood. That did not matter, he said, because it came from his head, not his heart; what ailed him I do not know, but I think

---

120. Howe, 130.

121. Ibid., 131

he lived under some great strain."[122] When Yeats was visiting, Mathers and his wife would sometimes play Enochian chess with him, a form of the game based on the older board game of Chaturanga that may have been invented by Westcott; or it is possible that it was delivered to Mathers psychically by the Secret Chiefs. It required four players, so while his wife, Moïna, partnered with Yeats, Mathers would take as his partner an invisible spirit. "Mathers would shade his eyes with his hands and gaze at the empty chair at the opposite corner of the board before moving his partner's piece."[123]

Yeats did not share Mathers' opinion that the Secret Chiefs with whom he communicated were living human beings. On the contrary, he expressed the view in his *Autobiographies* that they were thought-forms created and given tangible reality by the intense concentration of Mathers.

> Once, when Mathers told me that he had met his Teachers in some great crowd, and only knew that they were phantoms by a shock that was like an electrical shock to his heart, I asked him how he knew he was not deceived or hallucinated. He said, "I had been visited by one of them the other night, and I followed him out, and followed him down the little lane to the right. Presently I fell over the milk-boy, and the milk-boy got in a rage because he said that not only I but the man in front had fallen over him." He, like all that I have known who have given themselves up to images, and to the speech of images, thought that when he had proved that an image could act independently of his mind, he had proved also that neither it, nor what it had spoken, had originated there.[124]

Yeats believed that Mathers was deluding himself, but the poet does not seem to have considered that spiritual beings might manifest themselves to an individual through the unconscious levels of the mind of that individual, yet still be independent of the mind through which they manifested. To Yeats, the projection of the Secret Chiefs through the mind of Mathers meant that they were part of his ego, but this does not necessarily follow. Spirits use the mind of a human being to become perceptible in a way that human consciousness can recognize and interact with. But to say that for this reason they are

---

122. Howe, 114.

123. Ibid., 115.

124. Ibid., 130.

no more than personal artifacts of the ego of the individual perceiving them is to place arbitrary limits on the scope and complexity of the mind.

Astral Examination of Initiates

Astral projection was used in a variety of ways in the Golden Dawn and related occult orders that evolved directly from its teachings, such as the Society of the Inner Light founded by Dion Fortune (1890–1946), who had joined the Golden Dawn in 1919 while it was under the leadership of Moïna Mathers. Perhaps the most interesting application was in the testing of potential candidates for initiation into these orders. The writer Sir Arthur Conan Doyle (1859–1930), who created that memorable character of fiction, the detective Sherlock Holmes, experienced this astral testing firsthand. He related his experiences of 1898, the year in which he considered joining the Golden Dawn, in an article he wrote in 1924 for *Pearson's Magazine*. Doyle had an unnatural dream in which a member of the Golden Dawn visited him on the astral level for the purpose of testing him, to determine whether he was worthy of admission. It shook his nerves to such a degree that Doyle decided not to become a member.[125]

Two members of the Golden Dawn later visited Doyle in an attempt to change his mind. They told him of an astral journey they had made together to central Africa. Doyle wrote: "From what I learnt I should judge that the powers of this society included that of loosening their own etheric bodies, in summoning the etheric bodies of others (mine, for example) and in making thought images."[126]

This might be dismissed as merely an odd fixation in the mind of Doyle, who was a confirmed believer in spiritualism, were it not that others reported the same sort of astral experience. Ithell Colquhoun (1906–1988), who attempted many years later to gain initiation into both a descendant offshoot of the Golden Dawn and Dion Fortune's Society of the Inner Light, experienced an identical type of astral probing on both occasions. Both times, she was denied admission. During the 1920s, after filling out an application to join the Alpha and Omega Lodge of the Golden Dawn, but before she received word that her admission was denied, she went through the kind of testing mentioned by Doyle.

Colquhoun felt as though someone were exploring her on the astral level, trying to influence her will directly by an action that took place below the level of words, even be-

---

125. Howe, 200.

126. Ibid.

neath the level of thoughts. She had a strong sense of being invaded psychically and found that it required all of her powers to resist. She would later make use of this experience in her 1961 novel, *Goose of Hermogenes*, in which she wrote: "A kind of paralysis descended on my limbs as I fought; and so much energy was drained from my physical form that I found myself for some while unable to stir."[127] She wrote that she had no sense that the probing was hostile, "only searching" in an impersonal way. It was accompanied by what she described as a distant vibration. "Oddly enough, I did not immediately connect it with the A. O. or its Secret Chiefs: only after receiving the note of refusal did I begin to do so. Before that, I had scarcely taken the Secret Chiefs seriously."[128]

In 1954, she tried to gain admission to Dion Fortune's Society of the Inner Light. After being put through a correspondence course followed by a rigorous face-to-face interrogation, she was told that she was not a fit candidate for initiation, but that she should wait a year and she would be reconsidered. Thirteen months later, she again experienced the same sort of astral probing, although this time it was less intense than when she had sought admission to the Alpha and Omega Lodge of the Golden Dawn. Again she was rejected.

The spiritual leaders of the Society of the Inner Light were called Masters, after the practice in Theosophy, but it is evident that they were of a similar type to the spirits controlling the Golden Dawn. Colquhoun wrote that, in both instances, this astral probing was set into motion by those connected with the Secret Chiefs of the respective societies, and that it did not resemble the melodramatic type of astral projection usually described in occult literature, replete with exotic figures and echoing voices, but rather that it was characterized by an impersonal quality.[129]

Colquhoun mentioned that Yeats, writing a letter to a friend, told the story of how the ritualists of the London Isis-Urania Temple of the Golden Dawn once summoned a female member before them to question her concerning her relations with Aleister Crowley (1875–1947), who was something of a black sheep of the Golden Dawn. Colquhoun had always assumed that the woman had been summoned before them in the astral body, but she wondered if instead perhaps the astral probing technique that she herself had experienced had been employed. She wrote, "'astral examination' and 'astral judgment'

---

127. Colquhoun, 23.

128. Ibid.

129. Colquhoun, 33.

were standard practice in the heyday of the GD [Golden Dawn] for vetting both postulants and members aspiring to the Second Order. It seems that such methods were still in force long afterwards and may be so, to this day."[130]

The Sphere Group

When the Golden Dawn began to suffer conflicts among its leaders, various individual members tried to establish their own astral communication link with the Secret Chiefs, so that they could carry on the work of writing down the teachings of these spiritual masters. Florence Farr headed a group within the Golden Dawn that gathered regularly to do astral work. This was known as the Sphere Group. In 1897, Farr was made head of the London branch of the Golden Dawn by Mathers. Westcott had been forced to withdraw in order to protect his public reputation and his government job as London coroner. Mathers agreed with Farr that the practice of secret groups working within the Golden Dawn on projects of their own interest, such as her Sphere Group, should be formally accepted.[131]

The Sphere Group consisted of twelve members who met every Sunday at noon to "concentrate forces of growth, progress and purification."[132] They occasionally came together in the same physical place, but as Dr. Robert William Felkin (1858–1922), one of the original members of the group later testified, "meetings were not necessary for the work of the Group."[133] Felkin meant that physical meetings were unnecessary because the twelve met on the astral planes. The name of the group derived from the symbol of the "Star maps and Tree of Life projected on a sphere."[134] Maps of the celestial northern and southern hemispheres showing the spherical projection of the ten Sephiroth of the Tree of Life are reproduced in Israel Regardie's *The Golden Dawn*,[135] and it was these or maps very like them that were used by Farr and her group.

The twelve members stationed themselves at intervals around a circle. At the center was a being known as "the Egyptian astral" who was the Master from whom Farr received

---

130. Colquhoun, 34.

131. Howe, 170.

132. Ibid., 250.

133. Ibid., 251.

134. Ibid., 247.

135. Regardie, *Golden Dawn*, 605.

her group's teachings, and who controlled the work of the group. This rather mysterious figure was first contacted through a fragment of his Egyptian mummy case,[136] or so Ellic Howe was informed by F. L. Gardner, a Theosophist who joined the Golden Dawn and became a member of the Sphere Group. This initial contact was probably made by psychometry, a psychic ability supposed to enable sensitive individuals to divine, by touch, events connected with an object.

In 1901, the Egyptian astral announced that he must retire from the Group because he was about to ascend to a higher plane, which would make it impossible for him to carry on his former work. This was in keeping with the teachings of Blavatsky's Theosophy, which held that souls after death continued to evolve and perfect themselves, rising through the seven astral planes until they escaped them entirely to the higher planes of spirit. For some time thereafter, Farr and her followers met regularly on the astral level, but they substituted the Holy Grail in place of the Egyptian adept. In 1902, a prominent member of the London Temple, Annie Horniman (1860–1937), who believed herself in astral contact with one of the Secret Chiefs she called the Purple Adept, lobbied for the performance of a special banishing ritual to cleanse the Order of what she perceived to be the corrupting taint of the Egyptian adept. By this time, the Sphere Group had ceased to gather, but Horniman's resentment against what she felt had been favoritism shown to Farr by Mathers and Westcott lingered. Whether this banishing ritual was ever done is unknown.

Traveling in the Spirit Vision

Astral projection, and its closely related activity, astral vision, were key parts of the Golden Dawn training in the Second Order. The techniques were fairly simple. As is true of all methods of soul flight, there was little value in elaborate external structures when almost all of the work was done internally, using concentration, willpower, and visualization. In the Fifth Knowledge Lecture, a preliminary training for initiates, basic directions are provided for what is termed traveling in the spirit vision:

> The symbol, place, direction, or Plane being known whereon it is desired to act, a thought-ray as before is sent unto the corresponding part of the Sphere of Sensation of the Nephesch. The Thought-Ray is sent like an arrow from the bow, right through the circumference of the Sphere of Sensation directly unto the place desired. Arrived there, a sphere of astral Light is formed by the agency of the Lower Will, illuminated

---

136. Howe, xviii.

by the Higher Will, and acting through the spiritual consciousness by reflection along the Thought-Ray. This sphere of Astral Light is partly drawn from the surrounding atmosphere. This sphere being formed, a simulacrum of the person of the Skryer is reflected into it along the thought-ray, and this united consciousness is then projected therein. This Sphere is then a duplicate, by reflection, of the Sphere of Sensation. As it is said: "Believe thyself to be in a place and thou art there." In this Astral Projection, however, a certain part of the consciousness must remain in the body to protect the Thought-Ray beyond the Sphere of Sensation (as well as the Sphere itself at that point of departure of the Thought-Ray) from attack by any hostile force, so that the consciousness in this projection is not quite so strong as the consciousness when concentrated in the natural body in ordinary life. The return taketh place with a reversal of this process, and save to persons whose Nephesch and physical body are exceptionally strong and healthy, the whole operation of skrying and traveling in the Spirit Vision is of course fatiguing.

Also there is another mode of astral projection which can be used by the more practised and advanced Adept. This consisteth in forming first a sphere from his own Sphere of Sensation, casting his reflection therein, and then projecting this whole sphere to the desired place, as in the previous method. But this is not easy to be done by any but the practised operator.[137]

The Sphere of Sensation mentioned in this quotation relates to the ritual pattern adopted by the Sphere Group of Florence Farr. It is the microcosm of the Sphere's Group's macrocosm:

Thou shalt know that the whole Sphere of Sensation which surroundeth the whole physical body of a man is called 'The Magical Mirror of the Universe.' For therein are represented all the occult forces of the Universe projected as on a sphere, convex to the outer, but concave to man. This sphere surroundeth the physical body of a man as the Celestial Heavens do the body of a Star or a Planet, having their forces mirrored in its atmosphere. Therefore its allotment or organization is the copy of that Greater World or Macrocosm. In this 'Magical Mirror of the Universe,' therefore, are the Ten Sephiroth projected in the form of the Tree of Life as in a solid sphere.[138]

---

137. Regardie, 108–9.

138. Ibid., 100.

The Nephesch is the lowest of three levels of the soul, corresponding with the animal instincts of the microcosm and with the physical world of the macrocosm. For astral projection, the lower and more visceral emotions, sensations, and urges must be aroused and used to take advantage of their more tangible force. The Tree of Life is a Kabbalistic model of the universe in ten successive descending emanations, each of which comes forth from the one above it. The Golden Dawn applied these ten emanations, known as Sephiroth, to various parts of the human body. Each emanation has other associations or correspondences that can be used to link a part of the body with an astral plane or environment. For example, seven of the Sephiroth correspond with the seven spheres of the planets of traditional astrology. These Sephiroth also correspond with parts of the body. Through the connecting bridge of each of these seven Sephiroth, a part of the body can be associated with a planetary sphere.

The Ten Sephiroth

The Golden Dawn system is complex and a bit overwhelming for those unfamiliar with it. I do not propose to examine it in detail here, but I will list the ten Sephiroth on the Tree of Life and show how they join various parts of the body with various astral levels.

1.   Kether
    Above the crown of the head
    The Crown—sphere of the primum mobile

2.   Chokmah
    Left side of the brain
    Wisdom—sphere of fixed stars

3.   Binah
    Right side of the brain
    Understanding—sphere of Saturn

4.   Chesed
    Left arm
    Mercy—sphere of Jupiter

5.   Geburah
    Right arm
    Severity—sphere of Mars

6. Tiphareth
Torso
Beauty—sphere of the Sun

7. Netzach
Left leg
Victory—sphere of Venus

8. Hod
Right Leg
Glory—sphere of Mercury

9. Yesod
Genitals
Foundation—sphere of the Moon

10. Malkuth
Entire physical body
Kingdom—sphere of the four elements

Those familiar with the Tree of Life will notice that when applied to the human body by the Golden Dawn, it was reflected left to right. Chokmah, on the right side of the Tree, is placed on the left side of the brain. Hod, on the left side of the Tree, is located on the right leg. And so for the other Sephiroth on the sides of the Tree. Malkuth is often assigned to the feet, but it more accurately corresponds with the entire shell of the physical body.[139] Netzach and Hod represent, respectively, the left leg and the right leg, including the feet and toes. Kether is often applied to the crown of the head, but more properly belongs above the head and resting on it gently as would a crown.

Tattwa Doorways

As physical aids to help focus the mind during the practice of scrying and astral travel, the Golden Dawn employed various sets of symbols to act as astral doorways. Those most often used to initiate astral projection were the tattwas—five simple colored shapes derived from Hindu philosophy that embody the four lower elements of Fire, Water, Air,

---

139. Regardie, 102.

and Earth—and the fifth universal binding element, or quintessence, known as Ether or Spirit.

Akasa (Spirit)—black egg
Vayu (Air)—sky-blue circle
Tejas (Fire)—red equilateral triangle
Apas (Water)—silver crescent
Prithivi (Earth)—yellow square

These symbols were painted, or cut from colored craft paper and glued, on to cards, upon the backs of which were written the divine and angelic names corresponding with the tattwa. The symbols themselves were made about two inches in size upon blank cards around the dimensions of ordinary playing cards, for convenience of handling. The black egg is shown inverted with the small end down. The silver crescent reclines with both points upward. The red triangle has a single point uppermost. The sides of the yellow square are vertical.

Each tattwa symbol was placed on five cards, and upon each was painted or glued a smaller secondary symbol in the middle of the large primary symbol. This introduced an active seed element on the passive or receptive field of the main element, and mingled their qualities, with the main element still predominating. Since a smaller tattwa symbol upon the same larger tattwa does not show up, its physical placement may be omitted, but it should be understood to reside there. All twenty-five tattwa cards are compound and none are simple:

As no element on our plane can exist in an unmixed form, but contains within itself the constituents of all the others, or possesses several grades or planes of its own substance, so each Tattwa is subdivided into five divisions, currents or planes. Akasa of Akasa, Spirit of Spirit, would be the most Tenuous and purest form of that element, the integral nature of Spirit—its highest essence. Vayu of Akasa would refer to its airy quality; Tejas of Akasa to its fiery and dynamic aspect; Apas of Akasa, its fluidic and watery phase, while Prithivi of Akasa, its most terrestrial phase, or that aspect of its power which more nearly than the others contacts the earth. The same five-fold division, in the same five-fold order, applies equally to the other elements.[140]

---

140. Regardie, 458.

The method of using the twenty-five tattwa cards for both scrying and astral projection is fairly straightforward. The experimenter employing a tattwa symbol sits staring at it intently until it strongly fills the imagination. Then he closes his eyelids and attempts to transfer the image from the physical to the astral faculty of vision, without allowing it to fade away. Mathers wrote: "Transfer the vital effort from the optic nerve to the mental perception, or thought-seeing as distinct from the seeing with the eye. Let one form of apprehension glide on into the other. Produce the reality of the dream vision by positive will in the waking state . . . Then maintaining your abstraction from your surroundings, still concentrated upon the symbol and its correlated ideas, you are to seek a perception of a scene or panorama or view of the plane. This may also be brought on by a sense of tearing open, as a curtain is drawn aside, and seeing the 'within' of the symbol before you."[141]

Regardie described a technique that relied on retinal fatigue and generating opposite —what were known in the Golden Dawn as "flashing"—colors. First, the experimenter stares at the tattwa under good lighting conditions, then shifts his gaze to a white sheet of paper or to a white wall. The color fatigue produced in the eyes by the strong colors of the tattwa symbol has the effect of generating the visual impression of opposite colors as a temporary, fading afterimage when a blank white surface is viewed. For example, staring at the all-yellow Prithivi of Prithivi tattwa card will generate the vision of a mauve square when the gaze is shifted to a white surface.

The eyes are closed, and the afterimage in its flashing colors persists on the inner surface of the eyelids. Before it fades, the experimenter must mentally sustain and strengthen the image, and imagine that it is becoming larger until it is large enough for him to pass through as a kind of gateway. The experimenter should stand from his chair, and with eyes still closed imagine passing through this gateway. Regardie recommended the Golden Dawn ritual gesture known as the Sign of Horus—which is a reaching forward with the extended two arms as through groping in the darkness—as a way of facilitating this passage. From his comments, it appears that Mathers used the gesture known as the Rending of the Veil, which simulates the drawing open of two panels of a closed curtain. Both may be used: first the Sign of Horus, then the Rending of the Veil. It is useful to imagine the enlarged tattwa symbol moving toward you and engulfing you as you do

---

141. Regardie, 459.

this. Regardie quoted one contributor who observed, "Deliberately will to pass through the gateway. Let him imagine that he can hear it close behind him."[142]

The difference between scrying an astral vision and traveling to an astral landscape when using this tattwa technique is largely a matter of the clarity and sense of reality perceived. Within the Golden Dawn, the distinction was sometimes made between "astral vision" and "etheric vision." The first was scrying through the tattwa symbol remotely, and was described as flat and two-dimensional, with objects reversed left to right as though seen in a mirror. The second was projection into the scene, which became three-dimensional. Mathers wrote, "If instead of this simple vision a ray of yourself is sent out and actually goes to the place (astral projection) there is not necessarily the sense of reversal of objects . . . Scenes, things, instead of being like pictures, have the third dimension, solidity; they stand out like bas-relief, then haut-relief, then you see as from a balloon, as it is said, by a bird's-eye view. You feel to go to the place, to descend upon it, to step out upon the scene, and to be an actor there."[143]

Geomantic Symbols

Other objects were used as astral doorways. The most popular were the Tarot cards and the symbols of geomancy. Israel Regardie wrote: "It will be found a good plan to prepare cards of the Geomantic symbols painted in their appropriate colors, for these make perfect 'doors' through which the Seer can pass. And while these symbols are also attributed to the elements, the visions acquired from the Geomantic symbols using the names of the appropriate Rulers and genii will be quite distinct in character from those of the Tattwa cards. The Hebrew letters, the Tarot cards and Sigils, the planetary and zodiacal Signs, and Sigils of every description may be used to yield the symbolic door to a subtle plane."[144]

The geomantic symbols are formed by randomly poking four rows of holes into the ground with a stick and counting up the number of holes in each row. An even number of holes results in two small marks that usually resemble stars or crosses, but an odd number of holes in a row results in a single mark. The shape of these marks is not important; they merely represent a dot. In this way, a figure is generated consisting of four rows ranked one above the other—each row containing either one dot or two dots. There are

---

142.   Regardie, 459.

143.   Ibid., 463.

144.   Ibid.

sixteen possible figures that may be made in this way. During the Renaissance, geomancy was a popular form of divination. Each figure had a Latin name and was associated with astrological symbols such as the planets, zodiac signs, and nodes of the moon. The names were constant, but the astrological associations differed from system to system.

In their structure, the sixteen figures of geomancy resemble the sixty-four I Ching hexagrams, each of which is made up of six rows containing either a solid line or a broken line. The two dots in the row of a geomantic figure are symbolically equivalent to the broken line in an I Ching hexagram; the single dot in a row of a geomantic figure is equivalent to a solid line in an I Ching hexagram. The difference between the two sets of divination symbols lies in the number of rows of each figure: four in the case of geomancy and six for the I Ching. The greater number of rows allows for more complexity in the I Ching oracle. There is little doubt that members of the Golden Dawn employed the I Ching hexagrams as astral portals, although they are overlooked in the main documents published by Regardie. Aleister Crowley, a member of the Golden Dawn who derived his system of practical magic from the Order teachings, placed great emphasis on the I Ching.

Pathworking

Next to the tattwas, the most widely used astral doorways were the Tarot cards. They were widely employed throughout the Golden Dawn teachings, and in the grade rituals of the Order. The picture cards of the Tarot were used in conjunction with the Tree of Life to represent the pathways from Eleven to Thirty-two that connected the ten spherical emanations known as the Sephiroth. The Sephiroth themselves were numbered, rather confusingly, as paths One through Ten. A member of the Golden Dawn could not truly understand the Tree without exploring the linking pathways in the astral body, and the Tarot trumps were the most useful tools for defining the astral landscapes of the paths and the nature of their guardians.

Investigating each pathway on the Tree astrally is known as pathworking. The connecting paths were assigned in the system of the Golden Dawn to the Hebrew letters, which could also be used as astral gateways, either in conjunction with the Tarot trumps or alone. The final Hebrew letter Tau identified the lowest of the pathways on the Tree. "The idea was to re-read the rituals, and then endeavour to re-tread the Paths astrally. One example given, was that the Seer should formulate in imagination a vast pylon, and within its gates he should visualize the Hebrew Letter Tau, the Thirty-second Path . . . Then, imagining himself passing through this Letter Tau, and entering the Pylon, he should proceed to make the appropriate Pentagrams and Hexagrams, and vibrating the Divine Names appropriate to that plane . . . The same technique may be applied to every Path and to every Sephiroth."[145]

Rising on the Planes

A related activity that usually involved the picture cards of the Tarot known as the trumps was "Rising on the Planes." Regardie quoted from a document written by Mathers, in which the Tarot trump Temperance is mentioned. "By concentration and contemplation of the divine, you formulate a Tree of Life passing from you to the spiritual realms above and beyond yourself. Picture to yourself that you stand in Malkuth, then by the use of the Divine Names and aspiration, you strive upwards by the Path of Tau towards Yesod, neglecting the crossing rays which attract you as you pass up. Look upwards to the Divine Light shining downward from Kether upon you. From Yesod, leads upward the Path of Samekh, Temperance; the Arrow, cleaving upwards, leads the way to Tiphareth, the great central Sun."[146]

The path of the trump Temperance, which connects Yesod with Tiphareth on the central column of the Tree, was of special importance in the work of astrally ascending the Tree, because it was regarded as symbolically the rising arrow of a great bow formed from the lower part of the Tree of Life. This path could be ridden upward directly into Tiphareth, the central Sephiroth on the Tree that was occultly linked in the Golden Dawn system with the astrological Sun and with the Messiah, resulting in a significant degree of spiritual enlightenment (see the illustration in chapter 13).

Aleister Crowley was an enthusiastic advocate of both pathworking and Rising on the Planes, and emphasized the importance of these techniques in his 1929 work *Magick in Theory and Practice*. "The Aspirant should remember that he is a Microcosm . . . He should make it his daily practice to travel on the Astral Plane, taking in turn each of the most synthetic sections, the Sephiroth and the Paths. These being thoroughly understood, and an Angel in each pledged to guard or to guide him at need, he should start on a new series of expeditions to explore the subordinate sections of each. He may then practice Rising on the Planes from these spheres, one after the other in rotation."[147]

---

146.   Ibid., 464.

147.   Crowley, *Magick in Theory and Practice*, 203.

In these words of advice, we can detect an echo of Crowley's own daily curriculum of astral work while as a young man he studied the magic of the Golden Dawn. He was not happy with the training in astral projection that he received as a member of the Order, however. He wrote of himself in the third person, "He was rather encouraged in unsystematic working."[148] Crowley believed that a magician should not be susceptible to the whims of spirits or to emotional responses of either attraction or aversion for particular astral planes, but should instead explore them all as a form of exercise in astral projection, in much the same way that a classical musician practices scales until he is able to play any piece of music that is set before him. "Thus, it is necessary that the technique of Magick should be perfected. The Body of Light must be rendered capable of going everywhere and doing everything. It is, therefore, always the question of drill which is of importance. You have got to go out Rising on the Planes every day of your life, year after year."[149]

For Crowley, the daily exercise of Rising on the Planes involved a technique much like the Skrying mode of vertical astral ascent discovered spontaneously by the Theosophist Oliver Fox. It was to imagine his astral body rising straight up into the air, propelled ever onward at a terrific rate by the force of his concentration and the directed power of his will. The experimenter should not stop until compelled to do so by physical exhaustion. He wrote that this exercise could be started from any astral landscape or level. "One can go (for example) into the circle of Jupiter, and the results especially in the lower planes, will be very different to those obtained from a Saturnian starting point."[150]

Thus, in the Golden Dawn system that Crowley employed, each astral sphere or world is vertically subdivided into a series of planes that may be ascended by soul flight. The exercise of rising from the surface of the earth and continuing upward until compelled to stop from fatigue is merely a way of learning the general method of Rising through the Planes. "But, having obtained this power, it is, of course, legitimate to rise to any particular plane that may be necessary for the purpose of exploration, as in the case of the visions recorded in *Liber 418*, where the method may be described as mixed."[151]

---

148. Crowley, *Magick in Theory and Practice*, 204.

149. Ibid., 155.

150. Ibid., 154.

151. Ibid., 155.

The Vision and the Voice

The numbered book referred to by Crowley is otherwise titled *The Vision and the Voice*, in which Crowley's astral journeys to the Thirty Aethyrs of the Enochian angels are described in exhaustive detail. The text of the visions themselves was initially published in 1911 in Crowley's periodical *The Equinox* (Volume 1, Number 5 supplement), but was reprinted in 1929 with copious notes by both Crowley and Israel Regardie, who was then acting as Crowley's secretary. It represents the crowning fulfillment of Crowley's years of work as a member of the Golden Dawn, perfecting his ability to ascend the astral planes, and demonstrates what this type of rigorous training is capable of achieving when used by someone with a focused will and a natural aptitude for astral travel. Concerning Crowley's method, Regardie recorded in his introduction:

> The Seer had with him a great golden topaz set in a Calvary Cross of six squares, made of wood, and painted vermillion, which was engraved with a Greek Cross of five squares charged with the Rose of 49 petals. He held this, as a rule, in his hand. After choosing a spot where he was not likely to be disturbed he would take this stone and recite the Enochian Call and, after satisfying himself that the forces invoked were actually present, made the topaz play a part not unlike that of the looking glass in the case of Alice. (He had long learned not to trouble himself to travel to any particular place in his Body of Light. He realized that Space was not a thing in itself but merely a convenient category—one of many such—by reference to which we can distinguish objects from each other.) Frater O. V., the Scribe, would write down his words, and incidentally observe any phenomena which struck him as peculiar. [152]

Although Regardie signed his name to the introduction in which this passage occurs, the words appear to be Crowley's own. The same passage occurs in Crowley's autobiography almost word for word.[153]

The topaz set in the cross acted as Crowley's astral gateway. By reciting the Enochian Call, a kind of general invocation of the Aethyrs that is keyed into each Aethyr by the insertion of the name of that Aethyr, he attuned his consciousness to the particular world he wished to explore. Regardie wrote that Crowley did not trouble himself to first move his astral body—his "Body of Light"—to any particular astral location as his starting

152. Crowley, *Vision and the Voice*, 7–8.

153. Crowley, *Confessions of Aleister Crowley*, 616.

point to begin his ascent of the Enochian Aethyrs, but instead ascended directly from his physical body. This appears to have been a shortcut of the standard Golden Dawn technique. As Crowley experienced the successive Enochian worlds, he narrated what he was seeing and experiencing. One of Crowley's disciples who was traveling with him in North Africa, Victor B. Neuburg, whose magical motto in Crowley's occult Order of the Silver Star was *Omnia Vincam*, took down Crowley's words as a direct dictation. Crowley generally visited one Enochian Aethyr per day.

Crowley had begun this astral work in Mexico in 1900, but after exploring the lowest two Aethyrs, he found himself unequal to the task of continuing. "What I saw was not beyond my previous experience, but what I heard was as unintelligible to me as Blake to a Baptist. I was encouraged by the evident importance of these results, but I found that I could no more force myself to go on to the twenty-eighth Aethyr than I could have thrown myself from a cliff."[154] In the desert of North Africa in 1909, he discovered that he had made sufficient progress as an adept and that the work came easily to him.

The resulting descriptions of the thirty astral worlds of the Enochian angels are often enigmatic, frequently poetic, and contain a wealth of esoteric references and associations that shed light on both the Golden Dawn system of magic and on Crowley's esoteric writings. It was Mathers who introduced a simplified version of Enochian magic, first received from a hierarchy of spirits by the crystal scryer Edward Kelley in the late sixteenth century, into the Golden Dawn teachings, but it was not until the work by Crowley that it came to be investigated in a systematic way. Crowley's astral flights to the thirty Aethyrs represent the ultimate utilization of the methods of scrying and astral projection taught by the Golden Dawn, as perfected by its most controversial member.

---

154. Crowley, *Confessions of Aleister Crowley*, 613.

Remote Viewing
and the CIA

During the decade of the 1930s, interest in the paranormal experienced a rebirth under the umbrella term *extrasensory perception*, or ESP. The paranormal was taken out of the séance room of the trance medium and brought into the laboratory of the psychologist or parapsychologist, as he came to be known. A professor of psychology at Duke University named Joseph Banks Rhine (1895–1980) was the man most responsible for this rehabilitation of the study of "wild talents" that had first been observed in an analytical way during the séance by members of that venerable Victorian body, the Society For Psychical Research.

Rhine used the term *extrasensory perception* to describe the apparent ability of some individuals to acquire information by means other than the use of their five physical senses. He did not coin the term ESP—that term had been used by Dr. Rudolf Tischner

(1879–1961) in his book *Telepathy and Clairvoyance*, originally published in German in 1920 and republished in English in 1925—but Rhine transformed the term into a household word. He also employed the much less popular term *general extrasensory perception*, or GESP (which he did originate), to encompass both clairvoyance and telepathy, and the later term psi to cover both extrasensory perception and psychokinesis. Psi, a term inverted in 1946 by R. H. Thouless and B. P. Wiesner, was originally divided into the two parts psi-kappa and psi-gamma, for active or projective effects such as psychokinesis, and passive or receptive effects such as clairvoyance. It has since come to signify in a general way the mystery factor in psychic events that cannot be recorded or measured.

In his effort to transform the paranormal from occult to scientific, and to make it a respectable subject for university study, Rhine disregarded aspects that had anything to do with spirits of the dead, angels, demons, fairies, or ectoplasmic manifestations. He restricted himself to such phenomena as clairvoyance, telepathy, telekinesis, psychometry, and precognition—regarding them as latent abilities inherent in the physiology of the human brain that could be generated, studied, recorded, measured, and replicated. Over the course of his work, Rhine came to the radical conclusion that ESP could not be explained by ordinary physical means. In *New Frontiers of the Mind* (1937), he wrote: "An extrasensory force exists in another realty, and intersects and integrates with the physical world."[155]

ESP Cards

For the majority of his studies involving telepathy, clairvoyance, and precognition, Rhine used special decks of what are called Zener cards, named after one of Rhine's colleagues, the perceptual psychologist Karl Zener (1903–1964). They are about the size of ordinary playing cards, but are marked with five symbols in black on a white background—a circle, a square, a cross, a star with five points, and wavy lines. The original Zener cards were slightly different from those that eventually evolved into what were renamed ESP cards—the original deck had a smaller star than the later ESP version, and the original wavy lines were two sets of three lines, but were replaced by a single set of three thicker lines. Each deck consists of twenty-five cards, marked in sets of five with each symbol. Subjects of the Duke ESP studies were required to guess the identities of the cards as they were selected. Random chance is a score of five correct guesses out of twenty-five, or 20 percent accuracy.

---

155. Rhine.

The best-known series of tests is the Pearce-Pratt Distance Series that was conducted between August 1933 and March 1934. They involved a subject with unusual ESP abilities, Hubert E. Pearce, Jr., a student in the Divinity School at Duke University who had approached Rhine eighteen months earlier, saying that he had inherited his mother's clairvoyant abilities. Rhine subjected him to seven hundred standard runs through the Zener cards. Random chance predicted an accuracy of 20 percent, but Pearce scored 32 percent. Because of this much higher than average score, Rhine chose him for the distance series of tests. They were conducted by a graduate student in psychology, J. G. Pratt, with Rhine overseeing a portion of the tests in order to rule out collusion between Pratt and Pearce. The student and the person testing him were located in two different buildings on the Duke campus during the tests. The distances between the two varied from one hundred to two hundred and fifty yards.

After synchronizing their watches and agreeing on a time to begin a series, the two men took up their respective places in separate buildings. Each minute, Pratt selected a Zener card from a randomly shuffled deck and laid it facedown on a book without looking at its symbol. At the end of the minute, he set it aside and moved on to the next card in the deck. The subject, Pearce, attempted to identify the different card used in each minute of the test, and recorded his guesses. At the end of the run, Pratt examined the cards and recorded the symbols in the order that they had been laid on the book. A book, the appearance and title of which were known to Pearce, was used simply to give him a focal point.

The results were remarkable. In 74 runs through the Zener deck (1850 cards in total), Pearce scored 558 hits. Mean chance predicts 20 percent accuracy, or 370 hits. Pearce's score was more than 30 percent. In the 1954 report on the study authored by Rhine and Pratt, Rhine wrote: "The theoretical standard deviation derived on a conservative basis is 17.57. This total of 558 hits is 188 above the theoretical expectation and it gives a critical ratio of 10.70. The probability that a critical ratio so large as this would occur on the basis of random sampling is less than 10^{-22}."[156]

Parapsychology and the Nazis

The early work by Rhine was regarded with interest in Europe by German psychologists, but was never effectively duplicated by them. In Germany, the rise of the Nazis during

---

156.   Rhine and Pratt, 176.

the 1930s had a chilling influence on serious scientific research into the paranormal. The Nazis were infected with mysticism and superstition, but they did not attempt to cast these interests into the pseudo-scientific framework of laboratory ESP investigation. Even though occultism in the form of mystical beliefs and secret societies was found everywhere among the upper ranks of the Nazi party, scientists were viewed with suspicion and their speculative research was seldom encouraged unless it happened to support party opinion.

The man to whom Adolf Hitler dedicated his book *Mein Kampf* (1925) was Dietrich Eckart (1868–1923), a wealthy anti-Semitic publisher and an inner member of the Thule Society (*Thule-Gesellschaft*), whom Hitler had met in 1919. He may have instructed Hitler in the magical technique of projecting the power of his will through visualization, which Hitler would use so effectively in later years. He may even have introduced Hitler into experiments with peyote, the drug employed by the shamans of the New World for soul flight, as suggested by Wulf Schwarzwäller in his book *The Unknown Hitler*. However, there is no reliable evidence to support either of these conjectures. Hitler himself was not greatly interested in the ceremonies of ritual occultism. He manipulated occult symbolism and the intense emotion it generated for his political purposes, but he probably did not engage in overtly occult practices.

What is beyond question is that the Nazi party arose directly out of the Thule Society, an occult organization founded on August 17, 1918, by Rudolf von Sebottendorff (1875–1945). It adopted as its symbol a dagger surrounded by oak leaves, superimposed on a swastika with curved arms. Hitler would later use the swastika as the symbolism of Nazism. On November 9, 1918, just prior to Germany's acceptance of the humiliating armistice treaty that ended the First World War, the newly established Thule Society met and resolved to continue the struggle for German supremacy. Sebottendorff proclaimed as its new symbol a red eagle, declaring to his fellow members that the eagle was an Aryan symbol, and that its color symbolized its "capacity for self-immolation by fire," which, he told his audience, "warns us that we must die in order to live."[157] On May 9, 1945, upon hearing of the surrender of Nazi Germany to the Allies, Sebottendorff committed suicide by jumping into the Bosporus strait in Turkey.

In order to involve the common worker in his vision of a revitalized Germany, Sebottendorff had one of the Thule Society members, a newspaper reporter named Karl

---

157. Sebottendorff, *Bevor Hitler Kam*, 57 (cited by Baker, *Invisible Eagle*, chap. 1).

Harrer, form a "workers ring" near the end of 1918. This was renamed *Deutsche Arbeiterpartei* (German Workers' Party), or DAP, on January 5, 1919 and in February of the following year, was transformed into the National Socialist German Workers' Party, or NSDAP. One of its members was Adolf Hitler, who had been hired to spy on its activities, but who became its most ardent advocate.

Thule is a mythical island far to the frozen north that was first mentioned by the Greek geographer Pytheas of Massalia (fourth century BC). It reappears numerous times in ancient historical records, although its exact location is never certain. Sebottendorff believed that it was the center for a primordial race of pure blood, remnants of which still survived, guarded by beings of superhuman intelligence and abilities who were similar in conception to the Mahatmas of Theosophy or the Secret Chiefs of the Golden Dawn. By ritually establishing communication with the guardians of Thule, members of the society hoped to enlist their aid in creating a revitalized Aryan race that would exterminate the inferior races, which Sebottendorff and his followers believed to be descended from interbreeding between Aryans and animals.

It is apparent that the Thule of German fanatics, insofar as it can be said to have existed, was an astral land that could be visited by initiates of the Thule Society during ritual soul flight, and that the guardians of Thule were astral beings of considerable authority. As is so often true, its purely astral nature was not understood, and the Thule Society believed it to be an actual island in the far north of the world, which they sought in various ways to locate and possess. In 1925, interest in the Thule Society waned and it was dissolved, but its core beliefs lived on within the Nazi party.

Another secret society active among Germans during the decade of the 1920s was the Vril Society. The term *vril* originates in the novel *The Coming Race* by the English writer Edward Bulwer-Lytton (1803–1873). It is an early science-fiction novel, published in 1871. Vril is a mysterious and powerful force that in the novel has been harnessed by an advanced race of human beings living in a great cavern within the earth, who use it to accomplish a wide variety of functions. It is not unlike the Force in the *Star Wars* films—a potent occult energy. Many Germans during the period between the two wars who involved themselves in mystical theories were convinced that the earth is a hollow sphere, so the fanciful notion that an entire race of humanity could dwell in its depths struck them as plausible. It was believed in some quarters that Bulwer-Lytton's novel was fact disguised as fiction.

In a magical sense, vril is a blind force. It can be used for good or for evil, in a way similar to electricity, which also has no moral affiliation. One of Hitler's earlier advisors, the Rosicrucian and Freemason General Karl Haushofer, founded the Luminous Lodge of the Vril Society in 1925, the same year in which the Thule Society was dissolved. The author Wulf Schwarzwäller asserted that the purpose of the Vril Society was to investigate the roots of the Aryan race, and to perform ritual exercises designed to awaken the power of vril. He claimed that Haushofer was a student of the mystic Gregor Ivanovich Gurdyev, better known as G. I. Gurdjieff (c. 1866–1949). "Both Gurdjieff and Haushofer maintained that they had contacts with secret Tibetan lodges that possessed the secret of the 'Superman'. The Lodge included Hitler, Alfred Rosenberg, Himmler, Göring, and Hitler's subsequent personal physician Dr. Morell."[158]

Adolf Hitler and the Age of Horus

It is doubtful that Hitler himself ever engaged in astral projection or met the spiritual beings known as Masters that controlled the dark occult current of National Socialism. The sensationalizing writers Bauwels and Bergier, authors of the 1960 book *Le matin des magiciens*, mention an anecdote related by Hermann Rauschning, the governor of Danzig, who one day was chatting with Hitler about the problems in breeding a race of supermen. Danzig made the observation that animal breeders had only rarely succeeded in introducing significant desirable mutations into their bloodlines, and that the best that could be achieved is to assist Nature in bringing forth the new species.

> "The new man is living amongst us now! He is here!" exclaimed Hitler, triumphantly. "Isn't that enough for you? I will tell you a secret. I have seen the new man. He is intrepid and cruel. I was afraid of him."
>
> "In uttering these words," added Rauschning, "Hitler was trembling in a kind of ecstasy."[159]

Even if this quotation is historically accurate, it does not provide evidence that Hitler was able to travel on the astral level, or that he ever met spiritual beings who were the dark shadow-opposites of Mathers' Secret Chiefs—but it is suggestive that Hitler may have had visions of an astral nature. Hitler's admission that the "new man" made him afraid

---

158. Schwarzwäller, *The Unknown Hitler*.

159. Pauwels and Bergier, 149.

is interesting in the context of the belief of writer Gerald Suster that Hitler was the living fulfillment of the prophetic document received by Aleister Crowley titled *The Book of the Law*. This document, transmitted to Crowley psychically by his guardian angel Aiwass in 1904, formed the basis for Crowley's later cult of Thelema. It foretells of the coming of the Age of Horus that will sweep Christianity off the face of the world in a holocaust of warfare and bloodshed.

Summing up his views on the almost ceaseless military conflicts that characterized the twentieth century in the context of Hitler's rise to political power, Suster wrote, at the conclusion of his book *Hitler and the Age of Horus*, of his conviction that the violence had at its root a mysterious hidden force unknown to science, which he called an eruption of the demonic. After the example of Aleister Crowley, Suster personified this force in the form of Horus, Egyptian god of war. It was Suster's view that certain individuals had practiced magic as a way of controlling this demonic energy for their own political purposes, and that one of them was Adolf Hitler, whom Suster called "the greatest black magician of the century."[160]

A black magician Hitler may well have been, but it is my own view that he was a natural magician, similar in this respect to the mad Russian monk Rasputin, and was not instructed in esoteric practices by any occult society. Hitler and the other leaders of Nazism hated intellectuals, and there is no evidence that the Nazis ever sought to develop psychic abilities in a controlled and scientific manner to be used as weapons in warfare. Just as the anti-intellectual and anti-Semitic atmosphere of Nazi Germany inhibited the development of the atomic bomb, and even the completion of the V-2 rocket program,[161] it also inhibited the application of Rhine's ESP testing techniques in a practical military way. It can only be speculated what the Nazis might have accomplished with the paranormal had they devoted significant energies to its development.

Psi Prodigies of the USSR

There is reason to believe that, after the Second World War, the Soviets were more open to the idea of psychic soldiers and psychic assassins than the Nazis had ever been. The revelation that the USSR possessed the atomic bomb was a shock to the West in 1949. It was followed by the successful test of a Soviet fusion bomb in 1953 and the launch of Sputnik

---

160. Suster, 213.

161. Pauwels and Bergier, 170.

in 1957, raising the specter of orbiting nuclear weapons platforms. By the mid-1960s, para-psychologists were speculating what the Soviets might be doing in their secret psi laborato-ries, and how far ahead of the West they were in the development of psychic spies.

Every so often, a crack in the Iron Curtain let out a glimmer of information on So-viet psychics. Rosa Kuleshova, a twenty-two-year-old Russian girl, was featured in *Time* on January 25, 1963, for her amazing ability to read while blindfolded. *Life* did a story on her the following year. In 1968, another Russian woman, Nina Kulagina, amazed the world when film was shown of her moving objects using only the power of her mind at the First Moscow International Conference on Parapsychology. As a young woman, Kulagina found that objects would move around in her apartment, particularly when she was angry. She discovered that she could control these poltergeist activities using the power of her will. Kulagina was tested by Dr. Zdenek Rejdak, a prominent Czech scientist of the Prague Mili-tary Institute, who testified that he could find no trickery in her telekinetic abilities.

Kulagina became the favorite guinea pig of Dr. Leonid L. Vasiliev, a psychologist at Leningrad University who pioneered parapsychological studies at the Institute for Brain Re-search in Leningrad. He made over sixty films of her demonstrations of psychokinetic abil-ity. She was also studied by the Leningrad military physiologist Dr. Genady Sergeyev. It was Sergeyev who gave her an extremely unnerving experiment on March 10, 1970—she was told to stop the beating heart of a frog that had been removed from its body and suspended in a vessel of liquid. The result is described in detail in *Psychic Warfare* by Martin Ebon.

Ebon quoted Larissa Vilenskaya, who participated in Russian experiments involving Kulagina from 1971 to 1976, and who later wrote that under normal circumstances, a frog heart removed and suspended in solution in this way will beat for thirty to forty minutes, and sometimes for as long as ninety minutes. Kulagina was first instructed to make the heart beat faster, which she accomplished for a period of about two minutes. Then she was told to stop the heart while standing at a distance of approximately five feet. Vilenskaya wrote that it took her forty seconds to stop the heart. The electrocardiogram of the frog's heart showed a sudden flare-up of electrical activity that resembled an electric shock. Efforts to restart the heart were unsuccessful, although it is usually possible, by applying electricity, to restart a frog's heart after it has ceased to beat.[162]

In a separate incident, Kulagina terrified a skeptical Leningrad psychiatrist by speed-ing up the rhythm of his heart, demonstrating that her power was not limited to frogs.

---

162. Ebon, *Psychic Warfare*, chap. 6

She also had the disturbing ability to burn the skin of those she touched. The effect was said to resemble a very bad sunburn. She did this by laying her hands on the arms of the subject. After a short while, the pain became so intense that those undergoing the experiment would break the contact, unable to endure it. This ability was characterized as Kulagina's "counter-healing force," a malignant laying on of the hands. Its reality was verified in 1972 by the British parapsychologist, Benson Herbert, who published his account in the *Journal of Paraphysics* (Volume 7, Number 3).

Psychic Spies of the CIA

It is not difficult to imagine what effect these and similar studies on Russian psi prodigies had on planners in the CIA and American military intelligence. Rhine at Duke University had studied psychokinesis, but only in a statistical way using repeated throws of dice. He had no one remotely like Nina Kulagina to study. The nightmare of covert Soviet assassins, possessed of the ability to stop the hearts of American targets at any time over a great distance, must have made more than a few men in Washington with jobs that officially did not exist wake up in the night in cold sweats. It was reported in 1970 that the Soviets were spending sixty million rubles per year to study what was termed psychotronics.

A report written for the Defense Intelligence Agency (DIA) in 1972 concluded that not only had the Soviet Union gotten the jump on America in the area of parapsychological research, but they were outspending the U.S. and were well in advance of anything seen by American scientists: "The Soviet Union is well aware of the benefits and applications of parapsychology research. The term parapsychology denotes [in the Soviet Union] a multi-disciplinary field consisting of the sciences of bionics, biophysics, psychophysics, psychology, physiology and neuropsychology. Many scientists, U.S. and Soviet, feel that parapsychology can be harnessed to create conditions where one can alter or manipulate the minds of others. The major impetus behind the Soviet drive to harness the possible capabilities of telepathic communication, telekinetic and bionics are said to come from the Soviet military and the KGB." The DIA report even raised the possibility that Soviet psi agents were using mind control techniques to target "U.S. or allied personnel in nuclear missile silos."

The leadership of the CIA decided at the beginning of the decade of the 1970s that it had to discover what the potential was for penetration of American secrets by Soviet parapsychological operatives. They were mainly concerned with the ability to read minds at a distance, and to influence the thoughts and behavior of others by psychically applying mental pressure. The CIA began a research project called SCANATE. The project took on momentum when it was moved in 1972 to the Stanford Research Institute (SRI) in Menlo Park, California, and merged with a program of independent parapsychological research being carried out under the leadership of Harold Puthoff, who had recently been contacted by the New York artist and psychic Ingo Swann.

Swann, who had already engaged in ESP tests in New York in the laboratory of Professor Gertrude Schmeidler at City College, learned of Puthoff's interest in studying the boundary between the physics of living and non-living things, and suggested to Puthoff that he should look into parapsychology as a starting point. Swann visited Puthoff's lab in California, and there underwent a series of tests. Puthoff published the results, which came to the attention of the CIA, already engaged in its own parapsychological research. With CIA funding, they were able to bring in Puthoff's colleague, Russell Targ, to help run the program, and began to gather a small team of gifted psychics, most prominent among them Ingo Swann. The SRI program developed into two separate parts: a research branch and an active operations branch.

History of Remote Viewing

The term *remote viewing* was adopted for the primary activity of these psychic spooks— the extrasensory perception of scenes and events over extended distances. In the beginning, a person was sent to the remote location to be viewed to act as a kind of psychic beacon for the viewer. Swann discovered that a beacon was not really necessary when he did a remote viewing of the planet Jupiter just prior to the NASA Pioneer 10 flyby in December 1973, and discovered that Jupiter had its own faint ring system. The existence of this ring was later confirmed by NASA. Viewers began to work from nothing more than map coordinates of latitude and longitude in degrees, minutes, and seconds, and eventually even these coordinates were encoded to prevent possible second-guessing of data by the viewer based on geographical location.

The researchers at SRI were able to determine something that J. B. Rhine had suspected decades earlier—that remote viewing did not depend on the electromagnetic spectrum. They did this by first enclosing their viewers in what is known as a Faraday cage, a metal mesh cage that stops the passage of most electromagnetic waves. This was built into the walls of the test chamber occupied by the viewers. The Faraday cage could not block out wavelengths that were extremely long or short, however. The short wavelengths, those in the microwave range, were eliminated as carriers of remote-viewing information due to their limited effective distance of travel. To eliminate the ultra-long wavelengths in the ELF band of the spectrum, a remote viewer was taken deep beneath the ocean in a submarine. This effectively eliminated the electromagnetic spectrum as an explanation for remote viewing. In his book *Reading the Enemy's Mind*, Paul H. Smith wrote, "Apparently there was no known physical way to shield any target on earth from the prying 'eyes' of a remote viewer."[163] It was later discovered that the Soviets in their own parapsychological research had done a similar submarine test on remote viewing.

A concept developed within the program of something that was called the Matrix, a mysterious source of universal knowledge that could be somehow tapped into by remote viewers, who were able to draw upon specific portions of its data. "Getting information from the Matrix rather than from the target itself allows a remote viewer to access anything about a target site, whether it involves past, present, or (to some degree) future; inside; outside, intangible or tangible, all regardless of what the target's condition or circumstance may be at the instant of the actual remote viewing."[164] The Matrix is the same as what was known in Theosophy as the akashic records, which were held by Theosophists to contain both the past and future as well as the present.

Over the years, the program was associated with various ancillary investigations and it came under the auspices of several governmental organizations. In 1976, it was expanded and Ed May was added to the administration to help with the increased workload. In 1977, Army Intelligence set up Operation GONDOLA WISH to investigate just how vulnerable U.S. military intelligence was to Soviet psychic probing. This operation evolved into Project GRILL FLAME, which was actively devoted to collecting data on Soviet activities. It operated out of Fort Meade, Maryland, and was made up mostly of enlisted personnel who had demonstrated parapsychological abilities. The research program being run by the SRI was integrated into GRILL FLAME in 1979, and numerous long-range psi scans were run out of Menlo Park.

In 1983, the name of the program was changed to the INSCOM Center Land Project, or ICLP for short. By this time, Harold Puthoff, working with psychic Ingo Swann, had developed a training method that allowed anyone with a latent ability for remote viewing to return useful results. The accuracy was never perfect, but it was consistently above a

---

163.   Smith, 94.

164.   Ibid., 164.

statistical average, and it was this positive return of data that kept the program running for so many years.

What had been top secret suddenly became public knowledge when *Washington Post* reporter Jack Anderson broke the story in 1984. The U.S. Army found itself in an embarrassing position. When an evaluation of remote viewing by the National Research Council returned an unfavorable opinion, Army intelligence took the opportunity to distance itself from the program. Army funding ceased in 1985. The program was not allowed to die, but it was transferred to the Scientific and Technical Intelligence Directorate of the DIA under the redesignation SUN STREAK. In 1991, the program was moved to the Science Applications International Corporation, or SAIC, and it was renamed, for the final time, as STAR GATE.

Errors in management and poor morale within the program caused it to be transferred back to the CIA in 1995, with orders that it undergo a full evaluation. The two experts hired to do the evaluation were divided in their findings. The statistician Jessica Utts believed that a significant result above mere chance had been demonstrated, but the skeptical psychologist Ray Hyman, who was a prominent member of CSICOP, an organization devoted to debunking psychics, gave a negative review. The CIA closed the program down, with the conclusion—which has been hotly disputed—that in no case had the remote viewers provided information that had been used to guide intelligence operations.

The remote viewing program under its various incarnations was never large. In twenty-one years of operation, it cost the American taxpayers twenty million dollars and employed around forty personnel, among them the twenty-three individuals engaged in actual remote viewing exercises. At its peak in the 1980s, it employed seven viewers, but in its last five years during its decline in management and morale only three viewers were being used—one of them a Tarot-card reader, a fact that aroused considerable disdain among its detractors.

Three Techniques of Remote Viewing

Over the years, three different techniques were used by operatives. The first, employed during the original SRI work at Menlo Park during the early 1970s, was Coordinate Remote Viewing, or CRV, in which the viewers were required to give a description of a location identified to them only by map coordinates, which were at first given to them openly, and then later encoded. This procedure is very similar to pendulum dowsing, which is often done by psychics over a map to locate hidden or lost individuals or items. It is surprising that the CIA and Army Intelligence did not concentrate on dowsers when seeking operatives for their remote viewing experiments. Dowsers would have been naturally suited to the work, and as a group would undoubtedly have yielded the best results.

The second technique was known as Extended Remote Viewing, or ERV. This technique was perfected by Puthoff and Swann around 1983 as a way of systematizing remote viewing and making it into a science that could be taught to soldiers and spies with reliable results. It involved the induction of a meditative or trance state through physical relaxation, and the visualization of a kind of astral staging zone the operative entered prior to undertaking travel on the astral level to the site of the mission. It was called extended remote viewing for the simple reason that it took more time than coordinate viewing. This is the technique that concerns us since it was a form of astral projection, even though it was not recognized as such by those using it. This method was favored during the heyday of the remote viewing program, and it yielded the most impressive results.

The third technique introduced in 1988 was Written Remote Viewing, or WRV, in which information was derived from a spiritual agency through automatic writing. WRV was a form of mediumship or, to use the equivalent modern term, channeling. It was very much out of keeping with the desire of Rhine and other parapsychologists to distance their work from anything that hinted at spiritualism, but when the RV program was in its decline, those running it were willing to use anything they thought might provide the results they needed, including Tarot cards.

Extended Remote Viewing

The Extended Remote Viewing technique began with a period of stepped relaxation of the body and mind that was known in the STAR GATE program as the cool-down process. The viewer lay in a quiet, dimly-lit room on a comfortable recliner listening to classical music that played softly in the background. With the viewer was another person known as the monitor, who was there to ask questions and to write down the spoken responses of the viewer during the experiment.

The object of the cool-down process was to enter the theta state. In the jargon of STAR GATE, the normal waking state of the human mind is the beta state. When the mind is relaxed, it enters the alpha state. Eventually this drops into the theta state. In a 1997 interview for *Nexus Magazine*, David Morehouse, the author of *Psychic Warrior: Inside the CIA Stargate Program*, explained: "In theta-wave state, it appears that the conduits become open. It's called the 'thought incubation state', a time when that 'limen' which separates the conscious mind from the unconscious mind becomes thinner."[165] The limen is simply the threshold between the conscious state and the unconscious.

Morehouse worked as a remote viewer for American military intelligence. He describes the initial process of remote viewing as falling into the fourth dimension. He was taught to construct a special place on the astral level where he went after entering the meditative or trance state conducive to remote viewing. "We were taught to go into a place we called 'sanctuary'. It was a place where you would go to gather your bearings, to acclimate yourself. Each individual viewer created his own sanctuary. For some viewers it was some sort of a garden, or a safe house, or a safe place."[166] Morehouse explained that he would project into his sanctuary an apparitional or phantom self, a double of his normal physical form that was transparent.

Once safely within the sanctuary in his transparent astral double, Morehouse would begin what was termed "descent into the target area." His own sanctuary consisted of a cube in space surrounded on all six sides by stars. When he was ready to begin, a swirling vortex would form in the floor of this transparent box in space. Morehouse allowed himself to drop into this vortex, a stage in the process known as "jumping into the ether" and felt himself drawn headfirst down through this tunnel of light at an accelerating speed until his astral body struck a kind of membrane and punched through it to the target location.

There can be no question that this was a form of astral projection. The penetration of the membrane at the end of the light vortex is equivalent to the snapping shut of the "pineal doorway" described by the Theosophist Oliver Fox, and also calls to mind the Golden Dawn instruction that members should imagine that they clearly hear the astral portals of the tattwa cards close behind them after passing through. The construction of an astral place for ritual working is an accepted practice in modern Western magic, such as that practiced by the Golden Dawn. The sanctuary of remote viewers, which they built up in on the astral level to act as a kind of staging zone for their journeys, is very similar to the astral temple constructed by magicians for their ritual work on the astral level. It can take any form, since the substance of the astral world is malleable to the imagination.

---

165. Dowbenko, *Nexus Magazine*, vol. 4, no. 5–6.
166. Ibid.

Morehouse, however, strongly denied that he was engaged in astral projection, possibly because he was under the mistaken belief that astral projection is harmful and dangerous. "When you tear the spiritual body from the physical, what does that mean? It's harmful. That means that you leave the physical body open, allowing inhabitation by whatever else that wants to step in because the spiritual body is now gone. We're not talking about levels of consciousness. We're talking about spiritual separation."[167] Morehouse understood astral projection as a total separation of the spiritual body from the physical body. Spiritualists and Theosophists would strongly deny that the astral body can ever fully separate from the physical body, except in death, and therefore the physical body is never left empty and open to the entry of malicious spirits during projection of the astral double.

The process described by Morehouse of creating a sanctuary, entering it in an astral body, and then sending that body to distant locations on the astral level, can only be characterized as astral projection. Morehouse even referred to the phenomenon of repercussion, so well-known to those who project the astral double, although he did not know the spiritualist term. "The physical body is never left in remote viewing. There is always contact, but the physical body begins to manifest the physiological signs of what the projected consciousness is experiencing in the target area."[168] This is clearly a reference to repercussion, the belief that an injury done to the projected astral body will show itself on the physical body.

Morehouse, and presumably the STAR GATE team with whom he worked, preferred to use the term *bilocation* to describe the projection of his astral double. You will remember from earlier chapters that the term bilocation is used in the Catholic Church to describe the appearance of saints in two places at once. The STAR GATE team described it as folding space so that distant events came to the remote viewer, rather than the remote viewer traveling to distant locations. As I have pointed out, no form of astral travel actually involves travel since all projection is done into the astral world—and this is contained within the mind, which in its entirety embraces all points in the universe. The analogy used by the heads of the STAR GATE program to teach Morehouse and other remote viewers is that the unconscious mind is like the spine of a book, and the pages of that book are different planes of existence, all linked by the unconscious mind.

---

167. Dowbenko, *Nexus Magazine*, vol. 4, no. 5–6.

168. Ibid.

Remote Viewing Experiences

Remote viewing journeys were made not only to distant worlds such as Jupiter, but to the past and future as well. Morehouse viewed the Ark of the Covenant, which he described as a portal in four-dimensional space-time. It was discovered that the past could be examined but not changed. The future is more difficult to access because it is unfixed and variable, changing from moment to moment from the influence of present events as they unfold. Information gathered in both past and future, and even in other parts of the present, is never completely reliable. As the Theosophists pointed out, it is not the actual akashic records that are being accessed, but rather a distorted and incomplete astral reflection of the akashic records. For this reason, the information gathered during remote viewing, or during any other form of soul flight, must always remain unreliable. It may contain much useful data, but determining which parts are accurate and which are inaccurate is difficult or impossible, in the absence of some corroborating frame of reference.

Remote viewers sometimes encountered spirits while on their astral excursions, as would be expected. Morehouse described benevolent beings similar to angels that radiated a sense of warmth and light, but did not involve themselves in human beings traveling on the astral plane. He wrote that they would recognize the presence of remote viewers, but would not interact with them or guide them.[169] When Morehouse described these beings to his monitor, the monitor told him to approach them and engage them in conversation. The angelic beings merely smiled in a polite way and walked off. They regarded the remote viewer as harmless, but not worth talking to.

Morehouse also had his encounters with hostile beings that he regarded as demons. They would approach smiling, looking in every way like normal human beings, but when he began to suspect their true nature they would immediately attack him. On one occasion, they grabbed him by his feet and dragged him away upside down. He was sure he was about to be murdered. His screams alerted his monitor, who talked him out of his trance state. Morehouse made the very astute comment that these beings know what frightens a human being, and they attempt to amplify fears. This is correct. He arrived at the mistaken conclusion that they do this in an attempt to possess the physical body. This is not true. These malicious spirits amplify fears because strong emotions of a lower order are to them not only a nourishment, but a kind of intoxicant equivalent to alcohol. They

---

169. Dowbenko, *Nexus Magazine*, vol. 4, no. 5–6.

induce intense fear as a way of gorging themselves on the emotion and getting drunk on human terror.

The Verdict on Remote Viewing

The American Institute for Research report commissioned by the CIA in 1995 that marked the end of the remote viewing program STAR GATE is as significant for what it did not find, as for its direct recommendations. It did not conclude that remote viewing was a fraud, or that no parapsychological effects exist. It did not even try to claim that the re-mote viewers had never achieved accurate results. Rather, it condemned remote viewing on the grounds that it was inaccurate and not dependable—that it may work, but that it does not work all the time or with enough consistency to base a military action upon.

The conclusion of the Executive Summary of the report reads:

> The foregoing observations provide a compelling argument against continuation of the program within the intelligence community. Even though a statistically signifi-cant effect has been observed in the laboratory, it remains unclear whether the exis-tence of a paranormal phenomenon, remote viewing, has been demonstrated. The laboratory studies do not provide evidence regarding the origins or nature of the phenomenon, assuming it exists, nor do they address the important methodological issue of interjudge reliability.
>
> Further, even if it could be demonstrated unequivocally that a paranormal phe-nomenon occurs under the conditions present in the laboratory paradigm, these conditions have limited applicability and utility for intelligence gathering opera-tions. For example, the nature of the remote viewing targets are vastly dissimilar, as are the specific tasks required of the remote viewers. Most importantly, the informa-tion provided by remote viewing is vague and ambiguous, making it difficult, if not impossible, for the technique to yield information of sufficient quality and accuracy for actionable intelligence. Thus, we conclude that continued use of remote viewing in intelligence gathering operations is not warranted.[170]

This conclusion is hardly a dismissal of remote viewing. A similar sort of criticism might have been made about the use of electricity in the eighteenth century. It is possible that two centuries from today, something similar to remote viewing will be employed with

---

170. Mumford, Rose, and Goslin, *Evaluation of Remote Viewing*.

regularity for conventional purposes in daily life, and that those using it will never even consider that its very existence was once doubted, or that it was once held to be too unreliable to use.

CHAPTER NINE

UFO
Abductions

Accounts of UFOs (Unidentified Flying Objects) go back as far as human history. There have always been things seen in the sky that could not be identified, and such sightings continue unabated, although they are more numerous in some decades than in others. How they are interpreted depends on the culture in which they are perceived. For the ancient Greeks, UFOs were signs from the gods on Mount Olympus, given to mankind to guide its actions. The biblical Hebrews were more apt to view them as expressions of divine wrath. To medieval Christians, they were seen as forerunners of the apocalypse. In the modern technological age of science-fiction films and rockets, UFOs are described in a more mechanical way as vessels from outer space believed to carry intelligent alien beings, visitors from other worlds.

A specific event marks the beginning of the modern cycle of sightings of unidentified objects in the sky. On June 24, 1947, private pilot Kenneth Arnold was making the short flight from Chehalis to Yakima, Washington, a trip of about twenty-five miles, when he saw nine objects he described as "saucerlike things . . . flying like geese in a diagonal chainlike line."[171] Arnold estimated their speed at around twelve hundred miles per hour when he related his story to his local newspaper. Within a single month, reports of flying saucers were being received by the authorities in forty states. *Life* did a story on the craze in its July 21, 1947 issue.

What was not so well-known to the public is that at the close of the Second World War the Air Force had been receiving similar reports from all over the world. Donald H. Menzel, a commander in the U. S. Navy who headed the Section of Mathematical and Physical Research for Naval Communications, wrote: "Immediately after the end of World War II, sightings of mysterious flying objects began to multiply. More than one thousand such reports came from Sweden alone during 1946. I heard of these through classified channels but took no part in resolving them. Air Force Intelligence, however, fully alerted, had decided that the USSR, having taken over the German rocket program at Peenemünde, was responsible for the sightings."[172]

During the growing hysteria of the Cold War, these sightings worried the government enough to induce the Air Force to begin collecting information under a program titled Project Sign, but referred to in the popular media by the humorous name Project Saucer. On December 27, 1949, after more than two years of investigation, the Air Force dismissed all but thirty-four of the sightings as hoaxes, hallucinations, or misinterpretations of familiar objects; the thirty-four sightings they could not explain, they dismissed as "psychological aberrations."[173] But they could not get rid of UFOs so easily, reports of which continued to come in at the rate of one per day. Away from the microphones and cameras, the top brass were getting worried. They instituted another program, Project Grudge, to record and investigate these events.

---

171.   Darrach and Ginna, "Have We Visitors?"

172.   Sagan and Page, *UFO's: A Scientific Debate*, 130–1.

173.   Darrach and Ginna.

Investigations of J. Allen Hynek

These sightings were examined under the expert control of the astronomer Dr. Josef Allen Hynek (1910–1986), who in the spring of 1948 was teaching astronomy at Ohio State University in Columbus when he was approached by three military men from Wright-Patterson Air Force Base in nearby Dayton. They asked him what he thought about flying saucers. He responded that he thought they were a lot of "junk and nonsense." Immediately, they offered him a job as an astronomical consultant. He joined Project Sign, and stayed with the team investigating UFOs through Project Grudge and the subsequent Project Bluebook, right up until the Air Force investigation was terminated in 1969. In 1973, he founded the Center for UFO Studies, or CUFOS, and remained active in UFO investigations until his death in 1986.

Hynek began his work with the Air Force as a complete disbeliever—skeptic would be too neutral a term for his attitude. He dismissed cases as solved even though he could not explain them in any way. In a 1985 interview with writer Dennis Stacy, he admitted: "I stretched far to give something a natural explanation, sometimes when it may not have really had it." He mentioned a case from the Snake River Canyon, in which a man and his two sons reported sighting a metallic object in the air that caused the treetops to sway. Hynek explained away the sighting as some kind of atmospheric eddy, even though he admitted to Stacy that he had never seen such an eddy, and had no reason to believe that such eddies could even exist.

This negative attitude of Hynek in the early years of the Air Force investigation endeared the astronomer to his military overseers. When, in the 1950s, Hynek began to rethink his position, and was less willing to dismiss unexplainable reports as natural events, he fell out of favor with the brass; although he remained an advisor for Project Bluebook until the end, it was in name only. The Air Force was not interested in publicizing cases to which it could not attach a plausible, natural explanation. According to Hynek, intimately involved with the investigation for twenty-one years, it was never more than a whitewash. As he told Dennis Stacy, "They were under instruction from the Pentagon, following the Robertson Panel of 1953, that the whole subject had to be debunked, period, no question about it. That was the prevailing attitude."

Distant Sightings and Close Encounters

Hynek composed the following definition of a UFO that has since become the standard definition:

> We can define the UFO simply as the reported perception of an object or light seen in the sky or upon the land the appearance, trajectory, and general dynamic and luminescent behavior of which do not suggest a logical, conventional explanation and which is not only mystifying to the original percipients but remains unidentified after close scrutiny of all available evidence by persons who are technically capable of making a common sense identification, if one is possible.[174]

It is to Hynek that we owe the famous Hynek Classification System of UFO events, which was published in 1972 in his book *The UFO Experience: A Scientific Inquiry*. He divided reports of UFOs into two groups, each of which contains three subgroups.

Distant Sightings

1. *Nocturnal light*—any unexplained form of light seen in the sky at night

2. *Daylight disk*—any unexplained object seen in the sky during the day

3. *Radar-visual*—any unexplained radar blip verified by visual sighting

Close Encounters

1. *First kind*—a UFO seen at close range (within 150 yards) that does not interact in any way with the environment; may be seen in the air or on the ground

2. *Second kind*—a UFO at close range that interacts with the environment; quantifiable evidence of its presence remains after it has departed, such as scorch marks, impressions of landing gear, or elevated radiation levels

3. *Third kind*—a UFO at close range the occupants of which are observed; usually they are seen entering or leaving their craft, but sometimes the ship and the occupants are observed separately

Following the death of Hynek in 1986, two additional Close Encounter categories were added by those who study UFO events. These are the categories that have the greatest

---

174. Hynek, 10.

bearing on astral projection, involving as they do direct interaction between the occupants of UFOs and those who observe them.

4. *Fourth kind*—forced abduction of human beings against their wishes by UFO occupants; when held, the abductees are often examined or experimented upon

5. *Fifth kind*—direct contact between UFO occupants and human observers in which communication is established; the communication may be verbal or telepathic, and may convey information of a helpful or harmful type

Abduction by Aliens

There is a great degree of uniformity in accounts of alien abductions. The person taken is usually alone at the time, often lying awake or asleep in bed. A bright light or a glow may be seen, and strange noises heard. The abductee experiences physical paralysis and is levitated through the air, often in a prone position, by a beam of light or force, sometimes under the oversight of humanoid beings. The abductees feel themselves floating through the window or door and up into the air. The aliens sometimes pass through closed doors as though the doors did not exist. The abductee is taken to an enclosed chamber, usually rounded or domed, which is understood to be the interior of a spacecraft, placed on an examination table, and probed in various ways. Needles may be inserted into the abductee's head. Blood, sperm, or ova may be extracted, and tissue samples taken. Some abductees believe that small metallic or silicon objects are implanted in their bodies.

While aboard the alien craft, the abductees are sometimes raped by their abductors. Some are later shown babies developing in stalls or tanks, and are told that the babies are their hybrid human-alien offspring. A woman may be permitted to hold an infant, perhaps for the purpose of creating a bond between the baby and its human mother. The abductee is returned to the place where the abduction occurred. Often the memory is impaired, resulting in a gap in time during which nothing can be remembered. Only later do the memories of the abduction gradually surface. The recovery of the lost memories may be aided by hypnotherapy sessions. Some abductees observe small, cup-shaped depressions in their skin of which they have no prior memory. Others find strange scars at the base of their necks or elsewhere. Sometimes they develop burns on their skin similar to sunburns or radiation burns.

Types of Aliens

Descriptions of the supposed aliens vary, but they tend to fall into about half a dozen well-recognized groups and a few odder varieties.

1. *Grays:* The dominant type are small of stature with large heads and slender limbs. They have large, black, ovoid eyes that wrap partway around their heads, and are usually described as gray in skin color. Their fingers are long and slender, their mouths small and lipless, and their noses almost nonexistent. They usually have four fingers on each hand, but sometimes have six fingers. The females rarely have sex with male abductees, and the male Grays almost never have sex with female abductees. They prefer to extract mechanically the human sperm and ova for their breeding experiments.

2. *Hybrids:* Found only on the spaceships of the Grays, this second type of alien is larger and almost of human stature, with smaller eyes and skin that looks similar to human skin. They are thought to be human-alien hybrids that often act as assistants for the full-blooded Grays during the examinations of abductees, and they frequently have sex with abducted humans.

3. *Blonds, or Nordics:* The third type are more humanlike, with well-developed bodies, blond hair, blue eyes, and golden tanned skin. They are Scandinavian in appearance. They move with catlike speed and grace, have great strength, and are somewhat taller than the average adult human. In every respect, they resemble the Nazi ideal of the genetic superman. They often rape abductees.

4. *Insectoids:* A less frequently encountered fourth type are of human size but insect-like in shape, and are described as giant grasshoppers or giant praying mantises. Their eyes sometimes glow with intense red light. They are said to occasionally have sex with human women, and their sexual members are described as hard and ice-cold.

5. *Reptiles:* There is a fifth kind of alien that resembles a humanoid reptile with green scales over its body and large snake-like eyes of a yellow-green color. This type is around eight feet tall, muscular and possessed of great strength, with claws in place of fingers. They are aggressive and violent, and have been connected in some reports with acts of torture. They sometimes rape abductees.

6. *Goblins:* A sixth type consists of dwarfish, deformed little beings only a few feet tall, but broad and muscular, that like to deceive and play tricks. They are usually not connected with the abduction events.

7. *Robots:* This seventh type is made up of a wide variety of mechanical devices exhibiting a limited intelligence that are used by the Grays in their work. Some are mere mobile, articulated machines, whereas others resemble the human form.

8. *Balls of Light:* The eighth class of aliens takes the form of floating balls of intense radiance that are difficult to look at directly with the naked eye. They communicate by means of telepathy.

9. *Apparitions:* Sometimes aliens appear in a ninth class that is luminous and semi-transparent, and has the ability to walk through doors, walls, and furniture. It is speculated that these are artificial three-dimensional projections rather than living beings.

We can make a few general observations about this alien menagerie. The Nordics were commonly seen early on in the flying saucer craze, but were soon supplanted by the Grays, who have dominated the UFO scene ever since. It was the Grays who were featured most prominently in the 1977 film *Close Encounters of the Third Kind*. The Nordics perhaps owe their inspiration to Theosophy and related modern mystery traditions that feature perfected, spiritualized super-humans who dwell on a higher plane of existence. The Grays were probably inspired by illustrations of aliens in science-fiction magazines and on science-fiction book covers.

Science-fiction films and television series were almost certainly the inspiration for both the reptilians and the insectoids. A reptilian alien species known as the Gorn, having great strength, green scaly skin, and snakelike eyes, was featured prominently in the *Star Trek* episode "Arena" in 1967. Giant insects were a mainstay of Grade-B horror films in the 1950s and 1960s. The same can be said of intelligent robots. The hybrid species of alien arose from extrapolations of the widespread belief that the Grays are cross-breeding with humans. Naturally, Gray-human babies grow up to be Gray-human adults.

The dwarfish Goblins, the floating Balls of Light, and the Apparitions owe their inspiration to the traditional wellsprings in the human unconscious that have given rise for centuries to tales of fairies, will-o'-the-wisps, and ghosts. The mischievous behavior of the Goblin race coupled with their small size cannot help but connect them with the many creatures of legend that display similar traits—such as the pixies, goblins, dwarfs, brownies, but especially the fairies. In traditional lore, balls of light are often said to follow travelers in wilderness places, especially in marshes, bogs, and swamps. The natural occurrence of such things as foxfire and marsh lights probably gave rise to these tales, which have taken on their own mythic vitality. Ghosts of various kinds have been observed throughout human history, so it is not difficult to find the inspiration for the semi-transparent aliens that walk through walls.

Aliens Are Astral Entities

The key to making sense of this chaos of different alien types is to understand that none of them are physical in nature. They are all astral entities. Spirits in the astral world can take on whatever forms best serve their needs or adopted purposes. However, most frequently they adopt the forms that meet the expectations in the minds of those who perceive them, since doing so is the best way of establishing a relationship with those individuals. Most people today expect to see Grays when they encounter aliens, so naturally that is what most people see.

By stating quite unequivocally that all aliens are astral in nature, and that none are physical, I do not intend to deprive of their significance the differences between the various types. Those who have encountered over the past six decades spirits they believe to be aliens have divided them into these distinct classes in response to fundamental needs deep in their unconscious minds. These differences did not arise by accident, but rather were driven by some psychic imperative, and for this reason the details of their appearances are worth studying and the differences between the types worth comparing.

Although aliens are astral beings, and encounters with them always occur on the astral level, it is possible that they produce physical effects and artifacts, either directly or indirectly. Poltergeists are spirits, yet it is difficult to dismiss all physical poltergeist events as deceptions on the part of the adolescents around whom they usually revolve. There is observational evidence that spirits can generate physical events, and perhaps even produce physical objects and substances by drawing upon and channeling vital human energies. The mechanism by which this is accomplished remains a complete mystery.

Carl Jung Issues a Warning

One of the first observers of the UFO craze to suggest that it might not have a purely physical explanation was the psychologist Carl Jung (1875-1961). He pointed out in his 1959 book *Flying Saucers: A Myth of Things Seen In the Sky* that the shape of the average UFO was like a circle or disk, similar to the archetypal form of the mandala, a symbol of wholeness. Jung did not dismiss UFOs as imaginary, but he regarded them as a mystery that had a psychological component. He was not certain whether they were physically real or wholly psychological. In either case, he considered them the harbinger of a time of momentous and perhaps dangerous change in Western society that had been thrown up by the turmoil in the depths of the collective unconscious.

> These rumors, or the possible physical existence of such objects, seem to me so significant that I feel myself compelled, as once before when events were brewing of fateful consequence for Europe, to sound a note of warning. I know that, just as before, my voice is much too weak to reach the ear of the multitude. It is not presumption that drives me, but my conscience as a psychiatrist that bids me fulfill my duty and prepare those few who will hear me for coming events which are in accord with the end of an era.[175]

Jung observed that the UFO phenomenon had appeared just prior to the transition from the astrological Age of Pisces to the dawning Age of Aquarius. He regarded it as a synchronistic event, a mirroring in the outer material world of the tension within the human psyche that was generated by this transitional phase. Jung viewed the round shape of flying saucers as an unconscious compensation for the division of the Western world by the Iron Curtain, a futile attempt to restore wholeness by projecting symbols of wholeness into the heavens, the realm of the gods.

The beginning of the last great astrological age, that of Pisces, coincided with the founding of the Christian religion. Each age spans approximately 2,120 years. Jung intimated, without ever explicitly stating it, that the coming of the Age of Aquarius, accompanied by these spectacular signs in the sky, might herald the ending of the present Christian era in the West, and he feared its final end would be marked by a violent nuclear holocaust. It is curious to note that Aleister Crowley believed much the same thing—that the present Christian age was ending, and that a new age of independent thought brought

---

175. Jung, *Flying Saucers*, 15.

about by the emancipation of the individual was dawning that would be initiated by a horrific period of bloodshed and chaos. Jung did not mention Crowley, but he must have had some passing familiarity with Crowley's Cult of Thelema.

Prophecies of Aleister Crowley

In Crowley's prophetic *The Book of the Law*, the warrior god Horus in his form Ra-heru-khuti (Horus of Behutet), which Crowley chose to render as Ra-Hoor-Khuit, spoke through Crowley's spirit control, his guardian angel Aiwass, these words:

> I am the warrior Lord of the Forties: the
> Eighties cower before me, & are abased
> I will bring you to victory & joy: I will be
> at your arms in battle & ye shall
> delight to slay. Success is your proof;
> courage is your armour; go on, go on, in
> my strength & ye shall turn not back for any . . .
> I am in a secret fourfold word the blasphemy against
> all gods of men.
> Curse them! Curse them! Curse them!
> With my Hawk's head I peck at the eyes of
> Jesus as he hangs upon the cross
> I flap my wings in the face of Mohammed & blind him
> With my claws I tear out the flesh of the
> Indian and the Buddhist, Mongol and Din.[176]

The reference to the "warrior Lord of the Forties" needs no explanation. Remember, this book was psychically received by Crowley in 1904, long before the Second World War and the detonation of the atomic bomb in the 1940s. Jung perhaps feared the ill-defined approaching threat of the 1980s, which, as it turned out, was not marked by the nuclear holocaust of a Third World War, but by the collapse of the Soviet empire and the destruction of the Iron Curtain. It might be speculated that it is in this way that Horus asserts that the 1980s "cower before me and are abased."

---

176. Crowley, *Book of the Law*, 73–4.

As can be seen from the quotation, Crowley predicted a violent antagonism toward not only Christianity but toward all the major world religions. How much of a part Adolf Hitler plays in this unfolding of the transition between the Age of Pisces and the Age of Aquarius, and whether he is the magical child of Crowley predicted in the *Book of the Law* who would fulfill its prophecies, as suggested by Gerald Suster, is a matter of conjecture. My own view is that Crowley's magical child has yet to reveal himself, and that Hitler played only a part in the prophecies of *The Book of the Law*, not the central role.

Link Between Aliens, Fairies, and Witches

The astral nature of most, if not all, of the events of the UFO abductions, and their striking similarities with details of fairy abductions described centuries ago, was examined by the famous French UFO investigator Dr. Jacques Vallée, in his hugely influential 1969 book *Passport to Magonia*. Vallée is best known as the living model for the character of the French UFO expert in the film *Close Encounters of the Third Kind*, played in the movie by François Truffaut. Vallée began studying UFOs as a firm believer that they were alien spacecraft, but the lack of reliable material evidence caused his views to undergo a sea change in the late 1960s. In *Passport to Magonia,* he wrote: "When the underlying archetypes are extracted, the saucer myth is seen to coincide to a remarkable degree with the fairy-faith of Celtic countries, religious miracles, and the widespread belief among all peoples concerning entities whose physical and psychological descriptions place them in the same category as the present-day ufonauts."[177]

It is not difficult to draw these parallels. I will list some of the more obvious similarities between fairy abductions and alien abductions that have occurred to me in the course of my studies. It is by no means an exhaustive list, but it does suggest that we are looking at one phenomenon under two classifications—that fairy abductions and alien abductions are, at root, the same thing. However, we should no more jump to the conclusion that fairies are responsible than we should assume that it is aliens from outer space. Both classes of beings are spirits, existing on the astral level and accessible to human consciousness only when the state of mind is elevated from the physical level to the astral level.

1. Those abducted by fairies are taken into conical hills. The shape of flying saucers is often said to be domed or like a truncated cone.

---

177. Clark, "Vallée Discusses," 61.

2. The fairies take their abductees into rounded, windowless, womblike caverns. Aliens take their abductees into rounded, windowless, womblike metal chambers.

3. Those taken by fairies often have gaps in their memory during which they were unaware of the passage of time. Those taken by aliens experience "lost time" and gaps in memory.

4. Fairy abductees often have sex with fairies. Alien abductees often have sex with aliens.

5. Fairies substitute changelings for human babies—whom they resemble in every outward detail. Aliens breed hybrid babies half alien and half human.

6. Fairies place their changelings into the cribs of babies they have stolen so that mothers will nurse them, believing them to be their own. Aliens attempt to get female abductees to maternally bond with hybrid infants, telling the women that the babies are theirs.

7. Those taken by fairies sometimes suffer a pattern of marks known as "fairy bruising." Those taken by aliens suffer scars or cup-shaped depressions in their flesh.

8. Fairies give humans a potion or enchanted food to sap their will. Aliens sometimes give abductees a thick liquid to drink.

9. Fairies sometimes appear in glowing spheres of light. Aliens sometimes appear in glowing spheres of light.

10. Fairies sometimes leave circular marks on the ground where they have danced, called fairy rings. Alien spaceships that have landed sometimes leave circular burn marks or impressions in the ground.

11. Fairies sometimes vanish into thin air. Aliens sometimes vanish into thin air.

12. Fairies have been observed to pass directly into solid rock. Aliens have been seen walking through doors.

There are also obvious similarities between the experiences of those who believe themselves abducted by aliens and the experiences described by women accused of witchcraft during the Renaissance. Alien abductees are often marked; witches were marked by the Devil as a sign of their pact with him. Aliens try to get women abducted to care for hybrid infants;

witches nurse the familiars that are bound to them at a mark on their bodies known as the witch's teat. Aliens carry abducted humans through the air; the Devil, or the witch's imps, carry the witch through the air. Aliens rape abducted women; the Devil or his demons rape witches. Sometimes the sex is consensual between women and aliens; sometimes sex is consensual between witches and demons.

Reality of UFO Events

Jacques Vallée expressed the difficulty in clearly making a determination whether or not UFO events are "real" in a physical sense in a 1978 *Fate Magazine* interview he did with Jerome Clark:

> *Clark:* Can we infer from the existence of physical evidence, then, that there is a physical cause?
>
> *Vallée:* If the UFO phenomenon had no physical cause at all, there would be no way for us to perceive it because human beings are physical entities. So it has to make an impression on our senses somehow. For that to take place, it has to be physical at some time.
>
> *Clark:* So in other words there is such a thing as a solid, three-dimensional flying saucer.
>
> *Vallée:* No, I didn't say that. That may or may not be true. I don't think there is such a thing as the flying saucer phenomenon. I think it has three components and we have to deal with them in different ways.
>
> First, there is a physical object. That may be a flying saucer or it may be a projection or it may be something entirely different. All we know about it is that it represents a tremendous quantity of electromagnetic energy in a small volume. I say that based upon the evidence gathered from traces, from electromagnetic and radar detection and from perturbations of the electromagnetic fields such as Dr. Claude Poher, the French space scientist, has recorded.
>
> Second, there's the phenomenon the witnesses perceive. What they tell us is that they've seen a flying saucer. Now they may have seen that or they may have seen an image of a flying saucer or they may have hallucinated it under the influence of microwave radiation, or any of a number of things may have happened. The fact is that the witnesses were exposed to an event and as a result they experienced a highly

complex alteration of perception which caused them to describe the object or objects that figure in their testimony.

Beyond there—the physical phenomenon and the perception phenomenon—we have the third component, the social phenomenon. That's what happens when the reports are submitted to society and enter the cultural arena. That's the part which I find most interesting.

Clark: Before we go into that, let's clarify your views on the nature of the physical aspect. When I asked you if there was such a thing as a solid, three-dimensional flying saucer, I was thinking in these terms: Let's suppose that somebody says he has seen a UFO, the bottom part of which was flat and circular. He says he saw the object come down, settle on the soil and then fly off again, leaving a flat circular impression. Doesn't that clearly suggest the presence—at least for the duration of the sighting—of a solid object whose physical structure was more or less as the witness perceived it?

Vallée: Not necessarily. We have evidence that the phenomenon has the ability to create a distortion of the sense of reality or to substitute artificial sensations for the real ones. Look at some of the more bizarre close encounter cases—for example the incident from South America in which one man believed he had been abducted by a UFO while his companion thought he had boarded a bus which had suddenly appeared on the road behind them.

It is conceivable that there is one phenomenon which is visual and another which creates the physical traces. What I'm saying is that a strange kind of deception may be involved.

Clark: In other words the physical traces are placed there as ostensible confirmation of what the senses perceived?

Vallée: Yes.[178]

These remarks show that Vallée understood the impossibility of explaining the UFO experience in purely physical terms. Unfortunately, he had not quite succeeded in freeing his mind from the conventional view of reality that makes a clear understanding of interactions with spiritual beings on the astral level possible. He made the assertion that "if the UFO phenomenon had no physical cause at all, there would be no way for us to perceive it because human beings are physical entities. So it has to make an impression

178. Clark, 62–3.

on our senses somehow. For that to take place, it has to be physical at some time." This might seem self-evident to someone bound to a conventional view of reality, but it is simply untrue.

Sensory Metaphors

Information concerning spiritual beings does not reach us through our physical senses at all. It only *appears* to reach us through our senses. It is generated within the mind in the form of what I have termed *sensory metaphors* and then is apparently projected outward into what we like to think of as our external environment. I say "apparently projected" because the external environment exists within the mind, where the sensory metaphor was generated in the first place, so no projection is required. A dream is a kind of sensory metaphor. Spirits can talk to us in our dreams, and we hear them. We seem to hear them with our ears, but we hear only a sensory metaphor of their voices.

It might perhaps be argued that in order to excite the mind, in the process of generating a sensory metaphor to simulate its material presence, a spiritual being would need to affect the physical brain, and for this reason would itself need to be physical. But if that were the case, then the soul must be physical, since it affects the brain. Yet few theologians, and fewer scientists, would be willing to grant the existence of a physical soul. The important point to grasp is that information about spiritual beings does not come from outside the avenues of the five physical senses. Rather, it is generated within the mind, and it is given the illusory form of sense impressions through the use of sensory metaphors, so that the information appears to be obtained by the external senses.

This illusion can be absolutely perfect. If you think about the implications of this, you will soon see how significant they are. It is often impossible to tell the difference between a sensory metaphor and a sense impression. Let me give you an example. Suppose a spirit presents itself as a Gray alien. The spirit exists only on the astral level of the mind as it has no physical existence whatsoever. However, it can only interact with the mind of the person with whom it communicates by casting itself into the form of a sensory metaphor. It puts on a body and apparently projects that body into the outer environment, making it completely solid and real to the person who experiences the sensory metaphor of its existence. It is not really in the physical world at all; it has merely overlaid an astral form of itself that exists in the astral world on top of the physical world. Yet, to the person who perceives it, it has texture, shape, and warmth. It can be seen, touched, smelled, spoken to, heard, and when it touches or grabs the arm of that person, the touch is palpable.

That individual can quite easily have a full sexual encounter with the spirit, even though it does not in any way exist in the physical world.

Now we will extend the example, and presume that the spirit has the power to affect not only the sense awareness of the primary individual with whom it interacts, but also with anyone else who happens to be near that individual or watching that individual. Suddenly, the person no longer appears to be talking to thin air, but is seen to be speaking with a Gray alien. If the wondering friends approach the alien, they will be able to poke its gray skin with their fingers, assuming that the spirit is that tolerant of human stupidity. They will hear its words at the same time that the primary human contact hears them.

We will carry the example one step further. Suppose that one of the friends has a digital camera, and snaps a photograph of the alien. The spirit is able to create a sensory metaphor of the image on the display screen of the camera in the minds of all those who watched the picture being taken so that when the group gathers around the display of the camera, they seem to see the image of the Gray alien even though in a strictly physical sense no image was impressed upon the sensor of the camera. Yet how are these observers to determine that the image they look at is different from the image they see? Publish it in a national magazine? Yes, that might work. But how do we know how extensive the influence of a sensory metaphor is, or how greatly it can be extended? We do not know. Eventually, it might be presumed, the power of the sensory metaphor would reach its limit, and someone would notice that no alien was ever present in the photograph. But who can say when?

To complicate matters, there is the factor of mind control. Spirits can possess human beings quite easily, and use their bodies to manufacture physical evidence that supports their physical presence. For example, someone who believed that they saw an alien spacecraft land and then take off again, while possessed by a spirit representing itself as a Gray, might create a burned ring, or lay down a ring of sand, to mark where the spaceship supposedly landed. After the period of possession ceased, that person would have no memory of having created the ring, and so would swear in a court of law that it had been left by the alien spaceship.

A Classic Alien Abduction

The clearest evidence that alien abductions are astral projections comes from an account of the experiences of Albert K. Bender. In his 1963 book *Flying Saucers and the Three*

Men, he described his abduction, which took place on March 15, 1953, in terms that leave little doubt about its nature. As part of a general experiment conducted by the members of the amateur group known as the International Flying Saucer Bureau, to which Bender belonged, he lay down in his bed at six in the evening in Bridgeport, Connecticut, and repeatedly attempted to project from his mind a preset message of contact to any aliens who might be able to pick it up telepathically. Around the world, other members of the group were doing the same as part of their participation in what the group called World Contact Day.

After the third mental projection of the contact message, Bender felt his body suddenly grow icy cold. His head began to ache, as if with a severe headache, and he smelled an odor that resembled burning sulfur. He lapsed into a semiconscious state and the room around him seemed to fade. He got the impression of small blue lights swimming through his brain and blinking on and off. His temples continued to throb, but in addition his forehead directly over his eyes felt puffed up. The sensation of coldness continued. He opened his eyes, and was amazed to find himself floating in the air about three feet above his body. When he looked down, he saw his physical body still lying in the bed.

A voice spoke to Bender in his mind, telling him he had been chosen for a special mission. He responded telepathically, and seemed to drop back down onto the bed. The room was filled with what he describes as a yellow mist. He saw a shadow figure standing in the corner of the room, but when he made a motion toward it, the figure faded to nothingness. Gradually the mist disappeared, and Bender discovered that his radio had been turned on and was tuned to a part of the band where there was only background static. This whole experience occupied only five minutes. When he sat up, he found that he felt sick to his stomach. His head still ached and his forehead continued to feel puffy.

This abduction could also be described as a typical experience of astral projection. The only thing missing is the silver cord. The puffy feeling above Bender's eyebrows may have a relationship to what Oliver Fox termed his pineal doorway, which he believed to be located between his eyebrows at what is known in Kundalini yoga as the ajna chakra, the chakra of the body most associated with psychic abilities. The coldness of the body can be felt in communications with spiritual beings. The yellow mist is, again, a classic detail. Those who project the astral double often report that the air appears to be alive with tiny dust motes that dance and shimmer as though caught in a beam of sunlight. I have seen this myself during astral projection. It is very distinct. The air itself seems composed of minute discrete particles, giving it a kind of sandy texture to the visual perception. It is sometimes possible to observe a similar effect in a room at advanced twilight before the lights have been turned on, when the eyes are fully adapted to the dimness, except that during astral projection the air seems to glow golden.

As for the radio being turned on, the most obvious explanation is that Bender turned it on himself during his period of projection, in the same way a person sleepwalking will perform various actions with no knowledge, after waking, of having done them. The radio set to static served as a kind of metaphor signifying the presence of the aliens to Bender, as did the smell of sulfur. It is common for those having visions of spiritual beings to smell scents. When the spirits are perceived to be saints and angels, the smells are usually pleasant flower or incense scents. But when they are perceived as demons, the smell of sulfur is often reported. This smell may have been a cue from Bender's unconscious mind that he should not trust the aliens that subsequently appeared to him.

Returning from a two-week vacation, Bender discovered that his radio had been left on the whole while, tuned to an empty part of the band, and that the smell of burning sulfur lingered in his room. While preparing for bed, he felt a prickling at the back of his neck and his eyes began to water. Blue lights swirled around his room. He became dizzy, his head started to ache, and his forehead above his eyes felt puffy. As he stumbled over to the bed and threw himself across it, his body grew very cold. He reported that the room seemed to grow dark, yet he was still able to see. Three men dressed in black appeared, floating about a foot above the surface of the floor. Bender felt his body become lighter, and his fear departed. The eyes of the three suddenly lit up as they communicated with him telepathically.

Vanishing Metal Talisman

Informing Bender that he had been chosen to receive their revelations, they gave him a piece of metal with which he could summon them if he wished to communicate with them. Bender put the piece of metal—which he described as hard, light, and shining—into his "locked box" for the night; it was then around two in the morning. When he awoke the next morning, he went to the box to look at the metal object, only to discover that it had somehow vanished out of the locked box. Two days later, he again looked in the box, and there was the piece of metal in the same place that he had put it. He decided to use it to contact the three aliens according to their instructions, which consisted of holding the metal in his hand, turning on his radio to the empty part of the dial, and repeating several times the magic word (I cannot resist calling it that) "Kazik."

His body immediately became cold and his head began to ache. He lay on his bed, and almost at once found himself leaving his body. Looking back, he saw his physical body still lying on the bed. He felt as if he floated on a cloud, but the place above his eyes continued to hurt. After a sudden jolt, the darkness cleared away and he found himself surrounded by a golden glow. He saw that he was seated in a circular room with metal walls and a glass dome. Outside the dome was a night sky filled with stars. Bender immediately assumed that he was inside a flying saucer.

An alien activated a kind of circular picture tube, in which Bender saw scenes that were in full color and appeared three-dimensional. The alien proceeded to give Bender a kind of travel documentary of its home world and the various doings of the alien race that I will not relate, since it has no relevance to the subject of astral projection. However, the circular viewing tube is interesting because it parallels very closely the experience of Oliver Fox as a child, when the fairy came to him and showed him a circular projection of an animated farmhouse scene, in full color, which Fox from his Edwardian-era perspective could only compare to a magic lantern slide projection.

The appearance, disappearance, and subsequent reappearance of the piece of metal that acted as a kind of touchstone for Bender to establish contact with the aliens strongly suggests that it was an astral rather than a physical object. This is not absolutely certain, since it lies within the power of spirits to veil the visual perception of human beings, causing them to fail to see things that are right in front of them. Lower spirits frequently do this as a kind of joke, to make people waste time searching for personal items that are in plain sight the whole time. You may have experienced this trickery in your own life, if you have ever looked for your eyeglasses, or your pen, or your car keys, have been unable to find them, and subsequently have seen them sitting on the table or counter in open view where they would have been impossible to miss.

It is possible that the piece of metal was an object Bender picked up away from his house while in an entranced state of mind. Usually when metal that is supposed to have come from an alien implant or a space vessel is subjected to spectrum analysis, it is found to be composed of a common alloy. Unless spirits have the ability to cause apports and thus make objects pop into existence from empty space, either the metal object never existed, or it was acquired in the usual way from some terrestrial source by Bender.

The Men in Black

The three aliens are a version of the Men in Black who figure so frequently in the lore of UFO sightings. They usually appear shortly after an event to question the one who has seen the UFO, and to warn that person not to talk about the sighting. They wear black suits, black ties, black shoes and socks, but their shirts are usually said to be white. Bender's description differs in this regard. "All the other apparel such as ties, shirts, stockings and shoes was also black. They wore hats, of Homburg style, also black. Their faces were unpleasant to look at. Their eyes shone like tiny flashlight bulbs and the teeth were pearly white, set in a very dark complexion. I could not see their hands; they were covered by black gloves."[179]

It is possible that these astral spirits are part of the mind's own coping and survival mechanism, and are activated when an individual is in danger of experiencing sights and concepts during astral projection that might, in one way or another, prove dangerous to either his health or his sanity. This survival mechanism probably takes many forms. For Oliver Fox, it was the symbol of the Egyptian ankh—the symbol of life—that appeared in front of his inner vision and blocked his path whenever he tried to use his pineal-doorway mode of astral projection. It also took the form for Fox of his wife's voice warning him that he was in danger. I suspect that hearing this kind of warning voice is not uncommon for those who engage in serious experiments in astral projection.

There seems to exist within the depths of the mind either an automatic mechanism or an intelligent agent of some kind capable of preventing astral projection when there is the unconscious perception that some form of danger is being approached. It is difficult to know whether the danger warned against in these instances is real or an illusion. It appears similar to the blocks, which arise during psychoanalysis, that prevent a patient from facing up to certain key truths about his own mental state. In my opinion, the Men in Black are an astral manifestation of this coping mechanism. Whether they are protecting the consciousness of the astral traveler, or secrets held by entities dwelling in the astral world, is another question.

---

179.   Bender, *Flying Saucers and the Three Men.*

PART
TWO
PRACTICE

CHAPTER
TEN
Uses of Ritual

Shamans always use a ritual structure as a support for their soul flights. As we have seen, for the shamans of Siberia it often involved ascending the trunk of the world tree that is the living axis of the universe in a series of levels, represented physically by notches cut into the trunk of whatever tree or pole was used to embody the World Tree. A shaman may also mimic the movements and sounds of the totemic beast that carries his astral body away from his physical body, as a way of becoming one with the beast. In these and other ways, he pantomimes the initialization of soul flight, but the actual journey is done while he lies in a state of trance, motionless and insensible. Drumming, chanting, dancing, and the piping of flutes or whistling sounds made with the lips may also be a part of the separation ritual.

Once the soul flight begins, the ritual has served its primary purpose. It is a way of opening the astral gateway leading either upward to the heavens inhabited by gods and spirits, or down into the maw of the underworld where primitive peoples believed monsters, demons, and the souls of the dead to dwell. The shaman's use of ritualistic climbing is significant as a technique for separating the astral body. Both Sylvan Muldoon and Oliver Fox recommended that those attempting to project their astral bodies should imagine that they were climbing or ascending. Aleister Crowley advised that those seeking adepthood would do well to practice the Golden Dawn technique of Rising on the Planes once a day. Rituals involving acts of ascent are helpful in the initial stages of soul flight. The ascent may be physically represented by climbing a slope, stairs, or ladder in order to reach an elevated chamber or platform from which the actual projection occurs, but it should always be accompanied by the visualization of an ascent.

A repeated ritual builds habitual responses in the mind that spill over to the body so that, when done regularly, the ritual is capable of causing physiological changes, such as variations in heart rate, blood pressure, body temperature, and brain-wave activity. It is the change in brain function that most concerns us. Through repetition, a conditioned response can be created that is specific to the ritual, and occurs only within the ritual context. We see conditioned responses every day. The Russian physiologist Ivan Pavlov received the Nobel Prize in 1904 in part for demonstrating that a dog could be conditioned to salivate at the sound of a bell when the sound was associated in the mind of the dog with food. Because the response conditioned by a ritual does not occur at any other time except during the conduct of the ritual, the response can be isolated and separated from daily life. This is useful in order to generate a response that we would not wish to cause while doing such mundane tasks as driving a car, having dinner with friends, or working at the office.

Ritual serves the double function of helping to induce the separation of the subtle body at a desired time and place, while preventing the accidental separation from occurring when it is not desired. When a change in the mind-body gestalt is keyed specifically to a certain ritual, that change will not occur in the absence of the ritual trigger. Those with an abundance of psychic ability who practice the technique of astral projection at different times, in various places and in several ways, without enclosing it in any ritual pattern, may find that they are experiencing spontaneous soul flight when they do not wish it to occur, and do not seek to cause it. This lack of control can be frightening. The practice of astral projection only within a ritual context ensures that it remains controlled.

The ritual circle is a useful visual metaphor for ritual itself. The circle encloses a space, dividing the inside from the outside. The inside is exalted, elevated, and heightened in various ways for the purpose of accomplishing the ritual desire, whereas the outside is ordinary and unchanged. Esoteric potency or *mana* can be accumulated and stored within the ritual circle in the same way that energy is concentrated within a battery—because the boundary of the circle prevents it from flowing away. At the same time, the barrier of the circle excludes any discordant emotions, thoughts, or spiritual entities that might interfere with the realization of the ritual purpose. In a real sense, the entire structure of the ritual is an enclosing circle that divides the mundane universe from the heightened, special place conducive to the purpose for which the ritual is worked.

Use of Ritual Often Misunderstood

Spiritualists had little understanding of the use of ritual, either for transformation or for personal security. They conducted their astral experiments and séances in a casual way, disdaining what they conceived to be the outmoded trappings of the ceremonial occultism of the Middle Ages. They did not bother with a circle of protection, or with the use of symbols to act as gateways, or with names of power designed to command various types of spiritual beings, such as were used by members of the Golden Dawn. This indifference is encountered quite often in modern times. Channelers in general express contempt for ritual because they believe that they do not need it in order to establish communication with the spirits that speak through their voices. True enough. But they seldom consider that they may require ritual to prevent those spirits from speaking, or acting, through them.

Similarly, the remote viewers employed by the CIA and American military intelligence during the various incarnations of Project STAR GATE had, in general, a contempt for ritual, even though they employed a ritual of their own spontaneous design for their extended remote viewing sessions. They were so concerned about being scientific in their approach to remote viewing that they refused to admit or even to recognize that they were engaged in astral projection because of the negative connotation the term holds in the scientific community. Considering that one of them was a Tarot-card reader, this nicety of terminology appears a bit silly. Because they did not use a formal ritual structure, they were poorly protected when confronted by astral entities with malicious intentions. Their response was to retreat as rapidly as possible.

The formation of simple rituals is difficult to avoid when repeating the same actions on a regular basis. They define themselves spontaneously. We all have little rituals that help us get through our daily tasks. The morning grooming ritual. The first cigarette of the day ritual. The meet a friend in the street ritual. Each of these and a hundred others are like intricate little dances we do to facilitate the particular circumstances from which they arise. We do not consciously compose them. They shape themselves as behaviors that have served us well in the past, and which we rely on to serve us in the future. We have these little daily rituals stored away in our heads, awaiting only a particular set of triggers to start them running. Life would be much more difficult without them.

There is a quantum difference between a ritual that has created itself in an unconscious way, as a necessary and unavoidable response of the mind to repeated actions, and a ritual that has been deliberately and consciously structured for specific purposes, to both heighten desired responses in the mind and body and to exclude discordant influences that might hinder those responses. The one is a Model T Ford, and the other a Ferrari Testarossa. Since the natural formation of a ritual pattern of some kind is inevitable, it only makes sense to impose a pattern calculated to yield the best results.

Constructing Your Own Ritual

In constructing a ritual for soul flight, a factor that must always be considered is that the unconscious mind knows better than the conscious mind which symbolic forms are potent and which are weak. The unconscious cannot be relied upon to create complete effective rituals, but it knows what it likes. Sometimes a ritual that seems as though it should be effective in the abstract turns out to be lifeless in daily practice. When this happens, there is only one thing to do—the awareness must be opened to the unconscious mind so that it can express its needs, in the form of symbols, words, sounds, actions, gestures, and postures. A dead ritual can be made to live if changes in its pattern suggested by the unconscious are accepted and incorporated into it. There is nothing more pointless than the attempt to impose by brute force a ritual that the unconscious rejects.

You will know your composed ritual for astral projection has been rejected if, after you have performed it for two or three weeks on a regular basis, it remains lifeless. Then there are only two recourses—you must discard it entirely and compose a new ritual, or you must open your mind and allow changes in the ritual to suggest themselves during the course of its daily enactment. The second course is better because, if you permit it, your unconscious will rewrite your ritual for you and make it effective. If you choose to impose a second ritual, there is no guarantee that it will contain any greater measure of vitality than the first, and you may end up having to discard it also.

Your own ritual is always better than a ritual composed by somebody else because your own ritual arises from your preconceptions and requirements. I can suggest a ritual structure to you that is effective in its general principles, but I cannot ensure that it is perfectly adapted to your personal needs. It may be dead to you when you practice it and, if so, you will need to allow your unconscious mind to modify it until it comes alive for you. Ritual is the most intimate of activities. The reactions of each individual to each ritual are unique, and the factors that cause those responses are so complex that it is utterly impossible to predict them. The most effective ritual structure for each person must be arrived at through the use of intuition coupled with trial and error.

The process is made easier if a sound basic ritual structure is adopted in the beginning. Such a structure provides a stable symbolic foundation upon which to build your unique personal ritual. You can think of the basic ritual described below as a blueprint for a house. If designed well by the architect, the blueprint provides all the basic needs in a balanced way, but everyone who lives in a house built from a general blueprint will personalize such a house and make it unique.

Bear in mind that ritual is more than the mere repetition of a set of actions. This is a large part of its effectiveness, but some actions are inherently more meaningful than others. Some symbols are more potent than other symbols, either on a universal level as archetypes or on a personal level for the individual. The symbolic elements chosen to compose a ritual are not arbitrary, but arise from a sense of necessity that lies beneath the level of words. It may be impossible to express in an articulate way the reason one symbol is more effective than another symbol, or why one ritual action is powerful and another weak, but you will sense the difference when you experiment with the two.

Components of the General Ritual of Projection

Before presenting a general ritual of soul flight, to serve as a template upon which to build your own personal ritual, it will be useful to examine its component parts in the abstract. Many other ritual structures might be devised, but the form presented here contains the basic requirements needed for success and security. The parts of the ritual have been divided into two groups. The column on the left pertains to the house of ritual, which is erected around what is perceived as the boundary of the body. The column on the right pertains to the inhabitant of that house, and what is done with the body and mind during the enactment of the ritual.

1.	Chamber	6.	Posture
2.	Door	7.	Gesture
3.	Key	8.	Sound
4.	Corridor	9.	Imagery
5.	Elevator	10.	Will

Chamber

The ritual is conducted on the astral level, its parts created and sustained in the imagination. These astral components are reinforced by a physical space, material objects, and movements of the body. What is done on the physical level during ritual is reflected on the astral level, but the astral environment often differs in its details from the physical environment. For example, the physical space in which the ritual is enacted will seldom look the same as the astral space. Because the astral world can be shaped and transformed by the imagination and the will, the astral space can be made larger, richer, and more beautiful than the physical space, or it can be molded in specific ways to serve the purposes of the ritual.

You will remember that the remote viewers of the CIA adopted the practice of going to their "safe place" on the astral level in their extended experiments, as a staging zone from which to depart on their assignments. This "safe place" was nothing other than a ritual space created on the astral level. The formation of a ritual chamber or temple on the astral level that corresponds with the physical ritual space is universal in modern Western ceremonial magic. Since the CIA operatives had no clear idea of what they were doing—they probably believed they were the first to have invented the technique—their physical ritual space gave poor support to their astral space. Ideally, the physical chamber or place in which the ritual is enacted should have some correspondence with the astral chamber or place that is created and sustained in the imagination.

This correspondence is usually created by moving the body during the ritual in the same way the projection of the body in the astral chamber is moved so that, as the magician physically goes through the motions of the ritual, his astral form does substantially the same things on the astral level in the visualized place of working. For example, when a shaman of Siberia climbed the trunk of the tree or pole erected in the ritual enclosure, he simultaneously climbed up the astral levels of the World Tree. A modern magician will walk three times around the altar in his ritual temple in order to create an invisible vortex of force, while at the same time holding clearly in his imagination that he is walking around a corresponding altar in his astral temple, invoking a visible and tangible vortex on that higher level.

Ritual is thus enacted simultaneously on the physical level and on the astral level—that is, with the physical body in the material chamber and with the astral body in the astral chamber. Unless the mind is divided in this way between physical and astral perception, the ritual will have little efficacy. The point of consciousness cannot occupy both levels simultaneously, but it can jump back and forth between then so that it seems to occupy both levels. The ritual space is here referred to as a chamber, but on the astral level it may be a place out of doors, or even a place that bears no correspondence with any earthly environment. As a practical matter, it is useful to make the ritual place of working on the astral level somewhat similar to the physical place of working. Doing so allows it to be sustained more easily in the imagination. Most who experiment with soul flight will do so in a room of their house or apartment, so a room is a good choice for an astral place.

Whenever we imagine an environment in our mind, we create it on the astral level. This happens automatically. The mind of the average person is too vacillating and weak to create an astral environment that has any significant degree of duration. Astral places are formed and discarded by the restless thoughts of every man, woman, and child from moment to moment. No doubt even the higher animals generate astral landscapes of a simple type. However, when a magician trained in the techniques of Western magic creates an astral temple, he is able through the exercise of concentration to visualize it with greater than average clarity and in uncommon detail. Each time a magician works the ritual, he reinforces the astral place of working, so that it is sustained in the back of his mind between ritual operations. It becomes as real a place as any environment can be in the ever-shifting astral world.

The astral chamber is equivalent to the magic circle, in the sense that its four walls erect a boundary that separates the place of working from the greater astral world. The walls both contain the mental energies raised during the ritual, and prevent the entry of discordant forces that might hinder the ritual or even render it impossible. Even if the walls are not seamless in the physical room in which the ritual is enacted, they can be made so on the astral level because the astral chamber does not need to correspond with the physical chamber in all its details. Simply by not visualizing anything that lies on the other side of the walls, floor, or ceiling of the windowless astral chamber, those walls can be rendered completely impervious.

Door

The only opening in the astral chamber described in the following ritual is a single closed door. Just as the walls of the chamber correspond in a symbolic way with the barrier of the magic circle, so the door corresponds with the point at the center of the circle through which entry or exit of the circle is enabled. A magic circle can have only one opening: the point at its center. By expanding the point, it becomes an aperture into or out of the circle. It is necessary to create a doorway in the astral chamber to allow travel in the projected astral body to other places in the astral world.

On the astral level, it is possible to shift the central aperture of the circle to its circumference. This change is sometimes reflected in the physical temple of working magicians by moving the altar—which ideally resides in the center of the chamber—to one of the four walls of the room. It is usually done for convenience, to obtain a larger open floor area. The altar symbolizes the center of the magic circle, even when it is placed at its edge. The door visualized in the astral chamber does not need to have a corresponding door in the actual room in which the ritual is conducted because it represents not the physical door of the room, but rather the expanded central point of the ritual circle—which is understood to be embodied in the four walls of the astral chamber.

Key

The key does more than simply lock and unlock the door of the astral chamber. It determines by its symbolism what environment the door opens upon. On the physical level, there are many kinds of symbolic keys that can be used to access different astral locations and different astral planes. These will be treated in detail in later chapters. The tattwa symbols used to open astral gateways by members of the Golden Dawn are one type of key. The twenty-two picture cards of the Tarot are another type. The ancient Germanic symbols known as runes are yet a third kind of key.

The key, visualized in the form of a modern keycard on the astral level, is used to unlock the door of the astral chamber when you exit the chamber in your projected astral form. The door is conceived to be of a type that will relock itself behind you automatically. The locked door keeps your physical body safe from harm while your awareness is elsewhere. Because you are protected by the magic circle, the only access from the astral world to your physical place of working, where you sit or lie during the ritual, is through the astral chamber, and entry into that chamber is only possible through the door. When the door is locked, and you carry the keycard with you, no astral spirit can gain entry.

You might object that, since the astral chamber is only visualized in the imagination, its walls are not real, and so locking the door is meaningless. However, on the astral level, things visualized clearly in the imagination have as much reality and tangibility as any astral entity. Or to put it another way, a locked astral door is as real a barrier to a spirit as a locked physical door would be to a living human being. The stronger and the more tightly sealed it is imagined to be, the more substantial it becomes.

The symbol that serves as the astral key selects the particular type of astral environment to which the door will provide access. All other astral landscapes are excluded, or tuned out, by the specific occult vibrations of the key, which emits a kind of psychic musical chord that is different for each key. The key does not open the door of the chamber directly upon that astral environment, however. In order to reach the desired location in the astral world, it is necessary to travel there in the astral body. This travel is effected laterally or horizontally, so to speak, across the base level of the astral plane that corresponds closely with the physical world. When the door is opened by the keycard, it leads into a long, windowless corridor through which this journey may be safely made.

Corridor

There are various ways to express the transition from one astral landscape to another. A popular method is by flying through the air in the astral body until the desired location is reached. Shamans often flew on the backs of great birds, but the astral body can fly on its own, either with or without wings. A bird was helpful to the shaman as a kind of animal guide. A more mundane way is by walking to the location. In the astral world, it is possible to take giant gliding steps that cover large distances with each stride. You may remember having done this in your dreams.

The lower level of the astral corresponds very closely with the physical world. Indeed, it is often difficult for astral travelers to tell the difference. They believe themselves to be moving through the physical world. This is impossible, as the astral body cannot be present in our physical reality. Physical things stay on the physical plane, and astral things stay on the astral plane. Confusion arises when astral travelers projecting on the base astral plane that corresponds most closely with the physical plane are perceived by other human beings during waking consciousness. Then it appears to those who have seen the astral double that the double is present in the physical world. Not so. The double always remains in the astral world, but for a short time the observer has seen the astral double overlaid upon the backdrop of the physical world.

As members of Theosophy and the Golden Dawn clearly defined in their writings, there are two possible movements in the astral. A traveler can move across the astral landscape in the same way a traveler in the material world moves from one location to another on the face of the earth. This is the only way many individuals understand astral travel—as a change of location across the lower astral plane that corresponds with the physical world, so that the astral traveler seems to be moving through the physical world. However, in addition to horizontal movement across the base astral plane, there is vertical movement up and down the heavenly and infernal astral levels. The Theosophical system of seven distinct planes, one above the other, is an artificial imposition on the astral world, which has an infinite number of possible levels or zones of reality. Seven is a number laden with esoteric significance, and was often used in religious and occult texts to indicate related sets of realms, worlds, or ideas.

Division of modes of travel through the astral world into horizontal movement across a plane, and vertical movement through successive planes, was not invented by Theosophists, but is an essential part of the objective reality of the astral world. When a Siberian shaman of the Altaic people wished to visit the land of the dead, he first journeyed across the base astral plane, traversing barren steppes and high mountain ranges, to reach the gaping black pit known as the *yer mesi* (Jaws of the Earth) into which he descended to reach the underworld. Sometimes, access was by direct descent through seven lower levels, illustrating that these two types of movement through the astral world are independent of each other.[180]

Each location on the earth has its astral correspondences. The level of the astral nearest the physical world is virtually identical in appearance to the physical world. It is possible for an astral traveler to travel up and down the astral levels, while staying in exactly the same place. For example, you could travel vertically through the astral while remaining in a hotel room in Baltimore, and as you ascended or descended, the appearance of the hotel room would change. The farther you ascended or descended, the greater the changes would be, until the hotel room ceased to exist and was replaced by a completely different environment.

In the ritual structure presented in this book, travel across the lower astral, and hence travel across the surface of the physical world from place to place, is effected by means of a corridor extending from the doorway of the ritual chamber. Where the corridor leads is

---

180. Eliade, 200–2.

determined in a general sense by the symbolism on the keycard used to unlock the door. The corridor will lead to an environment that is in harmony with the nature of the key. When traveling across the landscape of the physical world, the key can be made quite narrow and specific—an address in a particular city, for example.

The corridor has no windows or doors on its sides. This provides secure travel, since there is no entry to the corridor, which leads only to a single place. At its far end, there is a single locked door that is accessed with the same keycard that opens the door of the chamber. Beyond this door is a smaller square room. In the opposite wall of the room is set a second door, and when this door is unlocked with the keycard, it opens directly onto the astral landscape or location defined by the key. The traveler takes the keycard out of its slot and retains it when exiting this small room.

Elevator

The small, square room at the end of the corridor is a special kind of elevator. Beside the second door, beneath the slot of the cardlock, is a keypad with five buttons arranged in the shape of a cross. The central button, marked with a circle, lights up when the elevator comes to a stop, and remains illuminated while it is at rest. The top button has on it an up arrow, and the one below a down arrow; the button on the left has an arrow that points left, and the one on the right an arrow that points right.

When journeying across the astral world on the base level that reflects the physical world, the elevator does not ascend or descend and none of these buttons are used. However, when the traveler wishes to rise or fall through the planes, he presses either the button marked up or the one below it marked down, in order to ascend or descend as far as desired. This vertical movement occurs at the same location that was reached by traveling through the corridor. For example, if the corridor led to the astral reflection of Paris, ascending the planes would take place in the astral equivalent of Paris. While the elevator is ascending, the up button remains illuminated. When it reaches its level, the central button lights.

The elevator travels not only up and down through the astral levels in the present, but can also carry you to the future or the past. The button with the arrow that points to the left is pressed to move back into the past; the button with the arrow that points right takes you forward into the future. Movement through time occurs on the base level of the astral world, at the location accessed through the corridor. For example, if the corridor led to Paris, pressing the back button would take you to the time in the past specified on your key. You might have written on your key, "Champs-Élysées, Paris, on June 21, 1851." The corridor would take you to the physical place, and the elevator would take you to the specified time.

Descent on the elevator leads to the infernal regions, and should not be casually undertaken. It is possible to reach the lower levels of the Christian hell, and to interact with the damned souls and demonic inhabitants of those levels, by descending in the elevator and exiting through the far door. Any level of any hell may be reached in this way—the levels of the astral world are infinite in number, despite the narrow templates that have been imposed on them by individual religions and cults. What you believe becomes your personal reality in the astral world. If you firmly believe that there are only seven astral levels, that is how many you will experience. If you believe that you will encounter only the spirits of once-living human beings on your travels, that is all you will encounter.

Posture

Soul flight is best accomplished in a reclining posture. A few gifted astral travelers, such as Emanuel Swedenborg, were able to project while walking around, but this is uncommon. The more usual posture is to fully recline on the top of a bed. Doing so makes it convenient to experiment with the projection of the astral double just before going to sleep at night, but this practice has its disadvantage, in that sleep usually comes before useful work can be done. The Golden Dawn preferred the sitting posture and employed it with good success. Most people find that they do not fall out of their chairs, as might be expected. This is also true for hypnosis—hypnotized subjects rarely fall from their chairs. The body automatically maintains its balance.

My own recommendation is that experiments of projection be done lying on top of a bed. You may, if you wish, practice while seated, but better results are usually gained by those who lie on their backs. I do not recommend that you practice while in bed under the covers, as a general rule, only because it is too easy to drift into ordinary sleep due to the sleep habits you have formed throughout your life. For the same reason, it is best to practice soul flight at a time of day other than your usual time for going to bed. I prefer the afternoon or early evening.

The room should be dim or dark. It is not necessary to have total darkness. The temperature should be moderate, so that you do not notice it. Wear loose clothing that leaves your breathing and the circulation of blood in your body unrestricted. You should avoid wearing jewelry and such things as a wristwatch, a hearing aid, eyeglasses, or shoes—

anything likely to feel tight or that exerts pressure on your body. However, if you are so comfortable wearing your hearing aid or watch that you never notice them, then you can leave them on. Do not worry that you will need your glasses in the astral world—you no more require eyeglasses when you engage in soul flight than you do when you dream. Soul flight is a kind of consciously directed waking dream. The trick is to induce a dream state without falling asleep. For this you need a peaceful mind, a comfortable and quiet environment, and a relaxed body.

It is best to lie on your back if you project while on a bed. It is possible to project the astral body lying on your side or stomach, but success with these postures is rare. Your legs or feet should not be crossed one over the other, as doing so tends to inhibit the free flow of energies throughout the body. Your arms may be left at your sides, but you may find it better to fold your hands over the center of your abdomen at your solar plexus. Energy and warmth are focused beneath the folded hands. If you are using a physical image or inscription as a key, as you should in most cases, you will want to place it beneath your folded hands, assuming it is something that cannot be damaged by perspiration or your movements on the bed, should it slip under you.

Gesture

Since the ritual of soul flight is done while lying down, the motions involved occur mostly on the astral level. I have reduced the ritual structure to its necessary minimum. There are three very basic gestures: casting the circle, the sign of departure, and the sign of return.

For convenience, the circle may be cast while sitting on the middle of the bed from which the projection is to be made. This is done by drawing a small circle in the air in front of your chest with your right index finger, at the level of your heart. The circle is drawn flat, as though you were projecting the tip of your finger up from under the surface of water and drawing the circle in the surface of the water from beneath. Slowly and smoothly, draw it sunwise, which is the same as clockwise from a perspective looking down at it from above. Join the end with the beginning so that the band of this invisible circle is seamless.

As you draw the small reclining circle, visualize at the same time as clearly as you are able a larger circle of light painting itself upon the air of your practice chamber around your bed, so that you are completely enclosed in the larger circle. This circle of light imitates the motion of your finger, moving around the room in a clockwise direction, and forms itself on the same horizontal plane as the tip of your finger, which should be at the level of your heart as you sit up on the middle of the bed. The circle of light is the real circle you draw—the small circle only symbolizes it. Sustain this glowing circle of golden light that surrounds your bed clearly in your imagination for a minute or so, and when at last you turn your thoughts to other matters, keep it in the back of your mind. It continues to float upon the air of your chamber, surrounding you and protecting you, throughout the exercise.

Lie back comfortably upon the bed, and prepare yourself to visualize the astral chamber. With your right index finger, draw upon the air in front of your face a small counterclockwise circle of blue light. Touch the center of this circle with your finger and extend a red line straight up through the circumference of the circle. The length of this line should be about three times the radius of the circle, so that the line projects above the circle for a distance equal to the circle's diameter. As you draw this symbol, be aware that the circle represents the circle of your body, and the line shows the departure of your consciousness from your body. Close your eyes, but hold the symbol of the blue circle and the red line in your inner sight for a minute or so, reinforcing it with your imagination when it becomes dim. Try to see it as clearly as you can, as though it were projected against the inner surface of your eyelids.

The blue circle also stands for the astral chamber. The red line begins at the center of the circle, which is its natural aperture, and represents the extension of the corridor from the door of the chamber. The red line terminates at the elevator. It is not necessary to be conscious of these correspondences during the practice of soul flight, but you should be aware that they exist. The red line pierces the blue circle at its center and flies beyond its boundary to its destination. It is a sign of going out of the body.

When you finish your exercise and lie on your bed in the astral chamber in your projected astral body, you must make the opposite sign of return with your right index finger upon the air in front of your face. This has the same shape and colors as the sign of departure, but is formed in a different way. The sign of return is made by drawing a blue circle clockwise upon the air, and then tracing a red line downward from outside the circle through the circumference to terminate at the center of the circle. This symbol represents the return of the astral body to the physical body. It is formed on the air of the astral chamber while still in the astral body, as a guide to its return, just as the sign of departure is formed in the physical chamber before the astral body departs the physical body, as a foreshadowing of its departure. The sign of departure is the first thing done in the physical chamber after the circle is projected, and the sign of return is the last thing done in the astral chamber before the circle is indrawn.

Indrawing the circle is an easy matter. Sit up on the bed in your physical chamber, so that the projected circle is once again at the level of your heart. Visualize it around your bed as before, glowing with pale golden light as it floats upon the air. Mentally cause it to shrink inward toward your heart until it is drawn all the way into your chest and forms a bright star in your heart center. Allow it to disperse its gentle warmth throughout your body, even to the tips of your fingers and toes, as it dissolves and melts away through your bloodstream.

Sound

Sound can act as a vehicle to carry the consciousness out of the body. It is possible to ride sound as you might ride a horse, and allow it to do the work of crossing the distance on the astral level. It can take the form of composed music, if you find that the music does not engage too closely your thoughts or emotions. Classical music is best for this purpose. Something should be chosen that can play in the background for an hour or so without any abrupt changes of tempo. You should avoid works with clashing cymbals and thundering drums. For the same reason, rock-and-roll music is not the best type of music for astral projection. Discordant sounds and jarring changes will cause you to lose your concentration, which must be focused on the visualization of the astral components of the ritual, not on the music. It is best to experiment with music, and if you find that it distracts you rather than provides you with a sound vehicle that carries your mind like a boat floating down a river, do not use it.

A more reliable sound vehicle is white noise, which is any hissing or fuzzy sustained noise, such as the sound of a television tuned to a channel that has no signal. True white noise contains all possible sound tones mingled together, but you can get much the same effect from any sustained background noise, such as the low rumble of a furnace. To be effective, the sound should be sustained. The ticking of a clock or metronome is not particularly helpful because the sound is interrupted rather than continuous, although a clock ticking may not interfere with your practice if you are so accustomed to it that you no longer consciously hear it.

You can create your own sound vehicle to ride into the astral by humming or whistling a single sustained tone very softly over and over. I find a low whistle effective. I sustain a tone on my breath and project it mentally outward, allowing it to carry my awareness away from my physical location. When I run out of air, I simply breathe in and renew the tone. Sometimes it can be effective to allow the whistle or hum to vary slightly, by letting it rise or sink in pitch. This must be done according to the directive of your intuition. It is not something you can plan ahead of time. If it feels right to you that you allow the tone you are creating to gently rise or fall in pitch, do so. It may make a sort of atonal melody, but you should not let your awareness focus on the sound as music, but instead continue to ride it farther and farther away from your body.

This sound technique is effective as a way of initially entering the astral chamber. Visualize the chamber as you sustain the tone, and allow yourself to be carried to the astral chamber, where you will find yourself lying on your bed, just as you are in your physical chamber of practice. When you feel yourself present in the astral chamber, you can allow the whistle or hum to cease. Do not be surprised if your low whistle has some curious effects on those in the same house or building where you are practicing. Even though the whistle may be much too low for anyone else to hear, the focus and projection of your mind will make others around you restless and uneasy. If someone is sleeping in the same house, they may begin to talk in their sleep, or they may even wake up. This is merely a side effect caused by the intense focus of your awareness, and should not be allowed to become a distraction in your work.

Imagery

The use of creative imagery is crucial to success in this ritual of soul flight. The protective circle, the sign of departure, and the sign of return must all be formed in the imagination so clearly that they seem present before your eyes. You do not need to actually see these symbols, but you must imagine them more clearly than you ordinarily imagine forms in your mind. The astral chamber, the corridor, and the elevator must be created in the mind, and sustained while you are present within them in your astral body. They are the ritual machine that launches you to your ultimate destination. How effectively they work depends on how well you create them on the astral level.

The way to create an astral object or environment such as the astral chamber is by continuing to visualize it over and over as it fades. This is best done by focusing the awareness on details, such as the pattern of the wallpaper, the shape of the overhead lighting fixture, the texture of the quilt or blanket beneath you on the bed, the way the light reflects from the floorboards or tiles, the colors of the rug, the shape of the molding around the door. All details of the chamber must be created by you, and re-created by visualizing them over and over.

In the beginning, you will have to invent details, but as you go back to the astral chamber day after day in the course of your regular practice, you will discover that it changes in subtle ways, and that new furnishings or details of its décor suggest themselves. It is an astral place, so its form is not fixed. You hold it together by re-imagining it, but if you are successful in creating the chamber on the astral level, it will begin to sustain itself, so that the process becomes less an exercise of creating the chamber anew each day, and more a matter of visiting a place that already exists.

Will

Your will is the driving force that projects you from your physical body to the astral landscape that you wish to inhabit temporarily. How effectively you are able to use it depends on your powers of concentration. There are exercises designed to enhance concentration, but we will not go into them, since they should not be necessary for the average person with a strong determination to succeed in soul flight.

A useful trick is to imagine that you project your astral awareness out of your body through your ajna chakra, the so-called third eye that is located approximately between your eyebrows. You can intensify your focus by turning your eyes to look at this spot with your eyelids closed, but you should not turn them so strongly that the strain becomes a distraction and reduces the effectiveness of your practice. A gentle turning inward and upward works best. Imagine that you see the sign of projection shining in the darkness, and will yourself to rise toward it. Do not attempt to visualize your astral body—simply use your willpower to lift your awareness toward the sign of projection, which recedes back into the darkness as you approach, drawing you out of your body. Eventually you will catch up to it, and when you do, visualize it changing into the astral chamber, and visualize that you are present within the astral chamber in your astral body.

The use of the power of the will is crucial in successful astral projection because it is the driving energy that allows you to progress and pass from place to place. But it cannot be forced. If you push too hard, you will defeat yourself and get nowhere. A gentle, constant, determined pressure is best. It is like the straining of the muscles of the body, only it occurs within the mind and the effort is directed at achieving the desired purpose. Dripping water will wear away the hardest stone, and a constant pressure of the will toward an objective will overcome any obstacle.

The Ritual of Soul Flight

Sit on the center of your bed with the lights dimmed. Mentally project the circle of light around the physical chamber clockwise at the level of your heart, while using a small symbolic circle made with your right index finger to guide its projection. When you have visualized the large circle clearly, lie back on the bed. Make the sign of departure in the air before your face with your right hand. Close your eyes and sustain the sign of departure in your mind, as though it were projected on the inner surface of your eyelids or upon the inner surface of your forehead at your ajna chakra. Be aware that the blue circle in the sign of departure is your body, and is also in an expanded sense the circle of light you have projected around your bed. The red line that extends upward from the center of the circle is your flight path into the astral world.

The symbolic key you have chosen to define the astral place or environment you wish to visit should be beneath your hands on your abdomen when you are lying down. If you find this positioning of the hands uncomfortable, you may wish to lay the key on your abdomen and leave your arms at your sides. The best location for the key is over the solar plexus. The slight pressure of the weight of the hands bearing on the solar plexus can assist the separation of the astral body. You will carry an astral double of the key with you when you enter your astral chamber. It is not identical to the physical key, but is always in the form of a plasticized keycard.

While holding the sign of departure in your mind, let the music or white noise you have set playing in the background carry you up and out of your body, or ride the sustained tone of a quietly whistled note. The use of sound is not essential—if you find it distracting, work in silence using only visual imagery. Let the sign of departure draw you onward. With your physical eyelids still closed, shape the astral chamber around you. See it as though you lie on the bed within the astral chamber with your eyes open. See through your closed eyelids. Place yourself into the astral chamber. You will probably still feel yourself lying or sitting in the physical chamber, but you will also be present in the astral chamber.

With the astral landscape you wish to visit held in your mind, get up in your astral body and walk to the door. It has a modern electronic card reader attached to the side of the frame, even though the door itself may not be that modern. Momentarily insert the card upon which your key is printed into the slot of the card reader to unlock the door. The key may be drawn or written on a piece of paper in the physical world, or printed or inscribed on some other material, but in the astral world it is always on a stiff, plasticized card. Step into the corridor beyond. It is well lighted, but has neither windows nor doors along its sides. Move down the corridor to the far end, holding the location you wish to visit firmly in your thoughts with the keycard still in your hand.

The corridor may seem quite long if the place you wish to visit is far away in space. You can assist your progress down the corridor by using your willpower to push your astral body along in enormous gliding steps, as though you were almost weightless. When you reach the door at the far end, insert your keycard through the slot of the electronic lock and enter the small, square room that is the elevator. Like the corridor, the appearance of the elevator is a matter you must decide for yourself. My chamber, corridor, and elevator are from the Victorian period, paneled in rich, dark mahogany, but you may find a modern décor more conducive to success.

If you are not ascending or descending on the planes, use the keycard to immediately open the opposite door of the elevator onto the place you have chosen to visit. It may not appear as you imagined it in every detail. Do not try to force the astral landscape to conform to your preconceptions, but instead allow it to express itself to you. Remember, you are traveling in the astral world not to experience what you already know, but to experience what you do not know. The door that leads to the elevator will disappear behind you, but you can summon it at any time merely by pressing the keycard to your forehead and willing it to appear.

If you are ascending the planes at the location you have chosen to visit in the astral world, perhaps to communicate with shades of the dead, fairies, or angels, then press the button with the up arrow while you are inside the elevator, and the elevator will ascend to the level you wish to reach. As it ascends, hold your desired destination clearly in your mind. When the elevator stops, use your keycard to open the far door and step into the astral world at that higher level. The first door through which you entered will automatically seal itself when the elevator is above or below the base level of the astral world, and you will not be able to open it until you have returned the elevator to the base level.

All other levels are higher or lower than the base level of the astral world that duplicates the physical world. The resemblance is never perfect because the astral world is a kind of mirror of the mind—and belief, expectation, and emotion distort its reflection, introducing errors. While visiting the base level of the astral, you can watch the astral doubles of the living as they go about their daily lives, and they will appear completely normal to you, so that you seem to be standing in the physical world with them. They will probably not see you or hear you, but if you touch them they will feel your touch as a cool sensation or a light breeze, or perhaps as a slight tickle on the skin. Since they are not inhabiting their astral bodies with their consciousnesses, which function in their physical bodies while they are awake, they usually remain unaware of your presence. Those with an uncommon degree of psychic ability may become aware of you. Sometimes a person with whom you share a close personal connection will see you.

On higher levels, the spirits that are the inhabitants will be aware of you, but may not take any notice of you if they decide that you are not of sufficient interest or importance to engage in dialogue. If you demand their attention, most spirits will give it—very much as a human being might take notice of a particularly noisy and insistent child. Those spirits who are closer to your own level of development, or who have some personal connection with you, will talk with you freely.

It really is not wise to press the down button of the elevator. The infernal levels of the astral world contain spirits of a coarse and sometimes malicious temperament. There you will find human spirits of an unhappy or aggressive nature, who cling to the physical appetites they enjoyed or were enslaved to during their mortal lives, as well as those inhuman spirits known as fallen angels or demons. Hell, if it can be said to exist at all, is an astral construction built by centuries of expectations on the part of the human race. There are different hells that correspond to the various belief systems of different cultures. None of them is a particularly pleasant place to visit.

When you wish to return to your physical body, press the keycard to your forehead and will the door of the elevator to appear. If you look around, you will generally find it in a short while. It tends to merge itself with whatever environment you are visiting, becoming a door in a brick wall, for example, or a door hidden amid a tangle of brush and branches if you are in a forest landscape. It will always be near at hand when you call for it. Insert the keycard into the slot to open the door, and if necessary, press the central button with the circle on it to return to the base level of the astral world. If you are above the base level, the elevator will always stop its descent at the base level—it will never go past into the infernal regions. Then, with your card, exit the elevator through the inner door to the corridor and follow the corridor back to your astral chamber, using the keycard again to open its door. Remember, all doors are opened by inserting the keycard into the slot, and all lock automatically.

Once in the astral chamber, lie down on the bed and make the sign of return in the air in front of your face. You make the sign of return by drawing a blue circle clockwise, then a vertical red line downward to the center of the circle, so that it pierces the circumference of the circle. Hold the sign of return in your imagination and place the keycard beneath your hands on your abdomen. Close your eyes in your astral body so that you see only the sign of return and focus on the center of the blue circle. Concentrate your will on descending back into your physical body by riding down the red line to the center.

When you open your eyes, you will once again be in your physical body. Sit up and mentally will the protective circle of golden light that surrounds your physical chamber in your imagination to constrict itself to a shining star in the center of your chest. Allow the light and warmth of this star to expand through your physical body to your fingers and toes. Do not neglect to indraw the circle at the end of the ritual. It returns your practice chamber to its ordinary state.

CHAPTER ELEVEN

Astral Doorways

The term *astral doorway* is used here to mean a symbol, object, or practice that aids consciousness to perceive the astral world or its inhabitants. Throughout history, certain things have been recognized to assist in both scrying and astral projection. These activities are closely related, and in my opinion are aspects of a single mental faculty that also shows itself in the form of lucid dreams and near death experiences. This psychic talent to gain awareness of the astral world is present in all individuals, but usually lies dormant unless triggered by a traumatic event such as an illness or a sudden physical injury. It appears to be related to the ajna chakra of the body, the mystical third eye between the eyebrows that may correspond with the pineal gland. The regular use of certain objects and practices can help to develop this latent talent.

The underlying unity between scrying and astral projection is indicated by the way in which these activities overlap. At times, astral travelers are aware of being in their projected bodies yet on other occasions feel themselves present in astral landscapes as a disembodied consciousness. Still other times, they observe astral scenes yet remain separated from them, as though they were viewing projected three-dimensional images.

Those who engage in scrying find that the boundaries tend to blur between visions viewed at a distance and visions experienced all around them in the same location they physically occupy. The alchemist Edward Kelley, who was the hired crystal gazer of the Elizabethan mathematician, cartographer, and spiritualist John Dee (1527–1608), would scry spiritual beings within a globe of rock crystal and relate their actions and words to Dee, who then copied the narrative down in his diaries. Kelley was also able to see complex astral landscapes in the crystal. Sometimes, the spirits came completely out of the crystal and were present to Kelley's astral vision in the chamber in which he scried, yet Dee could not see them because he lacked Kelley's psychic talent. On various occasions, they even touched Kelley so that he felt their contact: once pressing a heavy weight on his right shoulder,[181] and another time clawing him about the head.[182]

Not only was the boundary between seeing astral images at a distance and being surrounded by them blurred, but also blurred was the separation between the astral and the physical worlds. Once when Kelley deliberately ignored Dee's familiar spirit, Madimi, so that he could examine a book, the spirit repeatedly tapped the book on the cover to get his attention, and at last tried to pull the book out of Kelley's hands. Dee could not see the spirit, but he heard the taps on the parchment cover of the book.[183] Another time, a spirit knocked over an object in the scrying chamber, and both men saw it and heard it fall. The most singular event of a physical kind was the apport of a crystal-scrying globe that appeared out of thin air in the scrying chamber beneath the window. This globe subsequently became Dee's principal showstone, and was used by Kelley with excellent results.

Four Levels of Astral Awareness

You will remember that Emanuel Swedenborg distinguished three types of astral projection, although he did not use that term, but instead resorted to biblical references. The naked pro-

---

181. Casaubon, *True & Faithful Relation*, 25.

182. Ibid., 62.

183. Ibid., 31.

jection of his awareness into astral scenes he referred to as being "in the spirit," and regular astral projection, during which he was able to feel as well as see and hear, he called being "taken out of the body." The third type, which was a deeper and more complete experience of astral projection in which he remained in his physical body yet completely lost awareness of his physical surroundings while walking in an astral vision, he termed being "carried by the Spirit into another place."[184] If we add scrying to Swedenborg's three types of astral projection, the result is four successively deeper levels of astral awareness:

1. Scrying: visual perception of astral scenes at a distance

2. Projection in the spirit: direct disembodied perception of astral scenes

3. Projection out of body: direct perception of astral scenes in the astral double

4. Projection to another place: direct perception of astral scenes in the physical body

Swedenborg's final kind of vision—being present within an astral landscape in the physical body—is not really possible, but it can seem completely real to those who experience it. It happens when an astral scene is superimposed on the perception of physical surroundings, completely excluding that perception, so that the person experiencing it appears to walk through the astral landscape in the flesh. This is the level of astral perception described by those who report alien abductions. They have no way to distinguish between ordinary physical reality and the imposed astral experience, so naturally they assume that the astral events are physically happening. They believe the evidence of their senses, even though their senses are lying to them.

It is even possible that repercussion may occur in some cases, causing those who have alien abduction trauma to suffer some corresponding physical injury. The connection between mind and body is still a mysterious zone largely unexplored by science. Stigmata, the wounds of Christ, sometimes spontaneously appear on the bodies of Christians. If the mind can cause this degree of injury to the body, it is not difficult to accept that it can also open a lesion in the neck where an individual who suffers an abduction event believes an alien device was inserted.

---

184. Swedenborg, 625–6.

Soul Flight and the Moon

It is important to understand that scrying is not a psychic activity separate from astral projection, but merely the first level of the induced astral perception to which I have given the general title soul flight. The activities, materials, and objects that aid in scrying can also be used to aid in astral projection. In an occult sense, scrying falls under the influence of the moon, and the same lunar influence governs astral projection. By using lunar substances and symbols, soul flight in all its forms can be facilitated.

To say that something is under the influence of the moon is a bit misleading, although that is the way that the connection is expressed in the Western esoteric tradition. It is a holdover from a period when astrological terminology dominated the practice of ritual magic. In ancient times, the moon was believed to send down rays of occult influence that affected those individuals susceptible to them, as well as certain plants, animals, and substances classed as lunar in nature. These rays never physically existed, but were a kind of visual metaphor to account for the observed sympathetic response to active influences classed as lunar.

The Renaissance magician Cornelius Agrippa (1486–1535) summarized the nature of lunar things in his *Occult Philosophy*:

> These things are lunary, amongst the elements, viz. the Earth, then the Water, as well that of the sea, as of the rivers, and all moist things, as the moisture of trees, and animals, especially they which are white, as the whites of eggs, fat, sweat, phlegm, and the superfluities of bodies. Amongst tastes, salt and insipid; amongst metals, silver; amongst stones, crystal, the silver marcasite, and all those stones that are white, and green. Also the stone selenites i.e. lunary, shining from a white body, with a yellow brightness, imitating the motion of the Moon, having in it the figure of the Moon which daily increaseth, or decreaseth as doth the Moon. Also pearls, which are generated in shells of fishes from the droppings of water, also the beryl.[185]

Agrippa included among lunar plants hyssop, rosemary, the palm tree, and the olive tree. Among animals he mentioned the dog, chameleon, pig, deer, goat, panther, otter, baboon, cat, and any beast with horns that curve inward, such as the cow. Water fowl are also lunar in nature, as are mice, flies, beetles, and any creature that breeds in the mud. Sea animals particularly lunar in nature are the tortoise, crab, oyster, clam, and frog. He particularly

---

185. Agrippa, 80.

singled out menstrual blood as the most lunar of substances. He mentioned a number of other creatures, but this list will give an impression of the lunar nature.

Lunar elements are earth and water, making their combination in the form of moist soil or mud highly lunar. Earth was probably classed as lunar because the moon was believed to influence the germination and growth of all plants, giving plants in general a lunar quality—but not the onion, which according to Agrippa, is wholly under Mars, and is inimical to the things of the moon. Water is lunar for the obvious reason that the moon rules the tides. Hence, anything cool and moist is lunar, as is anything living in the cool, moist mud or generated in the mud, such as frogs and beetles. The colors white and silver are lunar because those are the general colors of the moon's face, yet black is also her color because she hides that face periodically. This monthly period of the moon links her to the menstrual cycle, but more generally to things that wax and wane, or open and close, particularly when they occur in darkness.

Rock crystal and similar crystalline stones such as beryl are lunar because they resemble water and are cool to the touch. Stones that are white or silvery, such as pearl or moonstone, express the moon's nature in their color, as does silver marcasite, also known as the mirror stone. All the cool, milky, and tasteless or slightly salty fluids or substances of the body are lunar, especially those that are cast off such as sweat and phlegm, because they wax and wane in quantity. The dew was believed to fall from the moon as a kind of lunar sweat, making dew lunar in nature. The cow is particularly lunar not only due to its curved horns that resemble the horns of the moon, but by virtue of its white milk. The cat is lunar because the pupils of its eyes resemble the lunar crescent, but can open into full disks just as the moon expands to show a full face.

It is no accident that the goddess of witches was held to be Diana, goddess of the moon, or that one of the primary activities of witches was the use of the flying ointment for travel to the sabbat gatherings. The active ingredients in the flying ointment were highly lunar substances. All narcotic or soporific plants such as monkshood and nightshade are lunar because they induce sleep or dreams and visions. It is no accident that the animal most closely connected to the witch as her familiar is the cat, one of the most lunar of all beasts. These things show the influence of the lunar virtue over witches. In paintings and illustrations of witches the moon is almost always visible in the sky, emphasizing the connection, which is understood by artists on the unconscious level.

By considering lunar things individually, and comparing them with each other, we can gain a general impression of the lunar virtue that rules over or governs the act of astral perception. Once this understanding is gained, the lunar virtue can be attracted and directed as an aid to soul flight through the conscious incorporation of lunar objects and materials into the projection ritual. The appropriate use of occult correspondences has almost been forgotten in modern times. Those practicing astral projection today might laugh at the idea of using lunar objects or symbols to assist in the separation of the astral double, yet such correspondences were employed with good results for thousands of years by philosophers, mystics, and magicians.

Lucid Dreaming

The moon rules over sleep and dreams as mistress of the night sky, when the world lies in sleep. Just as the sun, the great light of the day, symbolizes consciousness, so does the moon, the great light of the night, symbolize the unconscious mind. However, unlike the sun, the moon is variable, so she presides over partial consciousness as well. During waking, the awareness appears to be constant and unvarying, even as the light of the sun is unvarying. In sleep, there are various degrees of awareness that range from the complete oblivion of dreamless sleep to the full consciousness of lucid dreaming.

A lucid dream is a dream in which the dreamer has full control over his thoughts and actions. In my opinion, no significant distinction can be made between genuine lucid dreaming and astral projection. Most of the projections of Oliver Fox were lucid dreams, or extensions of lucid dreams. Fox became aware that he was dreaming without waking up, and once he had attained this self-awareness, he was able to move out of the dream setting into other astral landscapes. His primary technique for astral projection involved inducing self-awareness while dreaming, which he was able to accomplish by noticing anomalies in the dream, minor details that would not or could not exist in the actual physical world.

I have used a similar anomalous trigger to achieve consciousness in my own dreams. For me, it is the light switches in my house. If I am in a dream and go to turn on a light, and the light does not turn on, I think in the dream that it may be just a burned-out bulb. But if I try another light and it also fails to illuminate, I at once know that I am dreaming. Then if I choose not to remain on the astral level, I can compel myself to awaken, although it is difficult—rather like drawing myself up from the bottom of a dark, deep well. I become aware that my body is paralyzed. This is a natural condition known as sleep paralysis, a protective mechanism of the body to prevent self-inflicted injuries during violent dreams. I also become aware that my sense of hearing has been turned off. At some point as I force myself to wake up, my hearing will suddenly cut in as though a radio were switched on, and I am able to hear the background sounds in my bedroom.

I assume that, during sleep, sound is still being monitored by some level of my mind, but it is being filtered in such a way that ordinary background noises do not intrude upon my dream awareness. Sylvan Muldoon observed that it is only unusual sounds that disturb astral projection—common and familiar noises such as the ticking of a clock pass unnoticed. [186] This awareness of unusual noises is probably designed to guard against attacks or dangers during sleep, but common sounds that have been classed as harmless pass completely unheard during the dreaming state—not only unnoticed, but actually unheard on the conscious level.

Oliver Fox mentioned something he called the False Awakening.[187] It is when the awareness passes from ordinary dreams into a condition that seems to be normal waking, but is actually still deep sleep. When I experience the light-switch trigger, I am usually in a condition of false awakening. That is, I believe myself to have just woken up in the middle of the night, and believe myself to be reaching across to switch on the lamp beside my bed. When it fails to light, I seem to get out of bed to try the overhead light by means of the switch near the bedroom door. Only when this fails to light do I abruptly realize that I am not awake at all, but still asleep. At this point, I am in a state of astral projection in my body double, and fully conscious, even though still sleeping.

One method I use to wake up from this state is to lie down in my physical body, which I can see on the bed in the dimness of the bedroom, and then attempt to sit up and stand up, carrying my physical body with me. I usually have to do this several times—each time leaving my physical body behind me when I arise—before I pass into an awareness of lying within my physical body in a state of sleep paralysis. Then it is a matter of pulling myself up from the depths of sleep, which feels very similar to what must be experienced by a deep diver rising from the depths of a shadowy ocean to the surface. The apparent distance traversed in rising through the darkness can be considerable.

Induction of Lucid Dreams

However, we are not so much concerned with awakening from the condition of astral projection during sleep as inducing it. No induction method I have used to initiate a lucid

---

186. Muldoon and Carrington, *Projection of the Astral Body*, 198.

187. Fox, 47–8.

dream has been completely reliable. Consistent success probably depends as much on innate talent as it does on the technique employed. Some individuals are just better at astral projection than others, although with practice and the use of induction methods, the rate of anyone's success can be increased. Muldoon's advice was to hold your arm up as you are falling asleep, as a way of carrying consciousness into the sleep state. His theory was that as you start to drift off and your arm begins to fall, you can catch yourself and regain awareness. You can try this method, but I have found it to be worthless. Holding my arm balanced upright on my elbow tends to keep me from falling asleep for a longer period, but when at last I do drift off, it is not with conscious awareness.

Here is a symbolic lunar trigger that you can try, as a way of encouraging separation of the astral body. Cut a small twig from a water-loving tree or plant. Trees such as the willow or poplar, both of which love to grow in wet ground, would be appropriately lunar, but which plant is available will depend on the region in which you reside. Cut the twig from a living branch. It should be quite small and light—no more than a few inches long. Tie it in the middle to a length of white sewing thread and suspend it in the air about three feet above the center of your bed. Make sure you attach the thread firmly to the ceiling with masking tape or a pushpin so that it does not fall. The thread should be tied around the twig at its center of balance so that it moves in the slightest breeze or at the touch of your breath.

As you fall asleep in the darkness, be aware of the suspended twig above you and allow your consciousness to be drawn up toward it. Imagine it spinning and bobbing in the tiny currents of air stirred by your own gentle breathing. As you drift into sleep, recite this little verse, either aloud in a low voice or mentally:

> Diana of the silver bow,
> My soul has wings;
> Diana of the coursing hounds,
> My soul flies up;
> Diana of the leaping mare,
> My soul soars free.

Needless to say, you may compose your own invocation to the goddess of the moon. To be effective, it should be brief and rhythmic. It is a way of indicating to your unconscious mind that you are preparing to project your astral double while asleep, and of opening your mind to those influences that will contribute to this separation of awareness. As you recite this invocation, visualize the moon above the clouds in the night sky and see the wild hunt of the goddess pass as though racing across the tops of the wind-borne clouds—Diana on her pale mare rushing after her pack of hounds, her silver bow drawn to launch an arrow at her unseen quarry.

Another trigger that historically has been effective in inducing specific dream events is a charm placed under the pillow just before going to sleep. This can also be employed to produce a lucid dream state. The charm should indicate by its symbolism the effect it is intended to produce, and will be more potent for purposes of astral awareness and astral projection if it is lunar in nature. Such a charm may be called an astral doorway. An effective design would be a disk of black craft paper three inches in diameter, on which you have drawn or painted with silver ink or silver paint the waxing crescent of the moon, between the points of which is the oval of an open, staring eye. The crescent invokes the moon, as does the black color of the paper and the silver ink. The open eye indicates conscious awareness. Because it is between the points of the lunar crescent, it is awareness under the control or domination of the moon—awareness in sleep and during dreams.

If you are able to find the feather of a crow or raven, or better still the feather of an owl, it will serve as a potent lunar talisman for soul flight when placed beneath your pillow. The crow and raven are lunar birds primarily due to their color, which matches the darkness of night. The owl is a night bird that hunts in the darkness and has uncommonly keen night vision, so its feathers perfectly represent the desired conscious awareness during dreams. The feather is the preeminent symbol of soul flight, which is why it was favored by shamans the world over as part of their ceremonial costume.

Crystals and Crystal Gazing

Natural rock crystal (silicon dioxide) has been used since prehistoric times to induce astral visions and astral projection. Pieces of rock crystal have been discovered in caves amid the burial remains of shamans. Crystals were employed in Greek and Roman times for scrying. The crystals grow to a large size and can be polished into spheres or ovoid shapes. Pink quartz and smoky quartz are both common, but the most highly prized for scrying purposes are transparent and free from both coloring and inclusions. In ancient times, it was believed to be a form of petrified ice, created by intense and sustained cold.

The Roman naturalist Pliny the Elder repeated the popular view when he wrote "that it is a kind of ice is certain."[188]

Referring to the Persian magician Osthanes, Pliny observed: "As Osthanes said, there are several forms of magic; he professes to divine from water, globes, air, stars, lamps, basins, and axes, and by many other methods, and besides to converse with ghosts and those in the underworld."[189] Divination by "globes" is very likely a form of crystal gazing. The conversation with "ghosts and those in the underworld" may have been effected by means of astral projection, and travel to the land of the dead.

Science is at a loss to explain what power natural crystals may have to induce an altered state of consciousness that facilitates soul flight. It is sometimes suggested that staring at the shiny surface of a crystal may induce a self-hypnotic condition. This is undoubtedly correct, but does not account for the widespread use of rock crystals and similar clear gem stones, as opposed to other shiny objects, or for the degree to which crystals are prized for this purpose. Crystals are a strongly lunar substance, being like water in appearance and cool to the touch. The light shining through crystals resembles the silvery color of moonlight.

Almost all of the Enochian communications recorded by John Dee between the years 1582 and 1587 were scried by Edward Kelley in several small globes of natural rock crystal. The best results were obtained by the globe Dee referred to as his principal showstone, which was given to him in the form of an apport by the Enochian angels. During the Enochian communications, the crystal appeared to act not merely as a viewing window, but also as a power matrix and astral portal. It would glow at times with its own internal radiance. Spirits came through it into the scrying chamber with Kelley and Dee, and Kelley sent his awareness through it into various astral landscapes, so that he not only saw them but was also present within them.

Crystal balls of large size are expensive, particularly when they are clear with few or no flaws and inclusions. A ball of flawless rock crystal of three inches diameter or more would be considered large, and might cost two or three thousand dollars. Fortunately, good results have historically been obtained by scrying into crystal balls, globes, or natural unshaped crystals of relatively small size, and these are inexpensive. A few flaws or inclusions,

---

188.   Pliny, vol. X, p. 181.

189.   Ibid., vol. VIII, p. 287.

or cloudiness, does not inhibit the effectiveness of a crystal. Most crystal balls used in past centuries were imperfect, as perfect crystals were quite difficult to get.

Uses of Rock Crystal

A use of rock crystal that I find effective is to rest a natural crystal upon the hollow just above my solar plexus when I am lying on my back, with my hands clasped over the crystal. The crystal acts as a mental focus during soul flight. At the same time, I visualize a vortex opening in the air above the middle of my body and drawing me upward. This is a simple, unstructured method of projection that can either be used by itself, or incorporated into a ritual. You may wish to experiment with arranging crystals around your body as you lie upon your bed, or with placing them upon your chakra centers. Another effective trigger is to get a small, flat crystal that has been polished in a rock tumbler, and to lay it on your forehead between your eyebrows, over your third eye. The weight and coolness of the crystal aid in focusing awareness on the ajna chakra.

It would be impossible to demonstrate in any physical way why the mere touch of a crystal should encourage astral perception, but we are not dealing solely with the physical substance of the crystal, but with its astral substance as well—with the way in which the crystal affects not only the physical senses but also the emotions, imagination, and the unconscious mind. Crystals are power centers on the astral level. They accumulate and retain the potential force to cause change in the astral world. When seen with astral vision, they glow with internal radiance. It is as though a crystal, when it is contemplated and held in the thoughts, creates a gateway in the wall of separation between normal waking awareness and astral awareness.

One of the ways of scrying into a crystal ball was to hold it in the hands and gaze into it in total darkness, so that the crystal was not visible with ordinary vision. My grandfather, who was an accomplished crystal scryer, covered his head and shoulders beneath a black cloth when scrying into his crystal, which he placed into a box open at the top for the purpose. Since the cloth covered the box as well as his head, he could see nothing of the crystal, or at most its dim outline in whatever trace of light may have filtered through the cloth. My mother, who often watched her father scry when she was a little girl, assures me that he could not see even a trace of the crystal ball under the cloth.

This would seem to inconvenience the popular scientific theory that the crystal ball works by inducing self-hypnosis through prolonged staring at reflections of light in its shiny surface. My grandfather saw no reflections of light. He held the crystal in his mind as well as beneath his hands, and any brightness it possessed existed only on the astral level, since to his physical eyes it remained invisible in the darkness.

My grandfather's crystal globe was not crystal at all, but was made of common glass. He ordered it by mail from Chicago around the beginning of the 1920s, and it cost a considerable portion of his coal miner's paycheck at the time. He could never have afforded a genuine crystal globe. Fortunately for him and for countless other crystal scryers of limited means, clear glass is a wonderfully lunar substance. It is watery and cool to the touch, just like rock crystal. Glass is made from silica, often collected in the raw form of beach sand, and it provides another link to the moon. Anything connected with the beach falls under the influence of the ebb and flow of the tides, and hence is lunar.

A Lunar Accumulator

It is possible to construct a kind of accumulator of lunar virtue that can be of use in inducing astral projection. Take a clear glass flask or bottle and fill it with fresh seawater collected from an ocean beach. Seal the flask so that it will not leak. This instrument can then be left exposed to bright moonlight for several days. The best time to charge your lunar accumulator is during the three days of each lunar cycle when the moon shows a full face—the night before the full moon, the night of the full moon, and the night following the full moon. It should be stored away when not in use in a wrap of black silk or velvet, and never exposed to sunlight or even to the bright light of day. It can be taken out and used to good effect at twilight or in the evening.

The accumulator should be placed near to the head while lying down to practice soul flight. A good location is immediately behind the top of the skull. Another effective location is beneath the center of the bed on which you are lying during your projection. Even if you do not see the flask, you know where it is and what it contains. Indeed, even if you should forget entirely that the flask is there, your unconscious mind will continue to be aware of its existence.

Sometimes, those who are new to the concept of using traditional occult correspondences as an aid during ritual work form the mistaken notion that they must somehow trick their minds into believing that these objects are effective, or that they must infuse effectiveness into them by a kind of repeated brainwashing in which they tell themselves over and over that the object used has power of a certain kind. This is incorrect. The whole point of using such recognized esoteric materials is that they produce an effect on their own, by their own natures. Lunar materials will aid to induce a lunar state of mind, which is a state of mind conducive to astral perception. No one can explain how they do this, since whatever mechanism produces the resonance works below the physical level. But centuries of tradition testify that such an effect is real.

Mirror Portals

If anything may be said to be more lunar than a crystal globe, it is a mirror. They are uncanny objects that have always been accorded a measure of wonder and apprehension. By reflection, a mirror creates an image seemingly within its depths that is similar in outward appearance to the person reflected, but it is an image without substance. A reflected image is in this sense similar to an astral form. A mirror also appears to be a kind of doorway between the physical world and the reflected world that is its duplicate, just as the base astral world is the duplicate of the physical world.

This property was used by the writer Lewis Carroll (1832–1898) who, in his 1871 fantasy novel *Through the Looking-Glass*, had his protagonist Alice crawl through the surface of a large wall mirror into the reflected world, while she talked to her cat:

> "Let's pretend the glass has got all soft like gauze, so that we can get through. Why, it's turning into a sort of mist now. I declare! It'll be easy enough to get through—" She was up on the chimney-piece while she said this, though she hardly knew how she had got there. And certainly the glass *was* beginning to melt away, just like a bright silvery mist.[190]

This fictional account has several points of interest. The cat is a lunar beast, and the primary familiar of witches, as I have mentioned. Witches are proverbial for their ability to fly up the chimney, using it as a portal to the astral world when they set off for the sabbat gathering. Alice's mirror is set over the fireplace. Her description of the change in the surface of the glass is not unlike descriptions given by scryers concerning the apparent change in the surface of the crystal just before they begin to see astral scenes in its depths. A very common feature of such descriptions is the appearance of a mist. Carroll specifically wrote that the mist was "silvery" in color. Silver is the color, and the metal, of the moon.

Mirrors are lunar not merely because they seem to create astral images in their depths, but because the substances of which they are made—glass and silver—are both strongly

---

190. Carroll, 146.

lunar materials. Add to this their common rectangular shape, which resembles a window or doorway, and it is little wonder that they were used both for scrying and as astral portals. It is a common report that astral scenes are reflected left to right, in exactly the same way as mirror images. The members of the Golden Dawn made this observation while scrying in the spirit vision. Israel Regardie wrote:

> There was a good deal of glib parlance within the Order as to "astral vision" and "etheric vision." The former was described as the ordinary Tattwa vision, in which objects and landscapes, though vivid and alive, are yet "flat" as though reflected on a mirror, rather like a cinematograph film. "In this form of descrying, note that you see objects reversed, as to right and left, for which suitable allowance must be made." The use of the phrase "mirror-like vision" is actually a very adequate description. Yet this is capable, as development proceeds, of merging into another type of vision—a full-blooded clairvoyance, in which things and people are seen in three dimensions, and as though the seer were not merely watching the scene, but were actually in it. Some explained that as "etheric vision" although the actual Order documents describe this as the clairvoyance ensuing from astral projection.[191]

It is not very difficult to make the leap between describing a scried astral vision as mirror-like, and using an actual mirror as an astral doorway. To be most effective, the mirror should be large enough to easily step into, were the glass to become soft and mist-like, as it did for Alice. Although this is unlikely to happen in a physical sense, the astral body has no trouble stepping through the surface of a mirror. However, it is not absolutely necessary that the mirror be large. It can be enlarged in the imagination. This is what Golden Dawn members did when using tattwa symbols as astral doorways. "You may modify the earlier stages of the working by so enlarging the symbol astrally that the human being can pass through it. When very vivid, and not until then, *pass, spring or fly through it*, and do not begin to reason till you find yourself in some place or landscape."[192] The same course of action can be followed with regard to a small mirror.

---

191.   Regardie, 463.

192.   Ibid., 470.

How to Use a Mirror

A good location for a larger mirror that is used as an astral doorway is the wall at the foot of the bed upon which you lie when you practice soul flight. When you exit your physical body and leave it behind you on the bed, you can arise in your astral body and step into the mirror, which if you wish can be used as a conduit to carry you directly to your destination without the necessity to use the intermediary astral constructions of the chamber, corridor, and elevator. Needless to say, once you arise in your astral body, you are already on the base level of the astral world. It is helpful to imagine a vortex forming in the center of the mirror just before you step into it, a sort of whirlpool of silvery-gray light. In ceremonial magic, the symbol of the vortex, in the form of the two-dimensional spiral or three-dimensional cone, is employed to open gateways. The technical reason for this is that the vortex expands the point, which is the only entrance or exit from the circle. To fall into the mirror in your astral body, visualize a clockwise inward swirl which will draw you in toward its center.

To seal an opened portal created by a vortex, you can easily still the turning of the vortex by means of a cross inscribed within a circle. This is a highly effective symbol for halting change or freezing motion. The cross both preserves and defends. A regular Christian cross will work if you prefer to use it, but I employ a cross of equal arms—inscribing first on the air the vertical column downward, then the horizontal arm from left to right, and finally enclosing the cross in a clockwise circle. As this is drawn with the right hand over the portal you wish to seal shut, it should be visualized as glowing upon the air.

When using a large mirror as an astral doorway, it is best to keep it covered during the day, and not to use it for common purposes. It should be protected from the direct rays of the sun, and from strong daylight. To charge it with lunar virtue, set it outside or beneath a window where it can reflect the light of the full moon. Covering the mirror with a black cloth after it is charged will help retain this virtue.

To incorporate the lunar virtue of a mirror into the standard projection ritual, in which the chamber, corridor, and elevator are visualized, a small mirror may be combined with the symbolic key that specifies the astral destination. These can be held together with tape or a rubber band. The mirror and the key can then be placed over the solar plexus beneath the folded hands while lying on the bed during the projection. It is best to leave the surface of the mirror unobstructed and to place the key against its backing. When a small mirror is incorporated into the key, the keycard in the astral world should be visualized as having a mirror backing.

This small mirror can be used as an offensive weapon against astral beings. If you are confronted by an aggressive spirit and feel threatened, holding up the mirror surface of the keycard so that it reflects the image of the spirit will cause the spirit to withdraw in confusion, as its own hostility is reflected back upon it. In the astral world, a mirror reflects more than mere images. It also reflects emotions and subtle energies. For this reason it can be employed as a kind of psychic shield. It becomes a doorway only after it has been opened by a vortex, either consciously or unconsciously. When you conceive the mirror as a portal, you automatically open it even if you are not aware of this process. Hence, when using the mirror as a shield, it must be conceived as sealed and impervious.

The Black Mirror

Another kind of mirror that is used in magic is the black mirror. This is a sheet of glass to which an opaque black coating has been applied, rendering it into a midnight black surface that reflects shadowy images. Black mirrors were used in ancient times for common household purposes. They were made of sheets of polished volcanic glass, called obsidian, or a polished coal-like material known as jet. The black mirror is often preferred for magical purposes in our modern age because it is not found any longer in common use, having long ago been superseded by the much superior reflecting qualities of polished silver. John Dee owned a small black mirror that had supposedly been taken as plunder from the Aztec Indians.[193] It was made of obsidian and may have played a part in some of the early scrying done by Edward Kelley, although Dee and Kelley preferred crystal globes for this purpose.

The black mirror has a somewhat evil reputation in magic. This is a natural consequence of its color, which links it symbolically to the phase of the new moon, when the lunar orb is completely dark and hidden. This is the phase of the moon during which magic of a malevolent nature was worked. It is also suitable for works of necromantic magic, and for covert works of magic that must remain hidden. This association of the black mirror with evil is simplistic. Black is not a color of evil, but of negation. The dark is where the light is absent. A black mirror can be very effectively used for scrying and astral projection, by those who understand this distinction. Those seeking to project

---

193. Clulee, *John Dee's Natural Philosophy*, 206–7.

into the lower astral levels will find the black mirror particularly useful as an aid, since it resonates with the shadows of the infernal realms.

The Water Mirror

Another even more ancient magic mirror is the surface of water. It was employed for both scrying and divination in the form of natural springs and pools considered to be sacred. Such springs and pools were believed to be the dwelling places of spiritual beings and, without a doubt, spirits did appear and communicate with human beings through the astral doorways of these pools and springs. In a later evolution of this method of scrying, water was collected in a special scrying basin from such sacred water sources. Astral visions would be scried by peering down into the depths of the basin, which was often made of silver. The surface of the water might be stirred into a vortex by means of a wand. The great seer Nostradamus used a basin of water as part of his scrying apparatus, along with a wand, though exactly how they were employed remains a matter of conjecture.

We can adapt the ancient water mirror for the purpose of an astral doorway by filling a silver or silver-plated basin with clear fresh water on a table in the scrying chamber just prior to beginning the exercise of projection. A silver-plated basin is acceptable, since silver is plated over brass, which is predominantly copper, and copper as the metal of the planet Venus is not obstructive in any occult sense to astral projection. After leaving the body, the basin of water can be used as a portal by enlarging it on the astral level until it is large enough to dive into. The traveler should continue to descend deeper and deeper into the water of the basin until a light is perceived. He will gradually become aware that he is no longer descending into the depths of the basin, but ascending toward the light. As the light approaches, it enlarges itself into an opening through which the traveler emerges into the astral landscape he sought to reach. In this way, the basin of water can be used as a direct astral channel, bypassing the chamber, corridor, and elevator of the general ritual.

I have provided this method of direct passage into the astral world, along with the method of the mirror, because I know that some individuals who practice using the formal ritual of the chamber, corridor, and elevator may find it too elaborate and cumbersome to easily manipulate in their imaginations. The ritual of projection is not an essential part of soul flight, and if it becomes more of an impediment than an aid, it should be abandoned. This should not be done casually, however, since the ritual is structured in such a manner as to provide a high degree of both precision and security to the traveler.

The light at the bottom of the basin should be conceived as a kind of astral reflection of the open surface of the expanded basin that leads to the astral world, in much the same way that the reflection in the depths of a mirror may be thought of as the astral reflection of the physical world. Since the astral world is a reflection, the traveler is, by swimming down into the depths of the basin, actually swimming up on the astral side of the water surface. The basin does not have a bottom in the astral world, but it is a water-filled passageway similar to a submerged cave. It can be opened by making a clockwise stirring motion above the surface of the water in the basin with the hand, to initiate a vortex in the water. It is useful to conceive of the basin as a kind of silver bath when enlarging it on the astral level, prior to stepping or diving into it. Lean over this bath in your astral body and stir the water clockwise with your hand. Visualize a point of light in its distant, shadowed depths. Then enter the water and swim toward the light.

You can use water as an aid in the general ritual of projection by placing a silver or silver-plated basin or bowl filled with fresh, clear water beneath your bed prior to beginning the ritual. The silver and the water will both attract lunar virtue, and will facilitate the separation of the astral double during the ritual. Just before getting on the bed, you may wish to wet your fingertip in the basin and touch the water to your forehead, between your eyebrows, where your ajna chakra is located, so that this part of your skin will be drying and cooling as you visualize the sign of projection.

The use of these and all other astral doorways is optional. They should be employed where they are found to help, and discarded without a qualm when they are tried and found to be valueless or obstructive. Every person who practices soul flight is different, and no two human beings react to symbols in the same way. Some have an irrational fear of drowning, for example. Needless to say, the method of diving into the water-filled silver basin would be a poor method for those suffering from hydrophobia. Magic is the most practical of human pursuits, and soul flight is a magical practice. You should use what works, and discard what does not work. The various lunar doorways described above are likely to be helpful in some degree to most who try them.

CHAPTER TWELVE

The Tarot

The Tarot has been in existence since around 1425, possibly a few decades earlier. It was invented in northern Italy as a plaything for wealthy and noble families, and was based on the ordinary gaming cards used in Europe at the time. The Tarot was devised to play a trick-taking card game of the same name that is similar in some respects to bridge. In addition to four suits, each of which contains cards numbered from one to ten and four court cards, the Tarot has a special set of twenty-two picture cards, known as trumps, making a total of seventy-eight cards in the standard Tarot deck.

It was in France during the second half of the eighteenth century that the Tarot first began to be used for purposes of fortunetelling. They became a popular instrument for both divination and meditation once the notion began to circulate among French occultists during the following century that the cards had higher meanings hidden in their symbolism. The twenty-two picture cards received the most attention. They were linked by French occultists with the letters of the Hebrew alphabet, and with the esoteric associations that attach to those letters in the mystical system of the Kabbalah. Chief among the French exponents of the higher significance of the Tarot was Eliphas Lévi (1801–1875), who wrote in 1860 concerning the Tarot: "Now the extant Tarot is certainly that of the gypsies and has come to us by way of Judea. As a fact, its keys are in correspondence with the letters of the Hebrew alphabet, and some of its figures reproduce even their forms."[194]

This statement is noteworthy for the number of errors it manages to squeeze into so few words. The Tarot had nothing whatsoever to do with the Gypsies, did not derive from Judea, and does not reproduce in its images the forms of the Hebrew letters, except imperfectly and by mere chance in one or two cards. The only indisputable resemblance between the trumps of the Tarot and the Hebrew letters is that both are twenty-two in number, and even this association is imperfect since some Tarot packs have more than twenty-two trumps. However, the standard Tarot adopted by French occultists in the nineteenth century does indeed have trumps equal in number to the Hebrew letters, and this was enough to cause a connection to be formed between the two.

Teachings of the Golden Dawn

The esoteric analysis and magical use of the Tarot was not elevated to the level of high art until it became part of the system of the Hermetic Order of the Golden Dawn. Samuel Liddell Mathers, in the process of conveying the teachings of the Secret Chiefs that he and his wife received psychically by scrying, astral travel, and other means, delivered a complete set of occult correspondences for the Tarot of greater complexity and precision than any that had previously been created. It used the work of the French occultists as its foundation, but overshadowed them with its degree of sophistication. The teachings on the Tarot received by Mathers and his wife from the Secret Chiefs remain perhaps the greatest achievement of the Golden Dawn. They form the prevalent modern esoteric structure of the Tarot and are widely accepted as the standard, although other systems of correspondences exist.

The Golden Dawn was the first occult society to use the Tarot trumps as astral keys. By contemplating the image of a card, a member was expected not only to attain a mysti-

---

194. Lévi, *History of Magic*, 240.

cal understanding of the meaning of its symbolism, but also to be able to project consciousness into the astral plane represented by the card, in order to converse with the
spiritual beings that lived there and to learn to command them. This was done by means
of Kabbalistic divine names that were vibrated in a special way on the breath, so that they
resonated in the chest and in the bones of the head. Dion Fortune wrote:

> When one is deeply moved, and at the same time devotionally exalted, the voice drops
> several tones below its normal pitch and becomes resonant and vibrant; it is this trem-
> or of emotion combined with the resonance of devotion which constitutes the vibra-
> tion of a Name, and this cannot be learnt or taught; it can only be spontaneous.[195]

Fortune is a bit misleading, in that it is perfectly possible to teach anyone to vibrate a
word of power in a physical sense. What cannot be easily taught is the inner vibration of
the word, which occurs on higher levels of the mind. The general concept of vibrating
power words to control spiritual beings was derived from the magic of the Egyptians
and the Gnostics, who used words composed of vowel sounds as weapons and as instruments of compulsion on the astral levels. These words were meaningless in the ordinary
sense, and came to be known as barbarous words of evocation, since it was believed
that they derived from ancient and forgotten languages. However, the words used by the
Golden Dawn were not meaningless, but were Hebrew names of God that were sounded
by members of the Golden Dawn in a manner similar to the way that the Egyptian magicians and Gnostic priests vocalized their barbarous words.

Israel Regardie wrote that the supreme defense when traveling in astral realms was to
assume the god-form of Harpocrates, the Greek god of healing. "The astral image should
be formulated either as rising from a Lotus, or else standing erect over two crocodiles."[196]
A manner of testing the truthfulness of spiritual beings was to confront them with the
Golden Dawn symbol known as the Banner of the West, a black banner upon which is
an upright white triangle having within it a red cross. "Thus, should the being be of an
evil nature— 'thus far and no farther' is the message indicated to it by the Banner. The
interposition of the Banner would be immediately efficacious, by causing it to disappear
instantaneously. If, however, the entity is well-intentioned and not evil, no harm will

---

195. Fortune, *Mystical Qabalah*, 207–8.

196. Regardie, 465.

have been done by that formulation. No balanced force, no power of good, will object or resent legitimate forms of testing its integrity."[197]

I mention these Golden Dawn practices as a matter of general interest, since in scrying and traveling astrally into the Tarot trumps, these were some of the techniques used by members of that occult order. However, it is not necessary to adopt Golden Dawn techniques in order to imitate its practice of using Tarot trumps as astral doorways, or astral keys. Concerning the Golden Dawn method of scrying in the spirit vision and pathworking, Gareth Knight observed: "It was their practice, for example, to visualize themselves in full ceremonial robes and accoutrements and to have a complex system of checking whether a symbol or scene arising in consciousness was genuine or not by projecting upon it an appropriate Hebrew letter of a planetary sign to see if it dissolved the picture. . . . Such techniques can be useful but are really unnecessary given faith and pure intention."[198]

There are two ways the astral worlds of the Tarot trumps can be entered and explored. The first is directly, by using the trump as a doorway through which the astral body passes. This is the simplest method, requiring no ritual structure, but it may prove the more difficult method precisely for those reasons. The second way is to use the Tarot trump as a key within the context of the general ritual of projection.

Tarot Trumps as Doorways

In using the first method, sit comfortably with the Tarot trump you wish to enter positioned in front of you near enough so that you can see its details clearly. The room light should be dim, but not to such a degree that you find it difficult to see the image on the card. Study the card closely and consider its symbolism as a meditation. When you feel you have formed a connection with the card, close your eyes while holding its image in your mind, so that you seem to see it projected against the insides of your closed eyelids. When the image becomes indistinct, open your eyes and reinforce your mental image of the card by looking briefly at the physical image, then close your eyes and sustain the trump in your imagination.

Continue in this way for some time, striving to make the Tarot image ever more real and detailed in your imagination. Try to see beyond its edges in your mind, as though

---

197. Regardie, 465.

198. Knight, *Practical Guide*, vol. 2, 276.

it were a three-dimensional scene that you looked upon through a little window. Try to see behind objects in the scene. If details appear in your mental image of the trump that are not in the painting on the card, allow them to arise unhindered. If the leaves of trees begin to move in the breeze, or a stream or river in the image begins to flow, allow these animations to play themselves before your inner vision.

When you have managed to open the image on the card into a three-dimensional scene, mentally will the border of the card to expand until it is like the opening of a doorway and is large enough to step through. Arise from your chair in your astral body and step into the frame of the Tarot trump. The central image on the trump will be displayed before you, but you will also see much more going on to either side, and beyond that tableau. The trump is an entire world that is colored by the meaning and emotion of the central tableau that makes up the card image, with its own inhabitants whose natures and experiences have been shaped by that primary meaning.

At first, it is likely that these excursions into the worlds of the Tarot trumps will be exercises in creative imagination rather than astral journeys. Even at this level, they are an excellent way to understand the meanings of the picture cards of the Tarot. If you persevere and are successful with this technique, at some point it will no longer be necessary for you to deliberately create details in the astral landscape you imagine, but details will occur spontaneously, and you will begin to encounter the inhabitants of the astral world of the trumps. Every person who enters the trumps will experience different aspects of the Tarot worlds, because these landscapes are not fixed and unchanging, but are modified by the expectations and responses of the person who enters them. There is a certain objective level of experience that is enforced by the actual symbolism used in the Tarot image, but much of the perception of these worlds is subjective. The astral planes are reflections of higher realities, and like all reflections are subject to distortion.

When you have completed your exploration of the world of the trump, it is a simple matter to return to the doorway, step through it back into your practice chamber, and return your astral body to the chair in which your physical body sits with its eyes closed. Opening your eyes will end the projection. If you find that your astral body does not want to reintegrate with your physical body, which may happen when the astral landscape within the trump is finely detailed and self-animated, you should make the sign of the circle-cross over the astral doorway of the trump once you have exited it, and deliberately visualize it shrinking back down to the dimensions of the Tarot card. Banishing the doorway in this manner will make it easier to reintegrate with your physical body.

It is also a good practice on the grounds of security, although there is little danger to be encountered in the worlds of the trumps.

Tarot Trumps as Astral Keys

To employ a Tarot trump for an astral key, hold it beneath your hands to your solar plexus as you lie on the bed in your practice chamber after you draw the circle of protection around your bed, and just prior to forming the sign of projection above your face. It is a good idea to place the card in a protective envelope or wallet to prevent its damage from the moisture of your hands. You should meditate on the trump before beginning the ritual of projection, so that you can easily hold the image of the trump in your imagination. Conduct the general ritual of projection as described in chapter 10, using the Tarot card as a keycard to open the door of your astral chamber and the doors of the elevator. Even if the card is enclosed in a wallet on the physical level, its image is exposed on one side of the keycard on the astral level.

The astral landscapes of the Tarot trumps do not exist in either the past or future, but they are slightly above the base level of the astral world, so you must use the up button once you are inside the elevator. The landscapes of the trumps are not all on the same level, but are arranged one above the other in the mirror opposite of the way in which the trumps are ordered in the Tarot pack. That is to say, the final trump XXI The World is on the lowest of the twenty-two levels, and the first trump 0 The Fool is on the highest level. You can enter any trump you wish. There is no necessity to work your way through the series in successive rituals. However, this is a good way to gain an overall familiarity with all of the worlds of the Tarot trumps.

It might seem as though the trump of The Devil would lie on one of the infernal levels of the astral world, and be accessed by using the down button of the elevator, but that is not the case. The Tarot scenes should be thought of as dramatic tableaux, or stage sets, that exist for the purpose of education. It is not the real world of the Devil that you visit; it is a kind of dramatic presentation of that world that exists in harmony with the similar presentations of all the other trumps. That is why visiting the landscapes of the trumps seldom presents any danger to the traveler. The beings who inhabit these landscapes are actors whose purpose is to teach you. They will sometimes stage short, impromptu pantomimes for this purpose, which you must interpret based on your knowledge of the trump. The function of the Tarot is instruction.

Golden Dawn Correspondences for the Trumps

The order and attributions of the Tarot trumps below are based on the Golden Dawn system of occult correspondences, which is the standard system used in the modern Western esoteric tradition. It is necessary to have some familiarity with this material in order to use the trumps effectively during pathworking, which will be examined in the next chapter. This is not to imply that the arrangement is inviolable, and can never be improved upon, but the Golden Dawn order and attributions for the trumps are a good place to start when getting to know their astral landscapes, and when investigating their pathways on the Tree of the Sephiroth.

This set of correspondences for the trumps occurs in what is known as the Golden Dawn cipher document,[199] the supposed seminal outline upon which the Golden Dawn rituals and teachings were based. Unfortunately, it is impossible to know who wrote this portion of the cipher document or when, and in the absence of confirmation I prefer to attribute this material to Mathers, or more properly to the Secret Chiefs. A member of the Golden Dawn, John William Brodie-Innes was once heard to observe that it did not matter whether the gods or the Secret Chiefs actually exist. "The point is that the Universe behaves as though they do."[200] Those familiar with the astral world and its inhabitants will have little difficulty accepting that the Secret Chiefs do exist, or at least that they existed for Mathers and that they transmitted their teachings through him.

Once you are thoroughly familiar with the Golden Dawn correspondences for the trumps and their assignment to the paths on the Tree, you may be inclined to make changes in these arrangements that appear necessary, even as I have done in my own work. You will find my reordering of the Tarot trumps described at the end of my book *Portable Magic*. I do not propose to give it here since it is apt to cause confusion for those new to the study of the Tarot.

It does not matter which Tarot deck you choose to scry or travel into, but once a deck is selected you should continue to use it until you have investigated the astral landscapes of all the trumps. It is not a useful practice to mix trumps from different decks on successive days during experiments in projection, as the costumes, historical period, and general quality of the scenes vary considerably from Tarot to Tarot. For example, the Marseilles deck depicts figures and scenes of the Renaissance, whereas the Thoth deck of Aleister Crowley is abstract and more modern.

---

199. Küntz, *Complete Golden Dawn*, 116–7.

200. Ibid., 34.

The descriptions of the trumps below are based on the enormously popular Tarot designed by A. E. Waite, and drawn by the artist Pamela Colman Smith. My purpose is to convey the general atmosphere of each Tarot trump, and its essential or core meaning that will determine many of the details you will encounter when you enter its landscape. The Hebrew letter, its esoteric association, and the occult correspondence are drawn from the Golden Dawn system. Your own experiences within these worlds may differ from those I describe. This is to be expected.

0 The Fool

Hebrew letter: Aleph (ox)
Correspondence: Air
Path: Eleventh

The association of the ox to the trump of the Fool, through the first Hebrew letter, Aleph, indicates the stubborn nature of the Fool's quest. He forges onward, in search of he knows not what, heedless of the dangers that may lie in his path. The Waite trump emphasizes his airy nature by showing him on a high mountain precipice, the wind blowing the sleeves of his loose coat, the sun blazing down pitilessly like a great all-seeing eye from the blue heavens. The little dog at the feet of the fool may be barking a warning to him to pay attention to where he is about to place his step, yet from its posture the dog appears caught up in the enthusiasm of the Fool, and may be encouraging him forward with its senseless barking.

The world of the Fool in the Waite Tarot is a world of mountain trails, steep cliffs, and airy openness. Those who travel through it are apt to encounter wonders, but must have a care to avoid falling into snares and traps. Beyond the edges of the card may lie the stone cottages of mountain dwellers, caves that shelter dangerous wild beasts, and perhaps an abandoned fortress that once guarded a mountain pass. There are rushing streams and waterfalls, evergreen forests on steep slopes, and high meadows filled with wildflowers, upon which mountain sheep graze, unmindful of the wolves who watch and wait in the shadows.

The ruling intelligence of this world is an oracular voice speaking in riddles that may hinder or help, depending on their interpretation. This oracle is unseen, its form concealed within a shining whirlwind that dazzles with its radiance, but it may be the Holy Grail, common quest of the foolish and the wise.

I The Magician

Hebrew letter: Beth (house)
Correspondence: Mercury
Path: Twelfth

Unlike the Fool, who wanders through the wilds of the natural world, the Magician functions within the environs of men—interacting with them, matching his wits with theirs, amazing and deceiving their senses. The art of the Magician is illusion, yet his efforts to understand and control the ways of the world and the ways of mankind have given him a quick wit and a cunning mind. By striving to master others, he has succeeded in large measure in understanding and mastering his own human frailties and errors. The simple tools of his trade, symbols of the four elements that compose all things, allow him to express his command by the manipulation of the forces of nature.

His world is a public market square in an old-fashioned country town of cobblestone streets and shops and houses with steeply pitched roofs. It is possible to wander out of the square through its four gates, but the streets beyond, closed on both sides by the fronts of buildings and by high stone walls, bend and twist back upon themselves like the windings of a labyrinth. The inhabitants of the town are sly and knowing in their manner toward strangers, and the children enjoy playing tricks. Even the animals that may be encountered, such as horses, dogs, or cats, have a knowing light in their eyes.

The ruling intelligence of this trump is Hermes, the Greek god of commerce, communication, and wisdom. His oracle is a square pillar that has the bearded head of the god carved into its upper part, located near the central well of the marketplace. If you place a coin upon the stone ledge at the base of the pillar, the god may grant your wish.

*II The **High Priestess***

Hebrew letter: Gimel (camel)
Correspondence: Moon
Path: Thirteenth

The High Priestess is a mature, solemn woman who presides over a sisterhood responsible for the keeping of the books in a great library. Those who come to consult the library must gain her approval before they can pass between the pillars that guard its entrance, where she sits and interviews anyone who seeks entry. She has a penetrating gaze and is able to look past the superficial mask into the very heart of travelers. It is useless to try to deceive her. She dresses in a long robe that is the blue and silver of the moon, and wears a silver crescent at her forehead. A black cat, her familiar beast, is always nearby, watching and protecting her.

The unspeaking sisters who move like silver shadows between the high shelves in the main reading hall care for the books as if they were their own children, and there is no sign of dust or neglect anywhere within the vast building, which is arranged somewhat like a nunnery, with a dining hall and corridors of sleeping chambers for the sisters on the upper level. The appearance of the library is gothic, its pillars carved stone, its windows of colored glass tall and narrow. Everything is done in an orderly fashion. Those who request a book wait at a reading table in the main reading hall, and a sister brings the book to them, then returns it to its place when the reader is done with it.

The ruling intelligence is Diana, goddess of the moon. Her oracle is to be found in a small chapel dedicated to the lunar goddess. It has the form of a silver bowl filled with clear water that rests on a low stone pedestal. By gazing at the light from the round window above the altar that is reflected in the surface of the water, visions may be seen.

III The Empress
Hebrew letter: Daleth (door)
Correspondence: Venus
Path: Fourteenth

A gracious lady of the manor who is in the late stage of pregnancy sits out of doors in the sunlight in a field of ripe grain, enjoying the fine weather and the fresh air. Her skin is flawless and lightly tanned, so that it has a golden color; her hair is blonde and has been bleached to paleness by the action of the sunlight. It falls around her shoulders in natural curls. She has an expression of pleasant expectancy on her face, as though she is waiting the arrival of someone who will amuse or entertain her. Soft cushions and rich, embroidered cloths have been arranged on her chair to give her a place of comfort. Around her brow she wears a circlet cunningly fashioned into the shape of tiny white flowers, which almost have the appearance of stars.

Beyond the seated matron, a stream of rushing water divides the land, and on its far bank are visible the trees of a forest. The forest is wild, not cultivated—the cultivated land ends at the stream. What cannot been seen within the frame of the trump is the stately country manor house with its walled gardens, vineyard, and stables, toward which the Empress gazes with such delighted expectation. Soon entertainers will issue forth from the gates of the great house and put on a pantomime for her amusement. Everything has been arranged for her pleasure.

The ruling intelligence is Venus, goddess of love and sensual enjoyment—and also the goddess who presides over the health of beasts and the growth of crops. Her oracle is delivered in the form of the pantomime staged for the Empress by the minstrels who have been hired to entertain her. By observing the show, closely held truths may be revealed.

IV The Emperor
Hebrew letter: Heh (window)
Correspondence: Aries
Path: Fifteenth

The Emperor is an elderly but strongly built man with a white beard, who sits upon a throne in a place of natural fortification that encloses and protects his army. It is evident from the armor he wears beneath his tunic and cloak that he is engaged in some military campaign. He looks directly forward with an unwavering gaze and a determined and somewhat grim expression on his weather-worn face. His reserves of vital energy are deep, and he is in the process of applying them through the force of his will to the accomplishment of his purpose, which is not of a personal nature, but involves the well-being of the people under his authority.

It is evident that he has led his army into a canyon surrounded by steep rock walls and watered by a stream that flows across its floor, an ideal place to withstand a long siege. What cannot be seen beyond the edges of the card are the fortifications and ramparts that have been constructed to repel the hostile force from the entrance to this canyon, or the armed guards that constantly pace and keep watch on the walls of the keep. The contest will be a battle of wills as much as a physical confrontation, and the victor will be the side that does not lose sight of its greater purpose.

The ruling intelligence is the god of shepherds, who in Egypt took the form of the ram-headed deity, Amon. His oracular revelations are delivered directly to the Emperor, who relies on them for his strategies of warfare. By conversing with the Emperor on his throne, they can be discovered.

V The Hierophant

Hebrew letter: Vau (nail)
Correspondence: Taurus
Path: Sixteenth

The Hierophant is the pope of a religion of ancient origins and long-established traditions, who ensures that the divine laws are observed and who punishes those who violate them. He sits in an audience hall within a great stone cathedral on a golden and jewel-encrusted throne, a crown of gold upon his head, wrapped in official robes of royal purple. At his feet kneel two priests who have been selected to plead a religious controversy he is presently judging. One priest argues in favor of the defendant, and the other argues for the prosecution. The defendant is not present at this trial nor would he be permitted to speak in his own defense. The determination of orthodoxy is purely a matter for the church to decide, and the Hierophant has absolute power of judgment.

Around his throne rise the pillars of a great gothic cathedral. Sunlight streams in through the stained glass windows and lies in bright panels across the flagstones of the floor. Those who have come to hear the judgments passed by the Hierophant sit in respectful silence in pews extending down the length of the nave. They are permitted to hear the cases argued and judgments spoken, but are not allowed to speak.

The ruling intelligence is a golden calf that occupies a pedestal behind the altar of sacrifice, which shows rusty traces of dried blood. It does not offer oracles, but remains mute. All of its laws have already been uttered and written down in a book bound with black calfskin, and there are no new revelations. Those who seek guidance must do so by looking into the black book on its reading stand beside the altar.

VI The Lovers

Hebrew letter: Zayin (sword)
Correspondence: Gemini
Path: Seventeenth

A young man and young woman are united in marriage by a winged angel beneath the bright rays of the sun. In the Waite design, both are naked and represent Adam and Eve. The woman stands beneath the Tree of the Knowledge of Good and Evil, around the trunk of which coils a green serpent. The man stands beneath the Tree of Life, the leaves of which are flames. The angel, who may be the archangel Michael, blesses their union from a cloud of glory. When not portraying this pantomime of the marriage rite, they come and go beneath the trees of the orchard that lies off the edges of the card. The angel is not always present.

The field behind them is unfenced and uncultivated, and shows only a low green ground cover. The earth has yet to be plowed; the seed has yet to be sowed in it. Notice that the bodies of the couple are hairless apart from their heads, indicating immaturity. In the background is a conical mountain toward the peak of which the woman seems to gesture with her left hand. It may be the source of the clouds from which the angel has appeared.

The ruling intelligence of this trump is the oracle on the peak of the mountain, who when approached will speak from a shining cloud on questions of personal relationships and marriage.

VII The Chariot

Hebrew letter: Cheth (fence)
Correspondence: Cancer
Path: Eighteenth

Before the fortification wall of a town, a young man stands in a podium that resembles a chariot of war beneath a sheltering blue canopy decorated with stars. He wears ceremonial armor and a crown. It appears that he is just about to begin to address a multitude gathered in front of him, or has just completed his speech. It is evident that the chariot is not riding into battle by the strange creatures who are harnessed to it—they lounge indolently on the grass.

Beyond the limits of the card is a green meadow that has been prepared for a medieval knight's jousting tournament. Young noblemen sit their armored and decorated horses, while their squires hurry about preparing their weapons. The leaders of the town sit to watch the display in a grandstand of wood erected for the purpose.

The ruling intelligences of this trump are the sphinxes harnessed to the ceremonial chariot. When you ask a question of them, the answer, if it is favorable, is delivered from the mouth of the white sphinx. But if it predicts ill fortune, the black sphinx will utter it.

VIII Strength
Hebrew letter: Teth (snake)
Correspondence: Leo
Path: Nineteenth

A graceful woman in a long white gown, with a garland of roses in her hair, gently closes the gaping jaws of a male lion with her bare hands. The tongue of the lion lolls out the side of his mouth to lick her on the hand. On the Waite design, the garland of roses around her waist extends down to wrap around the neck of the lion, joining her to the lion.

The landscape in which they walk along together is pastoral and pleasant with rolling green grasses and stately shade trees in the background. In taking her pet lion for a walk, the woman, who is evidently of gentle birth, has not wandered far from the grounds of her country estate, to which she is returning. The lion has perceived a threat from a passing traveler and has snarled at the stranger in warning, but the woman admonishes her faithful guardian by closing his jaws. The danger is imaginary, not real. If you approach the woman to talk, she may invite you to her home for a feast in her dining hall.

The ruling intelligence of this card is a hunter dressed in a lion skin who carried a crude club for his only weapon, which he uses to enforce the peace and order of the countryside. He is inarticulate but sometimes gives rough yet practical advice.

IX The Hermit
Hebrew letter: Yod (hand)
Correspondence: Virgo
Path: Twentieth

In a snowy, mountainous region, a bearded man in a long, gray robe that is like the habit of a monk beckons with a lantern raised in his hand. His back is humped with age. He leans with care on his walking staff so that his feet do not slip in the snow on the edge of the steep slope that extends below him. In spite of his age, he shows no signs of cold.

Beyond this lonely figure, the sky darkens into night. It will not be long before the stars appear. He has been expecting your approach along the mountain path to the hermitage, and the late hour has caused the old man who is the sole keeper of the high spiritual retreat to use his lantern as a beacon so that you do not become lost and wander off the path and over a cliff in the darkness. The hermitage is a rough building of heavy timbers on a foundation of native stone, build to withstand the storms of winter. The old man invites you inside when he sees you, so that you may warm yourself before the fire in the common room. It is a lonely spot and he seldom gets visitors.

The ruling intelligence is the virgin goddess of the heavens, Virgo, whose statue stands within a small shrine inside the hermitage. If you light a candle in her honor, she may respond to your question by either nodding or by shaking her head.

X The Wheel of Fortune

Hebrew letter: Kaph (fist)
Correspondence: Jupiter
Path: Twenty-first

The Waite version of this trump is abstract and does a poor job of presenting its astral landscape. It is an old-fashioned wooden fairground wheel similar to a Ferris wheel, but turned by a crank at its axis. Various fantastic animal figures decorate the wheel. On a platform at the top is carved the image of a sphinx. A creature resembling a jackal is carved into the rim of the turning wheel and seems to rise as the wheel is cranked around by its sweating operator, and a creature like an undulating serpent is carved into the rim on the opposite side and appears to descend with the wheel's rotation. Children wearing the carnival masks of fantastic animals laugh with glee as they cling to the rungs on the edge of the wheel and try to ride it to the sphinx, who keeps as a prize a brass ring on the end of its sword.

A country carnival is in progress all around the wheel. Men are engaged in contests involving balance as they try to knock each other off a narrow rail. A primitive turntable is pushed by young men as several young women cling to it and shriek with glee. Confections are sold from carts with large awnings over them. Barkers at the doors of tents attempt to intrigue the fairgoers into paying a fee to enter. The entire town appears to be enjoying itself under the warm rays of the afternoon sun.

The ruling intelligence of this trump is the Roman goddess Fortuna, whose image is carved into the upright support of the wheel so that the shaft of the crank looks as if it passes between her legs, although her legs are concealed beneath the folds of her long dress. She has both hands raised and extended in invitation to an equal degree, and her gaze is expressionless and level. When asked her opinion about a future event, the turning of the wheel clockwise indicates a positive response, but the opposite turning is negative.

XI Justice
Hebrew letter: Lamed (ox goad)
Correspondence: Libra
Path: Twenty-second

A mature and serious woman sits between two pillars, robed in the costume of a judge. In one hand she holds up a set of weighing scales, and in the other, a sword—the symbols of her profession that signify respectively a fair and equal trial and the dispensation of punishment. Her artificial posture has the appearance of a formal pose as she walks into the courtroom with her instruments of justice in her hands, and sits upon the judgment seat before the audience assembled to witness the events of the trial. She soon puts aside her symbols, and the trial begins.

The environment of this trump is the interior of a courtroom. Behind the lady judge is an open window covered with a curtain that conceals the place of execution from the gaze of those in the courtroom. If her judgment is for a sentence of death, this curtain is withdrawn. The astral traveler may enter this scene as a spectator, a witness, or as the accused. The manner of the officers of the court is formal and reserved. Guards prevent precipitous exits through the doors at the sides of the chamber.

The ruling intelligence of the trump is the Greek goddess of justice, Themis, whose bronze statue adorns the back of the courtroom. She stands perfectly straight with a great executioner's sword balanced upright before her, its point resting on the floor at her feet, one of her hands clasping each side of its guard. She stares straight ahead. When questioned about legal matters, or matters of judgment, she inclines the hilt of her sword to her right-hand side for yes and to her left-hand side for no.

XII The Hanged Man
Hebrew letter: Mem (water)
Correspondence: Water
Path: Twenty-third

An enigmatic tableau greets the astral traveler into the world of this trump. A man hangs suspended by one ankle from a wooden scaffold with his arms bound behind his back, his head low over the mouth of a pit dug into the ground at the base of the scaffold. The leg that is free crosses behind the leg that is bound. He does not speak or seem to notice his surroundings. His face bears a rapt expression, as though he peers into some unseen distant reality and strives to comprehend its meaning.

The place of his trial of endurance is at a crossroads remote from human habitation. Forest trees lower their boughs close to the dirt roads, the spaces between their trunks filled with green shadows. The pit has mud at its bottom the depth of which cannot be guessed by looking at it. Were the rope around his ankle to snap, it is possible that the inverted man would disappear below its surface. Those who come walking along the roads stop and make gestures to the Hanged Man, trying to attract his attention. They even put on little pantomimes, but he ignores their efforts.

The ruling intelligence of the trump speaks oracles of wisdom through the mouth of the Hanged Man without his awareness of what is spoken. It is an angel that possesses his body while his spirit is absent.

XIII Death

Hebrew letter: Nun (fish)
Correspondence: Scorpio
Path: Twenty-fourth

The pallid, ghostly figure of Death, who in Waite's trump wears black armor and rides a pale horse, bears the black standard of a white rose. He carries no weapon—his mere touch, or even his deliberate gaze through the opened visor of his helmet, is fatal. He never speaks, but only gestures with the skull of his face fixed in a permanent grin. It is prudent for the astral traveler to give his horse the right of way, and not to look at his face.

Those who meet him along the road at sunset sometimes weep, or plead for mercy, or fall to their knees. The strength of their limbs leaves them so that they cannot flee. He spurns their lifeless corpses beneath the hooves of his white steed as he rides slowly past, deaf to all entreaties. The land on either side of the road is barren and blighted, showing only brown stubble of dead grass and a few dying trees in the distance that grow along the bank of a poisonous river.

The ruling intelligences of the trump are the three *Moires*, or Fates, who determine the length of human existence—Klotho who spins the thread of life, Lachesis who sustains it, and Atropos who cuts it. They cannot be prevailed upon to extend the term of existence but may reveal some of its mysteries if invoked by name.

XIV Temperance
Hebrew letter: Samekh (tent prop)
Correspondence: Sagittarius
Path: Twenty-fifth

An androgynous angelic figure stands at the margin of a pool, measuring the contents of one cup into another, so that the liquid makes a diagonal stream between the vessels. His—or perhaps it is her—attention is raptly focused on the task to avoid spilling even a single drop, so that the level in both cups may be made exactly equal. One cup originally held a strong wine, and the other was filled with pure water from the pool, but by pouring and repouring they have been combined. The angel will offer you one of the cups, and will keep the other to drink from as you sample yours, sharing this diluted wine with you in a spirit of harmony.

It is impossible to determine whether the sun near the mountains on the horizon behind the figure is rising or setting. Green marsh grasses and flowers grow all around the edge of the pond. The land is well-watered and fertile farmland. The air is mild, and the time of year has the feel of late spring. Frogs sound their notes from the lilies and birds sing in the grasses. On the other side of the pond, cattle approach the edge to drink. The water remains pure thanks to a stream that flows in and flows out. If you explore this landscape, you will find the farming folk pleasant and cheerful.

The ruling intelligence of the trump is Eirene, one of the Horae, the Greek goddess of peace to whom were made bloodless sacrifices. Her open-air shrine is not far from the pond, containing her stone statue. When invoked by name and asked a question, she may respond with a nod to answer in the affirmative.

XV The Devil
Hebrew letter: Ayin (eye)
Correspondence: Capricorn
Path: Twenty-sixth

Masquers come dancing through the town street in the darkness, flaming torches in their hands, their bodies painted and their faces masked so that they resemble the demons of the infernal regions. The central piece in their procession is a statue on a black pedestal on wheels that is pulled by a naked man and a naked woman who are chained by their necks to the pedestal. Both wear horns on their heads and tails protrude from their back-sides. The terrifying figure on the pedestal is a giant with bat-like wings and the curving horns of a goat. His torso and arms are bare, showing his red skin, but his legs are hairy and his feet resemble the talons of a hawk. An inverted pentagram adorns his head like a crown. He holds an inverted torch in his left hand, while his right hand is raised in a gesture of damnation.

As this procession makes it way through the town, the revelers keep up a constant din by beating on drums and pots with sticks, blowing whistles and flutes, and singing and hollering at the tops of their voices. Most of them are drunk. The townspeople watch them with amusement from the sidewalks. Now and then, the painted revelers seize one of the onlookers and refuse to release him until he ransoms his freedom with a coin. When the procession reaches the town square, the chains are symbolically struck off the necks of the naked man and woman by an imp wielding a sword, and the giant devilish figure is set on fire.

The ruling intelligence is Pan, god of nature. The flutes invoke his presence at the celebration in the form of a goat that is led along after the statue. For the price of a coin, the masked revelers will let you ask your questions of the goat, who will bleat to indicate an affirmative response.

XVI The Blasted Tower
Hebrew letter: Pe (mouth)
Correspondence: Mars
Path: Twenty-seventh

A tall tower of stone built upon a peak and accessible only by a steep and winding road is struck by a bolt of lightning during a storm. The crown of the tower catches fire and the blaze, driven by strong wings, begins to work its way down to the lower levels, its progress indicated by the flames that issue from successively lower windows. The inhabitants of the tower leap to their deaths from its windows to avoid the heat of the flames. There is no way for you to go to their aid because the entrance at the rear of the tower remains barred.

The townspeople who climb the hill to watch the progress of the flames are as helpless as you are. They inform you that the owners of the tower, a wealthy nobleman and his wife, were so fearful of being robbed that they built this impregnable citadel on the hill, where they could live with their children and trusted servants in complete security from intrusion. They may whisper rumors of dark doings in the tower concerning torture and black magic. As you watch, the tower collapses and falls into a heap of rubble.

The ruling intelligence of the trump is Mars, the god of warfare and destruction. If you listen, you may hear his voice speaking in the crackle and roar of the flames.

XVII The Star

Hebrew letter: Tzaddi (fish-hook)
Correspondence: Aquarius
Path: Twenty-eighth

An attractive, naked woman pours out the contents of two pitchers beneath a starry night sky as she kneels on one knee at the margin of a river. The liquid from one vessel falls on the land, and the stream from the other falls into the water. A single great star dominates the other seven above her head. It is evident that she is involved in some occult ritual that pertains to the fecundity and fruitfulness of the land and the water. In the tree visible past her shoulder, a bird sits and watches. The great star is Sirius, known as the Dog Star, which was venerated by the Egyptians because it rose above the eastern horizon at the time of the year when the Nile River flooded and overflowed its banks. In this way, the fertility of the farmlands of Egypt were annually renewed by a fresh deposit of river silt. The bird is the phoenix, which periodically renews itself and rises as a youthful bird from the remains of its former aged body.

When we gaze around at the world of this trump, we find that the land is part of a green floodplain beside a river. The remains of ancient stone columns and great statues lie broken and toppled into the rich black soil, so that they are half concealed by the grass and plants. Some distance away there is a temple to the Egyptian goddess Hathor, whose statues have the shape of a cow and also that of a woman with a cow's head, or a woman with a headdress of curving cow's horns.

The ruling intelligence of this trump is the goddess Hathor, from whose breasts flow the sustaining milk of the stars. The phoenix will act as her oracle, for if you pose it a question about some future event, it will cry out in its shrill voice if the answer is yes.

XVIII The Moon

Hebrew letter: Qoph (back of the head)
Correspondence: Pisces
Path: Twenty-ninth

The full moon shines down her light on a path that winds its way up from the edge of a stagnant pond into the distant hills that line the horizon. Droplets of night dew shower down with her silvery beams. On either side of the path stand two animals like dogs. Or one of them may be a wolf. They try to catch the falling dew on their tongues as they howl and bark at the moon. Behind them, unnoticed, a crayfish crawls silently out of the pool onto the path with its claws raised in menace. In the middle distance stand two similar watchtowers, so that the path undulates between them. Their windows are darkened. The scene gives an oppressive sense of danger and despair.

You observe these things while standing in the reeds and rank grasses that grow on the far side of the pool of murky, slime-covered water. It has a fetid smell of decay. By making your way quietly around the pool, you escape the notice of the snarling and howling animals, who appear half mad as they threaten each other across the imaginary barrier of the path. The moonlight makes the scene almost as bright as day. Glistening dew lies like a frost on every blade of grass and every leaf. When you reach one of the watchtowers, you find the door carelessly left unlocked. All the soldiers, who are evidently the military force of the nobleman that owns the tower, lie sleeping in their beds as though drugged, and cannot be awakened. Crossing to the other tower, you discover an identical situation, but the guards wear the crest of a different noble house. Something moves in the higher chambers of the tower.

The ruling intelligence of this trump is Hecate, triple goddess of the moon who presides over black magic, nightmares, and the use of drugs and poisons. Among her beasts are the dog and the wolf. If you sit on the grass with a bowl of water on the ground so that you can see the moon reflected in its depths, you can establish a communication with this goddess and learn of her many dark secrets of deception and glamoury (false appearance).

XIX The Sun

Hebrew letter: Resh (head)
Correspondence: Sun
Path: Thirtieth

Beyond a low stone wall grows a garden filled with tall sunflowers. Their heavy flower heads droop and nod in the warmth of a noontime summer sun. Bees and other insects move lazily from flower to flower. You hear childish laughter, and turn to see a naked boy galloping wildly toward you on a gray pony, waving a red banner in his hand. He rides bareback but seems in no danger of tumbling off as he flashes past you and continues along the wall of the garden.

You perceive an open gateway through which the child has disappeared. Faintly, you hear his laughter from within the garden, and you approach the gateway and enter beneath its stone arch. Inside are many flowers, plants, and trees, with sandy pathways winding between them. In the center of the garden is a hedge maze, and the plants that form its walls are covered with red and yellow flowers. Birds keep up a ceaseless chatter in the tops of the trees, and swoop down to peck at the seeds in the heads of the sunflowers. The air is heavy with heat and shimmers as it rises from the path. The sound of music leads you into the maze.

The ruling intelligence is the god Apollo, who is sometimes depicted in the form of a young boy. He is a god of healing, but can also cause sickness and death with the arrows of his golden solar bow. At his shrine in the center of the garden maze, you may consult his oracle through the mediation of his solemn white-robed priest, who utters the inspired responses of the god.

XX The Last Judgement
Hebrew letter: Shin (tooth)
Correspondence: Fire
Path: Thirty-first
Clouds roil in the sky—shutting out the rays of the sun, which lights them with lurid red and orange. From the clouds sound the tones of strident trumpets. In the ancient graveyard in which you stand beside an old stone church, a rumbling is heard from the ground. The sods above the graves split apart as the rotting coffins push their way to the surface and burst open, releasing naked men, women, and children whose bodies are miraculously restored and show no signs of decay.

The risen take little notice of your presence, but begin to sing joyously and lift their arms to the heavens. Some fall to their knees in prayer. Between the gray bodies of the risen walks a figure in white, his face radiant. As he touches each person in passing, they rise upward into the sky and vanish amid the clouds. Bear in mind that this is not the actual judgment you are witnessing, but a kind of dramatic enactment of it.

The ruling intelligence of the trump is the archangel Gabriel, who will sound his horn on judgment day, causing the dead to rise from their graves. Go to him and converse with him. He will give you good advice.

XXI The World
Hebrew letter: Tau (cross)
Correspondence: Saturn
Path: Thirty-second
A woman dances on a stage with a great python that wraps its gleaming, multicolored coils around her naked body and weaves its head and neck in time with the music of the flute and drum. Her long hair is bound up on the back of her head in a twisted braid, and

her legs cross as she leaps in time to the music from one bare foot to the other. She uses two small white wands to guide the serpent, holding one in each hand and applying them so skillfully that there is never a threat of her being bitten. On the stage curtain behind her are painted four heads that represent the four winds at the corners of the world—the heads of an angel, an eagle, a bull, and a lion.

The members of the audience in the small, dark theater strain with mingled wonder and horror as the python sways and hisses. It is evident that they are not accustomed to such worldly entertainments. Leaving the theater, you find that it is contained within a fairground tent. Other tents beckon, advertising their shows as the wonders of the world. Their lights shine brightly in the gathering twilight, but the fairground is strangely deserted.

The ruling intelligence of this trump is Urania, the Greek Muse who presides over the harmony of the heavenly spheres. She speaks only through her music and the graceful movements of her dancer.

CHAPTER THIRTEEN

Pathworking

Pathworking was a specialized form of astral projection developed within the Hermetic Order of the Golden Dawn for investigating astral reflections of the higher spiritual realities represented by the various parts of the symbolic diagram generally known as the Tree of Life. It is important to bear in mind that all this work was confined to astral levels, and that the environments experienced by those who ascended the Tree using this technique were not the actual higher spiritual realms, but rather astral impressions or simulations of those realms. Observing that the visual impressions of the astral world are but "representations at their own level of higher forces," Gareth Knight wrote. "However, if one sticks to astral imagery one is still on the astral plane, even if one seems to be floating in a brilliant blaze of glory in Kether, with the Kerubim circling all around."[201]

The Tree of Life is derived from the system of Jewish mysticism known as the Kabbalah, which Westcott and Mathers incorporated into the teachings of the Golden Dawn. The Kabbalah was developed mainly in Europe during the Middle Ages and the Renaissance, although portions of it, such as the text *Sepher Yetzirah*, are much older. The Tree was an attempt to represent in a single diagram the stages in the emanation of the universe from the undifferentiated godhead to the physical environment that most people think of as surrounding them.

Kabbalists understood the process not so much as a creation, but as a coming forth or extension of the divine essence in ten stages, which were called Sephiroth (singular form: Sephirah). These stages are conceived as spheres of light. The light is always the same within them—it is the undifferentiated light of God—but each successive emanation adds its own level of veiling or shadowing to that light, causing it to be perceived in a progressively more limited way. There is only a single spiritual radiance and it never changes, but it can be partially obscured or shadowed, lending it various different individual qualities or aspects, depending on how much of the light is able to shine through the veils, and in what way it is able to reveal itself.

The Kircher Diagram

The emanations were affirmed to be ten in number, and were arranged in various patterns by Kabbalists as a way of emphasizing different aspects of their collective nature and interactions. The Tree of Life adopted by the Golden Dawn is only one of these symbolic patterns for the Sephiroth, although it may be the most sophisticated. It appears almost exactly as it was used by Mathers and his flock in an illustration in the 1652 work *Oedipus Aegyptiacus*, written by the mystical philosopher and Jesuit priest Athanasius Kircher (1601–1680). Very similar Trees of the Sephiroth, though not in all their details, are older, but there exist numerous symbolic arrangements of the Sephiroth that do not resemble trees in the least. One of the more popular arrangements developed by Jewish Kabbalists was concentric, so that the Sephiroth are shown emanating outward in everwidening circles from a central point.

---

201. Knight, vol. 2, 278.

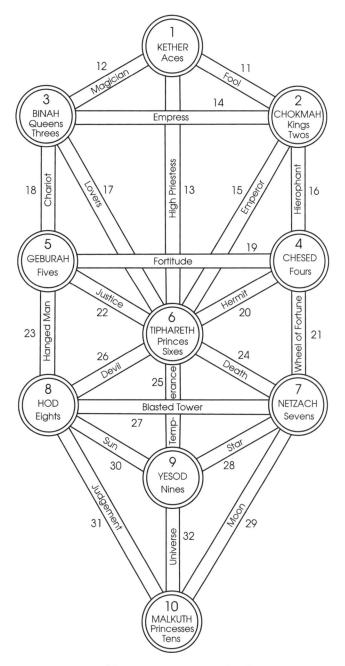

Golden Dawn Tree of Life

The Kircher and Golden Dawn glyph of the Tree is somewhat unusual for having three connecting pathways leading up from the lowest of the ten Sephiroth: Malkuth (the Kingdom), the sphere of the four elements that corresponds to the physical world. This appears to me to be an error in its structure. There are other glyphs of the Tree that show only a single path connecting Malkuth with the next higher Sephirah: Yesod (the Foundation), the sphere of the moon. It makes sense to me that all access to the higher spheres would be through the sphere of the moon, which, as the lowest of the astrological spheres that encircles the earth, functions as the gateway to the heavens. However, in the Golden Dawn Tree, it is possible to bypass the sphere of the moon by following paths that extend upward on either side.

The most significant aspect of the Kircher model of the Tree is that the connecting paths, or channels, between the ten spheres of the Sephiroth number twenty-two. This allows them to be associated with the twenty-two Hebrew letters. Indeed, it almost demands that such a link be made, and the Hebrew letters appear on the paths in Kircher's illustration of the Tree. Since Mathers and Westcott had developed an occult correspondence between the twenty-two trumps of the Tarot and the Hebrew letters, it was natural that they should assign the trumps to the paths on the Tree that were occupied by their Hebrew letters. This was something new in Western occultism, and it is perhaps the most significant innovation made by the Golden Dawn.

The connecting paths on the Tree became identified with their Tarot trumps, and their meanings colored by the meanings of the Tarot cards. During pathworking, the traveler astrally moves from Sephirah to Sephirah along the connecting paths. What is experienced on those pathways is determined in large measure by the Tarot trumps assigned to them in the Golden Dawn system. Whether this overshadowing of the paths by the trumps is justified is debatable. Traditional Jewish Kabbalists regard it with anathema. Whereas before its imposition, the meaning of a path was determined by the two Sephiroth that occupied its ends, and by its relative location on the Tree, the meanings of the trumps became predominant after the Tarot was applied to the paths.

All of these ten spheres have their astral equivalents. It is these astral reflections, not the actual spheres, that are visited during the projection of the double. The lowest of the ten spheres is not actually the physical realm, but is the astral reflection of the physical. It is the same as what I have called the base level of the astral world, through which astral travelers wander when they believe themselves to be traveling across the surface of the earth in the physical realm. It is an almost exact duplicate of the physical plane, and may be thought of as corresponding with the astral chamber that acts as the staging zone for soul flights in the general ritual.

Rising on the Planes

It is possible to move from this base astral level straight upward on the Tree by following the vertical paths. This was known in the Golden Dawn as Rising on the Planes.[202] Mathers wrote: "By concentration and contemplation of the divine, you formulate a Tree of Life passing from you to the spiritual realms above and beyond yourself. Picture to yourself that you stand in Malkuth, then by the use of the Divine Names and aspiration, you strive upwards by the Path of Tau towards Yesod, neglecting the crossing rays which attract you as you pass up. Look upward to the Divine Light shining downward from Kether upon you. From Yesod, leads upward the Path of Samekh, Temperance; the Arrow, cleaving upwards, leads the way to Tiphareth, the great central Sun."[203]

This brief direction by Mathers requires some amplification if it is to be understood by those unfamiliar with the Golden Dawn system of occultism. The glyph of the Tree of Life is to be visualized extending up from the body, and the traveler is to conceive himself standing within the sphere of Malkuth—this lowest sphere is to be entered in this manner on the astral level by the power of the imagination, as a starting place. The traveler then casts his astral awareness straight upward along the vertical path that extends from Malkuth to Yesod, the thirty-second path that is associated with the Hebrew letter Tau and the Tarot trump the World.

Standing in Yesod, the traveler than hurls his awareness upward along the twenty-fifth path, which leads vertically between Yesod and Tiphareth on the central pillar of the Tree, and is associated with the letter Samekh and the trump Temperance. This was known by those in the Golden Dawn as the Path of the Arrow, because they imagined the diagonal and horizontal paths around it as forming a great bow. Temperance is linked in the Golden Dawn system with the astrological sign Sagittarius, the Archer, which gave rise to the conception of the twenty-fifth path as a great arrow.

202.　Knight, vol. 2, 277.

203.　Regardie, 464.

The astrological sun was placed in the central Sephirah, Tiphareth (Beauty), which was understood to be the seat of Jesus Christ and all other divine human beings, or Messiah figures. To attain the level of Tiphareth in a true sense was believed to be as high on the actual Tree of spiritual worlds that the normal human consciousness was capable of ascending. Tiphareth is infused with divine radiance continually from the summit of the Tree, the sphere of Kether (the Crown), via the vertical path that links Kether with Tiphareth. To rise on the planes in this manner was to ascend in consciousness directly toward God as high as consciousness was able to rise.

The divine names mentioned by Mathers are the names of God assigned to the Sephiroth.[204] The divine name used by the Golden Dawn in Malkuth is Adonai ha-Aretz (Lord of Earth), those in Yesod are Shaddai and El Chai (Almighty and the Mighty Living One), and those in Tiphareth are Eloah Vedaath and IHVH (God Manifest and Tetragrammaton). Tetragrammaton was vocalized by means of its individual Hebrew letters as Yod-Heh-Vav-Heh, or sometimes as Yahweh. These names would be vibrated on the breath in a ritual way, and simultaneously visualized to float in Hebrew letters of glowing white fire upon the corresponding Sephirah of the Tree. By vibrating a name upon the breath, the traveler aspired in his consciousness toward it.

The "crossing rays" alluded to by Mathers are the horizontal and diagonal paths on the Tree. Were they to be followed, they would lead to the Sephiroth on the two outer pillars. This would be a distraction away from the purification of spiritual awareness that is the object of this form of Rising on the Planes. Dion Fortune wrote, "the Western magical operation of Rising on the Planes takes place up the Central Pillar of the Tree; that is to say, the symbolism employed to induce this extension of consciousness does not take the Sephiroth in their numerical order, commencing with Malkuth, but goes from Malkuth to Yesod, and Yesod to Tiphareth, by what is called the Path of the Arrow."[205]

Only the four central Sephiroth on the Tree are balanced in their nature. The Sephiroth on the other pillars of the Tree are polarized, and each can only be understood in relationship with their polar opposites on the other side of the Tree. They form three pairs: Chokmah-Binah, Chesed-Geburah, and Netzach-Hod. Since the purpose of Rising on the Planes in the Golden Dawn sense of the term is spiritual integration, to visit the other Sephiroth would be a distraction and would create imbalance and discordance in the mind.

---

204. Regardie, 64.

205. Fortune, *Mystical Qabalah*, 80.

Even the central Sephiroth may be thought of as polarized, but this polarization occurs vertically, forming the dynamic vertical pairs of Malkuth-Yesod and Tiphareth-Kether. Its tension acts to draw the mind upward from matter to spirit. The most balanced of the Sephiroth is Tiphareth, which is considered to be the center of the Tree and to express incarnate divinity, either as human consciousness ascended into divine consciousness or as divine consciousness cast down into human consciousness, so that the two mingle and become one. In a spiritual sense, Jesus lived in the sphere of Tiphareth, even though his physical body was reflected in Malkuth, since his consciousness was perpetually united with the mind of God.

This Golden Dawn understanding of Rising on the Planes is a bit limited. Rising on the Planes applies to any vertical astral travel—travel that occurs up through successive astral levels, rather than across a single level to different landscapes, particularly lateral travel across the base level that corresponds with the material world. The term was used in this broader general sense of passing upward through astral planes by Theosophists. However, in the Golden Dawn it acquired the very narrow and specific meaning of an astral ascent from Malkuth to Tiphareth on the Tree of Life.

Golden Dawn Pathworking

By contrast, pathworking in the Golden Dawn was the exploration of any connecting pathway on the Tree. It could be done by following up the paths in their reverse order from the thirty-second to the eleventh—the first ten paths are assigned in the Kabbalah to the ten spheres of the Sephiroth. This tracing of the paths in reverse numerical order was known as the Way of the Serpent because it was conceived as the winding ascent of a serpent up the Tree from its base to its crown. It was not absolutely necessary to explore the paths in order from lowest to highest, although this was the recommended way of getting an initial familiarity with them. Any path could be accessed directly by projecting consciousness into the Sephirah that formed its lower end. The lower end of the horizontal paths was the end attached to the lower numbered of the two Sephiroth that were its terminations, the left sides of these three horizontal paths.

For example, to explore the twenty-seventh path between Hod on the Left Pillar of the Tree, and Netzach on the Right Pillar, the traveler would project directly into Hod, and from there move across the Tree along the path from its left to its right side, and approach Netzach. It was advised that the Sephirah into which awareness was projected be conceived as a great pylon, or gateway. Inscribed upon the double doors of this gate was visualized the Hebrew letter of the path to be explored, and the traveler moved through the gate, and through the Hebrew letter, to gain access to the path.[206]

Gareth Knight gave a more detailed description of the procedure that was probably used by the descendant orders that evolved from the Golden Dawn, such as Dion Fortune's Society of the Inner Light.[207] The Sephirah at the beginning of the path is visualized as an astral temple having a gateway that exits the temple onto the path. Closing this gateway is a curtain or veil, upon which is painted the Tarot trump of the path. The divine name of the initial Sephirah is vibrated, followed by the name of its archangel. Then the traveler approaches the curtain of the gateway, and the image of the Tarot trump assumes a three-dimensional quality. The traveler steps into the Tarot trump as though stepping through a doorway, and finds himself on the path. Its details will depend on the mind that perceives it.

At the midpoint of the path, the traveler will encounter the Hebrew letter associated with it. Toward the end of the path he will see the astrological or elemental sign for the path, and will also perceive the Sephirah that marks the end of the connecting pathway in the form of the exterior of a temple. He may be able to pass through the open gates of this temple, but Knight wrote that the usual practice is not to enter it, even if it is possible to look through its open doors and see some of the details within.

Knight made the extremely important observation, which I have already emphasized in chapter 10 in connection with the astral chamber, corridor, and elevator of the general ritual, that nothing should be conceived beyond the boundaries of the path itself. "Also, in astral work, the boundaries must be clearly defined and kept to. A figure that is met *may* disappear from sight into a landscape or building but no impression should be fostered of it breaking bounds, thus risking leakage of psychic force or intrusion of alien factors."[208] When you do pathworking, the path you visit should be all that exists, apart from the interior of the temple of the Sephirah at its beginning, and the exterior of the temple of the

---

206. Regardie, 464.

207. Knight, vol. 2, 272–4.

208. Ibid., 274.

Sephirah at its termination. If you follow an astral entity off the path, its progress will create another astral environment. This is to be avoided.

Using the General Ritual for Pathworking

It is possible to employ the general ritual of projection for pathworking in the Golden Dawn tradition. The key used should be the Tarot trump of the path to be explored, or a representation of it. After projecting in the usual way into the astral chamber, and following the corridor to the elevator, exit through the opposite door of the elevator is immediate when working any of the three paths that lead upward from Malkuth; there is no need to ascend or descend in the elevator. The far door of the elevator opens into the temple of Malkuth at the beginning of these three paths, and from this temple the gateway of the Tarot trump is accessed. Which of the three trumps is visualized on the curtain of the temple gateway of Malkuth depends on which of the three paths is to be worked.

In the case of any path that begins with a Sephirah higher than Malkuth, the up button on the elevator must be pressed before the far door is opened onto the temple interior of that Sephirah. Malkuth represents the base level of the astral world, so no ascent is needed when seeking to enter the temple of Malkuth—the traveler is already on the base level of the astral when in the astral chamber. All other Sephiroth are higher than Malkuth, and hence higher than the base level of the astral world. They must be ascended to in the elevator before the pathworking can begin. They can, of course, be reached directly by a leap of the imagination, which is how it was done by members of the Golden Dawn, but the use of the elevator to rise up to these levels provides a useful ritual structure.

How the interiors of the temples of the Sephiroth are visualized for pathworking is left to the judgment of the traveler. Gareth Knight observed that they should each have a central altar with a flame burning both on it and the two pillars, one black and one white, that formed important ritual furniture of the physical temple of the Golden Dawn. My own feeling is that these Golden Dawn details are not really necessary. It is useful to have the astrological symbol that corresponds with each Sephirah inscribed prominently within the astral temple of that Sephirah. For example, Malkuth corresponds with the four elements, so the signs of the four elements in the form of four elemental triangles would appear within the temple of Malkuth. Hod corresponds with the planet Mercury, so the glyph of Mercury would appear within the temple of Hod.

One possible general form you might wish to use is a square room with two doorways, the one that exits the elevator through which you enter the temple of the initial Sephirah of the path, and a doorway in the opposite wall that is masked by a curtain painted with the image of the Tarot trump associated with the pathway you intend to explore. On the floor of the temple is inlaid the astrological symbol of the initial Sephirah of the path. To reach the doorway with the curtain, you must walk across this symbol. The details of each temple, such as the decoration or coloring of its walls, I will not describe, but will leave to your imagination, saying only that they must correspond to the nature of the Sephirah of that temple. The décor of the temple of Netzach, corresponding with Venus, would be sensual and voluptuous, for example, whereas that of Geburah, corresponding with Mars, would be spartan and military.

Since the paths are worked from their lower end to their upper end, and the temple of the Sephirah at the upper end is not entered, there is no temple to be visualized for Kether, at the very top of the Tree. This is appropriate because Kether is so exalted in its nature that it is sometimes said not to be a part of the Tree at all, but to exist above the Tree, which is said to have Chokmah for its first real Sephirah. Kether corresponds with the primum mobile, which does not have an astrological symbol or glyph. The symbol of Chokmah is the zodiac, so when exploring the very highest of the connecting paths, the path of the Fool that leads up from Chokmah to Kether, you would visualize the zodiac in the floor of the astral temple of Chokmah. The Tarot image of the Fool would appear on the curtain masking the second door. At the end of the eleventh path, you would see the temple of Kether only as a blinding and indistinct brightness, like the reflection of sunlight in a mirror.

The Thirty-Two Paths

The following list of the thirty-two paths on the Tree provides the essential information you will need to do pathworking. It is vital to have a good understanding of the Tarot trumps and the seven planets of traditional astrology before you begin this ritual work, since the trumps and planets play a large part in defining the nature of the connecting pathways and the spheres. The divine and angelic names are less important, but may be useful to know if they are needed to challenge an astral being you encounter on a path. I have provided the names and their translations as they were used by the Golden Dawn, even though not all of them are perfectly accurate. Some of the divine names are compound. Because the paths are numbered as they descend the Tree, the twenty-two paths that link pairs of Sephiroth are described descending from higher Sephirah to lower Sephirah.

Included with each path is the corresponding verse from a short Kabbalistic tract known as the *Thirty-Two Paths of Wisdom*, which was often bound under the same cover with the seminal work of the Kabbalah, *Sephirah Yetzirah*. The translation is from the 1887 edition of *Sepher Yetzirah* by William Wynn Westcott, one of the original human Chiefs of the Golden Dawn. Meditation on these verses is sometimes helpful in conceiving the astral appearance of the paths on the Tree.

1. **Kether** (Crown)
   Divine name: Eheieh (I Am)
   Archangelic name: Metatron
   Correspondence: primum mobile

"The First Path is called the Admirable or the Hidden Intelligence (the Highest Crown): for it is the Light giving the power of comprehension of that First Principle which has no beginning; and it is the Primal Glory, for no created being can attain to its essence."

2. **Chokmah** (Wisdom)
   Divine name: Yah (Lord)
   Archangelic name: Raziel
   Correspondence: zodiac

"The Second Path is that of the Illuminating Intelligence: it is the Crown of Creation, the Splendour of the Unity, equaling it, and it is exalted above every head, and named by the Kabalists the 'Second Glory.'"

3. **Binah** (Understanding)
   Divine name: IHVH Elohim (The Lord God)
   Archangelic name: Tzaphqiel
   Correspondence: Saturn

"The Third Path is the Sanctifying Intelligence, and is the foundation of Primordial Wisdom, which is called the Creator of Faith, and its roots are AMN; and it is the parent of Faith, from which doth Faith emanate."

4. **Chesed** (Mercy)
   Divine name: El (The Mighty One)
   Archangelic name: Tzadqiel
   Correspondence: Jupiter

"The Fourth Path is named the Cohesive or Receptacular Intelligence; and is so called because it contains all the holy powers, and from it emanate all the spiritual virtues with the most exalted essences; they emanate one from the other by the power of the Primordial Emanation. (The Highest Crown.)"

5. **Geburah** (Severity)
    Divine name: Elohim Gibor (God of Battles)
    Archangelic name: Kamael
    Correspondence: Mars

"The Fifth Path is called the Radical Intelligence, because it resembles the Unity, uniting itself to the Binah, or Intelligence which emanates from the primordial depths of Wisdom or Chokmah."

6. **Tiphareth** (Beauty)
    Divine name: IHVH Eloah Vedaath (Lord God Manifest)
    Archangelic name: Raphael
    Correspondence: Sun

"The Sixth Path is called the Mediating Intelligence, because in it are multiplied the influxes of the emanations, for it causes that influence to flow into all the reservoirs of the Blessings, with which these themselves are united."

7. **Netzach** (Victory)
    Divine name: IHVH Tzabaoth (Lord of Hosts)
    Archangelic name: Haniel
    Correspondence: Venus

"The Seventh Path is the Occult Intelligence, because it is the Refulgent Splendour of all the Intellectual virtues which are perceived by the eyes of the intellect, and by the contemplation of faith."

8. **Hod** (Glory)
    Divine name: Elohim Tzabaoth (God of Hosts)
    Archangelic name: Michael
    Correspondence: Mercury

"The Eighth Path is called the Absolute or Perfect Intelligence, because it is the means of the primordial, which has no root by which it can cleave, nor rest, except in the hidden places of *Gedulah*, Magnificence, from which emanates its own proper essence."

9. **Yesod** (Foundation)
   Divine name: Shaddai El Chai (The Almighty Living One)
   Archangelic name: Gabriel
   Correspondence: Moon

"The Ninth Path is the Pure Intelligence, so called because it purifies the Numerations, it proves and corrects the designing of their representation, and disposes their unity with which they are combined without diminution or division."

10. **Malkuth** (Kingdom)
    Divine name: Adonai ha-Aretz
    Archangelic name: Sandalphon
    Correspondence: Earth (the four elements)

"The Tenth Path is the Resplendent Intelligence, because it is exalted above every head, and sits on the throne of *Binah* (*the Intelligence spoken of in the Third Path*). It illuminates the splendour of all the lights, and causes an influence to emanate from the Prince of countenances."

11. **Kether to Chokmah**
    Hebrew letter: Aleph
    Tarot trump: 0 The Fool
    Correspondence: Air

"The Eleventh Path is the Scintillating Intelligence, because it is the essence of that curtain which is placed close to the order of the disposition, and this is a special dignity given to it that it may be able to stand before the Face of the Cause of Causes."

12. **Kether to Binah**
    Hebrew letter: Beth
    Tarot trump: I The Magician
    Correspondence: Mercury

"The Twelfth Path is the Intelligence of Transparency, because it is that species of Magnificence called *Chazchazit*, the place whence issues the vision of those seeing in apparitions. (That is the prophecies by seers in a vision.)"

13. **Kether to Tiphareth**
    Hebrew letter: Gimel

Tarot trump: II The High Priestess
Correspondence: Moon

"The Thirteenth Path is named the Uniting Intelligence, and is so called because it is itself the Essence of Glory. It is the Consummation of the Truth of individual spiritual things."

14. **Chokmah to Binah**
   Hebrew letter: Daleth
   Tarot trump: III The Empress
   Correspondence: Venus

"The Fourteenth Path is the Illuminating Intelligence and is so called because it is that *Chashmal* which is the founder of the concealed and fundamental ideas of holiness and of their stages of preparation."

15. **Chokmah to Tiphareth**
   Hebrew letter: Heh
   Tarot trump: IV The Emperor
   Correspondence: Aries

"The Fifteenth Path is the Constituting Intelligence, so called because it constitutes the substance of creation in pure darkness, and men have spoken of these contemplations; it is that darkness spoken of in Scripture, Job xxviii. 9, 'and thick darkness a swaddling band for it.'"

16. **Chokmah to Chesed**
   Hebrew letter: Vau
   Tarot trump: V The Hierophant
   Correspondence: Taurus

"The Sixteenth Path is the Triumphal or Eternal Intelligence, so called because it is the pleasure of the Glory, beyond which is no other Glory like to it, and it is called also the Paradise prepared for the Righteous."

17. **Binah to Tiphareth**
   Hebrew letter: Zayin
   Tarot trump: VI The Lovers
   Correspondence: Gemini

"The Seventeenth Path is the Disposing Intelligence, which provides Faith to the Righteous, and they are clothed with the Holy Spirit by it, and it is called the Foundation of Excellence in the state of higher things."

18. **Binah to Geburah**
    Hebrew letter: Cheth
    Tarot trump: VII The Chariot
    Correspondence: Cancer

"The Eighteenth Path is called the Intelligence or House of Influence (by the greatness of whose abundance the influx of good things upon created beings is increased), and from its midst the arcana and hidden senses are drawn forth, which dwell in its shade and which cling to it, from the Cause of all causes."

19. **Chesed to Geburah**
    Hebrew letter: Teth
    Tarot trump: VIII Strength
    Correspondence: Leo

"The Nineteenth Path is the Intelligence of the Secret of all the activities of the spiritual beings, and is so called because of the influence diffused by it from the most high and exalted sublime glory."

20. **Chesed to Tiphareth**
    Hebrew letter: Yod
    Tarot trump: IX The Hermit
    Correspondence: Virgo

"The Twentieth Path is the Intelligence of Will, and is so called because it is the means of preparation of all and each created being, and by this intelligence the existence of the Primordial Wisdom becomes known."

21. **Chesed to Netzach**
    Hebrew letter: Kaph
    Tarot trump: X The Wheel of Fortune
    Correspondence: Jupiter

"The Twenty-first Path is the Intelligence of Conciliation and Reward, and is so called because it receives the divine influence which flows into it from its benediction upon all and each existence."

22. **Geburah to Tiphareth**
Hebrew letter: Lamed
Tarot trump: XI Justice
Correspondence: Libra

"The Twenty-second Path is the Faithful Intelligence, and is so called because by it spiritual virtues are increased, and all dwellers on earth are nearly under its shadow."

23. **Geburah to Hod**
Hebrew letter: Mem
Tarot trump: XII The Hanged Man
Correspondence: Water

"The Twenty-third Path is the Stable Intelligence, and it is so called because it has the virtue of consistency among all numerations."

24. **Tiphareth to Netzach**
Hebrew letter: Nun
Tarot trump: XIII Death
Correspondence: Scorpio

"The Twenty-fourth Path is the Imaginative Intelligence, and it is so called because it gives a likeness to all the similitudes which are created in like manner similar to its harmonious elegancies."

25. **Tiphareth to Yesod**
Hebrew letter: Samekh
Tarot trump: XIV Temperance
Correspondence: Sagittarius

"The Twenty-fifth Path is the Intelligence of Probation, or Temptation, and is so called because it is the primary temptation, by which the Creator trieth all righteous persons."

26. **Tiphareth to Hod**
    Hebrew letter: Ayin
    Tarot trump: XV The Devil
    Correspondence: Capricorn

"The Twenty-sixth Path is called the Renewing Intelligence, because the Holy God renews by it all the changing things which are renewed by the creation of the world."

27. **Netzach to Hod**
    Hebrew letter: Pe
    Tarot trump: XVI The Blasted Tower
    Correspondence: Mars

"The Twenty-seventh Path is the Active or Exciting Intelligence, and it is so called because through it every existent being receives its spirit and motion."

28. **Netzach to Yesod**
    Hebrew letter: Tzaddi
    Tarot trump: XVII The Star
    Correspondence: Aquarius

"The Twenty-eighth Path is called the Natural Intelligence; by it is completed and perfected the nature of all that exists beneath the sun."

29. **Netzach to Malkuth**
    Hebrew letter: Qoph
    Tarot trump: XVIII The Moon
    Correspondence: Pisces

"The Twenty-ninth Path is the Corporeal Intelligence, so called because it forms every body which is formed in all the worlds, and the reproduction of them.

30. **Hod to Yesod**
    Hebrew letter: Resh
    Tarot trump: XIX The Sun
    Correspondence: Sun

"The Thirtieth Path is the Collective Intelligence, and astrologers deduce from it the judgment of the stars and celestial signs, and perfect their science, according to the rules of the motions of the stars."

31. Hod to Malkuth
Hebrew letter: Shin
Tarot trump: XX The Last Judgement
Correspondence: Fire

"The Thirty-first Path is the Perpetual Intelligence; but why is it so called? Because it regulates the motions of the sun and moon in their proper order, and each in an orbit convenient for it."

32. Yesod to Malkuth
Hebrew letter: Tau
Tarot trump: XXI The World
Correspondence: Saturn

"The Thirty-second Path is the Administrative Intelligence, and it is so called because it directs and associates the motions of the seven planets, directing all of them in their own proper courses."

CHAPTER FOURTEEN

Runes

There are many sets of esoteric symbols that might be used both as keys and as gateways for astral travel. The tattwa were extremely popular within the ranks of the Golden Dawn, as were the individual Hebrew letters. Astrological and alchemical symbols are effective, both the simple glyphs and the more complex compound symbols—it is quite possible to project the astral body into a scene depicted in an alchemical illustration. Indeed, the alchemical woodcuts and paintings that depict the various stages of the Great Work seem almost designed for astral investigation. They contain complex architectural structures with doors, corridors and windows, walled gardens, caves, meadows, roads and pathways, and are populated not only with human beings but with numerous strange creatures of dreamlike appearance. The strong resonance between dream symbolism and alchemical symbolism was studied in detail by Carl Jung in his work *Psychology and Alchemy*, a book that contains many alchemical images suitable for astral doorways.

The letters of the Enochian alphabet, received from the angels by Edward Kelley[209] on May 6, 1583, could certainly be used as portals, since each letter represents a unique spiritual being, or so the angels informed John Dee. The curious names of the individual Enochian letters, which seem to have no connection with the sounds the letters represent, may be the names of these spirits. Although there is no record that they were ever used for scrying in the spirit vision or astral projection by the original Golden Dawn, it is very likely that its members working in the Enochian system of magic, such as Aleister Crowley, experimented with them as astral portals, since the use of the Hebrew letters for this purpose was common.

Germanic Runes

---

209.   Laycock, *Complete Enochian Dictionary*, 36–7.

A set of symbols that did not form a part of the Golden Dawn esoteric system, yet deserves special examination due to its extreme potency, is the twenty-four Germanic runes. When used with a full awareness of their meaning, no symbols are more effective at evoking tangible astral landscapes. Perhaps due to the extreme simplicity of their shapes, the runes resonate in the depths of the subconscious with primal force. Each rune is a letter that may be used for writing, but as is true of Hebrew letters and Enochian letters, each is also a spiritual intelligence and its own astral world. The meaning of every rune expresses itself dynamically in these two ways—as a self-aware astral entity with whom it is possible to converse and interact, and as a landscape that contains and houses the entity, and reflects in its details the nature of the entity.

The Shamanic Ordeal of Woden

The god most closely associated with runes is Woden (the Norse god Odin), the one-eyed god of magic who became viewed as the father of the gods in the northern pantheon, on a similar footing with Zeus in the Greek pantheon. In his earlier Germanic incarnation, he was a shaman who wrested the runes from the roots of Yggdrasil, the World Tree, during a soul flight that was induced by a trial of physical endurance. The nature of his trial, and its reward, are described in a portion of the poem *Havamal* from *The Poetic Edda*, as translated by Henry Adams Bellows.

> 139. I ween that I hung /on the windy tree,
>   Hung there for nights full nine;
>   With the spear I was wounded, /and offered I was
>   To Othin, myself to myself,
>   On the tree that none /may ever know
>   What root beneath it runs.

> 140. None made me happy /with loaf or horn,
>   And there below I looked;
>   I took up the runes, /shrieking I took them,
>   And forthwith back I fell.[210]

The outline of the ancient Germanic shaman's initiatory trial of endurance, involving the projection of the astral body to attain the living wisdom of the runes, is evident in

---

210. Bellows, 60–1.

these few lines of poetry. Woden, the divine magician and the prototype of all the shamans who imitate his examples, gashed himself with a spear—his traditional weapon and the weapon favored by Germanic warriors—and then had himself suspended from Yggdrasil, the great ash that is the axis of the universe. For nine days and nights he hung on the tree without food or drink. The loss of blood and pain from his wounds and his bindings, coupled with his hunger and thirst, at last induced his astral double to leave his body and fly downward to the roots of the tree.

There are several significant details we may deduce from this important poem. The runes were an infernal device. They were not of the heavenly realms, but of the underworld, the dark realm of Hel, goddess of the dead, the hidden shadow world of monsters and devils, of necromantic sorceries and blood magic. Woden did not look upward when suspended from the tree; he gazed downward at the very roots of the tree, the depths of which no man has knowledge. The runes were carved into the roots of the tree. We know this because runes are not tangible things, but are symbols similar to letters of the alphabet. There is no such thing as a rune in a material sense unless it is inscribed on some physical surface.

The practice of the Germanic shamans was to carve runes into the bark of twigs and roots for various works of magic. Carving runes into the root of a tree was a type of death magic. It was done to kill an enemy. A tree was selected and given the name of the foe in order to magically unite the two. Death runes were carved on its root, and then the tree was deliberately made to wither and die. As the tree died, so died the man—or so the shamans who worked this magic believed. The twenty-four runes on the roots of Yggdrasil embody the living essence of the world ash. They express in their shapes the essential vitality of existence itself, and hence they possess the power to both give and take life.

It is significant that no source is specified for the runes. The poet, speaking with the voice of Woden, does not state who carved them. They are coeval with Yggdrasil itself, eternally existing at the foundation of all things. Indeed, it might be argued that the runes are the source of the world's vitality. They are the magical marrow upon which the tree feeds. For the ancient Germanic peoples, the underlying forces that sustain existence were twenty-four in number, and expressed in their shapes the twenty-four essential qualities of being.

The runes would have remained asleep and invisible at the roots of Yggdrasil, but the blood released by the spear of Woden, falling from his suspended body into the ground, fed the runes and made them active, causing them to glow in the depths of the underworld with lines of red fire, the color of embers. It was this glow that enabled the projected astral form of the god to see the runes and fly toward them. The runes called out to him mutely with his own life force. Because they lay buried at the very root of the tree, the primal beginning of existence, the astral body of Woden could only sustain the depths for the briefest moment, but it was long enough for him to snatch away the runes and return to his suspended physical form. The effort caused him to cry out in agony, and his bonds at once burst asunder with his newly attained power, releasing him from the tree.

Snatching up the runes from the roots of Yggdrasil did not deprive the tree of their nourishing energies—because they are not things but symbols. Woden caught them up and held them safe in his mind, as his astral double soared upward through the endless darkness to the light of day. The darkness beneath the ground is akin to the darkness of the unconscious, and the daylight is an expression of the waking awareness.

The parallels between this poetic fragment and the crucifixion of Jesus are obvious. Jesus was also wounded with a spear. He also hung from a kind of tree—the cross of crucifixion is frequently called a tree by poets. The identification of the cross of Christ with a tree is made in the great Anglo-Saxon poem *The Dream of the Rood*, where it is called the "glory-tree."[211] The poet of the *Havamal* calls the tree from which Woden hung suspended "the windy tree." That it was windswept suggests that it was located on a high place, such as the top of a hill, even as the cross of Jesus was located on a hill. As Jesus was a sacrifice to himself, in that as God incarnate in human form he gave his life to God the Father, so did Woden who was known as the High One and the All Father give himself to himself in the form of the shaman undergoing the initiation ritual, who assumed the identity of Woden for the purpose of receiving the runes.

Almost all of the practices of early Germanic shamans have been lost, and there is no way to know with assurance that this poem reflects an actual initiation ritual. Yet so practical is it in its details, from an esoteric standpoint, that I cannot regard it as other than an outline of the initiation rite of Germanic shamans who received the runes as their highest and most sacred mystery teaching. It may be argued that no man could endure nine days without water, yet there are religious rites still being practiced today that involve enduring nine days without water; Buddhist monks in Japan do so, for example. Nine days without water is an extreme test of human endurance, but it is not impossible, particularly if conducted under the open sky in a climate where rain is frequent.

---

211.   Alexander, *Earliest English Poems*, 106.

Runes and Necromancy

The location of the runes at the roots of Yggdrasil brings up a consideration that modern astral travelers should bear in mind when using the runes as astral keys or portals. They have the reputation as instruments of infernal or necromantic magic. This lends them a great physical power, but it also makes them somewhat dangerous. If not kept rigorously under control, they tend to act independently in unpredictable ways, not all of which may be desired by those who use them. It is something to consider when studying the runes. Woden was not a jolly, cheerful figure of fun, but a god of deception and guile who could bear malice and was never slow to exact retribution. This essential reality of his nature tends to get obscured by his later incarnation as the wise, benevolent father of all the gods. His name among the ancient Saxons was Grim, and this word best describes his true personality.

Woden's spirit familiars took the forms of two ravens and two wolves, creatures that express the kind of magic worked by the runes. They are both lunar creatures. The wolf is a beast associated with the fierceness of the natural world, and also with warfare. Wolves were reputed to be unrelenting, ravenous, and pitiless. The raven is particularly connected with the gallows and with graveyards because it is a carrion bird. It ate the flesh of the dead who were executed by hanging at crossroads. One rune charm mentioned by Woden in the *Havamal* is a charm to make the dead speak, showing that his magic was at least in part necromantic:

> 158. A twelfth I know, /if high on a tree
> I see a hanged man swing;
> So do I write /and color the runes
> That forth he fares,
> And to me talks.[212]

Those who travel astrally into the environments of the Germanic runes will encounter the raw forces of the natural world, anthropomorphized into the figures of twenty-four deities, and the corresponding wellsprings of these primal forces that arise within their own hearts and minds. Investigation of the worlds of the runes offers insight into the urges and fears in the unconscious mind. They are excellent as a way of coming to terms with your own

---

212. Bellows, 65–6.

individual human nature, for every traveler into the runes sees them in a unique way that resonates with his own deep motivations.

Woden speaks of staining the runes, as well as of carving them. The usual stain was blood, which fed the runes' symbols and rendered them active and aware. Until the runes are stained, they lie dormant as though asleep. The use of blood to awaken the runes is another indication that they were employed in necromancy. For purposes of astral travel, I do not recommend that you stain the runes with blood. This would cause their action to be more energetic and independent than would be desirable. It is better to inscribe them using red ink or red pigment, which in a symbolic sense represents blood. This was done in ancient times, so it is not a modern cheat—runes were stained with red ochre, a natural pigment dug from the ground that served as the blood of the earth itself.

Using a Rune Key

Draw the rune you wish to travel into about three inches tall on a small square of paper or a card, using red ink or red paint, and let it dry as you meditate upon its meaning. This will serve as the key during the general ritual of projection, and will be held over the solar plexus beneath your folded hands as you lie on your back on your bed and project yourself into the astral chamber. On the astral level, it becomes your keycard and unlocks the door of your astral chamber and the doors of the elevator. Traveling to the worlds of the runes is a rare instance when you will press the down button on the elevator. All of the runes are drawn from the roots of Yggdrasil and are in their fundamental essence infernal. The second door of the elevator may be conceived to open directly upon the world of the rune on the keycard.

Each rune world is dominated by its ruling god or goddess, whose name is the same as the name of the rune. These deities may also have other names by which they are more commonly known. It was usual in the mythology of northern Europe for the gods to have many names or titles that were descriptive of various aspects of their personalities. Woden in particular had dozens of different names. It is not possible to be certain that in their earliest beginnings all twenty-four runes were named after deities, but this seems likely. It was the usual practice to personify the forces of nature as spiritual beings. Many runes are explicitly known to have been linked to deities, and those in which the link is not explicit were also probably associated with a god or goddess of the natural world. In any case, the forces that energize and define the runes express themselves as intelligent beings when the runes are entered as astral landscapes.

Once within the land of the rune, it is important to seek out and confront the ruling deity. The rune itself, drawn upon the air in front of you with the index finger of your right hand, can be used as a sign of power. It will test the truthfulness in the appearance of the astral environment—if the land is out of harmony with the nature of the rune, inscribing the rune upon the air will cause the land to dim and become indistinct. The rune can also be used to subdue the deity of the astral world it governs. It is that god's highest sigil, and it has power over the god, should the god attempt to frighten or threaten you.

The following descriptions are subjective. The lands of the runes and their rulers will be different for each soul flyer who encounters them. These descriptions are based on my own early astral investigations of the runes, as presented in my book *Rune Magic*.[213] The earlier descriptions were quite brief, and they are here expanded, and in some details corrected to correspond with my more recent impressions of the rune environments.

1. Fehu

> Literal meaning: cattle
>
> General sense: possessions, ownership, wealth, submissiveness, slavery

The land of Fehu is a farming community dominated by herds of cattle. There is a small village of simple houses with a market square. It is overshadowed by a fortified keep, the ruler of which is the god of the land. He is a great bull of a man—stubborn, quick to anger, slow of wits, with a loud, bellowing voice, and glaring eyes beneath a shock of shaggy black hair. He bears a whip that he uses to drive the villagers from the path of his cart when he rides into the village. He is fond of fine clothes, gold and jewels, but always appears somewhat slovenly in appearance. When he remains within his keep, the villagers and farmers enjoy a placid though squalid existence.

2. Uruz

> Literal meaning: aurochs, an extinct species of wild ox
>
> General sense: virility, freedom, courage, manhood, trial of strength, power, the will

Uruz is a primal forest filled with wild beasts that stalk each other and engage in fierce battles. They are seldom clearly seen amid the leaves and shadows, but their presence is announced by the shaking of the undergrowth and their snorts and grunts. You may en-

---

213. Tyson, *Rune Magic*, 140–4.

counter wolves, bears, stags, wild boars, foxes, serpents, and creatures less natural in the dim and dappled light that filters through the forest canopy. There is a profusion of birds, and they keep up a constant chatter and song. The god is a barbarian hunter who carries a short spear and wears the mask of a bear. His body is nearly naked and painted with natural pigments. Around his hips he wears a bearskin, but his arms, legs, and feet remain bare. His deeply tanned face is noble, his eyes gray. He seldom speaks, and he never utters more than a few words at a time, preferring to grunt and gesture.

3. Thurisaz

Literal meaning: evil giant or devil
General sense: malice, wickedness, vengeance, hatred, spitefulness, slanders, underhanded dealings, evil

The land of Thurisaz is a land of shadows, an infernal realm of darkness in vast caverns beneath the surface. Steam and smoke rise from fissures in the rocks. Those who dwell in this place live in fear of the monstrous creatures that haunt the fathomless black pools and hidden clefts. The place has a strange greenish glow that emanates from fungus on the walls and rocks, and the inhabitants subsist on fish and on mushroom-like plants that sprout in abundance from the soil on the cavern floors. These dwellers in darkness have white skin, white hair, and large black eyes adapted to see in the dim glow. They are surly and not to be trusted. The god is a scaled creature that resembles a dragon, with a long tail, clawed feet, and many sharp teeth. The inhabitants and lesser creatures of the land flee its approach.

4. Ansuz

Literal meaning: the wise god, Woden
General sense: wisdom, eloquence, persuasiveness, authority, law-giving, magic knowledge

Ansuz is a land of gently rolling, wooded hills and lush meadows crossed by streams. Snow-capped mountains line the horizon. The inhabitants are a hardy northern folk who herd cattle and hunt wild beasts with spears. Within the depths of the forest is found a timber hall composed in part of still-living trees. A great tree rises at each of its corners. Its walls are rough logs with their bark still clinging to them, its roof thick shingles of enormous size split from the trunks of forest giants. The double doors of the hall always stands open, and sounds of a feast come from the interior, beckoning the traveler. The god is an old warrior chieftain with gray hair and a white beard, who sits at the head of a long wooden table, dressed in battle-worn armor, drinking from a horn set with silver. One of his eyes is covered by a leather eyepatch. On either side, young warriors eat and drink, amply supplied by young women with braided hair who carry food and ale on broad wooden platters.

5. Raido
> Literal meaning: a journey on horseback
> General sense: travel, a quest, seeking, exploration, communication

The land of Raido is a long road that winds its way between steep hills and dense forests. At intervals on the road are to be found inns for the accommodation of travelers. Many follow the road on foot and horseback, passing in either direction, bundles of their worldly possessions on their backs, or drawn behind ponies in carts. They are road-weary and seldom speak unless addressed. At the inns are to be found food and drink, along with a bed for the night and a stall for your horse. The god of the road is a wandering minstrel and storyteller flamboyantly dressed in brightly colored clothes, who rides from one hostelry to another, earning his way by entertaining the other guests.

6. Kano
> Literal meaning: torch, beacon
> General sense: a guiding star, the object of a quest, illumination on the path, truth, revelations, a guide or teacher

The rocks of the seacoast in Kano are crystalline, and shot through with the many colors that pulse in the sky like the moving bands of a vast rainbow, illuminating the sparkling crests of the waves on the ocean. Trees, grass, and other vegetation seems to glow from within as though the leaves were tiny panes of stained glass. The inhabitants of this strange iridescent coast are fisher folk, slender and elf-like in appearance, moving with grace along the stony beach, where they dwell beside their upturned boats in huts made of sod and woven grasses. On the rise of a headland stands a stone lighthouse. The god is a woman who keeps the light. She comes floating upon the air across the surface of the bay, a flaming torch in her hand and a book cradled close to her breast, her diaphanous white gown rising around her slender legs, her long red hair drifting as though alive above her shoulders. When she speaks, the entire world resonates like a vast crystal bell.

7. *Gebo*

Literal meaning: gift, sacrifice

General sense: a present, gift for service, something given or received, achievement, talent, avocation, devotion

Gebo is the bank of a great, slow-flowing river where religious mystics have placed themselves in various strained postures as tests of their devotion and endurance. One mystic lies tied to stakes in the earth with a wooden pallet laden with large stones resting on his chest. Another stands on one foot, his raised leg withered to thinness from long disuse. Yet a third holy man lashes his back with a flail so that the blood flies off in shining red droplets. Another sits naked and stares directly into the sun with unwinking eyes. Another plays the flame of a burning torch across the skin of his arms and torso. The inhabitants of the nearby village who come to the river to bathe and wash their garments scarcely notice the devotions of the men, so accustomed are they to witnessing such self-abuse. The god of the place is a mystic bound to the trunk of a withered tree that stands on the crest of a hill. His body is suspended by his bonds from the earth—his arms spread and tied to low-hanging, leafless boughs, for the tree is dead and has lost its leaves and most of its bark. Empty, bloody sockets stare blindly from his head where his eyes once were.

8. *Wunjo*

Literal meaning: joy or glory

General sense: ecstasy, heavenly blessings, rewards, recognition, fame, celebrity, renown, victory in contests, titles bestowed

The land of Wunjo is a mountain with gentle slopes clothed in woodlands and grasses that are grazed by flocks of sheep tended by shepherds who live in stone huts. At the end of the steep and winding road, at the crest of the mountain, rises a city of white stone walls. The sun-gilded clouds press close to its sides, so that at times the city almost appears to rise from the clouds themselves. It inhabitants are a cultured race of artists, athletes, and philosophers. Excellence of both mind and body is universally prized. Even the faces of the elders glow with good health. The goddess who rules the city as its queen is a slender yet athletic woman with long blonde hair held in place beneath a golden tiara, dressed in a white gown that resembles the style of ancient Greece. She speaks with a clear, melodic voice.

9. Hagalaz

Literal meaning: hail

General sense: destruction, violence, loss, deprivation, disaster, wrath, punishment, injury, fury, conflict, assault

Hagalaz is an evergreen forest in the midst of a raging winter storm of snow and hail. No security or haven is visible in the gathering twilight. The boughs of the trees bend low to touch the banks of snow on the ground under the weight of the snow that clings to them. In the distance, everything fades to a general grayness. The cold of the wind is bitter. Only the snow-covered trees offer a slight shelter. Movement is difficult, for the drifts of snow rise as high as the hips of the traveler. Sometimes an elk may be seen in the distance, huddled beneath a tree, and a glimpse gained of wolves circling behind it on stealthy steps. The god of the land is never seen, but is only heard as a moaning and roaring in the wind.

10. Nauthiz

Literal meaning: necessity

General sense: suffering, hardship, pain, need to endure, torture, servitude

The land of Nauthiz is dominated by a deep chasm of rushing white water, spanned by a wooden bridge. Laborers who are little more than prisoners toil ceaselessly to maintain the bridge. Their living quarters are built on the bridge itself, along one of its sides. The bridge exists in a constant state of disrepair. The planks newly laid upon it begin to weather and rot almost as soon as they are put down, and constant rumbling in the ground and trembling of the earth shakes loose the stones that make up its buttresses. Overseers with flails drive the workers on to ever greater efforts, but it appears that all their work may be in vain. The center of the bridge is burning. It is evident that it has been on fire for a considerable time. While laborers working on either side strive to extinguish the flames, others replace blackened timbers with new planks brought down from the hills in carts. There is great shouting and confusion, and no one appears in command. The god of this place is a vague form that shapes itself in the smoke rising from the fire so that its flaming eyes and gaping mouth may be seen, and it leans down and threatens and snaps at the backs of those who labor to maintain the bridge.

11. Isa

Literal meaning: ice

General sense: fascination, allure, enticement, entrapment, deception, false appearance, heartlessness, halt in progress, an enchantress

The land of Isa is a frozen lake in the midst of which is a small island covered with willows that stand leafless and naked in the winter sunlight. There is a house built upon the island. As it is approached across the surface of the lake, the traveler may gaze downward and see, through the depths of the transparent ice, the bodies of men, their sightless eyes staring upward and their hands frozen as they reach for aid that never comes. Smoke rises from the chimney of the house on the island, which is a large structure of two levels built from timbers, with a stone foundation. Those who knock upon the door are greeted by a manservant, who bows low and escorts them into the great hall, where a fire blazes in the fireplace. Women servants bring food and drink. The goddess of the place is a beautiful enchantress who owns the island and the house. She wears her dark hair gathered up on the back of her head with silver combs, but her features change with the flicker of the firelight, so that sometimes she appear young and naive, and at other times wise and mature of years. She is moody and given to flashes of anger that distort her mouth with rage. A white owl she keeps as a pet rides on the shoulder of her fox-fur cloak.

12. Jera

Literal meaning: harvest season, year

General sense: fulfillment, completion, end of cycle, turn of the wheel, change, reversal, reaping

The land of Jera is dominated by a mill next to a fast-flowing stream. The water turns a great wooden paddle wheel that provides the power to rotate the grinding stones. It is a busy place with many villagers coming and going, bringing their grain and leaving with their milled flour. The season of the year is eternal autumn, the time of the harvest. Part of the mill is a brewery, and the ale is sold in a common room on the lower level. Patrons can sit outside at tables under the overhang of the upper story and watch wagons and riders pass along the road. The god of the place is the owner of the mill, a giant of a man with a red face and balding head, who wears a flour-covered leather apron over his immense belly. In one hand he habitually carries a mallet, and in the other a cup of water for cooling the oak bearings of his millstones. He is cheerful and talkative, but always bustling about at his work.

13. *Eihwaz*

Literal meaning: yew
General sense: resilience, dependability, strength of purpose, a trustworthiness, magical might, command of occult forces

The land of Eihwaz is a medieval field of battle on the eve of conflict. Between the rustling canvas of field tents, campfires illuminate soldiers who lie asleep wrapped in their blankets or sit murmuring together as they stare into the embers. It gleams off stacks of spears and other edged weapons, and from the rounded polish of armor and helmets readied for the morning. The restless snorts and pawing of horses can be heard on the cool night air. Across the empty field, the dotted campfires of the enemy are visible in the distance like a scattering of stars. The god of the land is a stocky foot soldier with a longbow slung over his back, who walks restlessly between the campfires and speaks encouragement to the other men in a gruff voice. In spite of his unkempt black hair and brooding eyes, he projects an aura of nobility and authority that suggests he is more than he seems.

14. *Perth*

Literal meaning: apple
General sense: luxury, pleasure, sensuality, indulgence, intoxication, gambling, gaming, divination

The land of Perth is an extensive grove of apple trees at the time of the harvest. The harvesters climb the trees on ladders and pick the ripe red fruit into woven wicker baskets slung on straps over their backs. Others sit at long wooden tables eating freshly made bread and drinking smoky cider from wooden tankards, or red wine from pewter cups. There is a general air of good cheer. A few men cast dice across the tables for copper coins, or play draughts. One of the laborers, an older man with a white beard, sits on a great stump and works his bow across the strings of his fiddle, and a few of the younger men and women dance in the open space before him while others watch, keeping time by clapping their hands. The goddess is a noblewoman of middle years, voluptuous in body and beautiful of face, the owner of the orchard, who moves between the tables with a pitcher of wine balanced on her shoulder, offering to fill the cups of those whose cups are empty. Her dark hair has a disheveled look, and a faint sheen of sweat is visible on her bare shoulders and her flushed cheeks.

15. *Algiz*

Literal meaning: defense

General sense: warding off, protection, barrier, shield, avertive amulet, a defender

The land of Algiz is a high and narrow mountain pass, in which is set an ancient gate that is defended by guard towers on either side, and which has living quarters for its soldiers along its top. The gate is of stone cut from the sides of the pass, its shape a curved arch. The doors set in its frame are of heavy oak, darkened and made hard by years and bound by great straps of black iron. Travelers along the road must await the pleasure of the gatekeepers, since there is no other way over the mountains. They must pay a fee to pass, but for the amusement of the soldiers they are also required to answer riddles correctly. Until they can find the correct answer, they are not permitted to enter the gate. Those who attempt to force their way through when the gate is opened meet a rain of fiery arrows and naked sword blades that are hurled down upon their heads. The god of the place is the chief gatekeeper, who does not reveal himself directly, but stays in the shadows of the building above the gate while speaking in a deep, threatening voice to those below.

16. *Sowelu*

Literal meaning: lightning or solar ray

General sense: fire from the heavens, divine intervention, an omen, portent, righteous wrath, retribution, judgment, justice, fulfillment of karma

Sowelu is a land of desert sands that so shimmers and blazes with the reflected brightness from the noontime sun that no details can be distinguished through the rising waves of heat. Even the sky itself is bleached by the sunlight to a pallor that shows only a trace of blue. The wind sounds high overhead with a roar that is like distant flames, although nearer the ground the air is almost still. Even when it does blow fitfully, it feels like a blast from an open furnace. The god of this desert world remains unseen and unmet, but communicates with those who travel across his lands by means of haughty angelic emissaries who fly down from the heavens on great feathered wings that shimmer with iridescence. Their tone of voice is superior and their expressions are faintly disdainful, as though they resent the necessity to touch the ground.

17. Teiwaz

Literal meaning: Tew, god of oaths and battle

General sense: courage, war skills, weapons, honor, nobility, promises, principles, oaths, pledges, contracts

The land of Teiwaz is a battlefield cloaked beneath a heavy mist, so that nothing can be seen that is more than a few steps away. All around is the sound of the clash of steel on steel, the tortured cries of horses, and the shouts and curses of men. Sometimes a pair of combatants come into view, but fail to notice the presence of the traveler in their fierce confrontation. On the trampled brown grass lie the bloodied bodies of the dying, their faces and hair whitened by the settling mist. The god is a silent warrior in a long scarlet cloak who carries a drawn sword. His face is covered by a mask of beaten silver that has the shape of a bearded man. Around it, his golden hair streams free to his shoulders. He moves across the field, selecting who is to be slain, and those he gestures at with his sword die.

18. Berkana

Literal meaning: birch

General sense: sexuality, desire, lovers, virility, fertility, conception, new growth, awakenings, renewal, birth

A glade of silver birch trees covers the side of a gentle hillside in the land of Berkana. Morning sunlight slants through the new spring leaves, and dapples the soft green grass and mosses that cover the ground, making the wildflowers glow as if with an inner radiance. Birds sing in the upper branches, which are moved by a gentle spring breeze. Rabbits dart across the path at the feet of the traveler, or sit nibbling the flowers. The air is laden with the scent of moist earth and new growth. Between large boulders, a spring bubbles up and winds its way beside the path, making the sound of gentle laughter as it splashes over the stones in its bed. The goddess of the land is a maiden who walks naked through the soft grass, clothed only in her long blonde hair, which hangs down almost to her knees in a loose fan, half in front of her body and half behind. She leads a stag by a leather cord that is tied around its neck. At times, she leaps upon its back and rides it through the trees, laughing with excitement.

19. Ehwaz

> Literal meaning: horse
>
> General sense: swiftness, strength, grace, beauty, conveyance, vehicle, means to
> an end, instrument, the body

A rolling grassy plain stretches to the horizon in all directions in the land of Ehwaz. Thunder clouds can be seen in the distance, and occasionally lightning flashes from them, but they are so far away that the rumble of the thunder is slow to reach the ears of the traveler. The land is crossed by the moving shadows of clouds, and the wind bends the tall grasses in waves. Herds of grazing animals are visible on the plain, so far away that they are no more than a gathering of dark specks. Some move swiftly, and when they happen to wheel closer, they are seen to be wild horses, but there are other beasts more sedentary in their movements. A river flows between the hills, a silver ribbon upon the brown and green of the grassland. The god of the place is a youth with long black hair and wild gray eyes, who is dressed in rabbit skins. He never walks, but rides a white stallion, clinging to its back and guiding it with his bare heels and with his fingers laced in the long strands of its mane.

20. Mannaz

> Literal meaning: man
>
> General sense: human nature, microcosm, intelligence, the way to an end, solu-
> tion to a problem, mental virtues, the human mind, the magician, the trickster

The world of Mannaz is the interior of a great mansion that has innumerable corridors, halls, staircases, and chambers, so that it is impossible to explore all of it and it is easy to become lost. Servants move silently about, perpetually cleaning the house and maintaining it. They will not notice the traveler unless they are directly addressed, and their responses are usually unhelpful. Some of the doors are locked and others are open, but this cannot be known until they are tried. Each opened door leads into a different tableau, in which the inhabitants of the chamber enact a drama for the traveler as he enters. If they are questioned, they will respond and explain what they are doing. The scene out of each window in different—some show cityscapes, others mountains, others the seashore, others forests or country scenes. The god of this place is the keeper of the keys, the owner of the house who selects what rooms the traveler may enter. He is never met directly, but may sometimes be glimpsed moving away from a door or around a corner, and the rattle of his key in a lock as he unlocks a door can be heard even when he is out of sight.

21. *Laguz*

Literal meaning: water

General sense: the unconscious, the womb, dreams, fantasies, hopes, vanities, fashions, fads, impermanent things, fickleness, changeability

The world of Laguz is the depths of an ocean lagoon of transparent emerald water, with strange sea plants waving in the currents, and looming towers and hills of coral that create a confusion of moving light and shadow. Schools of colorful fish dart past and conceal themselves behind the coral growths. Strange creatures that are not quite human slide through the shadows on hands and flippers, watching with sly eyes. If you are patient, they will approach and converse with you, but their bubbling words are not to be trusted. Because this is an astral world, it is possible to hear them and speak to them through the water. The women of this race have lovely faces, and are sensual by nature, but fickle and apt to lose interest and dart away. Their goddess is a mermaid with bluish skin, more human in shape than the others. Only her fingers are webbed, and her feet end in small fins instead of toes. She sings haunting wordless melodies that evoke strange illusions and dreamlike vistas.

22. *Inguz*

Literal meaning: fertility god

General sense: home, hearth, family, patriarch, nurture, growth, development, evolution, decency, humanity, homely virtues

The world of Inguz is a country farm, with a stone farmhouse having a thatched roof and a wattle barn. The trees of the surrounding forest press the cultivated fields on all sides, apart from the rustic track that leads away between the hills. The squawk of chickens and the grunts of pigs can be heard at the back of the house. The farm is inhabited by an extended family consisting of a grandfather, a father, a mother, a grown son, a younger daughter, and an infant. There is a hired hand who does not speak. The god of the place is the grandfather, a robust old man with a flowing white beard who spends most of his time sitting before the fire in the main room of the house. He is always willing to talk to travelers who stop in for a meal or to rest the night in the spare bedroom upstairs, and is full of homely advice and wisdom.

23. *Dagaz*

Literal meaning: daylight

General sense: clarity, understanding, perception, openness, harmony, wholeness, enlightenment

The land of Dagaz is a windswept open plateau on which is situated a pagan temple consisting of a single standing stone surrounded by a ring of numerous smaller stones. Twelve ridges of earth, like low walls, extend away from the standing stone in twelve spokes, so that the construction has the form of a great wheel. The sun never sets in this strange world, but moves around the horizon in a complete circle each day, just as it does in the high arctic during summer, so that the shadow of the standing stone is cast into all twelve partitions of the wheel in turn. The inhabitants of the land do not live near this solar temple, but come to present offerings of wheaten cakes and ale in the various sections. Which section they choose appears to depend on their purpose, although it is not obvious why they should choose one over another. They come to pray and to present their offerings when the shadow of the stone enters the boundary of that part of the temple suitable to their prayers. They crumble the cakes over the grassy earth and pour out the ale. The god of the place is a strange multicolored bird with shining wings that perches atop the pillar when offerings are made, and sounds its approval with shrill and unearthly cries.

24. *Othila*

Literal meaning: native land

General sense: place of birth, homeland, roots, culture, tribe, race, nation, sense of identity, name, house and estate, the grave

The land of Othila is a countryside in which small holdings with houses upon them are divided by stone walls and hedgerows, so that in the distance, on the sides of the rolling hills, it gives a checkerboard appearance. Many of the fields are tilled into black furrows and are ready for planting. Large stones engraved with family symbols mark the corners of the holdings. There is a small stone church on the hill, and a graveyard behind it. The people are cheerful, but do not like trespassers, and will set their dogs on those who venture across their fields uninvited. The god of the place is a surveyor whose task it is to settle land disputes and determine the ownership of fields and other holdings. His word is the final law, to which there is no appeal. He walks the lanes and fields with a deliberate pace, carrying a long rod divided into inches, which he sometimes lies flat upon the ground to measure distances.

CHAPTER
FIFTEEN

Training for Soul Flight

The general ritual of projection given in this book provides a practical and secure structure that may be used for soul flights of all kinds. However, it does not explain how to actually separate your astral body from your physical body. No ritual can do this. The technique of separation must be learned through practice. It took the Theosophist Oliver Fox decades to perfect his methods. The magicians of the Golden Dawn worked on their techniques of scrying in the spirit vision and ascending the planes for years, and some of them were much more successful than others due simply to inherent natural ability for astral projection. Not all of us are as gifted as Sylvan Muldoon, who could separate from his body with ease, even in boyhood.

Unless some artificial method is employed, such as the use of drugs, soul flight must be learned through an extended course of practice, which has the advantage of providing a natural control over the experience that the use of drugs can never yield. Those who attempt astral projection with drugs, and who do so outside the supportive structure of a shamanic priesthood and in the absence of teachers, are inevitably going to get erratic and uncontrollable results that may be dangerous to their mental stability. The spirits who communicated with the medium Mrs. Minnie E. Keeler told her in 1916: "In the case of getting out by the action of anesthetics, the astral senses are dulled, so that the person rarely perceives anything while out, or remembers it."[214] Even when images are perceived, they tend to be disordered, and after the stupefaction of the drug passes away are found to lack meaning. It is strongly recommended that the temptation to assist the separation of the astral body with intoxicants or narcotics be avoided.

There are two sides to training for the projection of the astral double. One is physical and the other mental. The physical side involves those things you can do with your physical body to facilitate separation, either before or during your period of practice. The mental side involves training the imagination and using it in ways that encourage astral perception and projection—for the two are both aspects of the same process, and to perceive an astral scene is to be present within it, whether you are aware of your astral body or not.

Physical Considerations

Diet

On the physical side, one of the more important considerations is diet. This may seem completely irrelevant to Westerners accustomed to paying no attention to what they eat and when they eat, but the effect of diet on astral projection can determine success or failure. Heavy foods and overeating inhibit the separation of the double, while light foods and fasting encourage it. Consequently, those seeking to project astrally will do well to moderate their eating habits for a period of a week or two prior to beginning serious nightly practice, in order to create in their bodies a condition of sustained craving or tension that exerts a pressure tending to more easily release the astral body.

Fasting should never be carried to an extreme, or hunger will begin to dominate the mind to such a degree that it becomes a hindrance. You may wish to try fasting for twenty-four hours, taking only clear liquids during that period, as a way of initiating separa-

---

214. Crookall, *Techniques of Astral Projection*, 36, citing the *Journal of the American Society for Psychical Research* (1916), vol. X, 683.

tion of the double, particularly if you have practiced without success for several weeks. During the course of any sustained period of practice that may extend over months, taking solid food should be avoided for at least four hours before each practice session. For example, if you do your experiments at ten in the evening, it would be best not to eat after six. Drinking liquids should also be avoided for at least two hours before practice. Sylvan Muldoon found that a condition of thirst was helpful in initiating separation,[215] but in my opinion, this thirst should be so mild as to be almost subliminal, since otherwise there is a danger that it will constrain the astral experience.

Either a wholly vegetarian diet, or a diet that is very light on red meat, will yield good results. Beef, pork, lamb, and other solid, fatty meats do the most to inhibit success. Grease appears to be the primary factor involved. Rich pastries such as meat pies or dumplings cause a similar type of hindrance. Fish and other sea foods, such as shrimp and scallops, are not bad, and may be included in such meals as stir-fries without inhibiting success. Vegetables should be at least partially cooked, so that they are easy to digest. Meals that are fried should be avoided. Olive oil or other vegetable oils are not so harmful to success as are animal fats.

Avoid large infusions of sugar in the form of pies, sweet pastries, ice cream, chocolate, and so on. These generate a rush of energy, but this rush is followed by a crash of the body's vitality, often accompanied by mild emotional depression that further hinders success. Lunar foods are beneficial as a general rule. You will remember from the passage quoted from Agrippa that these include things that are bland, white, insipid in taste, or slightly salty. Pasta prepared in pale cheese is a good sort of meal, as are pale steamed or stewed vegetables, the white flesh of fishes such as halibut and haddock, and egg omelets.

Choosing the proper diet is mainly a matter of common sense. Avoid foods that remain with you for long periods, or make you feel heavy and bloated, or that give you a headache, gas, or an upset stomach. Eat what you enjoy, as long as it is light on your stomach and does not remind you of its presence in your body hours later. The kind of diet adopted for serious hatha yoga practice is ideal for astral projection work.

Posture

Another physical consideration is the posture you adopt during practice. The posture suggested in this work is to lie flat on your back on a bed, but astral projection is also possible, and has often been done, from a sitting position. In either case, comfort for a

---

215. Muldoon and Carrington, *Projection of the Astral Body*, 192.

prolonged period is essential. The feet should not be crossed. The reasons given for this are various. Some authorities claim that crossing the legs hinders the circulation of blood in the body. Others say that it interferes with the circulation of more subtle currents of energy. Another objection raised is that crossing the legs prevents the easy release of the astral double. A spirit in communication with the medium Mrs. Keeler told her: "Crossing the hands and feet is bad ... as it mixes up the nerve currents and hinders the exit of the Astral Body."[216]

Whatever the underlying cause, it is generally agreed that crossing the legs or the arms is to be avoided. The physical body acts in a manner somewhat similar to that of a hose carrying a stream of water—whichever way it is bent, the astral body follows its shape. Crossing the limbs may have an effect similar to kinking the hose so that the water can no longer flow. When the legs are crossed, the astral body may entirely withdraw for a time from the lower limbs below the intersection, even as an arm or leg falls asleep and becomes numb when placed in an awkward position. Just the opposite effect is observed in those who have suffered the amputation of a limb—the sensation appears to them to remain, as though the limb were still attached, and indeed, the astral body is sometimes perceived to project from the stump of the amputation, and takes the form of the lost limb.

The scholar Henry James wrote in an article for the American Society for Psychical Research titled "The Consciousness of Lost Limbs" that those who suffer an amputation sometimes assert that they can feel what is being done to the severed appendage.[217] It was a common superstition that when the severed limb suffered injury, its former owner would experience pain. This belief was perhaps encouraged by the pain that is often felt by amputees in a so-called "phantom limb"—a limb that is missing but that hurts as though it were still attached to the body. This close association between physical limbs and astral limbs suggests why such a simple posture as crossed legs may have a profound effect on the ability of the astral body to separate.

It is worth noting that in medieval times, crossing the legs was reputed to be a way to prevent oneself from being bewitched or otherwise influenced by magic. Men crossed their legs for much the same reason they made a hand gesture to ward off the evil eye. Today we have the superstition that crossing the fingers behind the back will prevent the truth from being drawn out of us by an interrogator. Folding the hands over the solar

---

216. Crookall, 34, citing the *Journal of the A. S. P. R.* (1916), vol. X, 679.

217. Muldoon and Carrington, *Phenomena of Astral Projection*, 22.

plexus, as I have suggested in the general ritual of projection, is not quite the same as crossing the arms since the folding is done at the extremities, and should not produce any problems concerning the release of the double.

Although astral projection is possible while lying on either the side or the stomach, separation of the double while in these postures is unusual. The experience of Oliver Fox was not the norm. He wrote: "Speaking for myself, it does not matter whether I lie on my back or on my side . . ."[218] Muldoon had the curious experience of accidentally projecting while lying on his stomach. "While lying on the stomach, the sensations while moving through the air are reversed. When you move upward, you think you are moving downward, and *vice versa*. The only way to tell the true direction of movement is by the sense of sight."[219] Muldoon regarded projection in this posture as "running contrary to the laws of projection."[220]

Environmental Factors

External environmental factors also play a part in either hindering or facilitating the separation of the astral body, though it is not always clear what does which. The French experimenter Dr. Charles Lancelin wrote in his book *Méthodes de dédoublement personnel* that for the best results the air should be clear and dry, with a high barometric pressure. The temperature should be slightly warm, but not uncomfortably so, and the air still and quiet. He found the best hours for success to be between eleven o'clock at night and three in the morning.[221]

In my own work with spirits, I have found that just the opposite conditions assist in my perception of the presence of spiritual beings, particularly my perception of their touch. This is true while I am wholly within my physical body. The best conditions to become aware of the near presence of spirits—by sight, sound, or touch—seems to be when the barometric pressure is low, and when rain is just about to begin to fall. The imminence of a thunderstorm, and the blowing of wind, seem if anything to increase the clarity of these perceptions. I mention this because it strikes me as significant that for the astral body to leave the physical body, high barometric pressure is asserted by others to be best, yet for spiritual beings to come close to the physical body and make their presence

218. Fox, 126.

219. Muldoon and Carrington, *Projection of the Astral Body*, 41–2.

220. Ibid., 41.

221. Crookall, xii.

known, or indeed to penetrate or enter the physical body, my own experience has shown that low barometric pressure is more favorable.

Controlled Breathing

Controlled breathing can aid significantly in bringing about the separation of the astral double. The spirits who communicated through the medium Mrs. Keeler asserted that "for getting out of the body, holding the breath is of value, but holding it out has no effect."[222] Two techniques come into play—the gentle, slow rhythm of breathing, which helps induce a condition of physical relaxation, and the deliberate retention of breath, which by the slight pressure it puts on the solar plexus assists the astral body to move slightly out of alignment with the physical body. This is felt variously as a dizziness, a sensation of spinning or falling, a buzzing throughout the body that resembles a sustained current of electricity, and a sense of drifting or floating. More than one of these conditions may exist simultaneously.

Using the inflated lungs to press the solar plexus with the diaphragm is easy enough to learn. Take a deep breath and lock the back of your throat so that your breath cannot escape. Push down and outward with your diaphragm and hold it in that position until you feel a slight dizziness. Allow this to grow for half a minute or so, then relax and release your breath. Use your imagination to ride the resulting floating sensation out of your physical body, just as though you were floating away from the shore in a small boat. After breathing slow, deep breaths for several minutes, you can repeat this exercise. It is best not to use it more than a few times in succession. It should be employed as a trigger, to initiate the separation of the astral body.

Take care never to do this exercise while standing up, or sitting where there are sharp corners or furniture on which you might fall and hurt yourself. It is very easy to pass into unconsciousness if pressure is sustained on the solar plexus for too long a period. That is counterproductive for the purposes of soul flight, and a sudden fall might be dangerous. Also, take care not to exert more than a gentle pressure, and never fill your lungs all the way—leave a little room at the top, so that it is not uncomfortable to hold your breath while you distend your diaphragm. As in true with most activities of life, moderation should be your guide. Eastern adepts often refuse to teach advanced breathing techniques because, if willfully abused and repeated excessively, they can sometimes cause injury to the body. This is not a danger if they are applied gently with limited repetitions.

---

222. Crookall, 33, quoting from the *Journal of the A. S. P. R.* (1916), Vol. X, 649.

This breathing exercise may be applied during the general ritual of projection while contemplating the sign of projection, as a way of assisting the entry into the astral chamber. Retain the breath, apply pressure with the diaphragm against the solar plexus, and then relax and do a dozen or so slow, deep breaths with a regular rhythm. You may feel yourself rising and falling during these regular breaths, as though lying in a small boat that rises and falls on gentle waves that pass under it. Do not resist this sensation; let it occur in a natural way.

Stepped Relaxation

Prior to beginning the breathing exercise, but after you have drawn the sign of projection, is may be helpful to engage in a deliberate technique to relax your body. The technique used by hatha yoga instructors works well. It is sometimes called *stepped relaxation* because it relaxes the body in steps or stages, one part at a time. It is usually employed in conjunction with a verbal hypnotic induction, as a way of causing students to feel pleasant well-being at the end of classes. However, the stepped relaxation can be used without an accompanying hypnotic monologue, and is effective at releasing tension from the body.

Lie comfortably in the posture you have adopted for soul flight, and while visualizing the sign of projection floating on the darkness of your closed eyelids, turn your attention to your left leg. Focus all your tactile perception on your leg, feeling its muscles and bones, the way the skin touches the bed, whether it is warm or cold, and the angle of your foot. Tense the muscles in your leg slightly to become even more aware of them, then relax your left leg completely and withdraw your attention from it, just as though it was no longer attached to your body. Do the same process of heightened awareness and withdrawal in succession for your right leg, your left arm, your right arm, your abdomen, your chest, and, lastly, your neck and head. Do not hurry these stages. Withdraw your consciousness to a point between your eyebrows.

Some of those who perform this form of stepped relaxation like to take it in smaller degrees, starting first with the toes of both feet, then the feet themselves, then the calves, then the thighs, and so on working their way up the body to the head and face. This is a matter of individual preference. If small parts of the body are successively relaxed, the exercise can consume a considerable length of time. When used in conjunction with the ritual of projection, it should not be allowed to dominate the ritual, but should form a brief preliminary stage designed to help consciousness shift from its ordinary waking state to a condition conducive to separation of the astral double.

Body Pressure Points

Another physical factor that can be helpful in initiating soul flight is pressure applied to key points on the body. I have already mentioned the usefulness of the weight of the folded hands resting gently over the solar plexus. The weight and warmth of the hands help to stimulate this body center, which some adepts of Kundalini yoga associate with the *manipura* chakra. Others say that the manipura chakra is located much lower on the torso, in the region of the navel. Whether or not the solar plexus is the manipura chakra, I have found it helpful to stimulate it during scrying and soul flight, both using the weight of the hands, and the pressure of the retained breath applied through the diaphragm.

A body center more widely recognized as important for astral projection is the point between the eyebrows, the ajna chakra, which can be stimulated in several ways. Perhaps the most effective method is to place a small, flat object on the forehead, so that its constant pressure stimulates the chakra and draws the awareness to it. A small silver coin such as a dime works very well. An older dime is better, because older coins contained silver, the metal of the moon, and astral projection falls under the general lunar influence.

S. L. MacGregor Mathers, leader of the Hermetic Order of the Golden Dawn, explicitly advised against using this technique. Describing the use of the tattwa symbols for astral doorways, Regardie, quoting from original Golden Dawn documents, wrote that "the process of working by placing the symbol upon the forehead, instead of imaginatively passing through it, is not a good practice. S.R.M.D. [Mathers] claims that it is liable to derange the brain-circulation and cause mental illusions and disturbance, headache, and nervous exhaustion."[223] In my own work, I have found that placing a small object on the ajna chakra is quite helpful. There is no reason why a symbol cannot be placed on the forehead, and yet still be used as an astral doorway. Contrary to what might be expected, unless the head is moved violently about, it has little tendency to slip or fall off, but will remain in place throughout the entire ritual.

If a small disk of silver is incised with the sign of projection, using a punch or other sharp instrument, it would is quite useful when placed on the forehead during the general ritual of projection. Another method I have used to apply this pressure is with a

---

223. Regardie, 462.

specially made circlet of copper. Silver would be a superior material, but copper is inexpensive and easy to work, and its qualities are in general harmony with those of silver. I shaped my circlet into a serpent biting its own tail, and wear it with the head of the serpent over my forehead. It does not press directly upon my ajna chakra, but it serves to draw my attention to this center by its continual presence. Any simple circlet of twine, fine chain, or wire that can be placed around the head will serve the same purpose. If you make a disk for this circlet that will hang over your forehead between your eyebrows, at your ajna chakra, its utility will be increased. If you inscribe this disk with the sign of projection, its effectiveness will be magnified still further.

One of the advantages of having a silver disk or diadem inscribed with the sign of projection is that it is worn only when you practice soul flight. After a few weeks of daily practice, your unconscious mind begins to associate the placing of the disk upon your forehead with the separation of the astral body. A useful habit is formed that aids in creating the correct internal conditions for projection. If you find that the use of a disk or circlet gives you a headache, you should stop using it, or at least change to a lighter disk, or looser circlet, that applies less pressure. The pain of a headache makes soul flight difficult or impossible.

Music

Music can be helpful in creating a unique sensory state that you associate only with the ritual of projection. Once it becomes habitual, it will strongly aid in causing separation of the double to occur. Common sense is needed when picking what music to use. The music should be pleasant, but not overly interesting. Background music is needed that can play yet be almost ignored by the mind. Vocal music is generally a poor choice to create atmosphere because the mind tends to become distracted by the words. If the words are unintelligible, such as is the case with Gregorian chants, this condition does not apply. Chamber music is generally appropriate. Longer works should be used, and a series of similar works played so that the mind is given no abrupt changes that would distract it. The volume of the music should be quite low.

The background music may be natural rather than artificial. Wind chimes, especially those made of crystal or silver, work well. Bird song may be used, if you happen to have birds outside the window of the room in which you practice. The sound of the wind rustling leaves, or the needles of pine boughs, makes a soothing background sound.

Scent

Those who enjoy incense may find that burning it during the general ritual helps to create a unique atmosphere, and develops a useful habit pattern. Any mild, pleasant incense may be employed. Avoid scents that are acrid and cutting, or that are too cloying and sweet in the back of the throat. Vanilla is a good lunar scent, and the lighting of a vanilla-scented white candle is excellent, as white is one of the colors of the moon.

Water Vessels

A useful trick you will not find mentioned elsewhere is to set a basin of clear, fresh water under your bed. A silver or crystal basin works best—the broader its opening, the better. Even plain glass is fine to use, since clear glass is lunar in nature. If you prefer, set this basin on a table or bureau in the physical chamber where you practice the general ritual. You can float a small, flat candle on the surface of the water, though you should never do this under your bed for obvious reasons of safety. The currents of air generated over the basin by the rising heat from the candle flame will help circulate the water vapor throughout your chamber.

Mental Considerations

Portal Exercise

As a mental exercise, visualize an astral doorway. This can be done at any time you have a few minutes to sit quietly and close your eyes. It does not need to be incorporated into the general ritual. Remember, the general ritual is designed to be an aid to soul flight; it is not a requirement. It is perfectly possible to project the astral body without using it. If you do wish to incorporate this exercise into the general ritual, perform the visualization just after forming the sign of projection, so that the image of the sign of projection merges and transforms into the image of the astral doorway. It can be used as an aid in entering the astral chamber.

Sit or lie quietly. Close your eyes. Visualize yourself as a disembodied awareness gliding through the blue heavens. All around you is blue sky. In the distance, something approaches. It is perceived first as a dot, but as it draws nearer, you see that it is a doorway. You are able to see the frame of the door, and the door itself. The details of the doorway are not important. You may prefer to visualize the same doorway repeatedly, or you may find that you naturally see different doorways, depending on your mood at the time of practice, or other factors in your life. The door can be single or double, simple or ornate, small or massive, the door to a cottage or to a pagan temple.

As the door draws near through the blue sky, it slowly opens, revealing a bright glow on the other side. The radiance is so bright that you cannot make out any details of what lies on the other side. Allow yourself to glide nearer to the door and pass through it so that the glowing light envelops you completely. This may end your exercise, or you may find yourself able to see details emerge of the place beyond the door as the bright glow slowly fades away. If so, you may wish to record them in your daily journal.

The opening doorway filled with white light is similar to the tunnel with light at the end that those who have had near-death experiences so often describe. Contrary to popular superstition, you will not die if you go through this tunnel. The tunnel, or the doorway of this exercise, are symbols of transition. They take your awareness to a different place. Do not be afraid to pass through the doorway. Such a transition of consciousness is essential for soul flight. You must pass into the astral world, and that involves passing through a portal of some sort. Even when we enter dreams, we first pass through what is poetically termed the "gates of sleep."

If you reach the stage where you begin to see details of the landscape on the far side of the doorway, you will find the appearance of the door frame, and the door or doors hung within it, to be in harmony with what lies beyond. A simple wooden door will probably open on to a rural landscape or on the interior of a cottage or shop; a gilded and ornately carved double doorway will open on a palace or temple or a walled garden. The same door will not always take you to the same place, but it will usually take you to a place of a similar nature.

Mantra

During the general ritual when seeking to enter the astral chamber, or during this visualization exercise when trying to open a doorway and pass through it, the repetition of a mantra is a good way to concentrate the attention. Mantras are words or brief phrases with magical significance, such as the famous "*om, mane padme hum*" of Tibetan Buddhism, said to translate into "Hail! The jewel in the lotus." This is a universal mantra, but mantras are often selected specifically for an individual student by a teacher as a key to enlightenment. The idea is that if the mantra is repeated often enough, enlightenment will dawn. Since you have no teacher, you must choose your own mantra. This can be done by meditating on your need, and then opening your mind to receive whatever mantra is given to you by your intuition.

In a sense, as the author of this book, I am your teacher, so it is only fitting that I provide an effective general mantra for the use of my readers. The mantra I have chosen for you is Enochian, a phrase based on real Enochian words that were transmitted through the scrying crystal of Edward Kelley to John Dee by the Enochian angels, but never put together into the phrase that appears here by the angels or by Dee. The mantra is "*Christeos Luciftias.*" It translates into English as the emphatic "Let there be Light!" (*christeos*— let there be; *luciftias*—brightness). It is a phrase of great power and authority.

If you know the astral world into which you wish to travel, you can pick a mantra that resonates with that world, such as the name of its ruling deity or spirit. Sometimes, the spirit of an astral realm may be abstract, a quality or condition that perhaps serves as its common name, and this can be used as its mantra. For example, "summerland" would make a good mantra when seeking to travel into the Summerland of myth. The name or title of a god or goddess particularly associated with an astral world might be used. Passage into the land of the rune Ansuz would be aided through the repetition of the mantra "Woden."

Whether a mantra should be voiced aloud or spoken only in the mind is also a matter of preference. I have experimented extensively with both techniques. I find that speaking the mantra with my voice so that it resonates in my chest makes it more potent, but also that speaking it can interfere with the rhythm of my breaths, particularly if I am using a breathing technique in conjunction with the mantra. I have developed a method that straddles the fence, being neither wholly verbal nor wholly mental. I voice the mantra silently, or almost silently, with my lips, and I allow my breath to express it without actually vibrating it in my larynx with my vocal cords. The result is a kind of soft, breezy whisper. This allows me to repeat the mantra on my breath both on the inhalation and on the exhalation.

This technique of subvocalization is common in magic, where mantras, names, or incantations must be voiced to release their power, yet are too sacred or too dangerous to voice aloud in such a way that others can hear what is said. The result was the "wizards that peep and that mutter" (Isaiah 8:19), as they are so poetically described in the King James Bible. The muttering of wizards was a way of saying something without actually voicing it aloud for everyone to hear. It works quite well when you wish to repeat a mantra where others who are sleeping in nearby rooms might be disturbed were it spoken in a normal voice. It was also used in religion. Shortly before the Temple at Jerusalem was destroyed by the Romans in AD 70, the Jewish high priests adopted the practice of speaking the name of God in such a manner that it could not be heard by the worshippers in the temple—in this way the power of the name was released by vocalizing it, but its sacredness was not diminished by revealing it to those who were not priests.

Symbol Visualization

A useful way to develop a talent for astral perception is to do regular visualization exercises. The visualization of simple symbols will help develop your inner sight. A few of the symbols suitable for this exercise are the cross, triangle, circle, square, pentagram, hexagram, sign of infinity, and spiral. Slightly more complex symbols that can be used are the Egyptian ankh, the Egyptian eye, the Masonic eye in the triangle, the Celtic cross, concentric circles, the pentagram within a circle, and the signs of the planets and the zodiac. These are all two-dimensional forms. They should be held in the mind with the eyes closed, as though they were being viewed floating on the darkness of space, formed from glowing light that has a soothing, pleasant golden-white color. This coloring is neutral in an occult sense.

As you lie down to go to sleep, adopt a comfortable posture on your back with your arms at your sides or folded on your abdomen and take a few slow, deep breaths. Close your eyes. Imagine the symbol you have chosen for the exercise floating in the air on the darkness. Pretend that you can look through your eyelids, which have become transparent, and that in the darkness of your bedroom the symbol floats before you. Imagine that you are actually looking through the ceiling of your bedroom into a larger darkness, and that you see the symbol at a great distance. It glows with soothing light, and flickers slightly round its edges as with some sort of electric fire. Hold it before your awareness for a few minutes, renewing it with your imagination when it begins to dim, and then release it and go to sleep. Do not worry if your mind drifts away from the symbol. Just bring it back and renew the symbol in the darkness.

You should be aware that when you do an exercise of this type, you are actually forming the symbol you imagine on the astral level, where it shines like a great beacon for any spirits who may be near you to notice. They cannot help but pay attention to the symbol you visualize. It is like a great searchlight stabbing its beam up into the night sky. Even though you are not present in any manifest way on the astral level, the creation of the symbol on the astral level announces your existence, and your desire to interact with the astral world and its inhabitants. This exercise will attract spirits to you, and you will become aware of their presence in various ways, even though you will probably not be able to clearly see their forms. A visualization exercise such as this is a way for students to proclaim that they are beginning practical work in astral perception. You will be noticed.

After you have practiced for several weeks using simple two-dimensional symbols, move on to simple three-dimensional forms. Instead of a triangle, visualize a shining pyramid of marble blocks floating in the darkness, a cube of stone, a sphere of crystal, a silver crucifix, or an Egyptian eye symbol made out of jet, ivory, and lapis lazuli. Experiment with causing the three-dimensional symbol to turn slowly so that you can see it from different angles. Practice turning it and stopping its motion. Practice zooming in with your astral vision to see its fine details and the texture of its materials. With your astral hand, reach out and touch the side of the object. This is just like extending your physical arm and hand, but you do not move your body—you reach out only with your mind. It is not necessary to visualize your astral hand. It can be left invisible. Feel whether the object you have created in your mind on the astral level is cool or warm, rough or smooth, dry or damp.

This kind of visualization exercise just before sleep each night is easy to do, and extremely useful in developing astral perception. As I have mentioned, it is also a way to announce to the inhabitants of the lower astral world that you are open to interactions with astral entities. There is no particular danger in such preliminary communications from spirits, which may be viewed as a polite way for these astral beings to announce their existence—a tap on the shoulder or a wave of the hand, so to speak, intended to attract your attention. These beings are always present all around you, so do not become alarmed when they take notice of you. It is only when you demonstrate to them, by repeated exercises in astral perception, that you wish more interaction, that they will make the special effort to reach you.

This, by the way, is what happens when an individual or group begins to play with a Ouija board or similar spirit communication device. It should come as no surprise when astral spirits notice this sort of activity, and respond to it. Nor is it dangerous. Those who proclaim the dread powers of the Ouija, and offer ominous warnings that you will be taken over and tormented if you dare to use it, are repeating a superstition. What happens is that, when you do something specifically designed to attract the attention of the inhabitants of the astral world, they will respond in kind by attempting to attract your attention, as a way of letting you know that you have reached them. There is seldom any malicious intention on the part of the spirits, but human beings playing around with a Ouija board or similar device who do not believe that such things as spirits truly exist become terrified when they feel the spirits' touch or see their forms for the first time. Such people are afraid of the un-known, not of any specific thing the spirits may do or say.

Astral Journal

Another important mental consideration is to begin keeping a record of your astral visions and encounters. It is a good practice to record your dreams also, since dreams and astral travel have a way of merging, as they are closely related experiences. A dream in which the dreamer becomes conscious and acquires the power of independent action is no longer simply a dream; it is an astral projection. Unless you record dreams and astral experiences, they will quickly fade from your memory. Oliver Fox observed this phenomenon, which I find to be true in my own experience. There is some mechanism of the mind that deliberately seeks to erase the memory of both dreams and astral projections. It is an active mechanism. The memory of a dream, for example, will slip away even as you are in the process of trying to remember its details.

What purpose this deliberate attempt by some level of the mind to erase the conscious memory of dreams and other astral experiences may serve is not clear, but if you wish to retain the details of your experiences, you must write them down in a journal. It is best to record them as soon after you experience them as possible, to preserve as many fine details as you can. It may seem to be a tedious chore because the last thing you wish to do when you are half-awake and half-asleep is to start writing in a notebook. However, if you leave it until the next morning, you will forget many details, so the effort is worth making.

Keeping an astral journal has the additional useful effect of making it possible to re-member more events. The very act of focusing the mind on recalling details of astral events makes the memories of them arise spontaneously. You may even find yourself remember-ing astral events that occurred to you during childhood or many years in your past. For ex-ample, until I began to think about astral projection in a serious way and experiment with various techniques, I had completely forgotten that when I was around five years old, I was in the habit of projecting myself astrally to two specific worlds, the world of the fairies and the world of the angels. It was my practice at that age to lie in bed before sleep and decide which of these two worlds I would visit, and then to project myself into whichever I had chosen for that night. The astral experiences were detailed and quite realistic. I did this for a period of at least a year or two, but until renewing my interest in soul flight, some part of my mind had blanked out that childhood practice from my memory.

CHAPTER SIXTEEN

Astral Guides

Modern astral travel is looked upon by most people as the mechanical projection out of the body of an esoteric double, which resembles the physical body but is insubstantial and usually invisible to others. It is hard to blame anyone for holding this view, since it has been put forward as the popular explanation for soul flight since the beginning of the spiritualist movement. A consequence of the expectations aroused by this simplistic model is that travelers will often see only human beings on their astral ramblings. Their expectations exclude the perception of more exotic spiritual creatures. After all, if we are going out of our body to wander the streets of New York City, we would expect to see the men, women, children, dogs, cats, trees, and stones of New York, not strange spirits or impossible architecture. Sylvan Muldoon wrote:

One of the greatest possible mistakes is to believe that, the instant one is outside his body, he sees thousands of spirits all about him. This is not the case, for although there are some, they are not numerous. Usually, one never sees a spirit during projection. Usually he finds himself alone—a stranger in a strange land, and yet a familiar land.[224]

Muldoon was writing from the spiritualist perspective, and had been taught to expect that astral projection involved actual physical travel by a subtle body across the everyday material landscape. He had also been led to believe that the only spiritual beings he was likely to encounter in the astral world were the spirits of the human dead. Since the nature of astral perception is so largely conditioned by expectation, both conscious and unconscious, this is the sort of astral landscape he found himself exploring. Only on rare occasions was this reassuring illusion disturbed.

Astral travel is sometimes arbitrarily divided into two kinds—on the one hand, the actual physical projection of the double into scenes of ordinary life as a kind of invisible ghost that observes other human beings; on the other hand, a mere fantasy of astral travel through impossible landscapes populated by spirits, elementals, angels, fairies, and mythological creatures. The hard-nosed remote viewers of the CIA would laugh at the second form of astral travel and dismiss it as dreaming while awake. It is more likely to be classed under lucid dreaming, where a distinction is made between lucid dreaming and astral travel.

This distinction is false. There is no difference in soul flight that appears to involve projection across the everyday physical environment of our planet and projection into strange and exotic realms populated with spirits and mythical creatures. In both cases, no actual travel of a physical kind is involved. The world the remote viewers of the CIA projected into, which seemed to them so normal and real, was an astral level that existed wholly within their minds. Even though it appeared to be solid, it had no more substance than the world of a dream. It was an astral reflection, not the physical world itself.

Astral Travel Occurs in the Mind

All astral travel is travel within the mind, brought about by a shift in consciousness from one level to another. As remote viewer David Morehouse observed with a surprising degree of insight during an interview for *Nexus Magazine*, "You're not really traveling.

---

224. Muldoon and Carrington, *Projection of the Astral Body*, 291.

It's like folding space. You are traveling, but you're not moving."[225] You do not actually project yourself to distant places; you access those places in your mind by the process he likened to folding space. One of the reasons descriptions of astral projection differ so radically is that the common concept of projection through space of some sort of subtle body is only a sensory metaphor adopted by the mind for the sake of its reassuring familiarity. Travelers are not describing a physical process, but a mental process.

The mind contains the physical body, the astral body, and the entire perceived world not only of the present moment, but of all past memories of the individual. It may also be connected with the minds of other human beings, or even with the minds of the entire human race, enabling an astral traveler to explore not only his own personal world, but the worlds of others. Indeed, there is reason to suspect that the mind is linked with all life throughout the universe, and that there exists only a single mind, which is perceived in a restricted way by each living being as its own mind, according to the expectations and limitations of that creature. If this is so—and many philosophers and mystics believe it to be true in a factual sense—then in soul flight we have the potential to go anywhere, through any period of time, beyond the limits of our personal experience.

Once we grasp that what appears during soul flight to be the ordinary physical world is really the base level of the astral world, we can understand why strange creatures or spiritual beings sometimes intrude on astral travelers, terrifying them into an immediate return to their bodies—that is, to their ordinary waking level of consciousness. Because the base level of the astral world is no different in its essential nature from the higher or lower astral levels, it is possible for spirits to enter it, either deliberately or by accident, in much the same way that a deep-dwelling sea creature can, if the needs arises, swim up toward the surface. Such encounters occur infrequently to those who explore the base level when they maintain in their minds the belief that they are actually traveling through the ordinary physical world, but they do happen.

Muldoon's Upsetting Experience

Muldoon described an upsetting experience of this kind that took place in 1923. In the evening, he listened to his mother converse with a woman about her recently deceased husband, whom the woman characterized as a brute and, in her words, "all bad." Muldoon formed a poor opinion of the dead man based on this dialogue. That night, he

225. Dowbenko.

projected his double while asleep, and discovered the ghost of the dead man waiting for him. The ghost fought with him and beat him, but could not prevent him from reentering his physical body and waking up. "Skeptics may say that this was a nightmare; but I know when I am conscious, and I know what is real when I am conscious. It was no nightmare!"[226]

Muldoon's astral experience was uncharacteristic for him. It illustrates two truths of astral travel. First, that the nature of the astral experience is conditioned by unconscious expectation. Second, that a spirit anomalous to the character of the astral landscape can intrude into that landscape—there is no natural barrier separating one astral level from another. Muldoon's brooding about the bad character of the dead man just before sleep acted as an invitation to the spirit of the dead man to visit Muldoon, and when Muldoon projected during sleep, the spirit took the opportunity to try to injure him. Fortunately for Muldoon, we are no more vulnerable during astral projection than we are during ordinary dreams, and he remained unhurt.

Whether the spirit that attacked Muldoon was indeed the spirit of the dead man, or was an astral entity who had taken on the appearance and personality of the dead man, is a difficult philosophical question. How it is answered depends in large measure on the views concerning the afterlife of the person who asks it. Those who believe in life after death, as it is often called —the survival of the personality after death—tend to believe that spirits of human beings who have died may be encountered in the astral world. Those who take the contrary view that there is no survival of personality or individual awareness after death regard such shades as astral beings who have adopted the appearance and personality of the dead individual for their own purposes.

I tend to hold the second position: that human personality cannot survive death, and that all spirits who claim to be dead individuals are playing roles they have taken on. Spirits, perhaps due to the malleable nature of the astral world, suffer great difficulty distinguishing truth from fiction. My own view is that they take on the identities of dead human beings to meet the unconscious expectations of those with whom they communicate, as a way of fulfilling their expectations, and perhaps as a way of generating a more intense personal bond with them. Spirits hunger for form, for identity, for a history, and will seize any personality that is strongly held in the mind of the living individual through whom they communicate. It is usually not a deliberate deception. They seldom

226. Muldoon and Carrington, *Projection of the Astral Body*, 293.

realize they are not the spirit of the person they claim to be. When they adopt the identity of a dead human being, it becomes their own identity.

What Muldoon encountered, in my opinion, was a spiritual being of a low or infernal type that became aware of the strongly held, well-formed conception of the dead man in Muldoon's mind, and put on that personality like a suit of clothing, making it a second skin—or to phrase it more accurately, making the personality of the dead man a first skin, since until then the low spirit had no strongly defined identity of its own. Once it became the ghost of the dead man, the spirit naturally acted as the ghost of the dead man would act and attacked Muldoon in retaliation for Muldoon's contempt and hatred toward the dead man.

Before the nineteenth century and the rise of modern spiritualism, it was common for astral travelers to interact with all manner of strange and exotic spiritual beings. One of the most common types was the fairies. Interactions with angels were also frequent. Ritual magicians and witches sometimes projected into infernal realms and held commerce with spirits they believed to be demonic. Mythic creatures such as the sphinx, harpie, satyr, centaur, and water nymph were also encountered on a regular basis, since Greek mythology was a part of any classical education. Expectation allowed astral travelers to reach the realms in which these creatures dwell and to interact with them. The general belief in the nineteenth century that these esoteric creatures do not exist was in large measure responsible for inhibiting spiritualists from reaching their realms or perceiving them.

The Spirit Guide

If you understand soul flight in the way it has been described here, as a transition of consciousness from one mental level to another, you will not face the same limitations as the spiritualists, but will be able to visit astral worlds of all kinds, and will interact with and have dealings with all manner of strange spiritual creatures. When traveling through unknown lands, it is always useful to have a guide who knows the territory, or at least one who is able to deal with any problems that might arise. When in the astral world, your guide must be an astral being, which I refer to here by the general term *spirit*. Dante, traveling through hell in his epic *Divine Comedy*, was guided by the ghost of the Roman poet Virgil. Although Dante's journey was fictional, it illustrates the utility of having a spirit guide to warn of dangers or to explain confusing events.

The spirit guide, often referred to as a *control* by spiritualist mediums, has a long and honorable lineage. The tutelary spirits of traditional shamans around the world were their spirit guides, as were the familiars of medieval European witches and the guardian angels of Christians. In modern times, spirit guides sometimes assume the forms of aliens to astral travelers who believe themselves abducted by UFOs. Although the type of spirits who act as guides may change from generation to generation, their role remains the same—to offer advice, guidance, and protection on matters relating to the astral world.

There are two general classes of spirit guide, those that are human and those that are inhuman. When I refer to human spirits, I refer to spirits who believe themselves to be the intelligences of living or formerly living human beings. By inhuman spirits, I mean all varieties of astral inhabitants who identify themselves as something other than human. Before spiritualism, it was relatively uncommon to encounter the first kind of spirit on the astral planes; after spiritualism, it became the norm rather than the exception. Perhaps both classes exist, and it is merely a matter of selective access to their planes, the result of expectation in the unconscious minds of astral travelers. Or perhaps, as I tend to believe, all astral spirits are inhuman and essentially formless in their root nature, and when first contacting human beings, they put on whatever forms and identities they find in the minds of those with whom they communicate.

This second hypothesis does not preclude the existence on the astral level of enduring realms and populations, or of spirits who have a fixed and sustained identity, since it is possible that once having adopted an identity as its own, a spirit may be enabled to keep it over a span of human generations with the support of shared human belief in the existence of that spirit. For example, a goddess such as Aphrodite may continue to exist on the astral level for many centuries because her nature and qualities are known to many human beings and are never absent from human thought. The same consideration applies to a being such as Santa Claus, or indeed, to Jack the Ripper.

Human Spirit Guides

The first class, spirits who appear to be human in nature—at least on the surface—make better spirit guides, simply because it is easier to communicate with a human being than with an inhuman being. The majority of spirit guides adopted by mediums over the past two centuries are of this type. Almost all trance mediums had spirit guides. In the early days of the American spiritualist movement, when the Old West was still being lived, it became popular to adopt guides who identified themselves as the spirits of dead Indians. In later decades, it grew more common for guides to identify themselves as Egyptian or Babylonian priests or sages. There was a huge rise of interest in anything Egyptian around the period that the Hermetic Order of the Golden Dawn flourished, so we find that the astral guide of the Sphere Group of Florence Farr was identified as the "Egyptian astral," and was believed by her group to be the spirit of a long-dead Egyptian adept.

Spirits who profess to once have lived as human beings are more inclined to sympathize with human problems, and are better adapted to interaction with humans on a regular personal level. In a practical sense, it does not matter whether the spirit is actually the shade or soul of a dead human being, or only believes itself to have been human—in either case, it acts with human emotions and from human motives. You will find yourself able to talk to this type of spirit, who will listen with sympathy. If the spirit was not sympathetic to your situation and problems, it would never have approached you to become your guide.

Another type of human spirit on the astral level that may act as the guide to travelers is not of the dead, but of the living. As curious as the notion appears on first consideration, it was believed by Theosophists and other esoteric schools that some of the guides and teachers on the astral level were living human beings that either in sleep or with full awareness projected themselves onto the astral planes for the purpose of aiding other human beings. Writing in his 1915 work *Invisible Helpers*, Charles Webster Leadbeater concluded about the nature of the astral beings who aid humanity: "At present, therefore, the main bulk of the work which has to be done along these lines falls to the share of those living persons who are able to function consciously on the astral plane."[227] Elsewhere in the same chapter he wrote:

> It becomes obvious then that such assistance as that to which we are here referring may most fitly be given by men and women at a particular stage of their evolution; not by the adepts, since they are capable of doing far grander and more widely useful work, and not by the ordinary person of no special spiritual development, for he would be unable to be of any use. Just as these considerations would lead us to expect, we find that this work of helping on the astral and lower mental planes is chiefly in the hands of the pupils of the Masters—men who, though yet far from the

---

227. Leadbeater, *Invisible Helpers*, ch. IV.

attainment of adeptship, have evolved themselves to the extent of being able to function consciously upon the planes in question.[228]

It was the belief of Theosophists that living individuals who had studied the teachings of the Society, and indeed any person of an advanced spiritual nature, performed good works on the astral level during sleep, even if that person had no recollection of their helpful deeds upon waking the next morning. Such work might well include acting as protector or guide to an astral traveler, although Leadbeater did not specify this function in his book. He asserted that exalted adepts have no time to help individuals with their everyday problems, and that nature spirits are usually uninterested in human affairs.

This idea that we may encounter other human travelers who are still living when we travel on the astral planes is frequently expressed in various forms. Mathers, leader of the Golden Dawn, was unsure whether the Secret Chiefs were living men, but he thought they were living, and reported that sometimes he met with them on the physical level, and at other times on the astral level. The Tibetan adept who dictated to Alice E. Bailey her shelf of bewildering esoteric writings identified himself to her as a man living in Tibet at the time he communicated with her. "I live in a physical body like other men, on the borders of Tibet, and at times (from the exoteric standpoint) preside over a large group of Tibetan lamas, when my other duties permit."[229] She did not believe herself to be receiving dictation from the spirit world but from a living human being in communication with her psychically, on the astral level.

When encountering inhabitants of the astral planes, it is impossible to know, without asking them outright, whether they are spirits or projections of living human beings. Even then, you may not receive a satisfactory answer, since those who project in sleep often forget their everyday human identity and assume a new identity while on the astral level, just as they forget their dreams after they wake up. Two complete lives may be lived simultaneously, one during the waking state in the physical world, and the other during dreams in the astral world, and neither of these personalities may be fully aware of the existence of the other. Sometimes all that filters through from our dream lives concerning this dual existence is a dim recollection of repeated yet progressive dreams that involve different events, but the same astral environment.

228. Leadbeater, *Invisible Helpers*, ch. IV.
229. Bailey, *Treatise on White Magic*, vii.

Inhuman Spirit Guides

The second class of spirit guide appears inhuman, or presents itself as inhuman, even though such spirits as a rule have many humanoid characteristics. Fairies, for example, are inhuman creatures yet resemble human beings quite closely. In their earliest legends, they are not tiny creatures with gossamer wings, but wingless and of the usual human size. They acquired their wings in popular paintings and illustrations of the nineteenth century from their association with the air, being insubstantial and apt to fade into the mist or disappear when the eye is momentarily averted from them. The four classes of elemental spirits defined by Paracelsus usually appear in humanoid form. Undines may closely resemble mortal women, but may have fins in place of feet or webbed fingers, for example. Humanoid forms allow these spirits to use human language to respond to astral travelers in a more familiar fashion than would be possible were they utterly monstrous.

Angels that interact with human beings are usually so nearly human in appearance and behavior that they cannot be distinguished from the living. The idea that angels must always have feathered wings is a fable that may have evolved from their association with the heavens, and their ability to rise into the air. Wings are a symbol that indicates an airy nature. In the Bible, those angels who visit and instruct men are usually very human, whereas the angels that are strange in appearance have little interaction with human beings. Angels acquired wings in popular modern art for reasons similar to those of the fairies—because they shine with inner light, appear and disappear unexpectedly, and descend from or ascend into the sky.

Angels can be trusted completely as guides on the higher astral planes, but they are focused mainly on spiritual matters. They cannot descend to the infernal planes because these astral environments are harmful or destructive to their composition. Even if they are able to survive the infernal levels, they suffer unceasing pain while upon them. The same is true of demons, who suffer constant pain when forced to ascend above the base level of the astral world. They even have a difficult time tolerating an environment on the base level of the astral that contains symbols of the higher mental and spiritual levels.

Angels and demons can meet and interact on the base astral level, which is the reflection and close correspondent to the physical world. When we see an angel while awake, we see the angel on this level, which sometimes overlaps the physical world to our waking perception. The angel appears to be in the physical world, but it is still on the astral level.

The same is true when we see a demon during ordinary waking consciousness—something that happens with gratifying infrequency. It never actually reaches the physical world, but remains on the base level of the astral world and only seems present in the physical world.

There is really not such a great difference between the physical world and the base level of the astral world. Both exist within the mind. When I assert that the physical world exists in the mind, I mean that all we can know or experience of the physical world is within the mind —mind knows nothing beyond mind. Our everyday waking consciousness can shift from one mental plane to the other fairly easily, and even unintentionally, during daydreams or under the effects of fatigue or mild medications. Drunks who suffer the horrible effects of delirium tremens experience vivid, tangible, real hallucinations, often of a horrifying kind. The creatures of these hallucinations are not physical in nature, but have risen to the base astral level, which the alcohol craving allows the sufferer to perceive by altering his mental state.

Demons make even poorer astral guides than angels. Here I use the term *demon* to refer to infernal spirits in general. They may be of some use when exploring the lower levels that lie beneath the base plane of the astral world, and indeed may even be necessary for this work, but they are not to be trusted. Those who are able to form a close personal bond of friendship with an infernal spirit may find that the spirit will help them to the best of its ability, and will show considerable affection toward them, but its emotional responses will always be capricious and unbalanced, its actions unpredictable.

Fairy Guides

Fairies and other spirits of the natural world are closer to humanity in their responses, and make better guides to the astral planes that are open to them than either angels or demons. The fairy personality is quite similar to the human, save only that fairies tend to be a little fey at times, as their name implies. They respond and act strangely, though seldom maliciously or violently, as can be the case with most other infernal spirits. They may appear somewhat odd, or a bit abstracted. Fairies of the common laboring classes tend to be short and stout of body, with dark skin. Those of the ruling class are taller, equal in height to human beings, and have generally fairer skin and hair. Fairy society is similar to human society, but maintains the social structure that existed centuries ago in Europe.

In a Kabbalistic sense, fairies dwell below the surface of the lowest Sephirah called Malkuth, the sphere of the four elements. Although much more benign that most other subterranean spirits, we know that they are infernal or chthonic because their dwelling places are under hills beneath the ground. On its surface, the astral world of Malkuth is almost indistinguishable from the common physical world of everyday life. Between Malkuth and Yesod is the realm of what are known as the earthbound spirits—the spiritual creatures of the natural world and the lower atmosphere who can never venture far from the sphere of the four elements. The zone between Yesod and Malkuth is given over to these spirits, and they are under the governance of the moon. When we see strange faces and shapes on the borders of sleep, or even while wide awake, we are usually seeing these lunar spirits that throng in countless numbers all around us.

Fairies dwell just beneath the surface of the earth. Other nature spirits such as nymphs and satyrs dwell on an astral plane that is just slightly higher in its vibration or energy level than the base level of the astral that corresponds with the everyday world. Both fairies and nature spirits can enter the base plane of the astral world with ease. Conversely, it is a very easy matter for astral travelers to cross from the surface plane of the four elements to the lower level of the fairies, or the slightly higher level of nature spirits. It can be as quick and as simple as opening a door, or turning a corner, and suddenly you are no longer in the ordinary landscape, but in a place that is strange and rich in sounds, colors, and scents.

Fairies have limitations as guides because they cannot ascend up the astral planes above the sphere of the moon, and cannot give their full interest or enthusiasm to matters of human interest. If a fairy has a strong personal affection for a traveler, that personal bond can take the place of a sense of duty. The love of the fairy for its human companion may sustain its loyalty and devotion when it is required to perform tasks it would otherwise regard with disinterest, or even distaste. Because of this bond of love, the pressing concerns of the human traveler can become the pressing concerns of the fairy guide, but of their own volition they do not persist in human affairs for any great length of time before becoming bored.

Elemental Guides

Those spirits that are predominantly composed of a single elemental essence, which Paracelsus divided into salamanders, sylphs, undines, and gnomes, are even less well suited to the role of general astral guide than fairies. The gnomes are elementals of Earth, and must remain on or beneath the base level of the astral world, on the ground. The undines ascend somewhat higher, and have their natural home in a band of spiritual Water that encircles the earth. Sylphs, composed of elemental Air, dwell in a band of spiritual Air that is a bit higher than the watery band of the undines. Salamanders, of elemental Fire, have a zone of habitation just above the zone of the sylphs. All three elemental bands are beneath the celestial sphere of the moon. They are termed earthbound spirits because, even though they inhabit zones above the earth, they are bound to it and cannot ascend above the moon.

The three elemental bands about the earth should be understood in a symbolic sense, as a way of dividing and ordering the elemental realms. Each is a pure elemental zone, in contrast to the zone of the earth itself where the four elements are always mingled together. All four elements have a higher aspect and a lower aspect. The lower aspects blend together on the earth, and the higher or spiritual aspects of the elements remain separated. The spiritual aspect of elemental Earth is so dense, it is difficult to distinguish it from its lower, more gross aspect, so the two are for practical purposes treated as the same, and elemental Earth does not receive its own separate zone.

In the Golden Dawn system of magic, the pure spiritual essences of the three higher elements are assigned to the three Sephiroth on the Tree of Life that are immediately above Malkuth. Elemental Air is placed in Yesod, sphere of the moon; elemental Water is assigned to Hod, sphere of the planet Mercury; and elemental Fire is located in Netzach, sphere of the planet Venus. It may be postulated that an extremely rarified and pure elemental spirit might be able to ascend above the moon to its own Sephirah, were it able to purge itself of all denseness and of the remnants of the lower aspects of the other elements. That is, a very pure elemental spirit of Air might ascend to Yesod, a pure elemental of Water as high as Hod, and a rarified elemental of Fire even as far as Netzach. Above this, no elemental spirit of any kind, regardless of how pure it may be, can ascend.

Practically speaking, elemental spirits cannot venture above the moon. The best astral guides are those that identify themselves as human. It is a peculiarity of human nature that we are able to travel into all three astral kingdoms—the heavenly, the earthly, and the infernal. No other being can do this without some sort of protection or higher authority, and it is a cause of envy in the hearts of some spirits, who resent the freedom humans have to move through the three realms with impunity. A spirit identifying itself as human will possess the same ability, by virtue of its belief. Whether it is truly the spirit of someone who has died, or is a spiritual being that has so immersed itself in its human identity that it truly thinks itself to be human, its faith in its own humanity will give it this power to move through the three realms.

Acquiring a Spirit Guide

You may be impatiently asking yourself, how do I acquire a spirit guide that will assist me in my exploration of the astral planes? Most commonly, you do not find such a spirit—the spirit finds you. When you engage in visualization exercises involving symbols, or the passage through astral doorways, you attract the attention of the lower astral world just as surely as if you had sent up a magnesium flare. By your visualization and the focus of your thoughts on astral forms, you become plainly visible in the astral world and all of your details become brightly illuminated, even though previously you may have appeared as no more than one of the countless millions of human beings who are present during their waking hours only as pale, entranced inhabitants of the base plane of the astral world, little more than unresponsive walking shadows.

It is very likely that you will be approached by a spirit as you practice astral visualizations, and as you make preliminary efforts to project your double. The spirit will make its presence known to you by appearing in your dreams, which is another reason why you should be keeping a record of your dreams in your astral journal. The spirit may also cause you to see its form, hear its voice, and feel its touch upon your body. The touch of a spirit can be completely indistinguishable from the touch of a human hand. Oliver Fox—among other astral travelers—reported that while he was projecting from his body, he was able to make others aware of his presence by touching them. Those he touched could not see or hear him, but they felt him. It appears that from the astral level, the tactile sense of the physical body is the easiest to affect.

When you become aware of the persistent presence of a spirit near you, it is important to determine its name, so that you can address it in a unique way that identifies it. Mentally send your thoughts outward to the spirit, and think very clearly your desire that the spirit reveal its name. If you possess strong psychic abilities, you may actually hear the name spoken, or see its letters written in astral fire. More likely, the name will come into your mind, and will have a sense of rightness. Record the name in your journal, and in all future communications with the spirit, address it by this name. If the name you have arrived at is not the name by which the spirit wishes to be called, it will eventually reveal to you a new name.

The name conveyed to you embodies the very identity of the spirit. It is as much the body of the spirit as the form that will eventually be revealed to your astral perception. By calling on the name, you can summon the spirit at any time of the day or night. How well you are able to perceive the spirit depends on the development of your astral senses—your ability to see, hear, and feel astral beings. It is important to understand that even if you do not clearly see or hear the spirit, there is every likelihood that it is present at your side when you call it by its name. The longer you use a name for a spirit, the more forcefully the voicing of that name—either mentally or aloud—will summon the spirit.

The link you have with your astral guide can be made even stronger through the use of a sigil that represents the identity of the spirit. A sigil is a symbolic pattern associated with a spirit. It acts as a kind of graphic signature. There are various ways to derive sigils from the names of spirits, but the simplest way is to ask to be given the sigil in the same way you were given the name, by inspiration. Very clearly and repeatedly, project your desire that the spirit should send you its identifying sigil. Then empty and open your mind. Whatever pattern of lines or shapes you perceive, draw it in your journal beneath the name of the spirit. Sigils are usually given by spirits as quite simple patterns, allowing them to be easily drawn, but if it happens that you see in your mind a three-dimensional shape or group of shapes, reduce it to its essential lines and use that simplified drawing as the sigil.

How you perceive your guide when you are projecting on the astral levels depends on your psychic ability. Ideally, you will be able to see the form of the spirit as a companion who accompanies you, and hear and understand the speech of the spirit. However, if your perception is less developed, you may only sense the presence of the spirit guide, and feel the occasional touch of the guide on your astral body. The ability of your guide to protect you will not be diminished by your inability to clearly see the form of the spirit or hear its words. Astral perception is not as predictable as the perception of objects with your physical senses. For example, it is usual for those projecting the double to see their physical bodies, but Oliver Fox was throughout his years of astral travel consistently unable to see his body. Similarly, some travelers report the existence of the silver cord and others do not. It should not be assumed, because you fail to see or hear your guide clearly, that your guide is not present.

Remain open to the presence of your guide during soul flight, ask for guidance or help whenever they are needed, and allow your guide to express itself to you in whatever ways it finds most useful for the purpose of communication. The spirit may guide you by touches, or sounds other than words, or lights perceived in the distance. You may feel only a strong pressure to move in a particular direction, or the sense that it would be best to go a certain way or do a particular thing. Allow yourself to remain open for these signs, and follow them. In this way, trust and a working relationship will be developed between you and your guide.

CHAPTER SEVENTEEN

Etiquette in the Astral World

In the early stages of your practice of soul flight, you may think that when you enter an astral world, you are in a kind of dreamland or fantasy landscape, where you can do anything that you feel the impulse to do without consequences. This would be an unfortunate mistake. It is true that a strong relationship exists between dreams and astral travel, but during a normal dream we automatically act in accordance with the dream, and for this reason never violate the integrity of the dream no matter how outrageous our actions appear. During soul flight, we function independent of the milieu that surrounds us, and may, if we choose, violate its natural laws. When we act irresponsibly, the result is confusion, fear, and outrage among the inhabitants of that astral plane.

Every astral environment has its own natural laws that can be learned by observation. Some are limited by their level of technology—there are many astral landscapes that appear medieval. They have somehow fallen out of synchronization with the time period of the physical world. Others, such as simple woodlands that contain no man-made structures, are limited by their lack of human inhabitants. Others are holy places composed of temples and courtyards filled with altars and statues of strange divinities, where it would be a violation to show signs of impiety. Travelers are expected to observe certain basic rules of behavior when they explore the astral levels, and if a traveler ignores good manners, the inhabitants of the level will very quickly cease to be friendly, and will become hostile and obstructive.

Behavior when traveling the astral world is mainly a matter of common sense. You act as you would act if you were visiting a foreign country. Treat the native inhabitants with respect. Listen courteously when they speak to you, and watch closely when they convey information by means of gestures or pantomimes. Try to accommodate their wishes, where such accommodation does not interfere in a serious way with your own purposes. Imitate their general behavior and customs. For example, if you are in a land where nobody speaks, you should remain silent. If you travel through an astral realm where spirits greet each other with bows, you should bow in return when a spirit greets you.

Nothing so disgusts and angers the spirits of an astral landscape as a traveler who acts with complete disregard for their presence, bullies them, speaks harshly, or strikes them. Do not try to play the great magus, and go around projecting pentagrams or vibrating words of power. Do not clothe yourself in imposing robes and costly jewels. This kind of bluster will not earn you friends, and is unlikely to help you acquire knowledge. Instead, it will mark you as a menace or a fool, and the spirits of the land will avoid you as they would avoid a madman. Always remember that you are a visitor, and be polite.

A Gift Demands a Gift

When seeking information or aid from a spirit, it is good manners to offer the spirit a gift as payment for its services. Fortunately, as a human being, you have the power to create objects and substances on the astral level using only the power of your imagination. Another way to accomplish the same end is to offer physical gifts before you begin your soul flight. The astral portion of the physical offering is received and used by the spirits for whom it is intended. The offering of physical gifts is the usual practice in religion, and indeed in ceremonial magic. However, the astral traveler, being actually present within the land inhabited by the spirits, will find it easier to shape his offerings mentally, and present them through the intermediary of his astral guide, or directly if he has no guide.

The idea of giving astral beings gifts composed of astral substance may appear strange at first consideration, but it is quite an ancient practice. The magicians of Babylon and Egypt used it when dealing with spirits in their rituals. Rather than travel to the astral realms themselves, they employed scryers to see and converse with the spirits, usually a young boy or girl. Children are naturally more mediumistic than adults. For the gathering and presentation of the astral offerings, they either had a spirit act as their agent, or they caused the spirits receiving the offerings to bring the offerings themselves. The intention of the magician allowed the spirits receiving the offerings to obtain them, which otherwise they could not do. The magician's conceptualization of the offerings created the offerings on the astral level.

In a ritual of Egyptian oil divination recorded centuries ago on a papyrus manuscript, the magician tells the young boy who acts as his seer to instruct the god Anubis to bring in offerings for the other gods who are invoked:

> You say to the boy, "Speak to Anubis, saying 'Bring in a table for the gods, and let them sit.'" When they are seated, you say "Bring in a [jar of] wine, broach it for the gods; bring in some bread, let them eat, let them drink," "let them eat, let them drink, let them pass a festal day." When they have finished, you speak to Anubis, saying "Dost thou make inquiry for me?" If he says "At once," you say to him, "The god who will make my inquiry to-day, let him stand up." If he says, "He has stood up," you say to him [i.e. the child], "Say to Anubis 'Carry off the things from the midst.'"[230]

In this ritual, Anubis is used as the agent who fetches the feast offerings, and even the table on which they are arrayed. He receives his instructions from the young boy who acts as the seer, who is in turn told what to say by the magician. The feast is wholly astral in nature. Later in the ritual, bread and salt are physically offered, but this first offering consists of astral bread and astral wine. It is the imagination of the seer that creates the materials of the feast on the astral level, allowing the god Anubis to acquire them.

---

230. Griffith and Thompson, *Leyden Papyrus*, 31.

In a ritual of Babylonian oil magic, recorded in a Jewish magical manuscript of the eighteenth century that is based on much older sources, the magician is instructed in the text to tell the child seer the following:

> And if he sees a man dressed in black tell him that he should put on white garments and return at once, and when he returns he shall say unto him: I command that thou shalt go at once to thy kingdom, and thou shalt bring a lamb and slaughter it and roast it and eat it, and after he has eaten he shall tell him: I command thee with the power and permission and command of my master and in the name of thy supreme master and by the command of thy king that thou shalt show me all that I ask clearly so that I should understand.[231]

This may seem a bit confusing, but is simple enough. The magician instructs the child seer to tell the spirit who comes dressed in black to put on white garments. The reason for the change of clothing is that symbols represent real qualities on the astral level. Black clothing is assumed by the author of the ritual to indicate evil intentions. When the spirit changes its garments, the shift from black to white renders benevolent its intentions toward the magician.

On the matter of the significance of the clothing worn by spirits, Regardie made the following observation in which he quoted Mathers: "On these subtler planes, or within the realms of these [tattwa] symbols, form takes on symbolic implication which we, on earth, have obscured if not lost. It is only human beings who swathe themselves in garments whose shape and colour bear no relation to their true character. 'Even on our own plane, the clothing of animals is pregnant with meaning, and on the astral plane this is far more emphatically the case. An elemental may, for some purpose of its own, masquerade for a time in alien garb, but we are given a certain definite procedure to follow in dealing with them.'"[232]

The methods of dealing with such deceptions in appearance mentioned by Mathers involved the vibration of divine and angelic names, the making of signs of the elemental grades of the Golden Dawn, and the formation of pentagrams upon the air with various elemental associations. Their purpose was to show to the spirit that the astral traveler

---

231. Gaster and Daiches, *Three Works* (*Babylonian Oil Magic*), 20.

232. Regardie, 460.

had authority over the spirit, and to compel the spirit to present itself honestly and in harmony with the elemental level represented by the name or sign.

Returning to our analysis of the Babylonian ritual, the magician tells the child what he is to say to the spirit who has put on white garments—that the spirit is to go to his kingdom, get a lamb, slaughter the lamb, roast it, and consume it, as an offering from the magician to the spirit. The lamb is wholly astral in nature. Even though the spirit fetches the offering himself, it is not an offering he could consume without the permission of the magician and the seer, because their expectations, acting through their imaginations, make the offering real and available to the spirit.

Once the spirit dressed in white has eaten the offering which he himself was forced to prepare, the magician tells the boy to command the spirit by various names of power—the first being the name of the magician, who is the boy's master, then by the master of the spirit, and finally by the king of the astral world within which the spirit resides. These names are not given in the ritual, presumably because they are specific to each spirit invoked, but during the practice of the ritual they would be voiced by the young seer.

The Use of Compulsions

I have quoted from these two rituals, one Egyptian and the other Babylonian, in order to show that this sort of astral offering was not unusual, but was a normal part of astral magic in ancient times. In my opinion, the second ritual suffers from a lack of good etiquette toward the spirit invoked. It seems poor manners to make a spirit fetch his own feast offering. This may have been the accepted practice, but it is better to rely on your guide, if you have one, to present the offering to the spirit you wish to question, or whose help you seek. The second bit of bad manners was the use of compulsion by means of names of power. If you are dealing with honorable spirits in the astral realms you visit, compulsion should never be necessary. The spirit will tell you what you ask if it wishes to tell you, and if it chooses to withhold its aid or advice, you should not seek to compel it, as this arouses resentment and is very apt to encourage deliberate deception on the part of the spirit compelled to serve.

The exception to this rule is when you have dealings with infernal or chthonic spirits —those that dwell on planes below the level of Malkuth. These underground spirits are by their inherent natures less trustworthy and should always be treated with care. They should never be abused, but it is wise to have ready names that you know possess authority to command these spirits. Always be alert for deception when interacting with the inhabitants of the lower levels. Elementals and nature spirits are less malicious than infernal spirits, but can be capricious and may try to deceive, as Mathers observed in the quotation by Regardie, given above. Regardie went on to write:

> It is but rarely that there will be necessity to resort to anything so drastic as the Pentagrams in these tattwa visions, for the vibration of the Hebrew name either of the element, or of the Archangel will restore order and harmony. The true form, colour, clothing, even adornments such as jewels and embroideries are consonant to the element and character of the beings under discussion. And unless they are, the Seer may be sure he is being imposed on, and should act accordingly—at once.[233]

Regardie does not mean that you should browbeat or attempt to intimidate the spirit you suspect may be wearing false colors—merely that if you are suspicious, you should test the spirit's integrity. This may be done most easily by voicing a name that you know has a natural authority over the spirit, and telling the spirit to reveal its true appearance in the name of that authority. There is no need to shout or bluster when doing this. If the name chosen is appropriate, and is indeed the name of a spirit with a rank above the spirit you are testing, it will have the power to compel the spirit to reveal its true appearance.

On the general subject of how to treat spirits encountered during astral projection, Mathers wrote: "Always treat these beings with courtesy and in accord with their rank. Pay deference to the superior orders, the Archangels, Angels, and Rulers. To those of lower rank, bear yourself as an equal; and to those lower still, as to servants whom you treat politely, but do not allow familiarity."[234] In the England of the nineteenth century, social rank was of much greater importance than it is today. It is good practice to treat all spirits with respect, but to avoid abasing yourself before those who come in splendid robes and bedecked in jewels, and to avoid equally displays of superiority toward those of a more humble, earthy appearance. Observance of rank plays a more important role in those astral lands that maintain a medieval social structure.

---

233. Regardie, 460.

234. Ibid., 461.

In my opinion, the Golden Dawn was somewhat obsessed with the possible deceptions of astral spirits. Perhaps this was due to the astral levels they scried and traveled upon—all of the tattwa levels are elemental in nature. The lower the level, the more likely its inhabitants are to trick the traveler, although displays of actual malice are rare on the sublunary levels between Malkuth and Yesod. The elemental zones on and immediately above the earth can be tested by vibrating the names of the four archangels of the elements—Uriel for the zone of elemental Earth, Gabriel for the zone of Water, Raphael for the zone of Air, and Michael for the zone of Fire. Uriel may be used for the realms of nature spirits, and for the land of the fairies, who dwell very close beneath the surface of the physical world and commonly walk abroad on the base astral level that corresponds with our world.

It is merely necessary to say to the spirit you wish to test, in a clear and firm voice: "By the authority of Uriel, archangel of Earth, show to me your true appearance." If the spirit is already in its true guise, there will be no change, but if it is seeking to deceive you with a veil of glamour, it will shimmer and dissolve into its true form. For the realm of the undines and other watery spirits, substitute the archangelic name Gabriel; for the realm of the sylphs and other airy spirits, the name Raphael; for the realm of the salamanders and other fiery spirits, the name Michael.

Appropriate Offerings to Spirits

You should not think that when you project yourself into an astral landscape that you must offer a great feast to everyone you encounter. An offering should only be given to the ruler of the place you visit, or to those spirits who assist you. In the first case, it is a sign of respect, and in the second, a payment for services rendered. An offering can be anything that will be well received by the spirit to whom it is given. Offerings of food and drink are traditional in both religion and magic, and will seldom be refused. An article of clothing can also be given, or a piece of jewelry, a book, a weapon, a musical instrument, a tool, or a flower. You should either send your astral guide to fetch the offering or, if you have no guide, get it yourself after creating it by imagining it present yet out of sight in a nearby location, such as behind a boulder or inside a cupboard. Whatever you visualize and imagine clearly on the astral level becomes real, and it has as much reality as the spirit to whom it is given.

The offering is not a mere token gesture; it has real value to the spirit that receives it. It is important to grasp this, as we are so accustomed to thinking of imagined things as unreal, and hence without value. Your gift should be given with sincerity, as a sign of respect or gratitude. When in doubt as to what is appropriate, bread and wine should be given. Only if you are sure that you understand the nature of the spirit with whom you are dealing, and the needs and desires of the spirit, should you attempt to make the offering more personal. If you know information that will be of use or amusement to a spirit, that can be given as a gift in place of an object.

It was the custom for members of the Golden Dawn, when they visited a tattwa environment, to wait for a spirit guide to present itself before exploring the landscape. "Under *no* circumstances should the Seer wander from his doorway *alone*; he should always wait until one of these elemental beings or 'guides' appears, and he should continue vibrating the names until one does appear, or until he obtains the sense that one is present."[235] This advice is prompted by a fear that the unwary astral traveler will fall prey to some sort of deception unless he is guided by a spirit whose integrity has been tested by names of authority or other symbolic instruments such as the pentagrams of the elements.

My own opinion is that it is not necessary to wait for a guide. The danger is slight or nonexistent. If you have your own general guide to the astral planes, your personal guide will supply all the protection and direction you need. If you are alone, it is very likely, as you begin exploring your surroundings, that a spirit will approach and interact with you. Ask this spirit to take you to the ruler of the place. As a matter of good manners, it is appropriate to pay a visit to the ruler of an astral world the first time you enter it. Sometimes, if the world is small and simple, the spirit who approaches you will be the ruling spirit.

You should allow the spirit who first meets you to guide you to the dwelling of the ruler of that astral land. If you are granted an audience or interview with the ruler, explain your intentions and politely offer a gift as a gesture of respect. If the spirit who first appears to you is the ruler of the realm, offer your gift to that spirit. Have your personal guide fetch it, or get it yourself from some convenient location that is nearby but concealed from sight. The ruler may express wonder at your powers of magic as you pull a bottle of wine from out of a cupboard or from behind a tree and present it in offering.

---

235. Regardie, 460.

This will enhance your standing. Resist the urge to make vain displays merely to impress the spirits.

Becoming Familiar with an Astral Realm

In order to really explore an astral realm, it is necessary to return to it again and again. At first, it is likely to be fragmented or vague, too much for your mind to comprehend, and a confusion of sounds and colors. Indeed, Theosophists describe the first perception of the astral world as nothing but vaguely defined forms. The Tibetan sage who instructed Alice A. Bailey wrote that "the appearance of the astral plane when first definitely *seen* by the 'opened eye' of the aspirant is one of dense fog, confusion, changing forms, interpenetrating and intermingling colors, and is of such a kaleidoscopic appearance that the hopelessness of the enterprise seems overwhelming. It is not light, or starry or clear. It is apparently impenetrable disorder, for it is the meeting ground of forces."[236] This description exaggerates the experience of most astral travelers, who find their initial views of the astral planes strange but not incomprehensible.

To some degree, this initial confusion of the senses occurs whenever we are presented with a truly unknown environment. The awareness is overwhelmed in its attempt to tame the chaos of new sights and sounds. Over time the mind begins to sort things out, and what we could not initially see at all, even though it was in plain view, becomes obvious, so that we wonder how we ever failed to perceive it. The same thing happens sometimes when we are shown a photograph of a jungle beast in its native environment. At first there is only a confused mass of light and shadow. Suddenly, the shape of the animal seems to leap out of the photograph as our mind makes sense of it. After that, it seems impossible to avoid seeing the beast each time we look at the photograph.

Regardie offered the rather poor advice that the traveler should imagine his astral body larger than the size of his physical body. "It is also said to be good practice, since form is symbolic in these regions, to imagine yourself as large as possible, always taller than the being confronting you. . ."[237] On the contrary, this is very bad practice. When the traveler does this, he is no different than a deceiving spirit who puts on a false set of princely robes, or the garments of a priest, or the wings of an angel, merely to impress the traveler. What is wrong for the spirit cannot be right for the human being. In my view, travelers should appear on the astral

---

236. Bailey, 221.

237. Regardie, 461.

planes in their natural form and normal height, wearing what they usually wear, and should in all things conduct themselves with honesty and integrity. If they do so, they are much more likely to earn the respect of the spirits they encounter.

Often a traveler finds himself returning again and again to the same astral realm. Something in its atmosphere or the behavior of its inhabitants resonates within his soul, so that he feels at ease in the place, as though he has returned home after a long absence. This is true in my own experience regarding a fairy realm that has the form of a small town located on the bank of a river. It is set in a time period several centuries before our own, a period roughly equivalent to the Elizabethan Age. There are farmlands and meadows surrounding the town. An old country road leads across them and through the town to the waterfront, where there is a dock for sailing ships that carry goods out the mouth of the river to the sea. I have visited this astral world dozens of times, and find myself completely at peace there. The inhabitants greet me pleasantly with knowing looks. It has become a sort of second home.

When visiting the same astral world repeatedly, it is important not to disrupt its natural functioning by intruding yourself too much into its affairs. It is better to remain somewhat withdrawn, and to play the part of an observer rather than trying to involve yourself in the politics or social life of the place. If you become deeply enmeshed in the affairs of that world, you may inadvertently destroy those aspects of it that lent it charm in your eyes and made it attractive to you. It is best to maintain a modest demeanor and to say little, but to nod and return greetings pleasantly. Your effort should be to make the inhabitants comfortable around you, but not dependent on you for any aspect of their lives. The world should function just the same when you are absent as it does while you are present.

It is an easy matter for you to create for yourself a place to live in this world, but do so in such a way that your new house does not interfere with lands held by the native inhabitants. Make your house similar in size and architecture to the houses of your neighbors. Resist the urge to play the part of the wealthy noble, since this is bound to cause disruption where you live. Either your presence will be resented, or natives will come to you for favors. Both types of disruption are to be shunned if you wish to preserve the integrity of the astral world. You may, if it is the acceptable practice of the place, hire one or two of the locals to keep your house while you are away, and to maintain your grounds.

Romantic Relationships with Spirits

Resist the urge to fall in love with a native of the astral world you have chosen as your second home. There is a great temptation to do so, since many spirits are quite charming and beautiful. However, if you join yourself closely to a spirit in a loving union, that spirit will become dependent on your presence, and will grieve and sicken when you are absent. It is kinder not to form such a bond unless you are very sure that you will be visiting that astral world on a regular basis for the rest of your life. A loving relationship with a spirit is a serious commitment, and it can have serious consequences.

It comes as a surprise to many people that spirits give birth to children, even though it is an accepted part of the folk tradition about fairies. The practice of fairies to substitute a changeling child in place of a human child was popularly believed until two centuries ago, and it was also held that young women were sometimes abducted by fairies to nurse fairy children. What is less widely recognized in folklore is that most female spirits, even those who are not fairies, can produce children.

Spirit mothers have spirit babies; human mothers usually have human babies. Until recent years, I would have said that human mothers always have human babies, but I have had my consciousness raised on this matter. It is possible for a man, when traveling in astral realms, to engender a spirit child on a spirit woman, who becomes pregnant and gives birth to that child within her native astral world. It is also possible, as strange as it sounds, for a woman, while projecting her double into an astral world, to become pregnant in her astral body by making love to a male spirit, and for her to give birth to that astral child while in the spirit world. The baby remains in the astral land of its birth, but its human mother can visit it whenever she travels to that land.

You may protest this as rubbish. At first consideration, it does seem absurd that a woman of flesh and blood could have an astral child. Yet I know a woman who was made pregnant by her spirit lover, and gave birth to a healthy baby boy. The child is presently being raised by his spirit father on the astral plane on which the father dwells, and is regularly visited by his human mother. Aside from not having a body, the child is in all other respects completely normal. Sometimes astral children mature very quickly, and then at a certain age reach their final form and remain at that age indefinitely. The spirit father of the child informed me that rapidly maturing spirits are of a type that is different from his son, who is maturing at the usual human pace.

Spirit children may exhibit otherworldly or slightly inhuman features, although just as often they are indistinguishable from human children. For example, a child born from the union of a spirit mother with catlike attributes and human father might possess eyes similar to those of a cat, or pointed ears. These secondary characteristics depend on the appearance of the spirit that is the mother. If the spirit mother is completely human in appearance, the baby will be completely human also.

Marriages with Spirits

Marriages between spirits and humans are possible. We know that they were recognized in ancient times, because records of these unions have been recorded in historical accounts and were regarded by the authors as factual. One of the most famous is the marriage between King Numa of Rome and the water nymph Egeria, who dwelled in a spring within a sacred grove near the Porta Capena in the south wall of the old city of Rome. The king went to her at night and received instruction in the making of religious laws, for which he was in later centuries renowned. Although the satirist Juvenal called Egeria the king's mistress, others refer to her as his wife. The Roman historian Varro believed that the marriage between Numa and Egeria was a mythic explanation for the king's use of water divination, as Saint Augustine reports in his *City of God*,[238] but in spite of Varro's cynicism, such unions did occur.

Plutarch, in his *Life of Numa Pompilius*, referring to Numa's "celestial wedlock in the love and converse of the goddess Egeria" was doubtful that spirits could unite with human beings in a sensual way, but remarked on the subject:

> Though, indeed, the wise Egyptians do not unplausibly make the distinction, that it may be possible for a divine spirit so to apply itself to the nature of a woman, as to imbreed in her the first beginnings of generation, while on the other side they conclude it impossible for the male kind to have any intercourse or mixture by the body with any divinity, not considering, however, that what takes place on the one side, must also take place on the other; intermixture, by force of terms, is reciprocal.[239]

---

238. Augustine, Saint, *City of God,* (bk. 7, ch. 35), vol. 1, p. 224.

239. Plutarch, *Noble Grecians and Romans*, 77.

Human-spirit marriages still take place today, although humans who marry spirits seldom advertise these unions. To do so would brand them as mentally unsound in the opinion of their family and friends, and might get them committed to an institution. These marriages, conducted on the astral level, are often enduring and happy. Indeed, there is an entire modern subculture of not only sexual relationships between human beings and spirits, but marriages that result in spirit children. This subculture is almost completely unknown to the popular media. It is never written about in magazines or talked about on television. It exists under the radar of our modern society, in spite of our constant lust to be entertained by new and outrageous diversions.

I sometimes speculate that many of the false pregnancies endured by women have, at their root, a relationship with a male spirit on the astral level. Such a connection can be established during sleep, when astral journeys occur that are not recalled upon waking in the morning. A woman may have a sexual relationship with a spirit in her sleep that she does not remember while awake, or that she remembers only in a vague and fragmented manner. It is not uncommon for a woman impregnated on the astral level by a spirit to exhibit some physical symptoms of pregnancy. The most common is the ceasing of menstruation. Morning sickness and a bloating of the abdomen are less likely, but they also occur.

These symptoms were noticed by the woman I mentioned who gave birth to the astral baby boy. She was kind enough to describe them to me in detail. They caused her no great apprehension because she was completely aware of her marriage with the spirit who was the father of the child, and knew that she was pregnant on the astral level. A woman who did not know she was astrally pregnant, suffering the same symptoms, would be perplexed, and might be inclined to seek some rational physical explanation in an effort to make sense of the situation—she would naturally assume that some man must have impregnated her while she was drugged or otherwise unaware.

The Care of Spirit Children

The ethical responsibility to care for such a child, once it has been created on the astral level, is no less rigorous than it would be for a child of flesh and blood. When the mother is a spirit, she can remain close to the infant and supply the child's needs, but it is only common decency for the human father to ensure that she is provided with nourishment to keep her strong. He can project vital energy from his own astral body into the body of the mother as a way of strengthening her, and she will pass a portion of the vitality on to the infant. Or he can infuse this energy into food and drink on the astral level, and present these to the mother. When the mother is human, she must rely on the love of the father for the child to cause him to watch over and protect the infant. To lighten his burden, she can supply him with vital energy.

If an astral baby is abandoned, it will not die, but it will blindly seek nourishment wherever it can find it, and is likely not to grow in a healthy or natural way. It is like a human infant abandoned on the streets of a slum that looks for food in the gutters. Such hardship can pervert the nature of a spirit that would otherwise grow to be kind and wise. A spirit child that starts its life in human form can, through this neglect, become bestial and deformed, its outward ugliness reflecting its inward corruption. On the astral planes, outward appearance is a true expression of inner nature, unless deliberately concealed for purposes of deception.

When they mature, astral children will go their own way in pursuit of their own unique destinies. Eventually, they will ascend to higher planes and may cease to have an active interest in the affairs of human beings. Part of this process of ascension may be an alteration of their forms, so that they would no longer be recognized by their human parent if encountered on the astral level. Yet these spirits always feel a bond with their human parent, and at times when the life of the parent is threatened, they may descend the planes to offer comfort or assistance.

Taking a spirit in marriage, or having a child with that spirit spouse, are serious steps to contemplate, and should not be entered into hastily. There is nothing inherently dangerous or immoral about such unions between spirits and humans, but they can result in misfortune and have unhappy consequences unless they are conducted with the same gravity and forethought that would be given to a human marriage, or the engendering of a human child. All actions have karmic consequences, whether done on the physical level or on the astral planes.

CHAPTER EIGHTEEN

Astral Self-Defense

The dangers of soul flight have been vastly exaggerated by those writing about the subject, particularly the spiritualists and Theosophists of the nineteenth century. One belief is that if the silver cord is cut, you will immediately die. Another is that a malicious spirit can prevent you from returning to your body, either by blocking your return on the astral level or by invading and claiming your body while you are gone. Yet another belief is that if you suffer some grave injury on the astral level, by a process known as repercussion it will show itself on your physical body and, if severe enough, it may cause death. There is the belief that you should not stray too far from your body, or you may become lost on the astral planes and never find your way back—your soulless body would then lapse into a state of permanent coma.

In addition to these mortal physical dangers, a host of more subtle and insidious threats are recited to frighten the prospective traveler. It is sometimes claimed that the unwary can become mesmerized by the strange beauty of the astral world and its spirits, and like those who eat and drink of the fairy feast, lose all interest in ordinary physical reality. Another fear raised is that astral vampires can suck the life force from the traveler, eventually weakening the traveler's body to such a degree that he succumbs to disease or infirmity. Yet another fear is that by venturing onto the astral planes, you will attract the notice of hostile spirits, who will then follow you back to the physical world and either obsess your mind or possess your body. There is also the ominous caution that the very practice of astral projection will drive you insane.

The good news is, direct physical dangers from soul flight of a life-threatening nature do not exist. You never actually leave your body; you merely shift consciousness from the physical state to the astral state. The silver cord is a metaphor for the sustained link between these two mental states. Sometimes it is perceived, but just as often it is not seen at all. Since it has no physical existence, it cannot be cut. Since you are never out of your body, you cannot become trapped out of it, or lose yourself on the astral planes and be unable to find it. The fable that repercussion can cause death is just as much false as the popular belief that if you fall off a cliff while dreaming, you will die. Neither is true.

Dangers of Repercussion

In rare cases, repercussion can produce minor injuries on the body such as bruises, welts, and scratches. These are not generated by spirits on the astral level, but rather by the traveler's own belief that injury has been inflicted upon him during soul flight. Strong belief can show itself in physical manifestations, the most famous of which are the stigmata, or holy wounds of Christ, which sometimes occur spontaneously to the hands, feet, forehead, and chest. They may simply appear, or they may follow an astral event such as an encounter with an angel. Stigmata wounds to the palms of the hands are the most common, and they happen most often to devout Christians. Sometimes they are found in those who protest that they have no religious faith, but it may be suspected that their faith is concealed beneath their conscious awareness. Strong faith can be formed in early childhood and then forgotten later in life, yet still remain in the unconscious.

Dion Fortune mentioned repercussion in her 1930 book *Psychic Self-Defence:* "It is a well-known fact that if an occultist, functioning out of the body, meets with unpleasantness on the astral plane, or if his subtle body is seen, and struck or shot at, the physical body will show the marks."[240] She described the patterned bruising found on her own body after an "astral skirmish" and quite wisely compared the bruises to the stigmata of saints and the swelling or bruising sometimes seen on hysterics. She wrote that "the mind, powerfully stirred, affects the etheric double, and the etheric double acts upon the physical molecules held in its meshes."[241] It is evident from this that she did not believe such injuries were caused by the direct actions of astral beings, but rather were generated reflexively by the mind of the sufferer.

The unpleasant encounter of Sylvan Muldoon with the ghost of his dead neighbor shows that while hostile spirits can confront and oppose travelers on the astral level, they are powerless to prevent reintegration of the astral double with the physical body. It is the same with dreams—many terrible things happen during our nightmares, but we always wake up. No spirit can prevent us from waking, and no spirit can prevent the return of the astral double. All they can do is attempt to frighten us. Some spirits are quite good at eliciting fear from humans traveling on the astral planes. They seem to know exactly which emotional buttons to push to cause the greatest possible panic. Actual harm is beyond their ability, and when we begin to reintegrate with our bodies they can only gnash their teeth in frustration.

As for the more subtle threats of fascination, vampirism, obsession, possession, and madness, it must be admitted that there is some basis to these dangers, but they are not nearly so prevalent or virulent as has been claimed by those who wish to discourage soul flight as a dangerous enterprise. It is useful to look at them each in turn, and to consider which dangers are real and which are inflated.

Astral Glamour

It was sometimes murmured in solemn tones by members of the Golden Dawn that poor Florence Farr and her Sphere Group had ventured too deeply into astral work, and had as a consequence become detached and lost interest in the more material pursuits of the Order. It was said that she had become caught in the spider's web of astral glamour,

---

240. Fortune, *Psychic Self-Defence,* 52.

241. Ibid.

with the implication that she was somehow no longer fit to bear the rigors of reality. Like a patron of a hall of mirrors who wanders too deeply and becomes lost in reflections, it was suspected that she had lost her way and would be unable to recover her normal personality, and would forever subsist in a half-dreaming state—half in the astral world and half out of it.

This is balderdash. It is true that Florence Farr, who was a beautiful and famous actress of the London stage, lost interest in her lovers and began to devote more and more of her time to her esoteric studies, but this may be set down more to the predictability and sameness of the men who pursued her than to her entanglement with astral visions. She simply became bored with sex, having had enough of it to last any woman a lifetime. The poet W. B. Yeats, who along with the playwright George Bernard Shaw and a dozen others had been her lover, referred to her increased pursuit of the esoteric as her "insatiable, destroying curiosity,"[242] but we may suspect the only thing destroyed was his masculine ego.

There is some truth in the fable that men and women who taste of the fairy feast can never return to the mortal world, but only in the sense that the astral planes are powerfully attractive to individuals of romantic sensibilities who are bored or sickened with everyday reality. Those seeking an escape from reality will find it somewhere—if not in astral travel, then in romantic fiction or drugs or religion. For this type of addictive personality, the astral world can exert a dangerous fascination, but the majority of those who explore its planes will be uninjured by the experience. It is similar to the effects of alcohol. Most people can drink, and even get drunk on occasion, with no ill effects in their lives, but a few cannot drink without drinking to excess. For these few, alcohol is dangerous.

No evidence exists to show that Florence Farr was of this addictive type of personality. She simply lost interest in the usual rounds of London society, and preferred to devote herself to esoteric studies at the British Museum. In 1912, she left England and traveled to Ceylon, where she accepted the position as head of a finishing school for girls. Allan Bennett, another member of the Golden Dawn who was the mentor of Aleister Crowley, had also left England more than a decade earlier to live in Ceylon, where he became a Buddhist monk. It is not uncommon for early fascination with practical occultism to evolve into an interest in religious mysticism. The study of magic reveals the

---

242. Howe, 68.

limits of everyday physical reality, and in individuals predisposed to religious thought, there is a tendency to move on to the study of spiritual reality.

Astral Vampirism

Astral vampirism is the theft of vital energy from the living, either by spirits or by other human beings. The person who serves as the vampire's host suffers from chronic and increasingly severe lethargy and physical exhaustion. This may result in the contraction of disease, since the defenses of the body are lowered, and when the body is so weakened that it cannot combat the illness, even death. However, the vampirism must go on for a long period of time—months, or even years—before such a drastic consequence becomes a serious threat. The physical body has large reserves of vitality, and it takes considerable time for it to become utterly depleted.

The myth of the vampire as a physical being who ingests the blood of its victims, and who sleeps in a coffin during the day, is only an externalization of the true vampire, who functions on the astral level. Astral vampires are real, but they are harmless unless they become fixated on a single host for their nourishment. This is not a common occurrence. Such spirits usually strike where opportunity presents itself, with no more forethought or discrimination than mosquitoes. A single vital meal drawn from the body causes no harm and is seldom noticed. It results in only a slight fatigue. This can be blamed on many factors—the last thing the average person is likely to consider is that he may have played host to an energy-sucking spirit.

The general ritual of projection is designed to prevent the intrusion of astral vampires. The walls of the astral chamber and corridor, coupled with the locked doors, insulate and protect the physical body during projection, while the traveler is interacting with spiritual beings. When entry is made to the astral levels only through the elevator during the general ritual, spirits that are encountered in soul flight find it almost impossible to locate the mind of the traveler during waking consciousness, or even during ordinary sleep. The ritual serves as a kind of magic circle that isolates and contains the period of interaction with astral beings, confining it to those times deliberately chosen by the traveler.

Spirit Obsession

Obsession and possession are related. Obsession is the persistent intrusion of a spirit into waking awareness, so that the spirit is perceived in various ways—usually as an image, a voice, or a touch. When a spirit appears in the physical world, it can seem completely real and solid, in every respect looking exactly as it would if it were standing before the observer in a living body of flesh and blood. When the spirit speaks, its voice sounds completely normal. When it touches the observer, its touch feels no different from the touch of a human hand.

There are cases in history where spirits have obsessed men or women for years, appearing wherever they go, and following them around. The person obsessed can see the spirit quite clearly, but no one else can see the spirit, except on rare occasions. In past centuries, those obsessed by spirits were naturally considered insane. They would stare at an empty chair and hold conversations with the blank air. Obsessing spirits pose little danger. They cannot injure those they obsess in any direct way, and indirect reflexive injuries caused by the unconscious belief in the attack of the spirit by the person suffering the obsession are usually minor. The danger lies in the reaction to obsession, which in extreme cases can be nervous breakdown or suicide.

When I refer to obsession, I am not talking about someone who believes that the spirit haunting their steps is a living person. These individuals are deluded, and have lost the ability to separate physical reality from hallucination. In true cases of spirit obsession, the person obsessed knows full well that the spirit is not a real, physical human being, and is in every other respect completely sane, but still cannot shake off the perception of the spirit.

Obsession is quite rare, and is extremely unlikely to befall those engaging in soul flight. Should it occur, one defense is to imagine that the spirit is slowly fading away. Each time you look at it, hold firmly in your mind that it is a little less solid than it was the previous time, a bit more transparent, and that its voice is more faint. This method is used in Tibet and other Eastern lands to dissolve what the Tibetans call tulpas, or thought-forms that can assume the shape of a human being, an animal, or an inhuman creature. In this way the spirit can be gradually diminished until it actually does fade into nothingness. Alexandra David-Neel created a tulpa in the shape of a monk that was so determined to sustain an independent existence that it took her six months to dissolve it. She wrote: "My mind-creature was tenacious of life."[243] Always bear in mind that on the astral level, imagination is real. It can both create and also destroy astral forms, provided there is a firm belief in its power and expectation of its effectiveness.

Spirit Possession

Possession is quite different from obsession. Instead of presenting itself externally to the perceptions of the person it has fixed its interest upon, the spirit assumes control of that person's body and displaces its intelligence, which enters a kind of dreamless sleep. Sometimes the displaced human awareness is still conscious, but helpless to affect the uses to which the possessing spirit puts its body, and remains in a half-trance, as though viewing events in a dream. In obsession, the spirit is interested in the human personality with which it seeks to interact, whereas in possession the spirit is mainly interested in the physical body that it has usurped and the enjoyment of sensations. Possessing spirits usually interact with the awareness of the person they take over only to the extent of tormenting the displaced human personality with shame and helplessness.

There is no more danger that a spirit will sneak into your body while you are off exploring the astral planes than that you will be possessed while you dream. You never actually leave your body during soul flight, so no vacant shell exists for the spirit to rush into. Possession is real; it does occur, but it is rare. In my opinion, the average person is in no greater danger of being possessed during soul flight than during the hours of normal waking consciousness. Being struck by lightning is also a real threat, but it would be foolish to avoid playing golf merely because this chance exists with a statistical probability above zero.

Loss of Sanity

As for the general danger of losing sanity through the practice of astral projection, it has been stressed by many authorities on Western esotericism that no one with an unstable mind should play with the occult in any of its aspects. Israel Regardie was particularly insistent on this point. He even went so far as to assert that before anyone engaged in the study of the Golden Dawn system, they should have themselves psychoanalyzed to determine their state of mental health. Regardie himself was a practitioner of Reichian

---

243. David-Neel, 315.

therapy,[244] and recommended that serious students enter psychotherapy as a general preparation for the practice of the magic of the Golden Dawn, which includes astral projection. "It is of small consequence what analytical school he selects. All are useful. All provide help for the student in his search for the Light, and serve as excellent preparation for the serious discipline of Magic and self-knowledge."[245]

Psychoanalysis enjoyed a much higher reputation at the time Regardie wrote those words. Since then, it has fallen out of favor among scientists, many of whom have come to look upon it as a quack profession, akin to chiropractic manipulation or aromatherapy. For Regardie, it was always a bit of a mania, a bee in his bonnet. I do not recommend psychoanalysis before the practice of soul flight, since it is unnecessary. However, anyone who has suffered from mental problems, either of a chronic or an acute kind, should be aware that astral travel can shake the foundation of their conventional view of reality. If they are determined to experiment with soul flight, they should do so with great caution, and if any problems arise of an emotional or perceptual nature, they should cease their practice immediately. Doing so is generally enough to restore a mental equilibrium.

Soul flight can be frightening at times. There arise moments of sheer terror. These are not the result of any real danger, but are an instinctive reaction to the unknown. The Greek god Pan was associated with the intense fear known as panic, which is the result of confrontation with something utterly alien and inexplicable. During soul flight, panic attacks in this ancient Greek sense can occur. It requires familiarity to overcome the instinctive response to flee back to waking reality. It is important not to overreact to this fear of the unknown. For most individuals, one experience of it is enough to cure them of ever wanting to engage in astral projection for the rest of their lives. The same may be said of experiments with the Ouija board, which can terrify the unwary. For a minority of others, the attraction of soul flight will be so strong that they will overcome their fear of the strange, and will force themselves to face it again and again until it ceases to have power over them.

Although there are no direct physical dangers in soul flight, there are dangers that arise from deception, misapprehension, confusion, and overreaction. It is these secondary dangers that must be guarded against. Spirits cannot harm you, but they can trick you into harming yourself by lying, startling you, threatening you, engaging in verbal

244. Regardie, xx.
245. Ibid., 5.

abuse, or bombarding your senses with noxious sights, sounds, touches, smells, and even on rare occasions, tastes. I once had a spirit transform the taste of a potato chip into something utterly foul. There was absolutely nothing in its appearance to indicate that it was contaminated in any way, and no other chips in the bag were affected by this foul taste. It was just an amusing little trick the spirit did for its own entertainment, to observe my reaction when I put the chip in my mouth. It is rare for spirits to modify the sense of taste, but it does happen, as demonstrated historically by all the accounts of sumptuous fairy feasts and delicious wines that suddenly vanish into thin air.

Dangers of Fairyland

Malicious spirits are mainly confined to the infernal levels of the astral world. If you avoid exploring these levels, you may never encounter such a spirit even after years of regular soul flights. Spirits of possession are all infernal spirits. It is much less likely that you will suffer possession if you remain on or above the base level of the astral world. Elementals are capricious, but not malicious. They play trick but mean no harm. The same is true of nature spirits that inhabit the mists and woodlands of the base astral level, remaining just out of sight unless actively sought. They are mischievous but harmless, although they can become willful and childish if their desires are frustrated.

Fairies are slightly different from elementals and nature spirits. They dwell just below the surface of the base astral level. They are the highest of the infernal classes of spirits and, as such, have the least malice in their natures of any of the infernals, but the innumerable frightening stories related in folklore about their malicious actions indicate that they are not to be trifled with or treated with contempt, and must be watched for signs of betrayal. They sometimes attempt to seduce the unwary traveler into fulfilling their purposes. In spite of the need for caution in dealing with them, visits to the lands of the fairies are filled with wonders and rewards of knowledge. If you travel to this highest of the infernal levels, do so with caution, forewarned about the deceptive nature of the spirits you will encounter there.

By the way, you should not expect fairyland to consist only of caves and caverns. This is where many fairies have their homes, but they also roam the countryside at will, and visits to their lands will often involve rural fields and woods that contain small villages and towns of an antique appearance. Merely because an astral level is infernal, or beneath the base astral level, does not necessitate that it consist only of caverns. Caves are the most natural symbolic expression of the infernal levels, but on many infernal levels you will not find caves.

Fairyland is somewhat behind the natural world in its time period—to travel there is to travel back in time several centuries. The exact period varies, suggesting that it may in part be a matter of the traveler's unconscious expectation. It is usually medieval or Renaissance, but can be as late as the Victorian period. Fairies do not seem to like the industrial age with its smoke and machines. They prefer a simpler and quieter landscape.

Although the exploration of fairyland can be rewarding, I recommend against descent into the lower levels of the astral world. These lower levels are the pagan places of the dead and the hells that are inhabited by demons. Even though the experience is no more dangerous in a physical sense than the exploration of the higher planes, the assault on the senses can be truly horrifying, with a power that can scar the memory for life. Another reason to avoid these levels is to lessen the likelihood that any demonic being will notice your existence and decide to take a personal interest in you. This would be bad. As much as possible, you are well-advised to shun the attentions of demons, even when they appear amusing or harmless. They are filled with malice and always seek some way to express it.

A Protective Amulet

A simple yet effective amulet of protection can be made from the rune symbol Algiz, which is shown in the illustration in chapter 14. It is shaped like the capital letter *Y* laid on top of the capital letter *I*, so that the *Y* has a vertical branch rising from its upright. It was used by northern Europeans as a symbol of protection. An amulet can be made by marking or inscribing the rune on any surface. That is one of the great advantages of the runes—they can be formed on anything, from any material. For example, the rune may be marked on a small square of paper in red ink and folded up, then placed in a locket and worn about the neck, or it may be inscribed on the outer surface of a pendant and worn so that it is exposed and visible. A paper with the rune drawn on it may be carried in the pocket or the wallet.

In an emergency, it is possible to evoke the protective power of the rune by cutting the rune into the surface of your right palm while on the astral plane, so that the lines of the rune bleed. This can be done with the fingernail of your left index finger, or with your left thumbnail. If you have a penknife in your pocket when you lie down to project your astral body, it will carry over into the astral world, and you can use the knife. The blood feeds and empowers the rune. Holding up your bleeding hand so that the rune is exposed and upright will create a powerful barrier. Needless to say, this should only be done on the astral level so that no damage is done to your physical body.

Another way of forming the Algiz rune with your hand is to fold your thumb against your palm and to spread your fingers with the two middle fingers together, so that your hand forms the shape of the rune. This takes a little practice, but it is not difficult. Extend your arm with your hand in this position and imagine a barrier between your astral body and whatever threat you seek to ward off. By forming two Algiz runes, one with each hand, and slowly turning on your own body axis with your arms extended to either side, you can create a protective circle around yourself. You should turn clockwise when forming the circle. This is a useful technique when you are surrounded by threats, and your retreat is cut off.

It is not a good practice to carry a weapon into the astral world when you engage in soul flight. Steel blades are effective weapons against spirits, but by carrying a weapon with you when you explore an astral landscape, you project a hostile aura that will automatically arouse resentment and hostility in the inhabitants of that place. A penknife is acceptable because it is more of a tool than a weapon, but a knife that might be used for fighting is better left behind when you project your astral body. A sword is a very effective weapon, but again it is usually ill-advised to take a sword with you on astral explorations, since its offensive purpose cannot be disguised. Guns are not particularly effective against spirits, so there is no point in carrying a gun over to the astral planes.

Names of Power

Another type of effective protection is the use of a name of power to command spirits. Such a name should only be voiced in a time of need. The Golden Dawn practice of repeatedly vibrating names of power until a spirit finally approaches that is obedient to them is unnecessarily aggressive, in my opinion, and is likely to stir up more trouble than it is worth. However, if you find yourself threatened or obstructed by a spirit, a name of power can be a useful way of achieving dominance.

When you voice a name of power, you are saying to the spirit you use it against that you are in harmony with its essential nature, and that you use it with the agreement of its owner, in the same way a herald or messenger to a foreign land might utter the name of his king as a way of invoking the authority of the monarch. Therefore, you should only choose a name to utter that you understand and with which you feel in harmony. Names of benevolent angels and deities are the safest to vibrate. If you are religious, naturally the name of a powerful figure in your religion would be a good choice.

Christians might select the name of an angel such as Michael, who is noted for his abilities as a warrior, or the name of Jesus, which has the potency to banish evil spirits. Names of God that are used in the Bible are effective for Christians, Muslims, and Jews alike. The divine name Shaddai means "the Almighty" and is an ancient name of great potency. It may be used in the simple phrase "Shaddai, protect me!" Similarly, an angelic name would be inserted into the phrase—for example, "Michael, protect me!" The invocation of the power of the name should be spoken emphatically, but there is no need to shout it out. Speak it firmly and clearly, while holding in your mind the nature and identity of the being that possesses the name.

Symbols of Faith

Religious symbols can make potent charms of protection for those who believe in their efficacy. The cross of Christianity, the Star of David of Judaism, and the lunar crescent of Islam are all forceful amulets of defense on the astral level, but only for those who have a firm faith in their power. Christians can also form the sign of the cross upon the air with their right hand, to act as a barrier. It should be visualized as floating upon the air, burning brightly with white flames.

Wiccans and pagans may prefer to employ the pentagram. The Golden Dawn pentagram known as the Banishing Pentagram of Earth makes an effective barrier, and can repel hostile spirits who try to approach too closely. "The Banishing Pentagram of Earth will also serve thee for a protection if thou trace it in the Air between thee and any opposing Astral force."[246] It is formed by drawing a pentagram upon the air with the right index finger using a continuous line that reflects back from each of the five points of the star and crosses over itself, to unite with its beginning. The Banishing Pentagram of Earth, as drawn by the members of the Golden Dawn, begins at the lower-left leg of the pentagram and is drawn in a clockwise direction. The first side of the pentagram is

---

246. Regardie, 282.

formed by making a line from the lower-left point to the upper point of the pentagram, and then continuing on to complete the symbol.

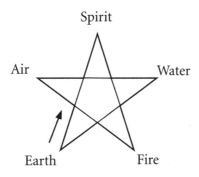

Banishing Pentagram of Earth

Returning to the Body

Always remember that there is no physical danger while you are on the astral levels. Your body remains safe, and you will inevitably return to it, even if you believe for a time that you have been prevented in some way from returning. It is a trick of malicious spirits to make you fear that you cannot leave the astral world, and that you are trapped outside of your body. If you become lost, or have trouble leaving the astral landscape you are visiting, remain calm. Eventually you will find yourself back in your body. This will occur naturally, even if you do nothing to cause it. Just as the mind naturally passes from dreaming sleep to wakefulness, so does the projected awareness naturally pass from the astral world back to waking physical reality.

You can assist this natural and inevitable process of return by lying down with your astral body, closing your eyes, and going to sleep. Adopt a posture that mimics the posture of your physical body. Just let yourself fall asleep while in your astral body, and you will awaken in your physical body. If you become totally confused and lost, and cannot find the door to the elevator used in the general ritual of projection, or if hostile spirits are keeping you from reaching the door, or if you have lost your keycard, or indeed if any mishap has taken place that prevents a normal return, this method will bring you back to your body.

Sometimes you will find that the more frantically you seek to wake up from astral travel, the more difficult it becomes. Anxiety prevents a reintegration with the body. During one of my first full projections, when I did not leave the room where my body rested on the bed, I lay back down into my body three times, each time trying with an act of will to reintegrate myself and lift my physical body up from the bed. Each time I failed—naturally enough, since I was doing all this while on the astral level. At last I saw that this method was not going to work, so I lay down into my body and allowed myself to drift downward through the darkness with my eyes shut. Then I willed myself to awake—not to sit up, as I had been trying to do, but to wake up. It was like swimming upward through the waters of a deep, dark well. The distance seemed quite far. When I reached the surface, I awoke in my physical body.

Had I been more relaxed about it, and used less force of will to awaken myself, the effort would not have been as great. I would have naturally risen to consciousness over a longer span of time. By forcing myself upward toward consciousness at an artificial rate, I created resistance, just as when you sweep your arm through water slowly there seems to be little resistance, but when you try to sweep it through quickly, the water presses back. If I had done nothing at all, nature would have followed its course, and my projected body would have reintegrated itself with my physical body effortlessly.

CONCLUSION

The End of the Journey

Soul flight in its many diverse forms is one of the great pillars of the Western esoteric tradition, and indeed of the esoteric tradition of the entire human race. It has been used for thousands of years to access alternative realities, to plumb the depths of the subconscious mind, and to establish direct communications with spiritual beings. Those who engage in soul flight always do so for the same reason—to acquire knowledge not readily available through other methods. It is only our cynical modern age, so obsessed with material things, that devalues this knowledge and treats its possession with contempt. In all past ages, it was sought as a precious attainment, a source of wisdom and power.

The concept of astral travel that evolved during the nineteenth century within the religion of Theosophy and the spiritualist movement was only a pale shadow of soul flight, shorn of most of its ritual and spiritual aspects, and reduced to the mechanical sending forth of the awareness across the ordinary physical plane, as a kind of invisible and powerless ghost—an ethereal Peeping Tom that could pass through walls and frighten friends asleep in their beds. The sad thing is that this crippled concept of soul flight has remained the popular understanding to this day, in the forms of modern astral projection and remote viewing.

Having read this book, you know that both astral projection, as it is generally conceived, and remote viewing are based on false assumptions, and for this reason can never yield completely reliable results. It is not possible to physically project a shell of awareness out of the body and across the face of the material world. Awareness is a part of mind, and forever remains within the mind. What a remote viewer sees is not the physical reality, but a resonance or reflection of that reality in the mirror of universal mind that is inevitably distorted in various ways. However, the information available to the soul flyer is not less useful than what is provided through the senses; it is merely of different kinds. Indeed, during soul flight the awareness can access many sources of valuable information unavailable to the physical senses alone.

Thanks to the work of the psychologist Carl Jung, with its emphasis on symbols and archetypes, we can no longer dismiss the astral world as unimportant, even if we persist in calling it unreal. It is the meeting place between human consciousness and spirit consciousness on all its levels, from the divine to the demonic. It is a realm of wonders and mysteries that remains largely unexplored and uncharted, a new world waiting to be discovered by those adventurous enough to enter its wilderness. I hope this book has provided some sense of how vast and strange this world truly is, and how significant a part soul flight has played throughout the spiritual evolution of the human species.

Bibliography

Adamski, George. *Inside the Space Ships*. New York: Abelard-Schuman, Inc., 1955.

Agrippa, Cornelius. *Three Books of Occult Philosophy* [1533]. Donald Tyson (editor). Translated from the Latin by J. F. in 1651. St. Paul, MN: Llewellyn, 1993.

Alexander, Michael (translator). *The Earliest English Poems* [1966]. Harmondsworth, UK: Penguin, 1975.

Anderson, Rasmus B., and J. W. Buel (editors). *The Norse Discovery of America: A Compilation in Extenso of all the Sagas, Manuscripts, and Inscriptive Memorials Relating to the Finding and Settlement of the New World in the Eleventh Century*. London: Norroena Society, 1906.

Apuleius, Lucius. *The Golden Asse*. Translated by William Addington [1566]. Reprint of the 6th Addington edition of 1639. Anonymous edition, no publisher or year.

Arnold, T. W. (translator). *The Little Flowers of St. Francis of Assisi*. London: Chatto and Windus, 1908.

Auden, W. H., and Paul B. Taylor (translators). *Norse Poems*. London : Athlone Press, 1981.

Augustine, Saint. *The City of God*. Translated from the Latin by John Healey [1610; revised 1620]. Two volumes. London: J. M. Dent and Sons Ltd., 1945.

Bailey, Alice A. *A Treatise on White Magic, or The Way of the Disciple* [1934]. New York: Lucis, 1997.

Baker, Alan. *Invisible Eagle: The History of Nazi Occultism*. London: Virgin, 2000.

Barnstone, Willis (editor). *The Other Bible*. New York: Harper and Row, 1984.

Bellows, Henry Adams (translator). *The Poetic Edda: Translated from the Icelandic with an Introduction and Notes*. [1923]. Lewiston, NY: Edwin Mellon Press, 1991.

Bender, Albert K. *Flying Saucers and the Three Men*. London: Neville Spearman, 1963.

Bentley, G. E. *Blake Records*. Oxford: Clarendon Press, 1969.

Besant, Annie, and C. W. Leadbeater. *Thought-Forms*. London: Theosophical Publishing House, 1901.

Blavatsky, H. P. *Isis Unveiled: A Master-Key to the Mysteries of Ancient and Modern Science and Theology* [1877]. Centenary Anniversary Edition (two volumes in one). Photographic facsimile reproduction of the original edition. Los Angeles: Theosophical Publishing, 1931.

————. *Studies In Occultism*. A collection of articles that appeared in the periodical *Lucifer* from 1887–91. Pasadena, CA: Theosophical University Press, no date.

————. *The Secret Doctrine: The Synthesis of Science, Religion and Philosophy* [1888]. Two volumes. Facsimile of the original edition. Pasadina, CA: Theosophical University Press, 1977.

Brewer, E. Cobham. *A Dictionary of Miracles: Imitative, Realistic, and Dogmatic*. London: Chatto and Windus, 1901.

————. *Dictionary of Phrase and Fable* [1870]. Seventeenth edition. London, Paris & New York: Cassell & Company Limited, no date.

Briggs, Katharine M. *The Anatomy of Puck*. London: Routledge and Paul, 1959.

Carroll, Lewis (pseudonym for Charles Lutwidge Dodgson). *Alice's Adventures in Wonderland, Through the Looking-Glass and Other Writings*. London: Collins, 1954.

Casaubon, Meric. *A True & Faithful Relation of What Passed for Many Yeers Between Dr. John Dee (A Mathematician of Great Fame in Q. Eliz. and King James their Reignes) and Some Spirits* [1659]. Glasgow: Antonine Publishing, 1974.

Castaneda, Carlos. *Journey to Ixtlan: The Lessons of Don Juan*. New York: Simon and Shuster, 1992.

Charles, R. H. *The Apocrypha and Pseudepigraphia of the Old Testament*. Two volumes. Oxford: Clarendon Press, 1913.

Clark, Jerome. "Vallée Discusses UFO Control System." Interview with Jacques Vallée. *Fate Magazine*, Vol. 31, No. 2 (February 1978), 60–68.

Clulee, Nicholas H. *John Dee's Natural Philosophy: Between Science and Religion.* London and New York: Routledge, 1988.

Colquhoun, Ithell. *Sword of Wisdom: MacGregor Mathers and the "Golden Dawn".* New York: G. P. Putnam's Sons, 1975.

Crookall, Robert. *The Techniques of Astral Projection: Dénouement after Fifty Years* [1964]. Wellingborough, UK: The Aquarian Press, 1977.

Crowley, Aleister. *The Book of the Law* [written 1904]. Montreal: 93 Publishing, 1975.

———. *The Confessions of Aleister Crowley: An Autohagiography* [1969]. Corrected edition of 1979. London: Arkana Books, 1989.

———. *Magick in Theory and Practice* [1929]. New York: Dover, 1976.

———. *The Vision and the Voice* [1929]. Originally published in *The Equinox*, Vol. 1, No. 5 (March 1911). Dallas: Sangreal Foundation, 1972.

Culpeper, Nicholas. *Culpeper's Complete Herbal, or English Physician.* Facsimile reproduction of the edition of 1826. Leicester, UK: Magna Books, 1992.

Cunningham, Allan. *The Cabinet Gallery of Pictures by the First Masters of the English and Foreign Schools.* London: George and William Nicol, 1836.

Darrach Jr., H. B., and Robert Ginna. "Have We Visitors From Space?" *Life Magazine*, April 7, 1952, pp. 80–96.

David-Neel, Alexandra. *Magic and Mystery in Tibet* [1932]. Originally published in French in 1929 as *Mystiques et magiciens du Thibet.* New York: Dover, 1971.

Denning, Melita, and Osborne Phillips. *The Llewellyn Practical Guide to Astral Projection* [1979]. St. Paul, MN: Llewellyn, 1988.

Deren, Maya. *Divine Horsemen: Voodoo Gods of Haiti.* New York: Chelsea House, 1970.

Dowbenko, Uri. "The True Adventures of a Psychic Spy: An Interview with David Morehouse." Two parts. Mapleton, Australia: *Nexus Magazine.* Part One: Vol. 4, No. 5 (August–September 1997); Part Two: Vol. 4, No. 6 (October–November, 1997).

Durville, Hector. "Experimental researches concerning phantoms of the living." *Annals of Psychical Science,* Vol. 7 (1908), pp. 335–43.

———. *Les fantômes des vivants: Anatomie et physiologie d l'âme: Recherches experimentales sur le dedoublement du corps de l'homme* [Phantasms of the living: Anatomy and physiology of the soul: Experimental research on the doubling of the body of man]. Paris: Librairie du Magnetisme, 1909.

Ebon, Martin. *Psychic Warfare: Threat or Illusion?* New York: McGraw-Hill, 1983.

Eliade, Mircea. *Shamanism: Archaic Techniques of Ecstasy* [1951]. Princeton, NJ: Princeton University Press, 1972.

Evans-Wentz, Walter Yeeling. *The Fairy-Faith in Celtic Countries* [1911]. New Hyde Park, NY: University Books, 1966.

Fodor, Nandor. *Encyclopædia of Psychic Science* [1934]. New Hyde Park, NY: University Books, 1966.

Fortune, Dion. (pseudonym for Violet Mary Firth). *Psychic Self-Defence* [1930]. New York: Samuel Weiser, 1979.

———. (pseudonym for Violet Mary Firth). *The Mystical Qabalah* [1935]. London: Ernest Benn, 1974.

Fox, Oliver. (pseudonym for Hugh Callaway). *Astral Projection: A Record of Out-of-the-Body Experiences* [1939]. Based on two articles in the *Occult Review,* 1920: "The Pineal Doorway" and "Beyond the Pineal Door." New York: University Books, 1962.

Gaster, Moses, and Samuel Daiches. *Three Works of Ancient Jewish Magic.* Contains *The Sword of Moses,* translated by Moses Gaster, London, 1896; *The Wisdom of the Chaldeans,* translated by Moses Gaster, Proceedings of the Society of Biblical Archaeology, December, 1900; *Babylonian Oil Magic in the Talmud and in Later Jewish Literature,* London, 1913. Chthonios Books, 1986.

Gerard, John. *The Herbal: Or General History of Plants*. [1597] Revised and enlarged by Thomas Johnson, 1633. New York: Dover, 1975.

Grieve, Maud. *A Modern Herbal: The Medicinal, Culinary, Cosmetic and Economic Properties, Cultivation and Folklore of Herbs, Grasses, Fungi, Shrubs and Trees with All their Modern Scientific Uses* [1931]. London: Tiger Books International, 1992.

Griffith, F. Ll., and Herbert Thompson (editors). *The Leyden Papyrus: An Egyptian Magical Book*. Original title, *The Demotic Magical Papyrus of London and Leiden* [1904]. New York: Dover, 1974.

Guazzo, Francesco Maria. *Compendium Maleficarum* [1608]. Translated from the Latin by E. A. Ashwin [1929]. New York: Dover, 1988.

Hansen, Harold A. *The Witch's Garden* [1976]. Translated from the Danish by Muriel Crofts. York Beach, ME: Samuel Weiser, 1983.

Howe, Ellic. *The Magicians of the Golden Dawn: A Documentary History of a Magical Order 1887-1923* [1972]. New York: Samuel Weiser, 1978.

Hynek, J. Allen. *The UFO Experience: A Scientific Inquiry*. New York: Contemporary Books, 1972.

James I, King of England. *Daemonologie* [1597]. London: John Lane The Bodley Head Ltd, 1924.

Judge, William Q. *The Ocean of Theosophy* [1893]. Pasadena, CA: Theosophical University Press, 1973.

Jung, Carl G. *Flying Saucers: A Modern Myth of Things Seen In the Skies*. Translated from the German by R. F. C. Hull. New York: Signet Books, 1959.

Kardec, Allan. (pseudonym for Léon-Dénizarth-Hippolyte Rivail). *The Mediums' Book* [1861]. Translated from the French by Anne Blackwell [1876]. London: Psychic Press Ltd., 1977.

———. (pseudonym for Léon-Dénizarth-Hippolyte Rivail). *The Spirits' Book*. Revised edition [1857]. Translated from the French by Anne Blackwell. Rio de Janeiro, Brazil: Federação Espírita Brasileira, no date.

Keightley, Thomas. *The World Guide to Gnomes, Fairies, Elves and Other Little People*. Reprint of the work originally titled *The Fairy Mythology* [1878]. New York: Avenel Books, 1978.

King, Francis. *The Rites of Modern Occult Magic*. Originally published as *Ritual Magic In England: 1887 to the Present Day* [1970]. New York: Macmillan, 1971.

———, and Isabel Sutherland. *The Rebirth of Magic*. London: Corgi Books, 1982.

Kirk, Robert, and Andrew Lang. *The Secret Commonwealth of Elves, Fauns and Fairies*. Lang's edition of Robert Kirk's *Secret Commonwealth* [1691]. London: David Nutt, 1893.

Knight, Gareth. *A Practical Guide to Qabalistic Symbolism* [1965]. New York: Samuel Weiser, 1980.

Kuhn, Alvin Boyd. *Theosophy: A Modern Revival of Ancient Wisdom*. New York: Holt, Rhinehart and Winston, 1930.

Küntz, Darcy (translator and editor). *The Complete Golden Dawn Cipher Manuscript*. Edmonds, WA: Holmes Publishing Group, 1996.

Laycock, Donald C. *The Complete Enochian Dictionary: A Dictionary of the Angelic Language as Revealed to Dr John Dee and Edward Kelley*. London: Askin, 1978.

Leadbeater. C. W. *Invisible Helpers*. American Revised Edition. Chicago: The Theosophical Book Concern, 1915.

———. *The Astral Plane: Its Scenery, Inhabitants and Phenomena*. Third edition, revised. London: Theosophical Publishing Society, 1900.

Leland, Charles G. *Aradia; or The Gospel of the Witches* [1897]. Custer, WA: Phoenix Publishing, 1990.

Lévi, Eliphas. *The History of Magic* [1860]. Translated from the French by A. E. Waite [1913]. London: Rider & Company, 1986.

Magnusson, Magnus, and Hermann Pálsson. *The Vinland Sagas: The Norse Discovery of America.* Harmondsworth, UK: Penguin, 1965.

Monroe, Robert A. *Journeys Out of the Body* [1971]. New York: Anchor, 1977.

Morehouse, David. *Psychic Warrior: Inside the CIA's Stargate Program.* New York: St. Martin's Press, 1996.

Muldoon, Sylvan, and Hereward Carrington. *The Phenomena of Astral Projection* [1951]. London: Rider & Company, 1975.

———. *The Projection of the Astral Body* [1929]. London: Rider & Company, 1972.

Mumford, Michael D., Andrew M. Rose, and David S. Goslin. *An Evaluation of Remote Viewing Research and Applications.* American Institute for Research. September 29, 1995.

Murray, Margaret A. *The Witch-Cult in Western Europe* [1921]. Oxford, UK: Clarendon Press, 1962.

Ophiel (pseudonym for Edward Peach). *The Art and Practice of Astral Projection* [1961]. New York: Samuel Weiser, 1973.

Paine, Albert Bigelow. *Joan of Arc, Maid of France.* New York: MacMillan, 1925.

Pauwels, Louis, and Jacques Bergier. *The Dawn of Magic.* Originally titled *Le matin des magiciens* [1960]. Translated from the French by Rollo Myers [1963]. London: Panther Books, 1967.

Pliny, the Elder. *Natural History.* In ten volumes. Multiple translators. Cambridge, MA: Harvard University Press, various years.

Plutarch. *Plutarch: The Lives of the Noble Grecians and Romans.* Translated into English by John Dryden, revised by Arthur Hugh Clough [1864]. New York: Modern Library, no date.

Regardie, Israel. *The Golden Dawn: A Complete Course In Practical Ceremonial Magic* [1938–40]. Sixth edition, four volumes in one. St. Paul, MN: Llewellyn, 1989.

Rémy, Nicolas. *Demonolatry* [1595]. Translated from the Latin by E. A. Ashwin. London: John Rodker, 1930.

Rhine, J. B. *New Frontiers of the Mind; The Story of the Duke Experiments.* New York: Farrar and Rinehart, 1937.

————— and J. G. Pratt. "A review of the Pearce-Pratt distance series of ESP tests." *Journal of Parapsychology*, 18 (1954), 165–177.

Robbins, Rossell Hope. *The Encyclopedia of Witchcraft and Demonology.* London: Spring Books, 1959.

Sagan, Carl, and Thornton Page (editors). *UFO's: A Scientific Debate.* New York: W. W. Norton, 1974.

Schwarzwäller, Wulf. *The Unknown Hitler: His Private Life and Fortune.* Translated from the German by Aurelius von Kappau. Bethesda, MD: National Press Books, 1989.

Scot, Reginald. *The Discoverie of Witchcraft* [1584]. Reprint of the John Rodker edition of 1930. New York: Dover, 1972.

Scott, Sir Walter. *Demonology and Witchcraft.* Second edition [1830]. New York: Bell, 1970.

Sebottendorff, Rudolf, Freiherr von. *Bevor Hitler Kam* [Before Hitler Came]. Munich: Grassinger, 1933.

Shakespeare, William. *Shakespeare: Complete Works.* London: Oxford University Press, 1905.

Sinnett, Alfred P. *Incidents in the Life of Madame Blavatsky.* London: Theosophical Publishing Society, 1913.

Smith, Paul H., *Reading the Enemy's Mind: Inside Star Gate, American's Psychic Espionage Program*. New York: Tom Doherty Associates, 2005.

Stewart, R. J. *Robert Kirk: Walker Between Worlds*. Shaftesbury, UK: Element Books, 1990.

Suster, Gerald. *Hitler and the Age of Horus*. London: Sphere Books, 1981.

Swedenborg, Emanuel. *A Compendium of the Theological Writings of Emanuel Swedenborg*. New York: New Jerusalem Publishing House, 1875.

Tyson, Donald. *Rune Dice Divination*. St. Paul, MN: Llewellyn Publications, 1997.

———. *Rune Magic*. St. Paul, MN: Llewellyn Publications, 1988.

Vallée, Jacques. *Passport to Magonia: From Folklore to Flying Saucers*. Chicago: Henry Regnery Co., 1969.

Virgil. *The Works of Virgil*. Translated from the Latin by James Lonsdale and Samuel Lee. London: Macmillan and Co., 1885.

Westcott, William Wynn (translator). *Sepher Yetzirah: The Book of Formation, with The Fifty Gates of Intelligence, and The Thirty-Two Paths of Wisdom* [1887]. Reprint of the revised edition of 1893. New York: Samuel Weiser, 1980.

Weyer, Johann. *On Witchcraft. An abridged translation of Johann Weyer's De praestigiis daemonum* [1583]. Translated from the Latin by John Shea. Edited by Benjamin G. Kohl and H. C. Erik Midelfort. Asheville, NC: Pegasus Press, 1998.

Index

A

abduction, vii, xvi–xvii, 6, 39, 42–44, 52, 135, 139–141, 145–148, 150–151, 181, 280, 301

Aberfoyle, 38

accumulator, lunar, 190

aconite, 29–30

Adam (biblical figure), 18, 52–53, 208

adepts, 85, 88, 92, 97, 264, 266, 281–282

Adonai ha-Aretz, 226, 233

Aeneas, 36

Aeneid, The, 36

Aethyrs. *See* Enochian Aethyrs

Agnes, Saint, 55

Agrippa, Cornelius, 23, 182–183, 261, 321

Ai Toyon, 6

Aiwass, 123, 144

ajna chakra, 94, 151, 173–174, 179, 189, 196, 266–267

Akasa, 109

akashic records, 90, 127, 132

alcohol, 12–14, 27, 132, 284, 308

Alfonso, Saint. *See* Alphonsus Liguori, Saint

Algiz, 253, 314–315

aliens, xvi–xvii, 6, 52, 135, 139–142, 145–147, 149–154, 181, 228, 280, 294, 312

Alighieri, Dante, 54, 279

All Hollows' Eve

Alpha and Omega Lodge, 102–103

alpha state, 129

Alphonsus Liguori, Saint, 48, 70–71, 73

Altaic, 6–7, 166

altar, 51, 57, 162–164, 206, 208, 229

altered state, x, 9, 56, 67, 188

Ambrose, Saint, 48

American Institute for Research, 133, 327

Amon, 207

amulet, 253, 314, 316

Anderson, Jack, 128, 321

Angela, Saint, 55

angels, 38, 48, 51, 53, 58–62, 65, 87, 109, 113, 115–116, 118, 123, 132, 144, 152, 175–176, 188, 208–209, 213–214, 219, 230, 240, 253, 270, 273, 276, 279–280, 283–284, 294, 296, 299, 306, 316, 326

animal magnetism, 67

ankh, 94, 154, 271

Ansuz, 247, 270

Anthony of Padua, Saint, 47–48

Anubis, 293

Apas, 109

Aphrodite, 280

Apollo, 218

apparitions, 39, 91–92, 130, 141, 233

apports, 66, 79, 81, 153, 180, 188

Apuleius, Lucius, 22, 26, 28, 321

Aquarius, 143, 145, 216, 237

Aradia, 21, 327

Ariadne, 75

Ark of the Covenant, 132

Arnold, Kenneth, 136

astral body, ix–x, xiii–xiv, xvii, 5, 8–9, 11–12, 14, 26, 33, 48, 51, 53–54, 56–57, 61, 67–77, 82, 85–86, 89–90, 93, 103, 112, 114–115, 130–131, 157–158, 163–165, 169–170, 172–175, 176–177, 186, 192–193, 196, 200–201, 239, 241, 243, 259–260, 262–264, 267–268, 277, 288, 299, 301, 303, 314–315, 317, 327

astral catalepsy. *See* catalepsy, astral

astral double, 8, 47, 67–68, 70–73, 77, 85, 91–93, 130–131, 151, 165, 168, 174–175, 181, 184–186, 196, 224, 242–243, 260–264, 266–267, 275–276, 278, 287–288, 307

astral gateway, 112, 115, 158, 164

astral key, 162, 164–165, 167, 174–177, 193–194, 198, 200, 202, 229, 244–245, 317

astral landscape, xiii–xv, xvii, 51, 53, 61, 76, 82, 111–112, 114, 163, 165–167, 173–176, 180–181, 184, 188, 192, 195, 201–204, 210–211, 214, 227–228, 241, 245, 269, 276, 278, 285, 291–292, 297–298, 314–315, 317

astral plane, xiii, 6–7, 51, 78, 81–90, 93, 97, 104–105, 107, 109–111 113–115, 132, 158, 164–167, 175, 199, 201, 222, 225–227, 259, 280–285, 287, 291, 294–295, 298–301, 304–308, 311, 314–315

astral projection, ix–xvii, 4, 8,